# The Leader,

## the Led,

## and the

## Psyche

Also by Bruce Mazlish

*A New Science: The Breakdown of
Connections and the Birth of Sociology*

*The Meaning of Karl Marx*

*The Revolutionary Ascetic*

*Kissinger. The European Mind in American Policy*

*James and John Stuart Mill:
Father and Son in the Nineteenth Century*

*In Search of Nixon: A Psychohistorical Study*

*The Riddle of History: The Great Speculators
from Vico to Freud*

*The Western Intellectual Tradition:
From Leonardo to Hegel*
(in collaboration with J. Bronowski)

Edited Works

*Revolution: A Reader*
(with A. Kaledin and D. Ralston)

*The Railroad and the Space Program:
An Exploration in Historical Analogy*

*Psychoanalysis and History*

Bruce Mazlish

# The Leader, the Led, and the Psyche

*Essays in*
*Psychohistory*

Wesleyan University Press

PUBLISHED BY UNIVERSITY PRESS OF NEW ENGLAND

Hanover & London

*The University Press of New England*
is a consortium of universities in New England dedicated to publishing scholarly and
trade works by authors from member campuses and elsewhere. The New England
imprint signifies uniform standards for publication excellence maintained without
exception by the consortium members. A joint imprint of University Press of New
England and a sponsoring member acknowledges the publishing mission of that
university and its support for the dissemination of scholarship throughout the world.
Cited by the American Council of Learned Societies as a model to be followed, University
Press of New England publishes books under its own imprint and the imprints of

Brandeis University
Brown University
Clark University
University of Connecticut
Dartmouth College
University of New Hampshire
University of Rhode Island
Tufts University
University of Vermont
Wesleyan University

1990 © by Bruce Mazlish

The poem by Ayatollah Khomeini translated by William Chittick is reprinted by
permission of *The New Republic,* copyright © 1989, The New Republic, Inc.

See page 321 for additional acknowledgments.

Library of Congress Cataloging-in-Publication Data

Mazlish, Bruce, 1923–
The leader, the led, and the psyche : essays in psycho-
history / by Bruce Mazlish.
p.  cm.
Includes bibliographical references.
ISBN 0-8195-5220-8 — ISBN 0-8195-6245-9 (pbk.)
1. Psychohistory. I. Title.
D16.16.M38  1990
901'.9—dc20        90-35351
CIP

5  4  3  2  1

# Acknowledgments

THIS book would not have come into existence without the suggestion of Jeannette Hopkins, the Director of the Wesleyan University Press, and her editorial skills have played a key role in shaping it. My debt to her is great. I also wish to record my thanks to Thomas L. McFarland, Director of the University Press of New England, who oversaw the promotion of the book once the Wesleyan University Press operations were put under his supervision.

In a book such as this, the product of many years of work and reflection, memories come crowding to the fore. My first go to my graduate school mentors, Jacques Barzun and Shepard Clough. The former, although he came to oppose psychohistory rather vehemently, taught me to move bravely across the terrain of interdisciplinary work in history; the latter instructed me in the virtues of keeping one's feet on historical ground while having lofty thoughts. Together, my two mentors, existing uneasily as joint supervisors of my thesis, "The History of Conservative Thought: Burke, Bonald, and De Maistre," unwittingly prepared me for living with ambivalences.

As I moved toward work in psychohistory, as part of my general interests in history and its methodology, Erik H. Erikson was a major inspiration, illuminating both psychoanalytic theory and its application to historical materials. Among many who taught me much about psychoanalysis were Francis de Marneffe and Arthur Valenstein. A good deal of my learning also took place at the Wellfleet Conferences, so called, where I was fortunate to have as colleagues not only Erikson but also Robert Lifton and later Kenneth Keniston (now, happily, my colleague at M.I.T.). The meetings of the Group for Applied Psychoanalysis (GAP) over the course of 15 years or so were a constant source of interest; of its members, Norman Holland and Abraham Zaleznik, who co-founded the Cambridge–Boston GAP with me, figure fondly in my memories.

In the area of personality and politics, or more specifically the study of political leaders, the International Society for Political Psychology has been the premier institution affecting me; and I have affectionate recollections of its moving spirit, Jeanne Knutson. The present editor of *Political Psychology*, Stanley Renshon, is both a longtime friend and a scholar whose judgment in these matters I respect highly. I have also benefited from the counsel of many other members of the ISPP.

Others to whom I would like to acknowledge a special debt in my peregrinations through the field of psychohistory, either for their friendship or scholarship—even when we might disagree, sometimes sharply—are Rudolph Binion, Kathleen Dalton, Peter Loewenberg, Gerald Platt, Lucien Pye, Andrew Rolle, Charles Strozier, Robert C. Tucker, Fred Weinstein, and Lewis Wurgaft.

A special thanks go to Melvin Lasky, editor of *Encounter* magazine, who many years ago first took a chance on publishing some of my writings in what was then a new field. And last, appreciation to my many students, undergraduate and graduate, over the years, who kept reminding me how skeptical and yet open one must be in a field where nuances and subtleties can play an unusually important role. They were also a constant reminder that psychohistorical insight can play a most meaningful part in the lives of individuals as well as in society at large.

# Contents

*Acknowledgments,* v

Introduction: The Science of Psychoanalysis,
the Social Sciences, and History, 1

## I. *The Applicability of Psychoanalysis*

1. Darwin, the Bedrock of Psychoanalysis, 13
2. Darwin, the Benchuca, and Genius, 31
3. Freud and Nietzsche, 38
4. The Hysterical Personality and History, 51
5. Autobiography and Psychoanalysis, 59

## II. *The Intellectual as Leader*

6. The Importance of Being Karl Marx, or
Henry Thoreau, or Anybody, 79
7. Jevons's Science and His "Second Nature," 95
8. The Iron Cage of Max Weber, 107

## III. *The Examination of Political Leadership*

9. Prolegomena to Psychohistory, 127
10. The Hidden Khomeini, 139
11. Orwell inside the Whale, 153

*IV. The Case of the USA*

12. The Iron of Melancholy, 165
13. Crèvecoeur's New World, 173
14. Leadership in the American Revolution:
The Psychological Dimension, 181
15. A Psychohistorical Inquiry:
The "Real" Richard Nixon, 198

*V. Toward a Group Psychology*

16. Leader and Led, Individual and Group, 249
17. The American Psyche, 267

*Notes, 287*
*Name Index, 313*
*Subject Index, 315*
*Bibliographical Note, 321*

# The Leader,

# the Led,

# and the

# Psyche

# Introduction:
# The Science of Psychoanalysis,
# the Social Sciences,
# and History

*I*S the use of psychology in historical studies legitimate? Put this way, it is obvious that the question is, in fact, rhetorical; for *all* history is necessarily psychological (it is also much else). How could it be otherwise? Historical inquiry deals with human beings rather than, say, with "natural history"; it concerns itself necessarily with desires and motives—and therefore with the psyche and the psychological.

Thus, the real question becomes: what *sort* of psychology is the historian to use? The possibilities are many, ranging from seat-of-the-pants psychology (the preferred posture of conventional historians) to various forms of academic and clinical psychologies.

In my view (and that of some others), the most useful psychological method to be applied to historical materials is the psychoanalytic.* Psychoanalysis is a general psychology, as well as a therapeutic procedure, which assumes the existence of unconscious as well as conscious mental processes and gives them a very powerful role in human behavior indeed. In addition to paying attention to the unconscious, psychoanalysis is also historical and developmental in its perspective and thus lends itself readily to the way

---

*Over the years, I have written a number of essays and articles that fall within what has come to be called the fields of psychohistory or personality and politics studies. In this book, I have tried to put these writings in a cohesive framework, to synthesize their arrangement so that they make a sustained argument. (This introduction and chapters 1 and 17 are, in fact, completely new.) What unifies them is that they are all concerned, though with different emphases, with the way theory relates to practice, i.e., application. In short, they are variations on a common theme.

1

historians see the world. It deals with actual human beings, in the full complexity of their lives, living not in laboratories but in real-life situations (though the patients in therapy are themselves studied initially in clinical settings). For these and other reasons, psychoanalysis is, I believe, the psychology of preference in historical work.

Put bluntly, a further question then becomes: how good, that is, how "scientific," is psychoanalysis? How valid is it for use by historians and other social scientists? What kind of "knowledge" does it bring that makes it especially useful and penetrating? And how reliable is that "knowledge"?

At this point, one then enters into dangerous thickets. The question of "What is science?" is not itself obvious. Is, say, physics the only model, or is there the possibility of new rules discovered by the human sciences, shaping their understanding out of the materials, the phenomena, with which they uniquely deal, rules that still fall within a valid scientific model?

In preliminary terms, it is important to realize that psychoanalysis is both a system of theory and a process, a science of mental processes and at the same time a process involving the scientist—that is, the analyst—and the patient or text or whatever is being analyzed, in a manner that becomes part of the science. One might say that, while a natural science theory is *about* a process, in psychoanalysis, as a "human" science, theory and process are so closely integrated that process *is* theory. Where the natural scientist looks outside him/herself, in a human or social science, the central subject, the "object," is humanity, of which the social scientist is a member.[1]

The process of psychoanalysis is, first of all, a relationship between the analyst and the analysand. That may, in practice, mean between the practitioner and a client, or between the practitioner and him/herself, or between the practitioner and a text. The way, as I shall try to show in Chapter 1, that this process becomes experienced as theory is in what Freud discovered almost in spite of himself and with some embarrassment: the telling of stories.

The story told by an analyst is highly individual, about a dream, a perception or misperception, or a piece of the experience of one person. The theory stands only partly outside the stories. It collects them, analyzes them, and organizes them into patterns and frameworks to be expected and looked for. Although a generalizing theory, it is a theory of the individual.

The individual is a *human animal*. I argue that absolutely fundamental to psychoanalysis is its basis in Darwinian evolutionary biology. Thus, the theory I refer to is grounded not only in human use of language and in human stories but in biological nature (of which language and culture themselves are evolutionary phenomena).

Of course, to explain something in terms of *origin* is itself a very Darwinian notion (though one must be careful to avoid the genetic fallacy).[2] Seen in this context, the psychoanalytic individual is a member of a species whose evolution has been shaped by both physical and cultural forces, though increasingly the latter has become the stronger force. The individual is part of a social group and cannot be understood apart from it. Biological nature, social existence, and cultural shaping all enter into the individual and into the theory and thus, ideally, into the process of psychoanalysis.

To deal with these issues, it is essential to begin with the problems and origins with which psychoanalysis has attempted to grapple. This is the major task of Chapter 1. Those who hold to an abstract view of what is science may find this process difficult and unappealing, for psychoanalysis can readily be faulted as not living up to rigorous standards of verification, accumulation, mathematicization, and the like, and, in fact, it can never be made to live up to them. I do hope to appeal, however, to those who have an interest in, a curiosity about, how psychoanalysis came to be and thus what its own character is—that is, what kind of knowledge it is in actuality. Unless the question of what kind of knowledge psychoanalysis is and what standards can be seen to apply to it are addressed, the reasons for which I urge the practice of psychohistory cannot be understood.[3]

It must be said, as forcefully as possible, that psychohistory itself is not a science; it is still a form of history. As such, it has all the problems of explanation attendant on that discipline: what is a historical "fact," how do we decide what facts to select, how do we understand past actors, do we operate under what are called covering laws, how do we test our evidence, how do we link evidence to inference, what form do we employ to express our understanding of the past? Such problems have preoccupied historians such as Marc Bloch, R. G. Collingwood, and E. H. Carr, to name only a few; and they must preoccupy all historians as well as all psychohistorians.[4]

What amazes me is how critics of psychohistory apply to it standards for historical explanation that they would never dream of applying to more traditional forms of history. In fact, most historians have been notoriously untheoretical, rarely thinking much about how "tight" their arguments are. The basic assumption is that the facts will more or less speak for themselves. Traditions of historical writing sanction the belief that adherence to facts, carefully established by the close scrutiny of documents, and then the linking of these facts by careful, detailed narrative constitute acceptable historical explanation. The use of footnotes, in turn, demonstrates a grappling with previous work. In this sense, history itself claims to be a sort of "science," in contrast, say, to myth.[5]

In fact, there is not all that much wrong with such an approach (many historians, incidentally, go much beyond it in conscious attention to methodology), and the results often rescue a sense of believable order out of the chaos of the past. The only point I am making here is that the same standards should be applied to the effort to use psychoanalysis, its "short stories," in historical studies. Of course, this must also include an understanding of psychoanalytic theory and how it operates vis-à-vis historical materials.

With this said, we can see that a consideration of psychohistory can be broken down into three questions: (1) how valid is psychoanalysis as a psychological science—I try to deal with that one, especially in Part I; (2) if valid, can such a science, conceived in experiences with patients, be usefully employed with historical figures or groups who are neither patients nor alive; and (3) how does one go about using it successfully?

Fortunately, there has already been much discussion of these issues (I too have tried my hand at them, especially in Chapter 9 of this book, as well as elsewhere); I need not summarize the literature but will add only a few brief comments here.[6] Although Freud himself cautioned privately against psychoanalyzing contemporary public figures—"psychoanalysis should not be practiced on a living [historic] individual,"[7] an injunction he himself violated with his flagrantly distorted book (William Bullitt was the principal author) on Woodrow Wilson—he did accept the use of psychoanalysis with dead historical figures, and he penned, for example, an interesting, if flawed, portrait of Leonardo da Vinci.[8] From such examples, we can see that as long as there are "texts," words, that can be analyzed, we have the possibility of psychohistory (although not practical psychoanalysis) with living as well as dead people, at least in principle.

Freud was not a historian and did not really work as one. Later historians, doing psychohistory, are not practicing psychoanalysis in the classical sense but employing a psychological science, exactly as they would use geology to deal with a landscape or economics to understand market and productive relations, in an effort to achieve greater *historical* understanding. The proof of the pudding is in the eating, and it is their work rather than any theoretical defense of it that should engage our major attention. Of course, as I have already suggested, an understanding of such work entails an earlier understanding of psychoanalysis so as to be able to evaluate properly what may serve as evidence and inference in its use in history.

Thus, the answer to question 2 points to the answer to question 3: how to use psychoanalysis in history successfully. Again, there are "theoretical" articles and books on the subject, and again I will say nothing more here but leave it that the actual work must serve as the testing ground.

At this point I turn to the rest of this book. A large part of it deals with individual figures—leaders—intellectual or political. Hence the first part of the title, "*The Leader,* the Led, and the Psyche."

In dealing with leaders, we are dealing with a fundamental biological inheritance of human beings as well as a specific social development. Herbert S. Lewis, for example, an anthropologist, states correctly that "there seems to have been an underlying assumption that decisions are predetermined by the social rules or the customs of a group and somehow are arrived at spontaneously." Closer examination, however, shows that this is not so. Among all of the higher primates, the evidence points to the essential role of leaders; Lewis concludes that "there are no known societies without leadership of at least some aspects of their social life, even though there are many that lack any single, overall leader with power to enforce his decisions."[9]

Schools of fish have leaders; so do flocks of birds. Pecking order among chickens is famous. Human animals are no different: they too have leaders. This observation may be even more true of complex than of simple societies. The sociologist Robert Michels, along with others, has powerfully argued that all large groups, even socialistic ones, necessarily become top-down structures: an iron law of hierarchy prevails. More recently, the political scientist Robert C. Tucker, in what I think is the best single book on the subject, has taken the position that "politics in essence is leadership, or attempted leadership, of whatever is the prevailing form of political community. . . . Leadership is not an ideal form of political rule [i.e., normative]; it is what we factually find when we study closely the political process." (P. 3) Going further, Tucker argues that "the conception of politics as leadership involves the recognition that whatever material interests and power interests figure in political life—as some always do—politics is basically a realm of the mind."[10] This last is a suggestive idea, which I shall pursue a little later as I relate intellectual to political leaders.

Political scientists have been at least as eager as historians to follow this lead. What is called "psychohistory" among the latter is generally known as "personality and politics" among the former. Hitherto, political scientists have tended to emphasize an Adlerian version of psychoanalysis, with its focus on power, and to use theories of superiority-inferiority and overcompensation rather than of libido. It really does not matter for present purposes which school, Freudian or Adlerian, is used: psychoanalysis, with its stress on the individual, can serve both historian and political scientist in analyzing great, and not so great, leaders. Thus, when Allan Janik and Stephen Toulmin (admittedly philosophers, though operating here as historians) write of Habsburg Vienna and its four major antiliberal parties, the Social Democratic, the Christian Social, the Pan-German, and the Zionist, they argue persuasively that "the charisma of Adler [Victor, the politician, not Alfred, the psychoanalyst], like that of Lueger, Schönerer, and Herzl, virtually established and sustained his party. In each case, the story of the man is the story of the party, and to understand the man is to comprehend the social forces that he personified."[11]

If one uses the resources of psychoanalysis in this understanding, then one practices a particular way (for there are, of course, others) of comprehending leadership. The importance of this effort, as a part of the human or social sciences, should need no underlining. I confess that at times I am tempted to believe that the origin of cultural differences—why one society differs so widely from another in its beliefs, values, and behavior—is best explained in terms of how one individual, sometime at the beginning, imprinted *his* personality, *his* individual structuring of the world according to *his* personal needs (in conjunction, of course, with environmental and other factors) on the group he formed around him.[12] One need only think of the influence of a Jim Jones on his Temple followers to see how the power of one personality can shape a small group.

Obviously, as societies grow more complex, the role and analysis of leadership also grows more complex. Historians and political scientists, along with anthropologists, join the inquiry. Yet all are still dealing with human individuals, who can usefully be seen in psychoanalytic terms. It is this effort that I have tried to join in essays ranging from Nixon and Khomeini to Marx and Weber. In such essays, I have tried to act as a scout, or guide, moving into relatively unexplored areas and leaving markers for those who might follow, intending to establish more fortified works.

The mention of Marx and Weber points to the fact that leaders are often primarily intellectual rather than political (although, as Tucker's "realm of the mind" reminds us, the two are often intertwined). I cannot refrain from quoting Keynes to this effect: "Madmen in authority, who hear voices in the air, are distilling their frenzy from some academic scribbler of a few years back. I am sure that the power of vested interests is vastly exaggerated compared with the gradual encroachment of ideas. Not, indeed, immediately, but after a certain interval. . . . But, soon or late, it is ideas, not vested interests, which are dangerous for good or evil."[13]

We need not take Keynes's "madmen" too literally. As Freud has convincingly shown, the line between the normal and the abnormal is constantly being crossed. Nor are academic scribblers free from the charge of "madness," in the sense I am using. The point is that intellectuals, along with politicians or statesmen, exercise leadership and that the elements of that leadership can be illuminated by the practice of psychohistory. Naturally, whereas with political figures we look primarily at patterns of action as well as at words and do so in a political context, with intellectuals the words, looked at in an intellectual context, are more central, though the patterns of action are not without meaning.

As is evident, I have tried, as part of my psychohistorical practice, to understand both political and intellectual leadership and the crossovers, in some cases, between them. I am also arguing in the course of the essays on intellectual figures (see especially Chapter 6, "The Importance of Being Karl Marx . . .") that, unlike the natural sciences, work in the human and social sciences is *intrinsically* linked with the personality of the individual carrying it out; that is, it enters not only into the motives for the creation of the work—Einstein, for example, clearly had personal as well as professional motives—but into the findings and evaluation of the work itself. I shall not reargue the matter here but simply state that this is what I struggled toward in Part II of this book, with results that the reader will wish to judge after reading the individual essays.

Increasingly, as I explored the possibilities of using psychoanalytic theory in leadership studies, I became aware that the results were still somewhat in a vacuum if one did not also study more intensely the led, the followers, and the cultural setting in which leadership and followership took place. Over time, I found myself attempting this task primarily in regard to American materials. In Part IV of this book I try to creep up gradually on the problem. In a sense, the essays here start addressing the question "What is an American?" It is natural that one essay should be on Crèvecoeur, the father of that phrase, and that another one should be on an intense experiential part of the Puritan background of the American past, and yet another on the psychological dimensions of leadership in the American Revolution.

One problem with Freudian psychology is that whereas it offers a viable *individual* psychology (though disturbingly weak in its founder's work in regard to women), it proffers little in the way of a reliable *group* psychology. Yet groups and group behavior are mainly what historians are interested in; and increasingly, as already suggested, I had become convinced that leaders could be fully understood only in detailed relation to those whom they led. Freud's *Group Psychology and the Analysis of the Ego* still remains within a limited individual framework, arguing that the leader leads by libidinal and narcissistic qualities.[14] Highly suggestive, it carries us only a very limited way. So too, Erikson's *Young Man Luther* and his *Gandhi's Truth,* although brilliant giant steps forward, still tell us only that the great leader, in solving personal problems, also solves those of many other people, the followers. Though immersing his hero in the social, cultural, and technological context of his time, Erikson remains within the realm of individual psychology, though pressing to its outermost limits.

How might one go further? How might I myself go beyond my earlier studies, such as of Nixon, where I only touched on the need for greater examination of the led? Where might lie the future of psychohistory? *Reculer, pour mieux salter*—to jump farther, one retreats a step. Thus, in Part V, I go back to some of the beginnings of leader-led studies and indulge in critical reflections. Then I jump. As a firm believer that theory must both precede and go along with practice, I have tried in the penultimate essay to explore what lines research into the leader-led relationship might profitably take. I conjecture that there exists for groups a psychic repository whose contents can be discerned through an exploration, not of individual psyches, but of myths, legends, folklore, literary constructions, rituals, monuments, and so forth, a different "text" from that normally encountered in Freudian analysis. I also surmise that leaders appeal to different segments of this repository, seeking to form a special group of followers by activating a particular part of the spectrum.

In the very last chapter of this book, I have sought to explore, very tentatively, the ideas concerning the psychic repository. I have tried to do so in the specific case of "The American Psyche," based on a course I have been teaching for the last half decade or more at M.I.T. In the course of this teaching, I came to focus on what I called polarities, as well as themes, running through the American historical experience and forming the American psychic repository. In Chapter 17, I merely offer a sketch as to how one might proceed; it is a work in progress.

My major interest throughout this book, as must be evident by now, is in exploring the theoretical possibilities of using one branch of the human or social sciences—in this case, psychoanalysis—in regard to historical materials. Because of this interest on my part, I have been willing to test my ideas on very diverse materials. Leadership, although a critical element in social science and history, is only one focus of my work, though it is the one central to this series of essays. However, as with the rest of psychohistory, leadership studies carried out in a psychological mode depend on convictions as to the worth of psychoanalysis. For that reason, I have spent a good deal of time, starting at the beginning of this introduction, as well as in some of the chapters that follow, examining the roots of psychoanalysis itself in Darwinian evolutionary biology and in the novelistic tradition.

In the end, I worked in the ways that I have discussed because I am interested in understanding the human species, my own, in all of its various manifestations. For me, the historical—that is, in the broadest sense, the evolutionary—mode is the most appealing and revealing way of reaching such understanding. Conceptually, this means that though the human is a "natural" animal and thus must be studied by means of the natural sciences, it also is an "unnatural" animal—that is, self-constructing, cultural—and thus must be studied by means of the human, or social, sciences. It is as an adventure in such a study that I hope the reader will finally experience his or her reading of this work.

# The Applicability
## of
# Psychoanalysis

# Darwin, the Bedrock
# of Psychoanalysis

THE starting point of psychoanalysis, as I have said, is Darwin. I start with him, while trying to understand Freud, because I believe firmly that Darwinian biology is the bedrock on which Freudian psychoanalysis stands. Freud said as much himself: "for the psychical field," he declared, "the biological field does in fact play the part of the underlying bedrock."[1] Although one can quote Freud as seeming occasionally to reject the biological heritage, these are stray variants on the basic theme: without Darwin, neither he nor we can imagine Freud.

Many subsequent observers, including psychoanalysts, have tried to detach psychoanalysis from its biological roots, rejecting such a base as crass and "materialist" and affirming only its hermeneutic, and thus humanistic, nature. This is a Cyclopean vision of psychoanalysis. The human is an evolutionary animal, a developmental and historical creature. Its nature must be understood in terms of a genetic, or Darwinian, viewpoint. As Freud's daughter, Anna Freud, said, "There never was any doubt about psychoanalysis as a *genetic* psychology."[2] The pervasiveness of Darwin's influence on Freud and his generation is so great that it became taken for granted and thus cannot be measured simply by the number of actual citations, though there are a goodly number of them to cite.

My aim here is not to go into the details of Darwin's work, nor even its effect on Freud, a work carried out by many scholars and deserving all of the attention it gets.[3] I wish simply to reassert the primacy of Darwinian evolutionary thought and practice for an understanding of Freud.

I will undertake here, however, a complementary task: to stress the way in which Darwin initiates the project of linking the body to the mind in an evolutionary sense and then how, in his own life and work, he offers tantalizing hints that lead on toward psychoanalysis.

The *Origin of Species* (1859) itself does not treat of the human animal. It is in *The Descent of Man* (1871) that Darwin finally turns to his own species, starting from the view that "man still bears in *his bodily frame* the indelible stamp of his lowly origin."[4] Darwin is, at this point, simply picking up where he left off in the *Origin*.

Such a view seemed to *reduce* the human to a mere animal, a bestial creature. Such was the worry of Darwin's old geology teacher, Adam Sedgwick, who, on receiving a copy of the *Origin,* wrote to his former student, deploring his having broken the link between the material and moral world: "You have ignored this link; and if I do not mistake your meaning, you have done your best in one or two cases to break it. Were it possible, which Thank God, it is not, to break it, humanity, in my mind, would suffer damage that might brutalize it, and sink the human race into a lower grade of degradation than any into which it has fallen since its written records tell us of its history."[5] It is a charge similar to that made against Darwin in the 1860 meeting of the British Association for the Advancement of Science by Bishop Willberforce, who would taunt him, indirectly, with the accusation that he had an ape as a grandfather.[6]

Sedgwick and Willberforce, and others like them, could not have made these charges if they had read, ahead of time, the to-be-published *Descent of Man*. Here Darwin conscientiously began to trace the evolution of the human as a moral as well as a physical creature. Here, in long and sometimes tedious philosophizing, Darwin speculated on human evolution, not only from the lower animals but from its own lowly primitive origins. There is, indeed, often an unfortunate racist element in Darwin's work; he echoes the prevailing view of the gradations of race, which is seen as starting with lowly primitive and negroid man and culminating in nineteenth-century Western Anglo-Saxon man. As he declares in his Introduction, one of the objects of his work is to consider "the value of the differences between the so-called races of man."[7]

He now also begins to give equal weight to sexual selection, along with natural selection, although he first is concerned to treat the former for its important role in differentiating races (by like choosing like, for example). The larger import of emphasizing this factor, the sexual, for a future psychoanalysis is clear. It is, however, in chapters such as "Comparison of the Mental Powers of Man and the Lower Animals" that Darwin hits his stride, stressing the continuity of emotions: animals too feel pleasure and pain, happiness and misery; they too dream; they use tools, and they even have language, though their language differs in degree from the human.

What then fully differentiates the human from the lower animals? It is religion, Darwin asserts, which, far from being innate, evolves over time and through stages. It is, even more importantly, "the moral sense of conscience" that is "by far the most important" distinction.[8] Where does this moral sense come from? Darwin's handling of this topic is somewhat murky, for he is obviously struggling across difficult terrain. It arises, he asserts tentatively, from each individual's "possessing certain stronger or more enduring instincts, and others less strong or enduring; so that there would often be a struggle as to which impulse should be followed." In addition to his theory of conflicting impulses, whose impact on Freud can easily be surmised, Darwin roots morality in "the social instincts."

Specifically, Darwin claims that the social instinct, "the feeling of pleasure from society," arises as an extension of "the young remaining for a long time with their parents." As he goes on, "With respect to the origin of the parental and filial affections, which apparently lie at the base of the social instincts, we know not the steps by which they have been gained." It is worth quoting the rest of his remark: "but we may infer that it has been to a large extent through natural selection. So it has almost certainly been with the unusual and opposite feeling of hatred between the nearest relations, as with the worker-bees which kill their brother drones, and with the queen-bees which kill their daughter-queens; the desire to destroy their nearest relations having been in this case of service to the community."

It is obvious that the animal whose young remain longest with, and in a state of dependency on, their parents is the human. Is it fanciful, further, to see the effect of these remarks on Freud as he pursued his path to the concept of an Oedipus complex? To anyone familiar with Freud's ideas, it seems likely that, consciously, or more likely unconsciously, it was in this evolutionary biology of Darwin, now extended to the human, that Freud found his immediate inspiration. He developed it in more psychological terms, of course, but the acknowledgment of Darwin's primal horde idea, in *Totem and Taboo,* reveals only in part the depths of Freud's indebtedness. It is in human *biological* nature that we find the "origins" of the Oedipal conflict; and for a most interesting speculation on how this might have evolved, I refer the reader to a stimulating article by Alex Comfort.[9]

A close reading of the whole of the *Descent* is essential for an understanding of Freud's Darwinian inspiration; I have touched only in a tangential manner on a few points. There is more, and a more direct, inspiration in *The Expression of the Emotions in Man and Animals,* originally intended by Darwin as part of the *Descent* but given separate form in 1872. Here, Darwin himself trembles on the edge of what we might now consider psychoanalytic insight. Freud read this work at least twice and marked it carefully. It is here that Darwin most forcefully makes the connection between mind and body and establishes the interactions of the two.

Observing infants and madmen, studying anthropological reports and composite photographs, Darwin argues that human emotions and their display are rooted in human evolutionary nature, where drawing back the teeth and snarling, for example, or having the hair bristle had a survival value. One can even say that, just as Darwin believed that ontogeny recapitulates physical phylogeny in the embryo, so the expressions can be seen as recapitulating emotional evolution in the child and adult. The most important point, of course, is that both mental and emotional acts arise on a bodily, evolutionary basis and remain so connected.

Yet, as Darwin develops this idea, he emphasizes the way in which the mind affects the body, giving a number of examples. One in particular is blushing (from which Darwin suffered). He analyzes blushing as a physical matter, where "the small vessels of the face become filled with blood," but he recognizes that the cause of this happening is an emotion, "the emotion of shame."[10] We cannot cause a blush by any physical means, even though the "tendency to blush is inherited," according to Darwin. As another example, Darwin cites his father, a medical doctor, as having noted that a patient of his, suffering from heart disease (from which he later died) and a habitually irregular pulse, invariably had a regular heart beat as soon as Dr. Darwin entered the room.

My own favorite, for its direct link to Freud's later work with hypnosis, is a footnote casually inserted into Darwin's text. It is a long quote, but I cannot resist giving it in full, for it is the most direct testimony of Darwin's own interest in the psychological. In a footnote, he observes:

> Dr. J. Crichton Browne, from his observations on the insane, is convinced that attention directed for a prolonged period on any part or organ may ultimately influence its capillary circulation and nutrition. He has given me some extraordinary cases; one of these . . . refers to a married woman fifty years of age, who laboured under the firm and long-continued delusion that she was pregnant. When the expected period arrived, she acted precisely as if she had been really delivered of a child, and seemed to suffer extreme pain, so that the perspiration broke out on her forehead. The result was that a state of things returned, continuing for three days, which had ceased during the six previous years.

Darwin then continues in a significant allusion, "Mr. Braid gives, in his 'Magic, Hypnotism,' &c., 1852, p. 95, and in his other works analogous cases, as well as other facts showing the great influence of the will on the mammary glands, even on one breast alone."

We are clearly on the way to Freud's psychoanalysis, though mediated through Charcot and Breuer, with both of whom Freud worked. We need only recall the first classic case, Breuer's treatment of Anna O., reported in *Studies on Hysteria,* where a similar case of false pregnancy is reported, to see in dramatic form the continuity. It is therefore not only in the grand strokes of Darwin's evolutionary theory—its geneticism, its linking of the human with the other animals, and its connecting of human sexual and emotional development—so well traced by other scholars, but also in the fine details of Darwin's own "psychological" observations and interests that Freud found inspiration, general and specific, for his own parturition of psychoanalysis.

Darwin knew whereof he spoke on psychological matters from his own personal experience.[11] In what follows in this book, I will argue, and then try to put into practice, the belief that intellectual constructs, while emerging from many sources, are also connected to the thinker's inner life. This is hardly an original idea. Nietzsche, for example, remarked that "philosophy is the confession of the philosopher"; and before him, Fichte had commented that "was für eine Philosophie man wählt, hängt davon ab, was für ein Mensch man ist" ("The philosophy a man chooses depends on what kind of man he is"). (One can't help comparing this with Feuerbach's "Man ist was er esst" ["Man is what he eats"], the materialist–body counterpart to the idealist–mind assertion; Darwin, of course, and then Freud after him, insists on the two being connected.) What is new, then, about psychoanalysis, and psychohistory, is the effort to examine the "confession" in a more than "religious" (i.e., in a scientific) fashion.

In his own life, Darwin knew a good deal about various forms of mental disorder and disturbance. His father, although a general practitioner, practiced what must be considered an intuitive form of psychological therapy with his patients and shared his insights with his son. Darwin's own relations with his father had strong psychological overtones. One does not have to go as far as Phyllis Greenacre in seeing a "murderous" Oedipal conflict between Darwin senior and his offspring to recognize that the father-son relationship played a strong shaping role in the development of Charles Darwin. In one of the essays that follows, "Darwin, the Benchuca, and Genius," I have tried to look at various explanations for Darwin's illnesses, including his relationship to his father, while emphasizing the creative outcome of his struggles.

Insanity, depression, stuttering—these were all "inherited" traits of the Darwin family familiar to young Charles. He was keenly aware of possible childhood roots of psychological development, proposing a "Natural History of Babies" in 1838 as a subject of further inquiry.[12] Darwin's own observations (observation was the trait he prized most in his father) covered cases of double consciousness, forgetting and involuntary recall, senility, and delirium. His own suffering was extensive, manifesting itself even before the voyage of the *Beagle* in heart palpitations and then in multiple symptoms of insomnia, headaches, eczema, and almost daily stomach discomfort (pains, belching, and, a little less frequently, vomiting), to name only a few. Darwin kept medical records on himself; using these, Ralph Colp, Jr., has written an invaluable book, *To Be an Invalid,* giving the details of Darwin's maladies, the possible explanations for them, and the attempted cures, which involved bouts of such treatments as water cures, clairvoyance, and the use of electric chains (shades of animal magnetism—in fact, however, Darwin tended to be critical of mesmerism), and even arsenic.[13]

When Charles Darwin spoke of the effect of the mind on the body, he surely had his own experiences in mind. Well might he have consulted, as he did, his own father (Charles was particularly upset at the diagnosis of hypochondria and turned to his father for a definite medical explanation), but he also could have profitably consulted a later doctor, Sigmund Freud. Of even more importance for our particular purpose, Darwin wrestled with his problems not only internally but in the form of notebook entries, speculating on psychological phenomena and trying to understand them scientifically.

We are fortunate that his notebooks have been preserved. We see him observing that "characters of dreams no surprise, at the violation of all [rules] relations of time [identity], place, & personal connections—ideas are strung together in manner quite different from when awake—peculiar sensation as flying" and recording three of his dreams, giving a provisional analysis of each. In another entry, he notes, "I often have (as a boy) wondered why *all abnormal* sexual actions or even impulses (where sensation of individual are same as in normal cases) are held in abhorrence," and he then adds cryptically, "It is because instincts to women is not followed; good case of instinctive."[14]

At another place, he writes, "My F. [father] says there is perfect gradation between sound people and insane—that everybody is insane at some time." Again, this is followed by the cryptic comments "My Grand F. thought the feeling of anger, which rises almost involuntarily when a person is *tired* is akin to insanity. (I know the feeling also of depression, & both these give strength & comfort to the body.) I know the feeling." (Incidentally, Darwin's son Francis tells us that Darwin suffered intensely from his own feelings of anger, feeling acute guilt over them.)

There are many more such entries that are of great interest, but I include here only two more citations. In his "Notebooks on Man, Mind and Materialism," Darwin writes, "Our descent, then, is the origin of our evil passions!!—The Devil under form of Baboon is our grandfather!—" How ironic that Willberforce was intuitively right, then, in his accusation! Only Darwin did not mean his grandfather as an ape literally but as the ape still within the human, that is, the evolutionary primate origins of human creatures and their emotional residual. Nor was Darwin prepared to settle simply for such an assertion. A few pages earlier, he had already written, "Origin of man now proved [i.e., his own theory of evolution by natural selection, still unpublished].—Metaphysics must flourish.—He who understand [*sic*] baboon would do more toward metaphysics than Locke [and his *Essay Concerning Human Understanding*]." Darwin's "metaphysics," of course, was to be his science of evolutionary biology. Its psychological development, I am arguing, was to lead to the psychoanalytic psychology, a new human science, of Freud.

Freud, of course, had not read Darwin's notebooks (for they were unpublished during Freud's life). He had, however, read the *Origin, Descent, Expression of the Emotions,* and various other, more technical works. All of these, I am contending, were permeated with Darwin's own personal psychological concerns, no matter how distant and underground, as well as emerging openly and forcefully in the *Expression of the Emotions* itself. More generally, Freud had studied Darwinian biology extensively in his university classes, especially those given by Carl Claus. It was Claus, who himself had worked on the development of the Copepoda, and thus on the class of Crustacea, who gave Freud his first research assignment: the examination of the gonadic (sexual) structure of the eel. The research was carried out at a marine research center in Trieste.

We know about Freud's studies with Claus, and thus of Darwinian biology, only as a result of recent scholarship.[15] Of course, there were other important influences on Freud's development of his science, and, though I have been stressing the biological as the bedrock, the others are also essential in any attempt to understand the full etiology and thus the nature of

Freud's effort at a science. A full historical study would have to deal with them at length. Here I merely touch on a few more, of special importance to my general thesis. One of these is the influence of another of Freud's teachers, Ernst Brücke, whose role was stressed by Ernest Jones in earlier work.

Brücke was Freud's hero, his model of a laboratory scientist. He was also a father figure, Freud's counselor, who eventually persuaded him to abandon laboratory work for medical practice (in order to make a decent living, which would permit him to get married). Brücke had been a member of a so-called school in physiology, made up of Emil du Bois-Reymond, Carl Ludwig, Hermann Helmholtz, and himself. In a letter to a friend in 1842, du Bois-Reymond wrote of a sort of manifesto: "[We] pledged a solemn oath to put into power this truth: no other forces than the common physical-chemical ones are active within the organism. In those cases which cannot at the time be explained by these forces one has either to find the specific way or form of their action by means of the physical-mathematical method, or to assume new forces equal in dignity to the chemical-physical forces inherent in matter, reducible to the force of attraction and repulsion."[16]

Freud spent much of his life struggling with this inspiration. It played a part in his early laboratory work, though this requires further discussion. It is the model on which he seems to have formed his "Project for a Scientific Psychology" (1895). It is the method he thought present in Fechner's measurement of pleasure–pain sensations. Even at the end of his life, Freud was hoping that physical–chemical forces would be discovered that could replace his own psychological explanations. This is the Freud who hankered after the physics' model I cited earlier as fueling the demand placed on psychoanalysis if it is to shape up as a true science. The vital question then becomes why Freud fell away from this model, though reluctantly, and whether it was a fall from grace or a tumble into a new science adequate to its phenomena.

The first thing that needs to be said is that by the time Freud was studying with Brücke, even Freud had come to realize that in practice the model didn't work. As Paul Cranefield has so nicely shown, "Freud's work under Brücke was histological in nature,"[17] not physiological. Nor was much of the mechanistic approach left in the researches of Brücke himself. Moreover, even the original inspiration, in the form of a revolt against the *Naturphilosophie* of their teacher, Johannes Müller, still left the "school" incorporating some of the earlier romanticism and holism into their own work. A provocative quote from Helmholtz can set our imaginations at work: Regarding psychic acts, he speaks of "the unconscious process of the association of ideas going on in the dark underground of our memory. Thus too its results are urged on our consciousness, so to speak, as if an external power had constrained us, over which our will had no control."[18]

Obviously, the Brücke mechanistic model, even if partly mythical, is not to be dismissed. It entered into Freud's mind set, along with the biological, and was a major influence in his effort to conceive of the mind as a kind of closed hydraulic system, or a pleasure–pain calculating machine, or a field of attraction–repulsion forces. As Freud said, the only Weltanschauung psychoanalysis brings to its work is the scientific, and in the late nineteenth century that frequently meant mechanistic physics. This Weltanschauung, or at least its physicalistic version, supplied the absolutely essential faith in a deterministic world that Freud needed (though it is no longer the one held even by physics itself; still, on the macro level it was essential for Freud). I am simply saying that if that was all that science meant, that is, that all science had to be on the simple deterministic model of nineteenth-century physics, we would not be discussing Freudian psychoanalysis here. Psychoanalysis would simply be a quaint, outmoded pseudoscience, an imitation form of physics, something like Henry Thomas Buckle's effort at scientific history, but of no further interest.

There is one other figure we must look at as having great effect on Freud, one we can see clearly through the important work of William J. McGrath in his book *Freud's Discovery of Psychoanalysis*. The subtitle of this book is *The Politics of Hysteria,* and McGrath persuasively argues for the role of nineteenth-century Viennese political life as shaping Freud's development of psychoanalysis. However, it is not this side of McGrath's work that concerns us here but rather his researches into the role of one of Freud's university teachers, Franz Brentano. Brentano was a Catholic priest as well as a professor of philosophy, who based his thinking on the English empirical tradition. A personally attractive man, Brentano cast a spell over the young Sigmund, altering his one-sided materialism.

In his *Psychology from an Empirical Standpoint,* published in 1874, the year Freud first enrolled in his course, Brentano declared that "just as the natural sciences study the properties and laws of physical bodies, which are the objects of our external perception, psychology is the science which studies the properties and laws of the soul, which we discover within ourselves directly by means of inner perception, and which we infer by analogy, to exist in others." And Brentano then announced: "The phenomena revealed by inner perception are also subject to laws." McGrath's conclusion, that "Brentano's methodology provided the foundation for Freud's whole approach to psychological investigation"[19] may be a little strong, but it does add another key piece to the puzzle.

By now it must be clear that Freud's scientific inspiration comes from diverse elements of the nineteenth-century endeavor to establish "laws." We can never actually explain his creativity, for creativity is the particular synthesis of intellectual and personal elements that, fused together, make for a previously nonexisting discovery. Nevertheless, we can identify some of the crucial elements that enter into his work. If we are to understand the nature of psychoanalysis as a "science," this becomes a critically important task, not a mere matter of biographical interest. In this task, as I have suggested, both a Brücke-type mechanistic physiology and a Brentano-type introspective psychology (here, too, many other names besides Brentano's could be introduced) take their place. Beyond them, however, I am arguing that the Darwinian is the crucial inspiration, for psychoanalysis is, above all else, a continuation of evolutionary biological science.

Darwin the scientist was fully aware that, as he put it, "scarcely a single point is discussed in this volume [the *Origin*] on which facts cannot be adduced, often apparently leading to conclusions directly opposite to those at which I have arrived."[20] Indeed, a few years after its publication, Lord Kelvin "conclusively" proved by the methods of physics and the use of mathematics that the earth was only 20–24 million years old, thus falling impossibly short of the hundreds of millions of years required by Darwin's theory. Yet Darwin persisted, while acknowledging that "anyone whose disposition leads him to attach more weight to unexplained difficulties than to the explanation of a certain number of facts will certainly reject the theory."[21] His own evidences and inferences were sufficiently persuasive to stand the assault of other evidences, from outside sources whose own accuracy might be challenged by newer scientific work.

So with Freud. As he announced in his *Introductory Lectures on Psycho-Analysis,*

> It would be a mistake to suppose that a science consists entirely of strictly proved theses, and it would be unjust to require this. . . . Science has only a few apodeictic propositions in its catechism: the rest are assertions promoted by it to some particular degree of probability. It is actually a sign of a scientific mode of thought to find satisfaction in these approximations to certainty and to be able to pursue constructive work further in spite of the absence of final confirmation.[22]

In this spirit, Freud had the courage to go on with his work. It is not that "anything goes" and no confirmation is needed. It is simply that a "particular degree of probability," which emanates from the *actual materials themselves,* is what we must look for. We must judge the "scientific" nature of our findings by the kind of evidence and inference that can characterize the phenomena that we, the inquirers, are attempting to understand. This was Freud's aim, and it should be ours.

I have been stressing the Darwinian and even the mechanistic basis of Freudian psychoanalysis. Why, then, can an acute observer declare that "practically all later changes in psychoanalytic theory have one common denominator *they move away from Darwinian thinking,*"[23] a move actually initiated by Freud himself. So far has the move gone in some cases that some, such as Paul Ricoeur or Roy Schafer, have declared it a strictly linguistic or hermeneutic study. After all, what the analyst deals with is "words," and at its extreme, psychoanalysis thus falls under the domain of literature, rather than science. A Jacques Lacan can then be hailed by some as a great analyst, offering "meaning" beyond that of more mundane, less structuralist practitioners and thinkers.

The fact is that "meaning" is at the center of psychoanalysis, setting it off drastically from the natural sciences, including even most of biology. Freud's great book is *The Interpretation of Dreams,* and *interpretation* is the key word.[24] As he moved out of Brücke's laboratory, as well as away from the dissection of Claus's eels, into medical practice and the treatment of nervous disorders, Freud discovered that his patients' hysterical symptoms were not organically based but "in the mind," symptoms of something deep in the unconscious. So too, dreams were not simply somatic events but were filled with latent meaning, beneath the overt, that could be interpreted through a new method, free association.

If free association became the microscope by which to examine the inner life of patients, literary works, among others, could be materials to be analyzed, to be interpreted for what they could tell us about unconscious mental products. The Greeks, for example, in many ways had been there before Freud. Listen to Plato in *The Republic:* Socrates, speaking of desires, refers to

> those which bestir themselves in dreams, when the gentler part of the soul
> slumbers and the control of reason is withdrawn; then the wild beast in us,
> full-fed with meat or drink, becomes rampant and shakes off sleep to go in
> quest of what will gratify its own instincts. As you know, it will cast away

all shame and prudence at such moments and stick at nothing. In phantasy it will not shrink from intercourse with a mother or anyone else, man, god, or brute, or from forbidden food or any deed of blood. In a word, it will go to any length of shamelessness and folly.[25]

When his interlocutor agrees, Socrates drops the matter, remarking that "we have been carried away from our point." For Freud, of course, such a dream becomes the starting point for a scientific inquiry, and he uses a Greek play, Sophocles' *Oedipus Rex,* as further inspiration for his construction of a scientific psychology.

Literature had always considered the dreamlike, the childlike, and the abnormal, whether in myths and fairy tales or in plays and stories. And before the institutionalization of psychology as a science in the late nineteenth century, psychology too paid attention to such matters, being more a kind of philosophical or literary inquiry than a laboratory one. As Wolf Lepenies reminds us in a suggestive article, psychology was only becoming a respected academic discipline when Wilhelm Wundt, its founding father—having taught a course at Heidelberg, "Psychology as a Natural Science," starting in 1862—published his *Principles of Physiological Psychology* in 1873 and established the first psychological institute, at Leipzig, in 1879.[26]

Wundt and his followers dismissed the childlike and the abnormal from psychological study and insisted that only the matter of consciousness was worthy of attention; psychopathology was solely about "the events of the diseased conscious." As is well known, Freud restored these subjects to psychology and took the unconscious as the focus of his inquiry into mental process. If Darwinian biology was the bedrock of his work, the unconscious became the cornerstone on which his whole conception of psychoanalysis rested; and interpretation became the method by which to comprehend the workings of the unconscious. Freud's genius was to make a rational science, admittedly of a very peculiar nature, out of the "irrational" materials found in literature as well as in the dreams, the symptoms, and even the everyday slips of normal as well as abnormal human beings. His "logic" was a "psychologic," in which the normal categories of logical thinking are no longer the language in which the unconscious "thinks" (the gravest mistake is made by Freudian critics when they ignore this point).

I do not rehearse the innumerable stumblings, the false starts, the revised theories, even wild concepts with which Freud pursued his way to psychoanalysis. Nor do I elaborate here the range of his concepts, theories, models, and so forth. Nor the way in which he did not leave the notion of unconscious mental processes as a mere assertion but detailed the way in which they work, dynamically, in terms of repression, projection, displacement, reaction formation, and so forth. The main point is that in the end Freud had established a new science, however tentative and however subject to revision—what science is not?—and he had done so by combining Darwinian biology with hermeneutic analysis.

The danger is that, emphasizing only one part of his inspiration, we may be tempted, for example, to reduce the human to mere animal heritage, making it a creature solely of biology—"red in tooth and claw"—devoid of culture; or, as did Pavlov, who developed one line of Darwin's thought, make it a creature solely of reflex actions that can be conditioned. On the other side, we may reduce the human to a mere literary creation, removed from animal nature, where any effort at science, whether natural or human, is a mere "social construction," a creation without any "reality" behind it, whose nature we may seek to understand "scientifically."

It was by holding the two parts—biology and hermeneutics—in creative tension, not reducing the human to either one, that Freud was able to work toward his new science. Its peculiarity stems from the fact that its subject matter is the human, a creature of both genes and culture (including both language and symbols), a most ambivalent and ambiguous creature. Such a creature, together with its mental workings and actual behavior, requires many approaches to understand "it"—mechanistic, chemical, physiological, to name a few, but also sociological, literary, and humanistic—of which psychoanalysis is, of course, only one. As I am arguing, however, it is a very special one, partly because it stands so dramatically at the boundary of the natural and the human.

One special aspect of this cusplike posture involves the notion of causality. In the natural sciences, causality figures prominently (even when expressed only in terms of probability theory), and a principal aim is prediction. Freud too sought to embrace causality and to carry out his work in terms of strict determinism. Paradoxically, by embracing determinism, he also hoped to lead his patients, and all of humankind as well, to freedom. In fact, by placing interpretation at the center of his science, Freud teetered on the edge of undercutting his own causal approach (though not its promise of freedom). As various of his followers, prominent among them Erik Erikson, have argued, psychoanalysis works in terms of corresponding processes and correlations rather than unicausality. One result, of course, is that it does not try, except in a most limited way, to be predictive.

In practice, Freud worked along a method derived from Darwin himself, who stood at the far end of the natural science spectrum of causality. As Stephen Jay Gould describes the method, such people, whom he calls "Mancunians," do not "usually employ the classical method of simplification and experimental replication; [they] use what the 19th century British philosopher of science William Whewell called 'consilience (or jumping together) of inductions'—the juxtaposition of sources so diverse and numerous that only one set of causes could encompass all the noted effects."[27] The method of "consilience" is the one used by Freud, just as it was used by Darwin. In Freudian terms, however, it takes on the shape of the famous, or infamous, concept of overdetermination, where numerous "sources"—phenomena—fall under "one set of causes," that is, a single theoretical explanation.

In sum, Darwin had given Freud a model of scientific method as well as scientific inspiration. It is a method that does not, as said earlier, provide prediction, but it clearly stands in close proximity to literary analysis and allows for greater understanding of the elusive human creature than was had previously. Such understanding I chose to call scientific (for some of the further arguments involved I refer the reader to Chapter 3, "Freud and Nietzsche").

Scientific discoveries are generally reported in research papers, as pioneered in the seventeenth century, for example, in the *Transactions of the Royal Society* (occasionally, there are the great books, such as Galileo's *Dialogues Concerning the Two Great Systems of the World,* or Newton's *Principia,* or Darwin's *Origin*). These papers typically describe research, which builds on previous work, detail the experimental procedures, report the observations and results, and explain how previous hypotheses may have to be modified or discarded unless they have been confirmed. In these ways, science is shared and accumulated. Ideally, the procedures and results can be verified by repeating the whole procedure.

How do Freud's research papers stack up against this ideal? Anyone looking at the published reports of his scientific discoveries with this model in mind will at first experience dismay (and for many this is the end of the matter). Such dismay was Freud's own first reaction to the form of his work. As he explained in *Studies on Hysteria,* "I have not always been a psychotherapist. Like other neuro-pathologists, I was trained to employ local diagnoses and electro-prognosis, and it still strikes me myself as strange that the case histories I write should read like short stories and that, as one might say, they lack the serious stamp of science."

How then could he justify his "case histories"? As he goes on, "I must console myself with the reflection *that the nature of the subject is evidently responsible for this.* . . . The fact is that local diagnosis and electrical reactions lead nowhere in the study of hysteria, whereas a detailed description of mental processes *such as we are accustomed to find in the works of imaginative writers* enables me, *with the use of a few psychological formulas,* to obtain at least some kind of insight into the course of that affection" (my italics). What Freud then discovers is "an intimate connection between the story of the patient's sufferings and the symptoms of his illness."28

All science is an effort to establish lawlike connections among phenomena. Freud is saying that in psychoanalysis the "connection" explaining a symptom is a narrative one, a "story"; the story itself, placed in the framework of psychological formulas (laws of a very special kind), offers us the observations, describes the procedures, and tells us how previous hypotheses, the formulas, have been confirmed or must be altered (or even discarded). The one thing it cannot tell us is how exactly to repeat this particular "experiment," for it is the very nature of the relationship involving the analyst and the analysand, with its powerful underpinnings of suggestion and confidentiality, that cannot be minutely replicated. Instead, we must tell other "stories," appeal to other, comparable materials, such as myths and dreams, and thus, by the comparative method, seek to construct and to test our psychological formulas—let us call them theories—which we then reapply to new materials (as well as old).

Let me flesh this out a bit further. The case history is, in fact, not just one narrative but the cumulation of hundreds or even thousands of narratives told during the course of an analysis. Although the final case history, as written by the analyst, appears to be about an individual, and idiosyncratically so, it is also about the species, common humanity. This is because of its biological basis; that is to say, the commonality of the human experience on which it depends stems from our inheritance. Our common needs, however, are not *just* biological but are always manifested in a social context, which determines their nature and expression. In turn, this expression takes the form of regularly recurring kinds of relations, which can be said to look like "laws" (though I think this is the wrong word for them). An example might be the Oedipus complex: though a constant relation exists, the subjects involved can be different, in the sense that it need not be an actual father and son but any parental figure and the child. Thus, my narrative or yours may have different facts, and they will certainly take different shapes in different cultures, but they will all speak to the same relationship.29

At this point we see why Freud, starting from a Darwinian basis, has had to move toward a hermeneutic science. It is a move mirrored in his shift from scientific monographs on eels, for example, to his "Just So" stories on humans (as his case studies were labeled by one critic). The importance of this move requires us to examine it further, just as we did with the Darwinian inspiration.

Our starting point has been the *Studies on Hysteria,* which contains both allusions to Darwin's *Expression of the Emotions* and an early statement of the case history method. In fact, Freud's letters show us how he was dream-walking his way to his new scientific reports. As early as 1883, in a long letter to Martha Bernays, he tried to understand and explain the suicide of one of his close friends, who was outwardly successful. But as Freud writes, "His death was by no means an accident, rather it was a logical outcome of his temperament; his good and bad qualities had combined to bring about his downfall; his life was as though composed by a writer of fiction, and this catastrophe the inevitable end." Freud concludes: "He all but screams for the novelist to preserve him for human memory."[30]

We are still far from the case history. The novelist may preserve a character for "human memory," but the psychoanalyst must use memories, the patient's, to construct a psychological science, though through the same device of narrative. The contrast with Freud's friend Arthur Schnitzler may help us to understand the difference. Like Freud, a medical student, who served as an assistant in the clinic of Freud's teacher, Theodore Meynert, and who also employed hypnosis in clinical situations, Schnitzler explored what Carl Schorske has called "the compulsiveness of Eros" (i.e., the power of instinct), but he did so in plays and novels. So penetrating were his insights that Freud hailed him as a "colleague" in the inquiry into the "underestimated and much-maligned erotic." Indeed, as Schorske tells us, "so strongly did Freud feel his affinity to Schnitzler that he consciously avoided the writer as his 'double' (Doppelgänger)."[31]

However, affinity is not the same as true similarity. What was lacking in Schnitzler, and in all of the other novelists of psychological intuition, was the Darwinian inspiration to science. Another doctor, this time a fictional one, can give us the hint we need. He is Lydgate, the flawed hero of George Eliot's *Middlemarch* (incidentally, one of Freud's favorite novels). In Eliot's words,

> He [Lydgate] had tossed away all cheap inventions where ignorance finds itself able and at ease: *he was enamored of that arduous invention which is the very eye of research, provisionally framing its object and correcting it to more and more exactness of relation;* he wanted to pierce the obscurity of those minute processes which prepared human misery and joy, those invisible thoroughfares which are the first lurking-places of anguish, mania, and

crime, that delicate poise and transition which determine the growth of happy or unhappy consciousness.[32] (my italics)

The fictional Lydgate became the real Freud. From the hazy intuitions of his letter of 1883, Freud moved to the beginnings of psychoanalytic science in the studies on hysteria of 1895. In between, he had learned hypnosis and studied its use, under Charcot, on hysterics. Such a technique and such a study taught him to believe in the power as well as in the existence of the unconscious (and not just Lydgate's consciousness). It also showed him that the line between the abnormal and the normal was porous, with neurotic symptoms (and a little later, dreams and parapraxes) having the same mechanisms as normal mental life. It allowed him, in the end, to use novelistic techniques and form in the service of psychological science.

That psychological science, I have been arguing, while incorporating the novelistic approach, is based on evolutionary biology. Simply to take one shocking fact, as stated by Mary Midgley, writing on sociobiology: "With no other species could a Freudian theory ever have got off the ground. Gorillas, in particular, take so little interest in sex that they shock Robert Ardrey: he concludes that they are in their decadence."[33] There is no getting around the fact that the human is the one animal that enjoys (if this word can properly be used) year-round heterosexual activity but has turned it into a source of acute anxiety, a psychological concern that manifests itself everywhere in an incest taboo. Darwin emphasized sexual selection; Freud went on to talk about sexual impulses. Although he probably over-emphasized the role of the libido, he was trying to fill a seeming vacuum in the culture of his time.

Unquestionably, Freud proceeded in a one-sided manner, with much of the subsequent development of psychoanalysis trying to right the matter. But then so does all science proceed this way. The important thing is that Freud was trying to start from the biological fact of the human being. Such a start quickly showed that whatever its genetic heritage, the human is a social–cultural creature whose evolution increasingly takes shape in those terms. Thus, we are really talking about sociobiology. Taken to occasional extremes by the brilliant zoologist, E. O. Wilson, it is handled with care and illumination by the philosopher Mary Midgley, the ethnographer Irenäus Eibl-Eibesfeldt, and the medical anthropologist Melvin Konner. A standard textbook, Henry Gleitman's *Psychology* (second edition), tells us that "to understand what is truly human about social behavior, we must understand how the built-in biological patterns laid down in our genes are shaped and modified by social experience as we grow up to become members of the society in which we are born."[34] It is this that is meant by sociobiology, and although Freud worked before its formal advent, he had clearly intuited some of its perspectives in Darwinian biology.

Now, I have called his mix of the latter, in the sense just given, and of hermeneutics a science. And at this point, the reader may well ask: Why bother stirring up a controversy? Why insist on the word *science*? I do so because science has a special meaning in our culture, an honorific aura that goes beyond its original meaning of knowledge. It embraces a method, the scientific, which is more than just the knowledge that can be acquired through sheer empiricism, that is, craft skill; or philosophical speculation, that is, wisdom; or religious feeling; or presumed revelation. The scientific method insists on the primacy of close observations, taken up then into a system of theory, whose parts must be logically consistent and whose hypotheses are played back against further observations and then modified.

In my view, that is what psychoanalytic psychology does. It is for this reason that the knowledge it conveys advances the social scientist, especially the historian and political scientist, in a way no other psychology does so fruitfully. Psychoanalytic science, as I have tried to show, is a human science, more tentative and ambiguous than the natural sciences or even such proclaimed social sciences as economics, but well suited to the materials with which it has to deal, the evolutionary animal, Man, filled with meaning. For those afflicted with "physics envy," this will not do; and I have no hope of shaking their "hard" views. For others, a greater openness will prevail, and a willingness to consider what a "new science," however soft, would look like.[35]

Let me put all of this in summary form. Freudian psychoanalysis, starting out in close proximity to the natural sciences and their outer edge of biology, moves toward the cultural sciences, shifting the boundaries of what we mean by science at the same time as it changes our sense of the normal and the abnormal; and it leaves us with a new way of thinking about inner nature, just as Darwin had done with outer Nature. In short, a scientific revolution has occurred, changing irrevocably the landscape of our mind.

# CHAPTER TWO

# Darwin, the Benchuca, and Genius

"DARWIN and the Benchuca" may sound like an anthropological saga. The Benchuca, however, is an insect, not a tribe. And thereby hangs a tale, for Charles Darwin was bitten by a Benchuca, which he referred to as "the great black bug of the Pampas." The attack occurred in South America, on March 25, 1835, as Darwin tells us in his account of the voyage of the *Beagle*. "It is most disgusting," he notes, "to feel soft wingless insects, about an inch long, crawling over one's body. Before sucking they are quite thin, but afterwards they become round and bloated with blood."

On the eve of sailing aboard the *Beagle,* Darwin saw, in a flash of intuition, that the voyage was, for him, a new birth, the beginning of a "second life." A few years after his return, however, Darwin, then in his late twenties, began to exhibit distressing symptoms that remained with him in varying degrees of intensity for the rest of his life: palpitations of the heart, gastric and intestinal pains, fatigue and lethargy, shivering spells, and insomnia. Thus almost all of his creative work was done in a state of illness, Darwin remaining quietly at his country home in Down, cared for by his devoted wife, Emma, and able to work in sustained fashion for only a few hours a day. His "second life," therefore, was characterized by chronic invalidism.

The doctors Darwin consulted could offer no useful diagnosis. In fact, he soon acquired a reputation for being a hypochondriac. The treatment prescribed was rest and the water cure, a regimen of daily baths in which the patient was swaddled in wet cloths for an hour or more at a time. For homeopathy and mesmerism Darwin had mainly scorn, claiming that neither was subject to scientific inquiry. The water cure was different: "No quackery," he wrote.

What do modern doctors have to say about Darwin's illness? A fierce battle has raged in medical and professional journals. Parasitologists and internists, fixing on the 1835 episode, claim the Benchuca as the cause. Since Darwin's time, they explain, the "great black bug," now known as *Triatoma infestans,* has been identified as the most important carrier of *Trypanosoma cruzi,* the causative agent of Chagas' disease,[1] whose characteristics closely match Darwin's symptoms. At this point, complex statistics come into play. For example, 70 percent of *Triatoma infestans* are infected with *T. cruzi;* parts of Chile through which Darwin passed, we are told by Professor Saul Adler, O. B. E., F. R. S., "show a 10 percent positive complement-fixation test in the population together with a considerable infestation with infected *Triatoma infestans.*" In short (the argument, of course, gets much more technical), it is definitely possible—for Adler, probable—that Darwin's illness was caused by the bite of the Benchuca.

Nonsense, respond a number of psychiatrists and psychoanalysts. The physiological etiology does not cover all of Darwin's symptoms and does not account for the fact that some of them—heart palpitations, for example—manifested themselves before the voyage of the *Beagle.* The true explanation, they contend, is that Darwin was a neurotic. His psychoneurosis was the result of his guilt about falling away from orthodox Christian belief; his unconscious resentment toward his "tyrannical father"; his Oedipal rivalry for his mother; his constant preoccupation with sex (*vide* his work on sexual selection).

What is the truth about Darwin's illness? His father, Robert, had tried to dissuade him from undertaking the *Beagle* voyage, pointing out its grave dangers. Did the son see the Benchuca bite as the fateful realization of his father's warnings? Darwin, as his son Francis remarks, had boundless reverence for his father, and "anything his father had said was received with almost implicit faith." As late as 1831, Darwin wrote his friend Professor John Stevens Henslow that "even if I was to go, my father disliking would take away all energy." Was his subsequent fatigue and lethargy a delayed retribution visited on Darwin for ignoring his father's advice? The evidence simply does not allow us to rule out flatly either the Benchuca bite or psychoneurosis as an explanation. What we can do, instead, is treat the question (if not the illness) as a misdirected effort. Not Darwin's pathology, but his genius, is what should interest us. That genius, in fact, was not crippled by his invalidism; it did, however, grow out of his own "life history," and that is something that psychoanalysis, or rather, psychohistory, can help us to understand.

Darwin's autobiography and letters are prime sources. He tells us his feelings toward his mother and father and reveals crucial themes in his own development. Of his mother he says little; his only comment, in the third paragraph of his *Recollections of the Development of My Mind and Character,* is "My mother died in July 1817, when I was a little over eight years old, and it is odd that I can remember hardly anything about her except her death-bed, her black velvet gown, and her curiously constructed work-table." Indeed it is odd: an eight-year-old can be expected to remember much, much more, if he is not intensely repressing his feelings.

The major theme associated with his mother is death. His concern with it emerges seven paragraphs after the comment on his mother; he writes, "I remember clearly only one other incident during this year whilst at Mr. Case's daily school,—namely, the burial of a dragoon soldier; and it is surprising how clearly I can still see [it]. . . . This scene deeply stirred whatever poetic fancy there was in me." What Darwin does not tell us in this paragraph is that he was at the Reverend Mr. Case's school at the age of eight, in 1817–1818, the same year as his mother's death. Although the soldier's burial would be a dramatic event for any little boy, it seems to have taken on heightened importance for Darwin.

Other evidence demonstrates Darwin's preoccupation with death. There is the dream recorded in his notebook in 1838, for example, where he recalls, "Thought that a person was hung & came to life, and then made many jokes about not having run away and having faced death like a hero." More to the point, however, are Darwin's pronounced feelings of guilt as a child. Two sentences after speaking of his mother's death, he confesses, "I believe that I was in many ways a naughty boy." A bit further on, he admits to a troubled conscience because of his habit of inventing falsehoods. Whatever the actuality—exaggerated, it seems—Darwin certainly viewed himself as a bad boy. The suspicion grows, based on comparable clinical data as well as on Darwin's admissions, that in an obscure fashion he felt partly guilty for his mother's death.

Concerned with the enigma and meaning of death since childhood, Darwin expanded his personal experience into a professional concern with destruction in general. Though he called his great work the *Origin of Species,* it is as much about the extinction of species as of their origin. Of course, many intervening experiences link Darwin's memory (or lack of it) of his mother's death and his work on evolution; what I am suggesting is that the theme of destruction—and with it, origin—takes root in Darwin's childhood.

To an eight-year-old boy the death of one's mother is a riddle. Darwin's answer to this riddle may lie in a letter he wrote to Asa Gray in 1860, expounding a theory of evolution in which no one is guilty.

> An innocent and good man stands under a tree and is killed by a flash of lightning. Do you believe . . . that God *designedly* killed this man? . . . If you believe so, do you believe that when a swallow snaps up a gnat that God designed that that particular swallow should snap up that particular gnat at that particular instant? I believe that the man and the gnat are in the same predicament. If the death of neither man nor gnat are designed, I see no good reason to believe that their *first* birth or production should be necessarily designed.

Haunted by his mother's death, Darwin consciously remembered little about his mother, but his father, loomed more than life-size. Darwin was constantly evoking his name, calling Dr. Robert Darwin "the wisest man I ever knew," "the kindest man I ever knew," and "the largest man whom I ever saw." Well might he say the last, for his father stood about 6'2" and weighed almost 340 pounds. This wisest, best, and most powerful of fathers, according to Darwin, was characterized chiefly by his powers of observation and sympathy, "neither of which have I ever seen exceeded or even equalled." His most remarkable gift, in his son's estimation, was "reading the characters, and even the thoughts of those whom he saw even for a short time." Exercising this ability in his medical practice, Dr. Darwin sounds like an early Freud. As Darwin explains, his father's patients, especially women, consulted him "as a sort of Father-Confessor."

> He told me that they always began by complaining in a vague manner about their health, and by practice he soon guessed what was really the matter. He then suggested that they had been suffering in their minds, and now they would pour out their troubles. . . . Owing to my father's skill in winning confidence he received many strange confessions of misery and guilt. He often remarked how many miserable wives he had known.

In the face of such an all-knowing and all-powerful parent, how did young Darwin feel? Though his father, exhibiting a family trait, often exploded in anger, Darwin never consciously had anything but the warmest and most loving feelings toward him. Instead, he turned against himself, feeling that his father's fears that he would be stupid, naughty, and an idle sporting youth—"You will be a disgrace to yourself and all your family," he was told—were, alas, entirely justified.

The extraordinary thing is how well Darwin learned to solve his problems, drawing from them, eventually, creativity (obviously there were other factors, too). Unconsciously, I believe, he learned to get back at his father while maintaining his feelings of love and respect for him. To his father's grave disappointment, for example, he did not do well at school and was unable to settle down to either a medical career at Edinburgh or a religious calling at Cambridge. He criticized his father subtly. Though he received anything his father said with implicit faith, his daughter recalls his saying that "he hoped none of his sons would ever believe anything because he said it, unless they were themselves convinced of its truth." Though he says his father "wisely" sent him to Edinburgh, Darwin thought his studies there a waste of time. Beginning a "second life" as a result of the *Beagle* voyage—undertaken against his father's advice—he finally achieved autonomy.

Darwin was able to accompany the *Beagle* expedition because he had become an ardent collector and amateur naturalist. His collecting was, I believe, a sublimated form of aggression discharged in a constructive way. Darwin was aware that he shared the family penchant for anger. Francis Darwin tells us that when his famous father felt strongly about a subject, "he could hardly trust himself to speak [Darwin, not incidentally, stammered], as he then easily became angry, a thing which he disliked excessively." In his *Recollections,* Darwin recalls how, as a little boy, "I acted cruelly, for I beat a puppy, I believe, simply from enjoying the sense of power." The episode lay heavily on his conscience. A little later, he became "passionately fond of shooting." When he killed his first snipe, his "excitement was so great that I had much difficulty in reloading my gun from the trembling of my hands." Later, at Cambridge, he picked up a bird not quite dead, and, disturbed, could no longer "reconcile it to [my] conscience to continue to derive pleasure from a sport which inflicted such cruel suffering."

The ardent sportsman thereupon became the collector. "Gradually," Darwin tells us, "I gave up my gun more and more, and finally altogether, to my servant, as shooting interfered with my work, more especially with making out the geological structure of a country. I discovered, though unconsciously and insensibly, that the pleasure of observing and reasoning was a much higher one than that of skill and sport." Darwin's aggression had turned into an identification with his father's "powers of observation."

However "neurotic" aspects of Darwin's personal life might have been, he was able to keep his scientific work free from crippling conflict. Indeed, he drew strength from his inner life. Though the sources of creativity can never be finally fixed, three elements in Darwin's own genius can be singled out. The first is his "scientific method." As Darwin modestly confessed, "I think that I am superior to the common run of men in noticing things which easily escape attention, and in observing them carefully." To his observational powers, Darwin added a constant play of thought. As his son Francis remarked, "no fact, however small, could avoid releasing a stream of theory"; and as Darwin himself wrote, "From my early youth I have had the strongest desire to understand or explain whatever I observed—that is, to group all facts under some general laws." One need only read Darwin's work to see how the play, and interplay, of observation and theory is constantly at hand. Robert Darwin, too, had extraordinary powers of observation, but he did not, as his son remarked, "try to generalize his knowledge under general laws." By both observing and theorizing, Darwin not only incorporated his father's talent but also went beyond him.

The second great element in Darwin's genius is his poetic vision. The poetic may seem, at first glance, a strange component of the scientific attitude. Yet the poetic ability to evoke imagination and see unusual connections is akin to the scientific endeavor. Certainly in Darwin it worked that way. Though he complained in later life of the loss of his aesthetic tastes— "my mind seems to have become a kind of machine for grinding general laws out of large collections of fact"—he was deeply interested in poetry in his formative years. He took great delight in Wordsworth and Coleridge, but his favorite poet was Milton, and it was *Paradise Lost*—a story of creation and destruction—that Darwin took with him for constant reading on the *Beagle*.

Darwin's account of his voyage is infused both with Wordsworth's poetic sense about nature and with Milton's concept of Creation. One long descriptive passage illustrates this combination. Darwin is crossing the Cordillera, in Chile, and he comes upon a raging river. He says:

> Amidst the din of rushing waters, the noise from the stones, as they rattled one over another, was most distinctly audible even from a distance. This rattling noise, night and day, may be heard along the whole course of the torrent. The sound spoke eloquently to the geologist; the thousands and thousands of stones, which, striking against each other, made the one dull uniform sound, were all hurrying in one direction. It was like thinking on time, where the minute that now glides past is irrecoverable. So was it with these stones; the ocean is their eternity, and each note of that wild music told of one more step towards their destiny.

Here the poetic and the scientific are fused, and in the next paragraph Darwin's imagination leads him to his scientific theory: "When listening to the rattling noise of these torrents, and calling to mind that whole races of animals have passed away from the face of the earth, and that during this whole period, night and day, these stones have gone rattling onwards in their course. I have thought to myself, can any mountains, any continent, withstand such waste?" We have seen how the burial of the dragoon in Darwin's ninth year had stirred his "poetic fancy"; now the rushing waters, reminding him that "whole races of animals have passed away," give him a key to the possible causal agent: time.

When the poetic vision is reinforced by Darwin's "ecological eye," we are well on the way to his great scientific theory. Darwin was not unique in his time when he talked about the "economy of nature." What marked him off from his contemporaries was both his sense of how one part of nature is connected to all other parts, how rivers, stones, and races of men are interdependent, and his ability to articulate that ecological connection in detail. One example is his rhapsodic description of the flora and fauna of Tierra del Fuego:

> I can only compare these great aquatic forests of the southern hemi-sphere with the terrestrial ones in the inter-tropical regions. Yet if in any country a forest was destroyed, I do not believe nearly so many species of animals would perish as would here, from the destruction of the kelp. Amidst the leaves of this plant numerous species of fish live, which nowhere else could find food or shelter; with their destruction the many cormorants and other fishing birds, the otters, seals, and porpoises, would soon perish also; and lastly, the Fuegian savage, the miserable lord of this miserable land, would redouble his cannibal feast, decrease in numbers, and perhaps cease to exist.

To this picture of destruction, Darwin needed only to add a similar picture of creation. It is a measure of his genius that he was able to do so, and to avoid sinking into the fatigue of his chronic invalidism. Perhaps the Benchuca was responsible for Darwin's palpitations of the heart. It played no role, however, in the impulses of his brain. These came from his life history, the "Development," as he tells us, "of my Mind and Character." It was out of this "Mind and Character" that Darwin, consciously and uncon-sciously motivated, forged the *Origin of Species*.

# CHAPTER THREE

# Freud and
# Nietzsche

$I$T is extraordinary how often one en-
counters the statement that Nietzsche was the forerunner of Freud and
psychology, anticipating by intuition the insight and theories the Viennese
doctor and his followers had so painfully to acquire by other means. Nietzsche was quite explicit about his pioneering preeminence. "Before me there
was no psychology at all," he announced. And Freud himself appeared to
support the assertion, repeating in a number of places his view that Nietzsche's "guesses and intuitions often agree in the most astonishing way with
the laborious findings of psychoanalysis."

With these authoritative statements from the two men involved, most
scholars have seemed content to let the matter rest and to forgo a critical
examination of the relationship itself. Thus, while a cursory glance at a
nearby major library discloses volumes on the relations of Nietzsche to
Goethe, Rousseau, Kant, Schopenhauer, Dostoevsky, Burckhardt, Tolstoy,
H. Spencer, Machiavelli, and Mussolini, among others, there is no comparable study on the relations of Nietzsche to Freud; nor, aside from a few
random pages in various books, are there any significant studies contrasting
Freud and Nietzsche.

I find my curiosity aroused by this state of affairs. Is the relationship so
obvious that further reflection is obviated? Or, to take a good Freudian
position, does the obvious simply prevent one from looking at what possesses in reality a deeper meaning than is indicated by the surface content?
At the very least, would not an analysis of the similarities and differences
between Freud and Nietzsche reveal to us something of importance about
the origin and nature of psychoanalysis? It is in this spirit, encouraged too
by Nietzsche's own injunction always to distrust "immediate certainties,"

that I plunge into a study of the relationship of these two great soul-searchers.

I begin with a catalogue of Freud's citations of Nietzsche. *The Interpretation of Dreams,* Freud's magnificent initial plunge into the psyche, was published in 1900.[1] It is important to juxtapose with this the fact that Nietzsche, insane since January 1889, died in August of the same year, 1900, and that his posthumous work, *The Will to Power* (published by his sister), appeared in 1901, with a further addition in 1904. These dates are rather interesting, for Freud's first definite public allusion to Nietzsche seems to occur in *The Interpretation of Dreams.* There Freud states that "a complete 'transvaluation of all psychical values' [in Nietzsche's phrase] takes place between the material of the dream-thoughts and the dreams."[2]

Where, by 1900, had Freud encountered this phrase of Nietzsche's? What of Nietzsche had he read? One problem is that the *locus classicus* of the phrase "transvaluation of all values" (or "revaluation") is the title of the final work Nietzsche wished to write, whose alternate title became *The Will to Power.*[3] Alas, on the basis of the dates given above, it is hardly likely that Freud encountered it there. Alternatively, Freud might have read Nietzsche's *Twilight of the Idols* (whose original title was to have been *A Psychologist's Idleness*) written in 1888 and published the very next year, just as insanity overtook its author. There, at the beginning of the Preface, Nietzsche speaks of "*a revaluation of all values* [*Eine Umwertung aller Werte*], this question mark, so black, so tremendous that it casts shadows upon the man who puts it down," and concludes with the postscript: "Turin, September 30, 1888, on the day when the first book [that is, the *Antichrist*] of the *Revaluation of All Values* was completed."

Unfortunately, even this as a source for Freud's quotation is neither certain nor even probable. The theme of revaluation (*Umwertung*) is sounded in almost all of Nietzsche's writings, from its cryptic expression in *Thus Spake Zarathustra* (1883–1885), through the clearer exposition in *Beyond Good and Evil* (1886), and up to the final works, *The Will to Power* and *Ecce Homo* (written in 1888 and published in 1908). Freud could have read it in any of these—or in none of them, acquiring it only on hearsay and as a tag phrase out of context.

As for the use of the phrase by Freud himself, however acquired, there is even an earlier possibility than the entry in *The Interpretation of Dreams.* Writing to his friend Wilhelm Fliess on September 21, 1897, after the failure of his seduction theory (based on the recital of supposed events in the early lives of his patients), Freud says, "In diesem Sturz aller Werte ist allein dar

Psychologische unberührt geblieben." Ernest Jones translates this as "In the collapse of all values only the psychological theory has remained unimpaired," and remarks that this is a paraphrase from Nietzsche.[4] In the authorized translation of the letters to Fliess, however, Mosbacher and Strachey offer a slightly different version: "In the general collapse only the psychology has retained its value," and they make no allusion to Nietzsche.[5] The whole thing is inconclusive and in any case refers to the same general ideas as expressed in *The Interpretation of Dreams*.

Apparently, Freud's next reference to Nietzsche occurs in *The Psychopathology of Everyday Life* (1904, though published as early as 1901 in a periodical). Freud records how one of his patients, trying to recall Jung's name, thinks instead of Oscar Wilde and Nietzsche. Next, Freud notes wryly, "As a common characterization of Wilde and Nietzsche she names insanity. Then she said chaffingly: 'You Freudians will go on looking for the causes of insanity till you're insane yourselves.'"[6] Clearly, this citation only shows that not Freud but his patient saw a link, and not a flattering one, between her analyst and Nietzsche.

Of far greater significance are the discussions of Nietzsche's writings at the Vienna Psychoanalytic Society on April 1 and October 28, 1908. On the first occasion, Dr. Hitschmann read portions of Section 3 (parts 5 to 9), "What Is the Meaning of Ascetic Ideals?" from Nietzsche's *Toward a Genealogy of Morals* (1887), while also briefly reviewing the first two sections of the book. His primary interest, however, was in analyzing Nietzsche's personality, and he concluded that, "It is interesting to note that Nietzsche discovers the crucial factor in the psychology of others, while he does not succeed in recognizing in himself that his own ideals correspond to his unfulfilled wishes." (This is a view, as we shall see, that Freud was to contradict at the second meeting on Nietzsche.) In the comments that followed, Adler hinted that Nietzsche's work was a sort of therapy, a view echoed explicitly in Max Graf's assertion that "Nietzsche's later philosophy is rooted in his struggle against his illness by means of self-analysis." Then, as the minutes record, Adler stressed that "among all great philosophers who have left something for posterity, Nietzsche is closest to our way of thinking. Adler [the Minutes are impersonal] once tried to establish a direct line from Schopenhauer through Marx and Mach, to Freud. At that time he omitted Nietzsche."[7]

Adler's line of thought was extended by Paul Federn, who stated that "Nietzsche has come so close to our views that we can ask only, 'Where has he not come close?'" He intuitively knew a number of Freud's discoveries; he was the first to discover the significance of abreaction, of repression, of flight into illness, of the instincts—the normal sexual ones as well as the sadistic instincts."

In the face of these claims for Nietzsche's priority by his own disciples, what was Freud's response? First, he stated "his own peculiar relationship to philosophy: its abstract nature is so unpleasant to him, that he has renounced the study of philosophy." Then, categorically, he announced that "he does not know Nietzsche's work: occasional attempts at reading it were smothered by an excess of interest. In spite of the similarities which many people have pointed out, he can give the assurance that Nietzsche's ideas have had *no influence whatsoever on his work*" (my italics). Having separated himself from Nietzsche, Freud then mildly passed to the attack. Nietzsche, he declared, "failed to recognize infantilism as well as the mechanism of displacement." Then, after a few more random remarks by Freud and others, the discussion ended.[8]

At the second meeting, October 28, 1908, the discussion revolved around Nietzsche's *Ecce Homo*. In his comments, Freud gave a psychiatric, or medical, diagnosis of Nietzsche as a paretic, accepted Jung's claim that Nietzsche was a homosexual, advanced his own claim that Nietzsche had a Christ fantasy, and then, surprisingly, declared that "there is no evidence whatsoever of a neurotic illness." After a few suggestive hints about the way philosophy may be seen as a projective system, Freud repeated his earlier denial that he had ever studied Nietzsche, in spite of the resemblances of some of their insights. Freud also stated that "the degree of introspection achieved by Nietzsche had never been achieved by anyone, nor is it likely ever to be reached again," a "handsome compliment" as Ernest Jones calls it.[9]

Indeed it is, one that I personally find Freud too generous in making. Hitschmann's comment on Nietzsche's ignorance of his own wishes strikes me as much nearer the mark (a view confirmed by Nietzsche's relations with other people, such as Lou Andreas-Salomé). Thus, with all due allowance for Nietzsche's tremendous intuitive perception I cannot see it as even remotely approaching Freud's self-analysis.

But what of Adler's and Federn's assertion, which has been echoed since that time, and which forms the starting point of the present article: that Nietzsche had anticipated most of Freud's ideas? At this point, we merely raise it anew as a question, deferring the attempt at a final answer until the record of Freud's citations of Nietzsche is complete.

The next entry in this catalogue is a footnote, added in 1910, to *The Psychopathology of Everyday Life*. Here, Freud admits that others have recognized the contribution towards forgetting made by the endeavour to fend off unpleasure. But none of us has been able to portray the phenomenon and its psychological basis so exhaustively and at the same time so impressively as Nietzsche in one of his aphorisms [*Jenseits von Gut und Böse,* IV, 68]: "'I did this,'" says my Memory. "'I cannot have done this,'" says my Pride and remains inexorable. In the end—Memory yields!"[10]

Was this mechanism, of a yielding memory, operating also in Freud's attribution of his ideas? Freud, who surely was one of the most self-conscious individuals who ever lived, apparently thought not. Thus, in 1914, in his *History of the Psycho-Analytic Movement,* he asserted categorically, "The theory of repression quite certainly came to me independently of any other source; I know of no outside impression which might have suggested it to me." Indeed, he tells us

> for a long time I imagined it to be entirely original, until Otto Rank [in an article in 1911] showed us a passage in Schopenhauer's *World as Will and Idea* in which the philosopher seeks to give an explanation of insanity. What he says there about the struggle against accepting a distressing piece of reality coincides with my concept of repression so completely that once again I owe the chance of making a discovery to my not being well-read.

Continuing his remarks, Freud comments that "yet others have read the passage and passed it by without making this discovery, and perhaps the same would have happened to me if in my younger days I had had more taste for reading philosophical works." In this context, Freud then disassociated himself from his supposed philosophical shadow, Nietzsche.

> In later years, I have denied myself the very great pleasure of reading the works of Nietzsche, with the deliberate object of not being hampered in working out the impressions received in psychoanalysis by any sort of anticipatory ideas. I had therefore to be prepared—and I am so, gladly—to forego all claims to priority in the many instances in which laborious psychoanalytic investigation can merely confirm the truths which the philosopher recognized by intuition.[11]

Later, we shall try to evaluate the "mere confirmation" which Freud seems so modestly to add to intuition. Meanwhile, another of the many cases in which Freud's friends eagerly pointed out to him literary or philosophical companions in the discovery or exposition of a psychological idea is recorded in "Some Character-Types Met with in Psychoanalytical Work" (1916). Discussing the phenomenon of "criminals from a sense of guilt," Freud remarks:

A friend has since called my attention to the fact that the "criminal from a sense of guilt" was known to Nietzsche too. The pre-existence of the feeling of guilt, and the utilization of a deed in order to rationalize this feeling, glimmer before us in Zarathustra's sayings "On the Pale Criminal." Let us leave to future research to decide how many criminals are to be reckoned among these "pale" ones.[12]

It is hard to know whom "future research" will number among the criminals from a sense of guilt, but the reader need only glance at Nietzsche's passage in *Zarathustra* to see how difficult it is to recognize the "Pale Criminal" as one of them. Freud, although in the earlier versions of the quoted passage calling Zarathustra's sayings "obscure," seems to have perceived more in them than the average reader—I for one—may be willing to admit.[13]

The next mention of Nietzsche by Freud seems to occur in 1919, when Freud added a passage to *The Interpretation of Dreams* in connection with the subject of regression in dreams. Having written *Totem and Taboo* in 1912–1913, Freud had become more and more concerned with the large historical and social setting of his individual subjects. Thus, in 1919, he declares that

dreaming is on the whole an extension of regression to the dreamer's earliest condition, a revival of his childhood, of the instinctual impulses which dominated it and of the methods of expressions which were then available to him. Behind this childhood of the individual we are promised a picture of a phylogenetic childhood—a picture of the development of the human race, of which the individual's development is in fact an abbreviated recapitulation influenced by the chance circumstances of life.

Freud then adds a reference with which by now we have become quite familiar. "We can guess how much to the point," Freud continues, "is Nietzsche's assertion that in dreams 'some primeval relic of humanity is at work which we can now scarcely reach any longer by a direct path.'" The passage from Nietzsche occurs in *The Birth of Tragedy*. Had Freud read this work by 1919 in its entirety, or had some obliging friend once again pointed out the similarity of thought?

With *Group Psychology and the Analysis of the Ego* (1921), Freud continued his investigation of what he called "man's archaic heritage." Again, as in *Totem and Taboo,* he tells the "Just So" story of the primal horde, ruled over by a despotic male, the father, who controls all of the females (and who is ultimately to be murdered by the sons, leagued together, and then turned by them into the totem ancestor and thus the originator of morality and religion). But this time Freud elaborated on the character of the despotic male. We must assume, Freud tells us, "that his ego had few libidinal ties; he loved no one but himself, or other people only in so far as they served his needs. To objects his ego gave away no more than was barely necessary." Then, in perhaps a surprising (and mistaken?) attribution, Freud continues:

> He, at the very beginning of the history of mankind, was the "superman" whom Nietzsche expected from the future. Even today the members of a group stand in need of the illusion that they are equally and justly loved by their leader; but the leader himself need love no one else, he may be of a masterful nature, absolutely narcissistic, self-confident and independent.

The 1921 work was much concerned with the notion of the ego; it received its companion term in 1923, when Freud wrote *The Ego and the Id*. According to Freud, he derived the term *das Es* (translated into English as "id"), to describe the entity which earlier he had called the "unconscious," from George Groddeck, a practicing physician who had recently become interested in psychoanalysis. But behind Groddeck, there is also our old friend Nietzsche. As Freud noted in a footnote, "Groddeck himself no doubt followed the example of Nietzsche, who habitually used this grammatical term for whatever in our nature is impersonal and, so to speak, subject to natural law." This double genealogy of the term is given again by Freud in his *New Introductory Lectures on Psychoanalysis* (1933), when he says he will no longer speak of the unconscious," but, "borrowing, at G. Groddeck's suggestion, a term used by Nietzsche, we will call it henceforward the 'id.'"[14]

To my knowledge, Freud significantly mentions Nietzsche only twice more. The first is in *An Autobiographical Study,* which repeats an assertion we have heard a number of times before.

> The large extent to which psychoanalysis coincides with the philosophy of Schopenhauer—not only did he assert the dominance of the emotions and the supreme importance of sexuality but he was even aware of the mechanisms of repression—is not to be traced to my acquaintance with his teaching. I read Schopenhauer very late in my life.

The inevitable associate of Schopenhauer is then also brought into the account. "Nietzsche," Freud declares, "another philosopher whose guesses and intuitions often agree in the most astonishing way with the laborious findings of psychoanalysis, was for a long time avoided by me on that very account; I was less concerned with the question of priority than with keeping my mind unembarrassed."[15]

The second, and last, additional entry about Nietzsche occurs in relation to Freud's comments on the plan of Arnold Zweig to write a book on Nietzsche's mental collapse. Zweig asked Freud for his ideas about Nietzsche's life, and Freud, in a letter of May 11, 1934, pointed out the difficulties in writing biographies. Then he added that "with Friedrich Nietzsche there is something that goes beyond what is usual. There is also an illness, and that is harder to explicate and reconstruct; that is to say, there are no doubt psychical processes in a certain sequence, but not always psychical motives generating them, and one can go very much astray in trying to unravel these." Next, obviously seeking to warn Zweig off, Freud remarks casually, "Anyhow a non-expert has not much interest in the details of an illness."

Having said this, Freud, with his usual self-awareness and introspection, especially on this sensitive matter, continued rather candidly:

> I cannot say whether these are my true reasons against your plan. Perhaps they have something to do with the way in which you compare me to him. In my youth he signified a nobility to which I could not attain. A friend of mine, Dr. Paneth, had got to know him in the Engadine [probably around 1885] and he used to write to me a lot about him.

The "non-expert," Zweig, must obviously have persisted, for in another letter of July 15, 1934, Freud answered rather peevishly:

> You overrate my knowledge concerning Nietzsche, so I cannot tell you anything of much use for your purpose. For me two things bar the approach to the Nietzsche problem. In the first place one cannot see through anyone unless one knows something about his sexual constitution, and with Nietzsche this is a complete enigma. . . . In the second place he had a serious illness and after a long period of warning symptoms a general paralysis became manifest. Everyone has conflicts. With a general paralysis the conflicts fade into the background of the etiology.[16]

Clearly, Freud was not going to admit to a special knowledge about Nietzsche. Did Freud have such a knowledge?

In looking back over the list of citations, I have reached a few simple conclusions:

1. Freud obviously repeated or borrowed a few catch phrases from Nietzsche: "transvaluation of all values," "pale criminal," "primeval relic of humanity," "superman," and possibly the id.

2. Freud obviously admired, or at least expressed admiration for, Nietzsche, along with Schopenhauer, T. Lipps, and others, as an intuitive forerunner of some of the insights of psychoanalysis laboriously acquired by other means. At an early date, Freud also stated that Nietzsche possessed great self-knowledge; later in life, Freud admitted that he really knew very little about Nietzsche's psyche.

3. Freud obviously felt annoyance at attributions, especially of influence and sometimes of insight, of his own work to Nietzsche.[17] Freud finally admitted as much in his letter to Arnold Zweig.

4. Freud repeatedly and categorically denied that he had secured any of his ideas or inspiration from Nietzsche (or Schopenhauer, for that matter); in fact, he simply had not read him until late in life, after his own basic work. In this mood also, Freud pointed out the gulf between his work and Nietzsche's philosophizing: for example, Nietzsche's ignorance of the role of infantilism, displacement, and so forth.

I see no reason to doubt Freud's explicit statements. The problem, it seems to me, rather revolves around the question of why Freud cited Nietzsche as often and eagerly as he did, and why he did not react more sharply against the comparisons and the allegations of anticipations, drawn even by his disciples, between his work and Nietzsche's. Two possible answers are at hand. One is that Freud, launching his bold, new science, could use as much "protection" and "confirmation" as he could get from a figure like Nietzsche. By 1900, for all his queerness, Nietzsche was an acknowledged great man and thinker; and the unknown and unaccepted Freud would therefore be in good company. The second possible answer builds on this first: Nietzsche was not only a world-famous philosopher; he was a Christian (even though a nonbelieving one). Freud's "Jewish science" desperately needed support in the non-Jewish world, and we know how eagerly Freud promoted Jung to prominence in the movement, partly for this reason. Nietzsche's openly expressed admiration for the Jewish "race," for example, in *Beyond Good and Evil,* and his call for their inbreeding with Prussian noblemen to produce the superman of the future would hardly have alienated Freud, with his own pride of race.[18] In short, from a number of viewpoints the support of someone like Nietzsche could be most valuable.

Whatever the reasons, Freud's own acceptance of the link of his name with Nietzsche has contributed to the view that sees the German philosopher and philologist as the "first psychologist of Europe" (Nietzsche's own phrase), expressing in his aphorisms and parables what Freud more prosaically collected and wrote down in his case histories. As we have seen, however, the evidence presented above removes any question of direct influence or inspiration by Nietzsche on Freud. Should Nietzsche's claim to preeminence as a psychologist, then, be based on the originality and scope of his work, irrespective of whether or not he influenced Freud?

My interpretation, to state it at the outset, and it is, of course, something of a truism, is that the differences between Nietzsche and Freud mark the decisive step in the advance from philosophy to science in the field of depth psychology. Therefore, to call Nietzsche "the first psychologist" is to obscure this fundamental revolution of thought. One can find prototypes of this sort of major revolution in the change from natural philosophy (though the term persisted) to modern physical science in the seventeenth century, and from moral philosophy to economics in the late eighteenth century. So too, but now in the late nineteenth century, from moral philosophy a science of depth psychology emerged (though developing and spreading only in the twentieth century). In this light a confusion of the roles of Nietzsche and Freud is as unfortunate as not recognizing the difference between Giordano Bruno and Galileo or, say, Bernard de Mandeville and Adam Smith (who, starting as a teacher of moral philosophy, ended as an economist). In the case of the Brunos, Mandevilles, and Nietzsches we have philosophical (or theological) positions arrived at by the method of intuition, with their confirmation or verification sought after either by the same method or by a form of faith. Opposed to this is the attempt at forming a "new science" by men like Galileo, Smith, and Freud.

Nietzsche, it is true, speaks of his "Gay Science" and of his attempts at experimentation. By experimentation, however, he meant only introspection, the plunge into his own psychic depths. There is no other clinical basis (unless one wishes to classify his work in classical philology as "clinical") for Nietzsche's observations. Confirmation of his intuitions and insights, therefore, only means "self-confirmation"; and this is simply not to be compared in rigor and control to Freud's self-analysis.

Nietzsche's real disinterest in establishing a scientific psychology also manifests itself in his abhorrence of systems. "The will to a *system*," Nietzsche says scornfully, "in a philosopher, morally speaking, a subtle corruption, a disease of the character; amorally speaking, his will to appear more stupid than he is. . . . I am not bigoted enough for a system—and not even for *my* system."[19] Instead, Nietzsche's way, brilliantly pursued, was the way of a philosopher: critical inquiry into the very premises of psychology, morality, and religion. He conducted the inquiry by dialectical means, and in this sense his distaste for systems is valid; Nietzsche wanted no part of the traditional philosopher's systematic and rigid deduction from unexamined premises. But his dislike of systems misled him into confusing them with *systematic reasoning,* and with the perception by means of the latter of logical inconsistencies and of possible irreconcilability of theories with the factual evidence. The circular path of data to theory and then back to data, the endless dance of the creative scientific mind, was not Nietzsche's way.

We can see this clearly, for example, in Nietzsche's perception concerning the Superman, who is able to cut loose all of his libidinal ties. In so doing, according to Nietzsche, the Superman is giving full effect to his will to power, and on this basis Nietzsche extrapolated his observation of a presumed psychic mechanism into a moral injunction. What Nietzsche did not see, because he never took his "theory" back to the data, is what effect this liberation from libidinal ties might really have on a prospective Superman. Does the Superman, ruled only by his own desires, freed, so to speak, of the superego, in fact lapse into Dionysian barbarism? If not, why not? Or else, does the prospective Superman in reality find that he cannot free himself from libidinal ties except by the straitjacket of intense repression, for which he and society must pay an unusual price? Does he discover that his guilt feelings are aroused by his "will to power," that there are ambivalent feelings involving his passive wishes as well? These were impossible questions for Nietzsche, because he was not interested either in systematically examining the scientific implications of his insights or in reconciling and changing them in the face of additional data.

Instead, Nietzsche was interested in being a moral philosopher, who attempts to solve the tormenting problem of seeking values in a world where God is dead. Psychological intuition was the underpinning of his critical inquiry, but psychology as a body of scientific knowledge was not his aim.

It was Freud's aim. This is not to say that Freud had no interest in morality or religion. His work is filled with reflections on these subjects, starting in his earliest letters to Fliess, becoming stronger in *Totem and Taboo,* and culminating in *Moses and Monotheism.* A note of his, for example, in 1897 could almost be mistaken for one of Nietzsche's long aphorisms:

> *Definition of "Saintliness."* "Saintliness" is something based on the fact that, for the sake of the larger community, human beings have sacrificed some of their freedom to indulge in sexual perversions. The horror of incest (as something impious) is based on the fact that, as a result of a common sexual life (even in childhood), the members of a family hold together permanently and become incapable of contact with strangers. Thus incest is antisocial

and civilization consists in progressive renunciation of it. Contrariwise the "superman."[20]

But Freud had no interest in moral *philosophy* as such; as he kept repeating, philosophy with its abstract nature was unpleasant to him.

In one sense, of course, this attitude connected Freud to Nietzsche. Like the latter, Freud disliked systems and system builders. For example, writing to Lou Andreas-Salomé, Freud expresses concern lest she may have slipped away from him "to the system builders, to Jung, or rather to Adler." Instead, he cautions her, "Through the ego–libido you have observed how I work, step by step, without the inner need for completion, continually under the pressure of the problems immediately on hand and taking infinite pains not to be diverted from the path." Again, in another letter, he repeats, "I so rarely feel the need for synthesis. The unity of this world seems to me something self-understood, something unworthy of emphasis. What interests me is the separation and breaking up into its component parts what would otherwise flow together into a primeval pulp."[21]

Freud's disaffection for systems and for what he called "synthesis" did not mean, however, a rejection of systematic reasoning. The latter was essential for the "breaking into component parts." Thus, in the same letter to Lou inveighing against systems, Freud talks of "building up his theory." Indeed, Freud insisted time and again upon the imperative need for hypotheses, which were then to be tested against the evidence.

The evidence, of course, was not only Freud's self-analysis, scientifically conceived, but the "talk" of his clinical patients. Unlike Nietzsche, Freud was a doctor, scientifically trained. Thus, in addition to the materials of the poet and the mythmaker, with their extraordinary intuitions, Freud could avail himself of the more prosaically expressed revelations of his patients as disclosed in their "case histories." He had a real "laboratory," whence he could derive and where he could test his hypotheses.

In constructing his theories, Freud, as is well known, was strongly influenced by his early training in biology, physics, and physiology. His masters here were not Schopenhauer and Nietzsche but men like Helmholtz, du Bois-Reymond, and Freud's own teacher, Brücke. These men instructed him in positive science, and provided him with a model of physicalistic psychology that resembled early nineteenth-century energy systems. Thus, Freud sought to "ground" his theories in a truly physical entity—sexual impulses, observable in children—and to "connect" them to psychological behavior by what were, at least in theory, quantitative paths. As Freud sanguinely anticipated, the theory of conservation of energy in physics was to be matched by a "law of constancy" in psychology; and thus inspired, he filled his early pages with such metaphorical remarks as "the expenditure of force on the part of the physician was evidently the measure of a *resistance* on the part of the patient."[22]

Freud's use of models and metaphors from nineteenth-century physics may sometimes lend an air of scientism to his work, but it also indicates beyond question his desire to link his psychological investigations to the great tradition of the natural sciences. As he stressed in his *New Introductory Lectures on Psychoanalysis* (1933), psychoanalysis, "as a specialized science, a branch of psychology . . . is quite unsuited to form a *Weltanschauung* of its own; it must accept that of science in general."[23] True, his materials seemed odd: the free associations, the "chimney sweepings" from the minds of his subjects, but Freud's approach to them was rigorously scientific in intent. Nietzsche, on the other hand, more or less intuited the importance of dreams, understood the significance of errors, and recognized in himself the meaning of neurosis; but he never sought to analyze his dreams nor his neurosis nor to think systematically about the dynamics involved in them. It was Freud, with his vision of psychoanalysis as a branch of science, who looked upon mental life as a new form of dynamics to be analyzed and thus understood.

The success of Freud's venture into science is manifested in the followers whom he inspired. By 1910, the International Psychoanalytical Association was formed, and scientific journals like *Imago, The Psychoanalytic Review,* and others soon grew up. Thus, Freud, unlike Nietzsche, had pupils, in the sense of scientific followers who attempted to go beyond the master in both theory and data.[24] Whatever reservations we may hold about the *successful* scientific nature of psychoanalysis, we must admit that its practitioners aimed at developing a true science (which, of course, was also to serve as a guide to therapy).

It is no derogation, surely, of Nietzsche to say that he did not aim either at such a continuing body of knowledge or at scientific followers. His greatness is as a seer and an inspired moral philosopher. There is no need, in an effort to underline his contributions, to claim for him a role as psychologist that obscures the nature of the tremendous gap that separates him from Freud. Nietzsche's psychological insights find their place in the illustrious tradition of penetrating soul-gazers like Maine de Biran, Stendhal, and Schopenhauer. Freud is the first scientist in the new discipline of depth psychology. To state what should be a truism but ultimately appears not to be: between the two men, Nietzsche and Freud, an intellectual revolution has taken place.

# CHAPTER
## FOUR

# The Hysterical Personality
# and History

W<small>HY</small> should historians be interested
in a psychological monograph on hysteria? When the book is Alan Krohn's
*Hysteria: The Elusive Neurosis,*[1] there are two good reasons. The first is
that the book presents a first-rate history, not of hysteria itself (that is done,
for example, by Veith in her book, *Hysteria*[2]) but of recent psychiatric,
mainly psychoanalytic, theories about it. Krohn seeks to reestablish the
diagnostic usefulness of this most ancient of diseases, the neurosis par
excellence for Freud. The origins of psychoanalysis are inextricably caught
up with conceptualizations about it and obsessional neurosis. Historians
reading Krohn will have a clearer idea of the theoretical setting in which
Freud worked and of the vicissitudes of the theory since.

The second reason lies in the application of psychology to history. The
historian is sometimes faced with hysterical phenomena, either an individual who shows pronounced signs of the neurosis or groups who seem
possessed by it. A Hitler may serve as an example of the first, according to a
number of observers, and sixteenth-century participants in witchcraft of
the second. In fact, one of Krohn's major points is that hysteria is uniquely a
neurosis that takes on the coloring of a specific historical and cultural
setting—hence, its "elusive" nature. We will be misled if we concentrate
only on its varied symptoms; we must focus on a constant hysterical personality, which can take multihued forms. Thus, hysteria is, or should be,
of special interest to historians because it is omnipresent data and, to return
the favor, because comparative history is so essential in understanding hysteria's fundamental, unchanging core nature. The psychohistorian and the
psychoanalyst join hands.

Krohn's procedure is to review Freud's theory of hysteria, to analyze
various definitions of hysteria, to discuss the etiology of the disorder, to

explore hysteria from cross-cultural and historical points of view, and to conclude with the presentation of a comprehensive model of the hysterical personality and hysteria, building on the previous presentation. In an article not cited by Krohn, Smith-Rosenberg informs us that "psychoanalysis can historically be called the child of the hysterical woman."[3] And so it was. Freud's first major publication, *Studies on Hysteria,* appeared in 1895. His collaborator, Joseph Breuer, treating Anna O., the first great pseudonymous character of psychoanalysis, fled from the emerging conception of hysteria when his attractive patient, in love with her doctor–father, experienced the symptoms of a false pregnancy during one of their sessions.[4] Freud, made of sterner stuff, stayed, so to speak, and became the true father of the new mental "science" of psychoanalysis. He came to understand that what had occurred between Anna O. and Breuer was a matter of "transference"—and "countertransference," for Breuer was unduly and unconsciously drawn to his attractive patient—that Anna O. was manifesting "conversion symptoms," and that behind the symptoms lay a sexual etiology. Freud connected that etiology to his notion about an Oedipus complex: the unwelcome sexual impulses were "repressed," for they violated society's sense of propriety. Was such violation merely because nineteenth-century Victorian society was unusually repressive, or because the intrapsychic struggle would always run up against real or fantasied prohibitions? Freud pronounced for the latter: after all, the one universal taboo is against incest. Critics of psychoanalysis prefer to view Freud's "science" as culture-bound, a mere reflection of a parochial European society.

Almost everyone now admits that hysteria, in its classic nineteenth-century form, is becoming extinct. Analysts today rarely see such patients. Narcissists, it appears, rather than Freudian-like hysterics and obsessionals fill their offices. Does this prove the critics right? No, says Krohn: hysterics are as numerous as a century ago. What has changed is the form in which they present themselves. Conversion symptoms are out, but the hysteric is still with us. In fact, the "most basic feature" of hysteria is its "complex use of contemporaneous cultural and social forms," for more than any other psychopathology, "the forms of the disorder . . . have shifted with changing social and cultural currents" (p. 6).

We need to move from attention purely to symptoms to a focus on character—the hysterical personality—to understand what is constant in hysteria. In the 1920s, Reich (of unfortunate orgone box fame) formulated the first comprehensive psychoanalytic psychology of character.[5] In 1923, with *The Ego and the Id,* Freud broke through the constraints of his own earlier work, with its emphasis on the libido, and established the foundations of structural theory (with its well-known id, ego, and superego) and thus of ego psychology. The result was that a new way of looking at hysteria, a new ideal type definition, could come into place, not only retaining what was valid in the work of Freud and his early followers but going beyond. The hysteric could be defined as "simply a personality with characteristic ego style, defenses, cognitive structure, superego structure, and interpersonal modes" (p. 213).

Freud was right that in hysterical personalities, both female and male, there "tends," as Krohn puts it, "to be a classical, unresolved Oedipal conflict" (p. 126). Out of such conflict may come conversion symptoms, but not necessarily so; for example, symptoms may take the form of maladaptive patterns of life choices—a woman constantly becomes involved in hopeless relations with unsuitable men. Generally, the hysterical personality has successfully gone through the pregenital stages of libidinal and aggressive development; it has not become stuck in narcissism. Ego capacities are fairly normal and adaptive. It is capable of "solid secondary-process thinking," though seldom capable of rich verbal ideation or freewheeling fantasy (p. 216). Its ego style is characterized "by a use of passivity to disguise, inhibit, and disown personal resources and accomplishments" (p. 216). In fact, the hysterical personality aligns itself with the prevailing "myth of passivity" of its culture—shamanism, witchcraft, and Victorian conversion symptoms—to hide the libidinal and aggressive strivings from itself: I am the "passive" vehicle of the gods, or of the Devil, or of my twitchings, which make me do these things, not my own desires. Along with its particular form of "passivity," the hysterical personality functions relatively smoothly; it has the capacity for delay and planning, and for socially acceptable behavior, though often dramatized in an exaggerated fashion. Its prime defenses are "not knowing," "not seeing," and "not recognizing": denial figures largely, as does displacement (p. 219). It can form and maintain relationships, but has trouble with them according to the amount of intimacy or sexual responsiveness demanded by the partner. Its superego has a basic integrity.

One could go on with the details of Krohn's updated definition of the hysterical personality. The historian working on this subject will want to read these pages carefully (pp. 213–232). What one has is an "ideal type," a diagnostic aid to be applied with much caution and without heavy-handedness to a historical subject. The analyst can appeal to psychodiagnostic testing, such as the Early Memories Test, with a living patient (p. 233); the historian has a harder time obtaining such data from the records of those long dead. (Yet I do not believe that the historian must completely give up hope: the diagnostician interprets memories with an eye to variety–narrowness, warmth–coldness, subtlety–bluntness, etc., of the images of self and others, and perhaps the historian could do the same with, say, an autobiography.)

Krohn's book offers not only an abstract definition—a diagnosis—of the hysterical personality but insists on the fact of its taking on culture-specific forms as part of that definition. To secure a resolution of the Oedipal conflict, the hysterical personality resorts, unconsciously, to the "myth of passivity" of its culture.

Krohn deals only briefly with witchcraft, as one of the "myths of passivity" in which the hysterical personality clothed itself at a given time. In the period from the Middle Ages to the seventeenth century, the myth gave credence to the notion that "the Devil or a witch could wrest control of the body and use it for its own purposes. . . . The fits, anesthesias, and hallucinations of the victims of witchcraft were then not the victim's but the Devil's doing. These people were hysterics in that they called upon the culture's myth of the Devil working his evil through innocent victims in their effort to disown the intent behind their own acts and thoughts" (p. 164). It is the victims of witchcraft who represent examples of hysteria, not the witches; on closer examination the latter are narcissists with "an unabashed conviction of [their] own omnipotence, including the immense power of [their] thoughts, deeds, and rituals" (p. 165).

It is of interest to compare John Demos's account of witchcraft in Salem. In this fine article, there is only one mention of the term "hysteria," and the concept "hysterical personality," as described by Krohn, is absent. Instead, Demos plays down the sexual element so omnipresent in European witchcraft accounts and focuses on what he considers a key difference in the American variant: aggression. "Most striking of all," Demos tells us, "is the absence of allusions to sex; there is no nakedness, no promiscuity, no obscene contact with the Devil. This seems to provide strong support for the general proposition that the psychological conflicts underlying the early New England belief in witchcraft had much more to do with aggressive impulses than with libidinal ones."[6]

Krohn's definition of the hysterical personality would insist on the central role of the libidinal impulses along with the aggressive. Demos, who, in fact, is very receptive to psychoanalytic theories and uses them in his work, might well reply that the historical materials simply do not support that insistence. Krohn, in turn, might say that a fresh, more insistent look at the data will necessarily disclose the sexual element, though in a cultural form peculiar to New England. Such an imaginary dialogue points to the vexed question of how the historian is to use psychoanalytic theory in relation to historical evidence.

There are many related questions to be asked. Why were the witches and their victims almost all women? Did not the men also have strong aggressive impulses, and how were they expressed? Krohn, for example, offers a fairly extensive analysis of shamanism as one cultural form of the hysterical personality. By and large, shamans, such as the Apaches and Eskimos, were men. In theory, then, if the culture had favored it, the New England witches and their victims could also have been men. Was it because women in European Christian culture were distrusted by the paternalistic society, seen as threatening men with castration, on one side, and betraying them, on the other (i.e., being more carnal than men and ready to enter into prurient league with the Devil)? Then why not a sexual emphasis, too, in New England witchcraft? Why, incidentally, does fecundation of a woman by a god win approval from the Greeks, in general, and at the birth of Christianity, whereas in later Christianity (in the Middle Ages) it takes the form of intercourse with the Devil—God's rival and challenger—and is a matter to be detested? The questions circle back on themselves, in that wonderful interplay of theory and evidence that must constitute the heart of historical research.

By the seventeenth century, in any event, witchcraft was under serious challenge as a culturally accepted form of hysteria. It no longer legitimately filled a social function. Skeptics and scientists increasingly offered naturalistic explanations. Though Joseph Glanvil and Cotton Mather, both fellows of the Royal Society, still held to the orthodoxy of witchcraft, other voices spoke of it as "but an illusion of crasie imagination" and pointed to the role of contagion in the outbreak of witchcraft episodes.[7] With the triumph of what we have come to call the Enlightenment, witchcraft phenomena flickered out.

In its place stood a disease, hysteria. The brain, not the uterus, became the center of the affliction. Doctors now began to speak of "nervous" disorders, of "neurosis" (a term introduced by William Cullen in the mid-eighteenth century), and, a century later, of "psychotic" and "psychiatric" (introduced by Baron Ernst von Feuchtersleben).[8] Philippe Pinel treated, rather than punished, hysterics and other neurotics in the Salpêtrière, formerly a prison and now, in the early nineteenth century, an asylum. The way was opening wide for Jean-Martin Charcot, Pierre Janet, and then Freud.

If we follow Foucault, in his *Madness and Civilization: A History of Insanity in the Age of Reason,* we will believe that a heavy price was paid in shifting from a "divine madness," played out in society, to a "mental illness," incarcerated in a "benevolent" mental institution. It is not clear how witches, burned at the stake, would feel about Foucault's thesis; perhaps the flames fed their narcissism in a way Pinel's playacting therapy could not. In any case, hysteria could no longer resort, acceptably, to witchcraft. By the nineteenth century, as a mild neurosis, harmful to families perhaps but no longer threatening to society at large, it could generally escape incarceration. It could play out its impulses in the rather benign form of Freud's hysterical Victorian patients.[9]

If women in sixteenth-century Europe were seen as sexual and threatening figures, by the nineteenth century they had changed into pure, delicate beings. Instead of being evil, they were perceived as all good. Faced with an intense need to repress her libidinal and aggressive feelings, expected by her culture to be passive, naive, and a bit dumb, while at the same time strong, in command, and a help to her husband, Krohn tells us, the Victorian woman often took flight into hysteria. By falling into fits or exhibiting amnesias and conversion reactions, she could express thoughts and feelings not admissible to consciousness. "The Victorian woman," Krohn explains, "could thus feel as if she were fragile and meek, while, in her behavior, the meaning of which her ego was able to shield from awareness, she betrayed her passion for power, erotic pleasure, and moral control" (p. 183). The prime residue of the Victorian form of the hysterical personality, for Krohn, is in the American South, where it persists more than anywhere else.

Largely because of Freud (although many others were concerned), we are all familiar with the individual psychodynamics of the Victorian hysterical woman; the story need not be told anew. Social historians, however, can emphasize further the connections with sex roles (see Smith-Rosenberg) and with larger social issues. Krohn's emphasis on the prevailing "myth of passivity" fits well with this sort of emphasis.

It is when we come to the present cultural manifestation of the hysterical personality, at least as depicted by Krohn, that controversy may set in. First, of course, we must accept Krohn's thesis that the hysterical personality is as prevalent as ever, though rare today in the form of a conversion neurosis. Such latter cases, he informs us, tend to occur, when they do, in rural areas. Although at one point Krohn seems to reject the explanation of its relative disappearance in terms of increased social sophistication—having a hysterical fit hardly works any more because we all know what's *really* behind that symptom—in the end he seems to allow for such a causal factor. We would also instance the changed image, as well as reality, of woman emerging after the two world wars: the shy, delicate girl of purity has given way to the aggressive working woman.

According to Krohn, whatever the outward changes, the hysterical personality is still with us. It merely adapts itself to our present culture's myth of passivity. "To be the helpless victim of one's society, the stars, one's unconscious, or mental disease," Krohn points out, "are now our culturally sponsored myths of passivity and thus form the basis of current hysterical alternatives" (p. 188). Krohn adds that the modern hysteric, "making use of her new social options, has come to use the avenues of object choice and vicarious identification to express unconscious strivings and maintain the ubiquitous hysterical illusion of passivity" (p. 192). Some women liberationists are unlikely to be assuaged by Krohn's qualification that reevaluation and criticism of the culture is not "without merit," when his main assertion is that "the hysteric is consequently coming to locate the source of her problems in political and social oppression" (p. 197). Krohn's probable response is that only that small number of women liberationists who, in fact, do tend to the hysterical personality would take more umbrage than is involved (such people, it should be remarked, are not likely to present themselves to Dr. Krohn as patients): placing the blame on society *can* be, though it need not be (and generally is not) a "culturally fostered response to personal discontent, anxiety, and conflict" (p. 197).

Not only hysterical personalities but episodes of mass hysteria—temporary outbreaks that spread by contagion, taking advantage of the propensity of hysterical personalities in a society to lend themselves as instigators and carriers of the "disease"—are more clearly understood in the light of psychological theory. Edgar Morin, in *Rumour in Orlèans,* for example, reminds us that in May 1969 (not in the Middle Ages) a report spread that girls were being drugged in six women's dress shops in the center of a major French town and being spirited away. The idea of the white slave trade took on new, mythical life as the rumor contagiously spread. Morin and his fellow researchers were aware that the rumor "sprang from the subterranean depths of the unconscious," but they mention the term *hysteria* only once.[10] Morin chooses to analyze the rumor primarily as a sociological phenomenon. Morin, I feel, would have benefited from a more explicit awareness of theory, as propounded by Krohn, while retaining his original perspective. Such a joining of the sociological and the psychological would have deepened our understanding of this 1969 hysterical outbreak.

Krohn's work makes one other contribution. It redeems hysteria and the hysterical personality from the scrap heap of history. It is modish nowadays in psychoanalysis, and becoming so in psychohistory, to pooh-pooh the classical Freudian emphasis on the libido and sex and to speak only of ego psychology and object relations theory. The conversion symptoms of the hysteric have been replaced, as I stated earlier, in the analyst's office by the laments to the loss of self and identity of the narcissist; psycho-historians have begun to follow the clinical fashion. In fact, this is an important and necessary development, and historians must become increasingly aware of the new theories. The most interesting work in the future will probably be in these terms. Yet Krohn, building on the work of others, shows us how to retain the libidinal while adding the insights of ego psychology and object relations theory—how to understand that the hysterical personality is still with us, though in changed costume. A libidinal conflict is at the center of that hysterical personality, exactly as Freud had analyzed it. This is a sobering reminder about the origins and the continuing nature of psychoanalysis—and thus of psychohistory.

# CHAPTER FIVE

# Autobiography and
# Psychoanalysis

THERE is little doubt that autobiography as we know it came into being in the early nineteenth century. The *O. E. D.* claims 1809 and Robert Southey as the origin of the term in English itself. This may be so, but a closer look at Southey's employment of the term suggests it is an accidental, and, as used by him, rather meaningless neologism:

> The life of Francisco Vierira, the painter [Southey wrote in *The Quarterly Review*] . . . composed by himself. Much has been written concerning the lives of the painters; and it is singular that this very amusing and unique specimen of autobiography should have been entirely overlooked.

Yet, Southey probably spoke better than he knew, for the combination of traits that stood in back of the word "auto-biography," in its modern sense, had already come into being during the decade or so preceding 1809, a decade which we can call loosely the early Romantic period.

It is, indeed, in romanticism that the concern with the self takes on new attributes, different from the preceding soul-searching of the religious. Thus, if I had to give a compacted definition of "modern" autobiography, I would say that it is a literary genre produced by romanticism, which offers us a picture from a specific present viewpoint of a coherent shaping of an individual past, reached by means of introspection and memory of a special sort, wherein the self is seen as a developing entity, changing by definable stages, and where knowledge of the self links with knowledge of the external world. Both together provide us with a deep and true grasp of reality.

Romanticism is often thought to have been concerned with the exotic and the illusionary, and so it often was. Much more central to it, however, was what I shall call "romantic empiricism": the effort to come to grips with

59

reality in a more intense and truthful way than by means of philosophic and scientific abstractions. Certainly, this was the case with knowledge of the self, where the various associational psychologies were built upon and surpassed by Wordsworth's "on the pulse" sort of knowledge. Thus, in his Preface to the *Lyrical Ballads,* Wordsworth talks of his poetry as an "experiment," wherein he selects "the real language of men," which can best be examined in "low and rustic life" because there "our elementary feelings coexist in a state of greater simplicity." These feelings are not experienced in isolation, separated from all other feelings, but rather "are modified and directed by our thoughts, which are indeed the representatives of all our past feelings." Hence, we perceive reality in terms of individual memory, and it is the only way that we can *truly* perceive it. As John N. Morris remarks of Wordsworth's *The Prelude:*

> The very high claim that the act of retrospection and composition is in itself the source of a knowledge higher than the particular truths of the experiences recorded marks Wordsworth's autobiography off from all previous English examples of the form.[1]

For Wordsworth, such "higher" knowledge of the self gives knowledge of the external world as well. As he says, the Poet "considers man and nature as essentially adapted to each other, and the mind of man as naturally the mirror of the fairest and most interesting qualities of nature."

Wordsworth's stress on self as the key to reality is also sounded by the man who, as Arthur Lovejoy puts it, first, in 1798, launched the word *romantic* on its modern career: Friedrich Schlegel. "All so-called *Romane*," Schlegel informs us, should be valued "in proportion to the amount of direct personal observation and of the representation of life which they contain." Alas, even of the novels of Richardson and Fielding, good as they are, Schlegel must exclaim: "How sparingly and in driblets do these books mete out to us the little portion of reality (*das wenige Reelle*) which they contain! And how much better a *Roman* than the best of these is almost any book of travels or collection of letters or autobiography, to one who reads them in a romantic spirit!"[2] It is autobiography "in a romantic spirit" that puts us in greatest touch with reality, and, as we have seen with Wordsworth, the method or means by which this is accomplished is memory or retrospection of feelings and thoughts. At this point, then, we have at least two of the elements of my "compacted definition" of autobiography.

Goethe provides another element, the view of the self as a *developing* entity in a *developing* world. In a famous passage he writes that the chief task of biography (I substitute here autobiography) is

to depict a man in the circumstances of his times . . . how he shaped out of
it an outlook on the world and on mankind . . . how he in turn reflects it
. . . so that one may well say that each man, were he born a mere ten years
earlier or later, would have become a quite different person, as far as his
own inner *development* and his effect on the outer world are concerned.

A *Bildungsroman,* the novel of development, is what Goethe and his contemporaries have in mind, and they have merely extended to the self the
notions of development concerning mankind and society elaborated by
thinkers as varied in their orientation as Condorcet (with his ten stages of
mental progress), Saint-Simon (with his law of three stages, shortly to be
expanded upon by Comte), and Hegel (with his Reason, unfolding through
various national spirits, dialectically on increasingly higher levels, shortly to
be "materialized" by Marx).

Where do the particular stages of development envisioned for the self
come from? Here, we are on less secure ground. The notion of childhood,
Philippe Ariès tells us, is only affirmed and confirmed in the nineteenth
century, and for most of the century it is more a battleground of conflicting
views than a settled terrain of time. Wordsworth's child comes "trailing
clouds of glory" from God; Rousseau's child is Emile, and Rousseau himself
(who, he admits, is "still a child"); and Dicken's child is Oliver Twist and the
circus people of *Hard Times.* If by child we mean the first six or seven years
of life, even Rousseau accords it only about three pages (1712–1718) in his
*Confessions*! If by child we mean the age until, say, sixteen or so, Rousseau
preserves for it all of Book I, or somewhat over thirty pages out of a total of
six hundred. As he says at the beginning of Book II (1728–1731), "Although
no more than a child," yet he ends the long sentence by talking of himself in
the same breath as a "youth."

Clearly, this question of the child as a stage in individual development is
of enormous importance and complexity. For our purpose here, we can
only note its existence as a "problem area" and pass on to another stage of
self-development making its appearance at this time: adolescence, first pre-
figured perhaps in the idea of a *Sturm und Drang* period. Yet adolescence,
too, is a most unclearly defined stage during the whole of the nineteenth
century, only coming fully into its own in the early twentieth century. As
vaguely perceived a hundred years earlier, however, it is colored by dark
clouds of melancholy and by a sense of life's meaninglessness and emp-

tiness. The individual is often seen as out of tune with the age, or out of step with its development. Thus, the notion of "alienation" can frequently be attached to this stage of adolescence. Paradoxically, too, the introspection that pervades this stage is viewed as, in part, the cause of this alienation and, in part, the only way back to a healthy connection with life and society.

Once past *Sturm und Drang,* life is generally perceived as a single stage of developing maturity—and professional achievement—marked as it may be, of course, for some, with continuing melancholy and occasional break-down but homogeneous as a stage until old age and death. Such is the view of the self, changing by definable stages, I believe to be most characteristic of the early nineteenth century. It is the view of the self that also becomes a stylized way of organizing, as well as of perceiving, the self when one comes to writing autobiography. Correct or not in its details, such an exposition nevertheless points truly to the conviction of the times that the self at least develops, and develops by stages. To this we must now add that such a development could be perceived by taking up a definite point in time—say, middle age or the moment of professional success—and looking back in retrospect over one's life. Thereby, one could see that it had a definite shape and a particular meaning. A different vantage point, and, as Chateaubriand demonstrated in the three different occasions on which he rewrote his memoirs, it would have a different meaning.

By now, I hope, we have come full circle back to my compacted definition of autobiography:

> The coherent shaping of an individual past from a specific present view-point, achieved by means of introspection and memory of a special sort, wherein the self is seen as a developing entity, changing by definable stages, and where knowledge of the self links with knowledge of the external world, and both together provide us with a grasp of reality.

If we elect to follow John Morris in his *Versions of the Self,* we can add to this that the chosen method of perceiving the meaning of the self is by the individual having passed through the vale of suffering, gloom, and pain generally embodied in the *Sturm und Drang* period—the "introspection" that I alluded to above. As Morris reminds us, William James spoke for the experiences of the previous two or three generations when he asserted that only the "sick soul," the "divided self who has in his own person become the prey of a pathological melancholy, can know the world for what it is." In Morris's thesis, "the experiences recorded in nineteenth-century autobi-ography are . . . secular counterparts of the religious melancholy and con-versions set down in the autobiographies of earlier heroes of religion . . .

'self' . . . is the modern word for 'soul.'" The discipline that claims today to speak most knowingly of the "self," especially of the "sick" and "divided" self, in the process displacing the notion of soul altogether, is the "science" of psychoanalysis. It would seem useful, then, to examine what effects the psychoanalytic conception of the self has had on the literary genre that presumably offers one of the most revealing and "real" portraits of the self: autobiography.

Autobiography before Freud, no matter how introspective, was concerned only with the conscious mind. Memory, in this view, consisted of "the representatives of all our past feelings," but these "representatives" could be recollected merely by moving tranquilly across the surface of our thoughts. Freud changed all of this by showing that consciousness is only the tip of the iceberg of our mental processes, and that underneath lies the vast mass of our unconsciousness. Penetration to this mass is not easy. As Freud, in his *Autobiography,* phrased the matter:

> How had it come about that the patients had forgotten so many of the facts of their external and internal lives but could nevertheless recollect them if a particular technique was applied? Observation supplied an exhaustive answer to these questions. Everything that had been forgotten had in some way or other been painful; it had been either alarming or disagreeable or shameful by the standards of the subject's personality. The thought arose spontaneously: that was precisely why it had been forgotten, i.e., why it had not remained conscious. In order to make it conscious again in spite of this, it was necessary to overcome something that fought against one in the patient; it was necessary to make an expenditure of effort on one's own part in order to compel and subdue it. The amount of effort required of the physician varied in different cases; it increased in direct proportion to the difficulty of what had to be remembered. The expenditure of force on the part of the physician was evidently the measure of a resistance on the part of the patient. It was only necessary to translate into words what I myself had observed, and I was in possession of the theory of repression.

Repression and resistance—these are the forces that block the way to our unconsciousness and hinder our remembrance of the deepest parts of self-experience. Under hypnosis we might effect a partial recollection—but without conscious control. The real train of explosive powder by which we might remove some of the repression and resistance covering our past turned out to be "free association." This method, especially as applied to the analysis of dreams, opens up a tunnel to our unconscious from which we are then able to dredge up our deepest memories. Psychoanalysis, like Hamlet, offers us "more things in heaven and earth . . . than are dreamt of in our philosophy." And—how fitting this is—it does so precisely through the very dreams themselves!

What memories, then, do our dreams most strikingly reveal to us? As Freud explains,

> In my search . . . I was carried further and further back into the patient's life and ended by reaching the first years of his childhood . . . the impressions of that remote period of life, though they were for the most part buried in amnesia, left ineradicable traces upon the individual's growth. . . . But since these experiences of childhood were always concerned with sexual excitations and the reaction against them, I found myself faced by the fact of infantile sexuality.

Memories as repressed, free association as the means of reaching them, and infantile sexuality as the source of the initial memories that so powerfully affect our future growth—these are the now familiar ideas of Freudian psychology. How do they affect autobiography? If we go back to my original definition, we can see that three elements of it have been refined or redefined by psychoanalysis: the "means of introspection and memory"; the self "as a developing entity, changing by definable stages"; and, at least implicitly, our knowledge of the self and of the external world, and thus our "grasp of reality."

Introspection and memory have obviously been afforded new methods by which to accomplish their task of achieving greater knowledge of the self. Whether at the hands of a professional analyst or by self-analysis, or merely by a loose awareness of psychoanalytic theory—and this last is undoubtedly the prevailing method—autobiographers today are forced to confront memories with which their predecessors were, fortunately or unfortunately, unblessed. Even if they choose not to incorporate such awareness in their books, autobiographers must reckon with a reader who may demand such incorporation and, where it is missing, supply parts of it. Thus, even what is left out takes on a new significance.

Perhaps the most obvious, though neglected, influence of psychoanalysis on autobiography concerns the concept of the self developing by definable stages. With Freud, the stage of infantile sexuality becomes central to any account of self-development. Indeed, in the orthodox Freudian scheme, there is a tendency to see the rest of life as an inexorable working out of the impulses and "complexes"—especially the Oedipus complex—necessarily experienced in infancy, (i.e., until about the age of five or six). The latency period that follows is merely that: a pause. Puberty and adolescence are simply new battlegrounds on which the old war is fought out; and one has the impression—although this is to distort Freud to some extent—that the outcome has already been decided earlier. Adulthood and its achievements seem only to exemplify the particular neurotic, if not psychotic, means of working out or acting out our earlier complexes. Partial freedom from the determinism of our "memories," so to speak, can only be gained, if at all, through the therapeutic "reeducation" provided by psychoanalysis.

The effect on autobiography of such a scheme, if carried out, is to have a huge first chapter on infancy and its accompanying sexual impulses, a small chapter on the trivia of the latency period, a larger chapter on adolescence, and so on through professional successes or failures. To this "ideal type" of autobiography, writers seem to have only partially responded, either out of the difficulty of obtaining their earliest memories, or from discretion, or out of disbelief. Nevertheless, the influence of Freudian thought on our conception of stages of development has been profound. The mere three pages devoted to his infancy by Rousseau in the *Confessions* no longer convince us as true and deep introspection. More typical today, for example, would be Arthur Koestler's dedication of the first eighty or so pages of his book *Arrow in the Blue* (1952) to a psychoanalytically oriented description of the first sixteen years of his life, including many observations on his infancy.

It would be a mistake, however, to believe that psychoanalysis itself has remained fixated on Freud's earliest formulation of the stages of individual development. He himself, as is known, began to shift the emphasis from the id impulses to the ego defenses and adaptations in his book of 1923, *The Ego and the Id*. And this task was taken up and furthered by his daughter Anna Freud (*The Ego and the Mechanisms of Defence,* 1936), and numerous others, especially Heinz Hartmann (*Ego Psychology and the Problem of Adaptation, 1937–9*). With this shift, consciousness in a sense comes back into its own. It is not the raging impulses of the id that alone shape us forever after but the interplay with the id of the ego as it tries to master the impulses and relate them to reality. While infancy remains a dominant stage in development, psychoanalysts have come subtly to view it in a new light and, moreover, to balance its effect by an awareness that what goes on in infancy is not merely held in abeyance or replayed in latency and puberty periods but subject to a true *development* and thus change. Psychoanalysts do not reject the past of infancy; rather, they build upon it. And the architecture of identification in adolescence, while grounded on the identification of infancy, has a shape different from the foundations themselves.

Erik H. Erikson has been prominent in this reevaluation and in a further revision of the theory of stages in the development of the individual, what has come to be called the life cycle. To the stress on both the id and the ego, he added an emphasis on the superego. He has combined all three processes—the biological drives, the conscious mental activities, and the "conscience" of culture (the ego ideal and the superego)—in a fascinating and subtle correspondence, one that holds for all stages of development. To top off his approach, he has given more or less equal weight to the various stages of the life cycle: in his typology, there are "eight ages of man"— oral–sensory, muscular–anal, locomotor–genital, latency, puberty and adolescence, young adulthood, adulthood, and maturity—and each has development possibilities of its own. All of this was and is potential in Freud. Erikson has had the artistic imagination and genius to bring it out, fully formed, into the open.

I cannot help feeling that there will be a "cultural lag" in this matter and that for a while longer autobiographies may be written, and undoubtedly will be read, in terms of Freud's earlier formulations. Thus, id and infancy will be unduly and uncritically stressed. Gradually, however, the extrapolations and refinements of Freud's own theories by such of his followers as Anna Freud, Heinz Hartmann, and Erik Erikson will become better known.[3] Then ego and superego, and states other than infancy, will share equally in our heightened attentions. The more recent formulations are still theories of "depth psychology," but they have risen to new heights. It is especially in the concern with the interaction of id and ego with superego, and the effort pragmatically and effectively to get at the nature and process of the latter, as exemplified in the work of Erikson, that we approach Goethe's call for a depiction of "a man in the circumstances of his time . . . how he shaped out of it an outlook on the world and on mankind . . . how he in turn reflects it." In this effort to depict such a man, autobiographies, to convince us, ought ideally to deal with the self as a developing entity, developing through an Erikson-like life cycle and in correspondence with a changing world.

Now, psychoanalysis also sheds additional light on the question of what is true and real about both the self and the world. Roy Pascal, for example, in his *Design and Truth in Autobiography* devotes an entire chapter, "The

Elusiveness of Truth," to it. Here he quite rightly insists that truth of fact and truth of feeling are both necessary. The former, presumably, can be publicly verified, although simple omission of fact is more difficult to detect and frequently more significant than commission of error or lie. Truth of feeling is a more private matter, and generally we are persuaded as to the truth of the autobiographer's emotions by the total artistic conviction that the autobiographer is able to establish, rather than by any one assertion. With psychoanalysis, this problem takes on a newer coloring in terms of what we may call "actual" and "psychic" reality.

In his early dealings with his patients, Freud was shocked to hear them describe scenes of infantile seduction by their parents. He was even more shocked when he discovered that these scenes were actually untrue. "When I had pulled myself together," he tells us in his *Autobiography*,

> I was able to draw the right conclusions from my discovery: namely, that the neurotic symptoms were not related directly to actual events but to phantasies embodying wishes, and that . . . psychical reality was of more importance than material reality.[4]

It is in this light, then, that we must approach such autobiographical accounts as, say, Charles Darwin's, when he tells us that "it is odd that I can remember hardly anything" about his mother "except her deathbed, her black velvet gown, and her curiously constructed work-table." We can only believe that Darwin believes his statement as a matter of psychic rather than actual reality. So too, with the statement in his next paragraph, that "the passion for collecting . . . was very strong in me, and was clearly innate, as none of my sisters or brother ever had this taste." In actual fact, as he elsewhere recalled, his brother collected plants, probably as ardently as did Darwin. Once again, we are aware of psychic reality taking precedence over actual reality. With the advent of psychoanalysis we are more keenly aware of, and more equipped to cope with, what must always be at the heart of autobiography: the interplay of the truth of fact and feeling, of the actual and psychic reality.

If we take autobiography as I have defined it and as modified by Freudian theory, are there any psychoanalytic autobiographies extant to which we can point? Before we touch on two examples, one by Sigmund Freud and one by Ernest Jones, a preliminary note: Psychoanalysis ordinarily presents its findings in a "case history."[5] Typically, such case histories start from the neurosis that has brought the patient to the therapist. In "Frau Emmy von N," the first case written up by Freud, in *Studies on Hysteria* (with Breuer), he begins, "On May 1, 1889, I took on the case of a lady of about forty years of age, whose symptoms and personality interested me so greatly that I . . . determined to do all I could for her recovery"; in the famous "Little Hans" case, he says, "In the following pages I propose to describe the course of illness and recovery of a very youthful patient"; and in the equally famous "Rat Man" case, he begins, "A youngish man of university education introduced himself to me with the statement that he had suffered from obsessions ever since his childhood, but with particular intensity for the last four years." The *neurosis* offers the "specific present viewpoint" which I mentioned earlier in my definition of autobiography, and it is from the *analysis* of the neurosis that the whole previous life of the patient is then unfolded.

Now, in "normal" autobiography, such an unfolding generally takes place in a linear, narrative, and highly chronological fashion;/and, of course, its starting point is not in a neurosis (or at least not an overt one). Case studies, too, do read in part as if they were pure narratives; or as Freud put it, as if they were Kiplingesque "Just So" stories. There is, however, an essential and large-scale difference between autobiographies and case histories; the latter have at their core a nonlinear analysis, by means of dreams and free association, of a character, seen through its present neurosis. Further, the material is presented in a time scheme, which, while embracing some elements of actual chronology, is mainly concerned with psychic time and with occurrences therein. Also, in place of the linear, we have an emphasis on the "systematic going around in circles," as Erikson puts it, that is involved in clarifying the process whereby the id, the ego, and the superego of an individual have been interacting.

In the light of this preliminary note, we ought perhaps not to be surprised that Freud and Jones, when they come to write autobiographies instead of case histories, write standard, linear, narrative, chronological accounts.

Freud's *An Autobiographical Study* (*Selbstdarstellung* in the original) was published in 1925, when he was sixty-nine, with a Postscript added in 1935. It was written, on request, for a series called *Die Medizin der Gegenwart in Selbstdarstellungen* (Contemporary Medicine in Self-Portrayals) and thus from the beginning had a professional aim. Yet it is interesting to note that Freud converts this "occasion" viewpoint into the real, central viewpoint of his life by what he himself says. He begins by remarking that he has already "published papers upon the same lines," (i.e., autobiographical) as the present one. Specifically, he instances his *On the History of the*

*Psycho-analytic Movement* (1914) and *Five Lectures on Psycho-analysis* (1909–10). One cannot help concluding from this that Freud saw his life primarily as the "life" of the psychoanalytic theories and movement that he had created, and to a large extent, vice versa. If we were to use a modern catch phrase, we might say that Freud's "identity" was achieved with psychoanalysis. Clark University in America first accorded him public recognition by its invitation in 1909 to deliver the *Five Lectures,* and Freud acknowledged in his opening statement that "no doubt I owe this honour only to the fact that my name is linked with the topic of psychoanalysis; and it is of psychoanalysis, therefore, that I intend to speak to you." As we have seen from the *Autobiography,* however, for Freud to speak of psychoanalysis is to speak of himself. He admits there that the 1909, 1914, and 1925 papers all "have dealt more with personal considerations than is usual or than would otherwise have been necessary." And in the 1925 effort as autobiography, he adds only that "I must endeavour to construct a narrative in which subjective and objective attitudes, biographical and historical interests are combined in a new proportion." His next paragraph begins, "I was born on May 6th 1856, at Freiberg in Moravia, a small town in what is now Czechoslovakia."

But surely many standard autobiographies aim at a narrative in which subjective and objective attitudes are combined (Freud's "new proportions," of course, refers only to his two earlier expositions). As for Freud's treatment of the "subjective" attitudes, we are disappointed in our hope for a deeper psychoanalytic treatment of these in the *Autobiography.* Let me cite two instances. Freud's only reference to his wife, Martha, is in a paragraph where he explains how she caused him to miss becoming the acknowledged discoverer of local anesthesia by cocaine. In his words, "I may here . . . explain how it was the fault of my *fiancée* that I was not already famous at that early age [1886]"; then, after explaining the incident, he concludes, "but I bore my *fiancée* no grudge for her interruption of my work." Can we seriously believe that Freud would let off any of his own patients with so light-hearted a statement? A glance at Jones's longish chapter, "The Cocaine Episode," Chapter 6 in his *Life and Work of Sigmund Freud,* reveals a rather different story. Beyond this, of course, one must note that in the light of Freud's own emphasis on sexuality and the choice of a wife, the turmoil through which he passed in securing the woman of his choice might well come under the heading of "subjective attitudes" in a true depth-psychology autobiography. But it is all missing in the *Autobiography.*

Turning to the psychoanalytic movement itself, we notice Freud's statement in the *Five Lectures,* "If it is a merit to have brought psychoanalysis into being, that merit is not mine. I had no share in its earliest beginnings." Instead, Freud assigns the credit to Dr. Josef Breuer. By the time of the *History,* we have a different story. "In 1909, in the lecture-room of an American university," Freud now remarks,

> I had my first opportunity of speaking in public about psychoanalysis. The occasion was a momentous one for my work, and moved by this thought, I then declared that it was not I who had brought psychoanalysis into existence: The credit for this was due to someone else, to Josef Breuer. . . .
> Since I gave those lectures, however, some well-disposed friends have suggested to me a doubt whether my gratitude was not expressed too extravagantly on that occasion.

Now sharing this doubt, Freud spends the rest of the paragraph retracting most of the credit he had previously assigned to Breuer. By the time of the *Autobiography,* Freud was emphasizing the fact that his psychoanalytic theories and methods were vastly different from Breuer's, and explaining that "for more than ten years after my separation from Breuer I had no followers. I was completely isolated." Freud alone, in short, from the perspective of 1925, had become the unique and lonely creator of psychoanalysis.

What sort of analytic explanation does Freud offer for his changing attitudes toward his share in the creation of psychoanalysis, a question that involves intense feelings toward the matter of priority and the desire for fame, as well as toward his former friend Breuer (and later toward Adler and Jung)? The answer is, almost none. Freud demonstrates a vague awareness that a changed viewpoint—his being unknown in 1909, a challenged leader of the psychoanalytic movement in 1914, and an unchallenged father of psychoanalysis in 1925—has influenced his account, but he does not go below the surface of this vague awareness. In effect, Freud's *Autobiography* could as well have been written by a nonanalyst!

Yet, interestingly enough, Freud has left us basically a psychoanalytic account of his life embodied in his *Interpretation of Dreams* (1900). There, with incredible boldness, he exposes not only his revolutionary theories to the scorn of the official medical world but also the content of his own self in its most "subjective" attitudes, for an extraordinary number of the dreams that he analyzed there were his *own* dreams. As he finally admitted in 1908 (in the Preface to the second edition),

> This book has a further subjective significance for me personally—a significance which I only grasped after I had completed it. It was, I found, a portion of my own self-analysis, my reaction to my father's death—that is to

say, to the most important event, the most poignant loss, of a man's life. Having discovered that this was so, I felt unable to obliterate the traces of the experience.

Thus, in *Interpretation of Dreams,* Freud bared and analyzed the deepest springs of his psyche: his experience of the Oedipus complex, his feelings about the sibling rivals who anticipated the Breuers and Jungs of his later years, his aggressive impulses, his worldly ambitions, and so forth.

Should these revelations, properly speaking, have also appeared in his *Autobiography*? And, if not in the particular piece he wrote to satisfy an official professional request, in some master work summing up his life? Or is the psychoanalytic "case" material intrinsically unsuitable to the auto-biographical genre?

Ernest Jones began to write his own autobiography in 1944 and completed a manuscript draft of eleven chapters, *Free Associations,* with a provisional title of "Early Memories," covering his life up to 1918 (one wonders if the juxtaposition of the ending of two world wars is purely accidental). As his son informs us in an epilogue, Jones suspended his writing because of the difficulties in dealing frankly with the "disagreements and rifts which accompanied the growth of psychoanalysis and the shortcomings of some well-known figures. To present these from his own angle might seem unduly subjective." His solution to this difficulty was to write his monumental biography of Freud, wherein his own involvement with psychoanalysis—as his son puts it, "The story of Ernest Jones is essentially that of psychoanalysis"—is submerged and mingled with the story of its founder. Only in 1957, with the *Life* of Freud completed, did he turn to a revision of his own autobiography, cut short by death the next year.

Now, the one thing Jones's autobiography is not is an exercise in "free association"! It is, instead, a most careful and precise linear, narrative, and chronological account of Jones's life, with a maximum of attention given to the public events of his career and a minimum to his personal, inner life. This is so even though Jones claims otherwise in his first two paragraphs in the first chapter, "Origins":

> I was born, the first child and only son of my parents, on the first of January 1879, in the parish of Llwchwr, in a village called Rhosfelyn; the Great Western Railway had in 1852 rechristened it Gower Road, a name my

father later got changed to the hybrid Gowerton. It is situated in the centre of Gwyr (Gower), the ancient kingdom between Swansea Bay and Caermarthen Bay, and is about six miles away from both Swansea and Llanelly, though the direct road between these towns does not pass through it.

It is the common experience of psychoanalysts that a patient intimates in the first hour of the treatment, and often in the very first sentence, the most important secrets of his life, although this is done in such a veiled way that it may take months or years of arduous work before it is possible to read the inner meaning of them. Were I in the position of such a patient, the opening sentence of this book could be put to a similar use.

Jones then adds, "I know that the essential story of my life lies hidden in these sentences, though they need a minute examination to decipher it or even discern its elements. Let me see; it may prove worth while to follow this train of thought; to do so should at all events illustrate the psychoanalytical attitude of mind."

Alas, in this only instance in his autobiography where Jones really claims to follow his "train of thought," we get neither free association nor, I believe, real insight into the psychoanalytic attitude of mind. Instead, we get a highly contrived, logical, and consciousness-oriented account of his familial and geographical origins and their presumed effect on the rest of his life. Of course, Jones is too good an analyst not to have achieved some insight into himself, bits and pieces of which he offers to his readers. But as we read through his account, we get the growing feeling that most of what he says is a screen, in fact, a *defense*, against our penetrating into his unconscious life. The chapter and the book are filled with trivia, such as his statement about his own father, Thomas Jones, who "early became converted to Baptism . . . by the great preacher of the same name as himself, Thomas Jones, the father of three famous sons, one of whom was Principal of the University College of South Wales, in my student days there." This is dust thrown in our eyes. What does it matter that the man who converted Ernest Jones's father had three famous sons? Yet much of Jones's memoirs is filled with allusions to and paragraphs about people whose only claim to entry seems to be that they became "famous" in terms of the British Establishment (especially medical, of course). What we appear to have is closer to name-dropping than to self-revelation; though, as a result, perhaps the latter comes through unconsciously.

What we do not have is any insight into Jones's deepest feelings achieved by free association. For example, he tells us that "my mother had wished to give me the name of Myrddin, but my prosaic father cavilled at this and chose instead to name me after Queen Victoria's second son, Alfred Ernest.

. . . It was a decision not easy to forgive, and when I grew up I at least discarded the first of these unwelcome royal appellations." Why was the name "unwelcome" and "not easy to forgive"? Did Jones resent the "second son" aspersion (in his first sentence he has informed us that he was "the first child and only son")? We are not told.

In one more example, Jones reveals, perhaps inadvertently, a definite pattern in his love life. The first episode reminds us a bit of Freud's cocaine episode. In 1902, Jones met a girl friend of his sisters who, he tells us, "confided in me so sympathetically about her unhappiness at being engaged to the wrong man—it was her fourth such attempt—that I was moved to remove her distress by gallantly offering to take his place . . . it was a mistake which I had much cause to rue before long." The "rue" involved was that the engagement cost Jones his initial brilliant start in medicine. This came about because, a year or so after his impulsive engagement, Jones's fiancée underwent an operation for appendicitis. "Although it meant a six hours' journey," he tells us, "I naturally wanted to be with her." As a result, Jones, who was resident at a hospital whose rules prohibited him from spending a night away from it, but thinking he had a dispensation from the rule, went off to be with her. His absence discovered and judged to be without the correct permission, Jones was dismissed from his post and blackballed from similar posts. "Success" had turned to "Failure" (the titles of two of his chapters), and thus, by apparent accident, Jones was turned toward psychoanalysis, a field outside the medical establishment of his time.

Not until twenty pages later does Jones tell us more about this engagement—as he puts it, to "Maude Hill (one of the well-known Birmingham Hill family). Years older than myself . . ." It broke up. Beyond that, he tells us nothing about his feelings in the love affair that caused him to lose his prized "success." In 1916, Jones married a young Welsh musician: "The third time we met, I proposed to her." After her death, Jones remarried in 1919. As his son of this marriage tells us in the Epilogue, Jones and his mother "were engaged in three days and married within three weeks."

Now, no one has the right to pry into Jones's personal life and to demand from him an explanation for the precipitateness with which he became engaged to three women. One can only say, however, that without such an explanation, and similar ones, we cannot talk seriously of "free association" nor of a psychoanalytic autobiography. I am emphatically not suggesting that Jones's autobiography is without value, although in the little I said of him, to prove a particular point, it might have seemed that way. Nor am I saying that Jones was not a brilliant psychoanalyst and a man of large character. Quite the contrary, he was an eminently qualified analyst, a major (if not the major) strength in the international psychoanalytic movement, and a peerless biographer of Freud. I am simply saying that Jones's autobiography, along with Freud's, suggests that psychoanalytic autobiography at the best of hands may not be possible at all. Or if it is, it is so only as a case history.

My first conclusion is that autobiography, even after Freud, is what it has always been: primarily a consciously shaped *literary production.* As such, it cannot simply offer free associations, or analyses of dreams, or any other part of a standard case history in lieu of a highly stylized and structured account of an individual's development of self, as perceived from a specific present viewpoint other than neurosis. True, it is possible that the writing of an autobiography might conceivably be a substitute for actual therapy. Roy Pascal hints at this when considering the possibility of writing his own autobiography: "One could be content if one could feel one's self to be consistent, to have developed naturally and organically, to have remained 'true to itself,' and if within this framework, one could order certain intense experiences whose significance defied analysis[!] but which were particularly one's own." Nevertheless, therapy and analysis do not thereby become autobiography.

My second conclusion is that psychoanalysis, rather than a potential enrichment of autobiographical writing, may be a hampering influence. It may indeed become a defense against true self-revelation. Rousseau earlier had used his *Confessions* as a device whereby he might expiate his sins, and as one of his recent psychological biographers, William Blanchard, has pointed out, had also discovered that "a full confession, in which he threw himself tearfully at the feet of his father and declared his helpless dependency, reduced this fearful figure to remorse and brought forth the demonstration of love he so ardently desired . . . there is no mistaking this same tendency in his writing."[6] Thus, Rousseau's increased psychological insight went hand in hand with a use of that insight that then operated to block real acknowledgment of his self. Utterly different in nature, but similar in being defensive, is the frequent use, for example, by Freud and Jones of their own psychoanalytic insight to prevent too intimate or indiscreet an exposure of themselves in their autobiographies. Where a more naïve person might blurt out the deeper truths about himself, analysts such as Freud and Jones know, *consciously,* what to repress as an expression of their *unconscious.*

Paradoxically, then, the autobiography that professes to offer the most free association may, in fact, offer the least.

A third conclusion, however, balances this judgment by calling attention to psychoanalysis's positive contributions to autobiography. Once we accept that autobiography is a carefully structured literary production, we can see that psychoanalysis offers the genre a new, secular vocabulary to replace the old religious words describing the soul's experiences, as well as a new definition of the "sick" and "divided" soul. Psychoanalysis also proffers a newly stylized series of developmental stages of the self; and for these stages it also offers both new weights, for example, an additional importance to infancy, and new significances, for example, a stress on infantile sexuality as formative of later character. The subject of autobiography, in short, becomes increasingly "psychoanalytic Man." However, as I have said, the autobiography itself does not become psychoanalytic, either in form or substance.

The fourth, and last, conclusion is that the most meaningful impact of psychoanalysis on autobiography is probably in terms of the reader, not the writer. The theories of psychoanalysis, even if only "in the air," teach us to read autobiographies in a new way. They instruct us to make new demands. To one who is even partially informed about its theory and technique, psychoanalysis creates a compulsion to approach autobiography in a "psychoanalytic" way. Hence, we are alert, at least potentially, to the deeper meanings—Erikson's "The Meaning of Meaning It"—both of what is said, and what is not said. We insist on taking depth soundings from the unconscious as well as surface readings from the conscious. The writer of an autobiography may not be able to present these to us effectively and consciously; yet we, as readers, can and must create them for ourselves out of the experiences that he or she presents to us. In sum, the increased demands are more on us, the readers, than on the writer.

In this increased demand on ourselves, a deeper knowledge of our own psyches, as well as that of the autobiographer's, becomes imperative. As Erik Erikson has so brilliantly pointed out in his article, "On the Nature of Psycho-Historical Evidence: In Search of Gandhi," a new typology for the understanding of autobiography must be worked out, and central to it must be not only the autobiographer's own problem of "transference," but our problem of "countertransference" as well. As Erikson suggests,

> Transference is a universal tendency active wherever human beings enter a relationship to others in such a way that the other also "stands for" persons as perceived in the pre-adult past. He thus serves the re-enactment of

infantile and juvenile wishes and fears, hopes and apprehensions. . . . This plays a singularly important role in the clinical encounter and not only in the dependent patient's behavior towards the clinician. It is also part of what the clinician must observe in himself; he, too, can transfer on different patients a variety of unconscious strivings which come from *his* infantile past. This we call *counter-transference*.[7]

Now, autobiographers are not patients, and we, the readers, are not clinicians. Yet, one of the principal reasons for a person's writing an autobiography is to discover, in the writing of it, what one *has* been and thus what one *is*; what one's life *has meant* and thus what it *means* in the present moment. So too, the reader of the autobiography discovers, or should discover, in the "clinical"-cum-"literary" encounter with the autobiographer's self some insight both into *that* self and into the reader's *own* self. It is the gift of psychoanalysis that it aids the reader in acquiring this insight on its deepest level by, for example, an understanding of transference and countertransference, projection and displacement, and so forth. Thus, autobiography, psychoanalytically viewed, is binocular; it offers us equal knowledge of the development and meaning of ourselves as well as of our "other self," the writer of the autobiography. The encounter, then, is not only clinical and literary; it is creative in a newly special sense.

# The Intellectual as Leader

# The Importance of
# Being Karl Marx,
# or Henry Thoreau,
# or Anybody

KARL Marx was a great and protean figure of the nineteenth century and was the inspiration for the revolutions in his name that exploded in the twentieth century. He was also a private person, in the sense of having his own life. Born in the Rhineland to a Jewish family that converted to Protestantism, he received a typically Prussian-Christian education in Gymnasium, went on to study philosophy at university level, became involved with the radical Young Hegelians, and, as a result, lost the opportunity to enter on a professorial career.

Instead, he entered upon a journalistic and revolutionary career. Married, with children, he was almost always in financial straits, rarely working at a suitably rewarding job financially; fortunately, his friend and collaborator, Friedrich Engels, kept supporting him. Together, the two men wrote the great works of Marxism and organized an international revolutionary movement.

Most of what I have said so far concerns the public Marx. On a more private level, there is much of interest in his early efforts to write poems, plays, and novels, his relations with his father, his own fathering of an illegitimate child whom he did not acknowledge, his possible Jewish self-hatred, his soaring ambitions and irascible temperament, and so on.

Biographers generally seek to establish the public and private details of Marx's life, along the lines I have given above, but only as a good story in itself or as a context for the great writings that stand independent of those squirmy details. The questions they ask are all with these aims in mind. I want here, however, to pose a different sort of question: Does it really matter who Karl Marx himself was? Does it matter that he was a person such as his biographers have depicted him and lived the life they have described and not some other? Do we not have his doctrines, independent of his actual existence, which speak for themselves? Even if someone else had written them, would not their effect on us be the same?

Common sense would seem to nod its head in the affirmative to the latter queries. Yet I suggest we examine this set of questions more closely. I think we will find a series of complicated and interrelated issues wrapped up in the seemingly simple set. The importance of being Karl Marx and not, say, some other Marx (one of my waggish friends has suggested as a title "The Grouchy Marx") or indeed some other named person entirely is worth further examination. It can best be approached, however, by indirection.

Marx was the founder of a great secular religion (although now seemingly falling apart). I compare him to Jesus, Buddha, and Muhammad. I should like to draw an analogy especially with Jesus in order to raise the necessary questions about the meaning of ideas and doctrines. Does it matter who Jesus was? That he lived the life we are told he did? I suggest a number of thought experiments, in spite of their seeming, initially, to be blasphemous. First, imagine that we had only one surviving account, St. Matthew's, for example. Would this affect our view of Christianity? Next, imagine that we have all of the existing accounts but that, suddenly, another authenticated document appears, which gives new details of Jesus' life and behavior, somewhat at variance with the present received accounts. Say, that, in fact, it shows beyond possible doubt that Jesus was actually a charlatan, a person like Jim Jones of the People's Temple, misleading and traducing his followers, that he had taken bribes from the moneylenders on the side and had actually had an affair with Mary Magdalene.

Would this change our view of Christian doctrine? After all, the existing doctrines might be exactly the same, the words in the New Testament as we have always had them. I believe that most Christians would experience a tremendous shock at such revelations. While some Christians would undoubtedly and undoubtingly close their eyes to the new evidence and continue to believe—"believe because it is absurd," said St. Thomas Aquinas—many others would lose "faith."

In the case of Christianity, of course, a special factor is involved. Part of the doctrine, in fact, is to follow the example of Jesus. The imitation of Christ is central to the religion itself. We are exhorted to follow him, abandoning our fathers and mothers in the process, both doctrinally and existentially. If his life turned out to be a mockery of his doctrines, an obvious problem would be created.

In historical fact, we know almost nothing of Jesus the person. Many have gone in search of him, but he is lost in the mists of time and tradition. One who made an earnest and interesting effort is Albert Schweitzer, with his *The Psychiatric Study of Jesus*.[1] Dr. Schweitzer's book reads like a case study. Various scholars, working from the existing accounts "as gospel," have portrayed Jesus as a disturbed young man, suffering from visions, hallucinations, and a split personality: a classic schizoid case. Schweitzer discusses these accounts, but at the end he rescues Jesus from the asylum by declaring that the young man's behavior was completely "normal" in 33 A.D., in terms of his culture. What would be bizarre in twentieth-century America was commonplace in Israel two thousand years ago, and Christ's mission could only be undertaken and carried out in the prevailing modes. Nevertheless, our fanciful thought experiments and Schweitzer's examination do suggest that it would matter who the real Jesus was.

Our analogy to Jesus takes us only a little way. An air of unreality hangs about it, for we know so little about the actual man. A more contemporary example may sharpen the issue. Indeed, it was in relation to Henry David Thoreau that I first found myself thinking seriously and sustainedly about the problem. One book, *Young Man Thoreau* (1975) by Richard Lebeaux, suggested that a close look at the hero's life revealed a disparity between the exhortations to independence and "life in the woods" of *Walden* and the actual experiences and behavior of the author.[2] A subsequent faculty seminar, given by one of my colleagues at the Massachusetts Institute of Technology, dissolved into a contentious discussion as to whether the new evidence made, or should make, any difference in our reception of the book's ideas.

Now Thoreau is a particularly apt comparison to Marx. As it happens, he was a direct contemporary, born in 1817, a year earlier than the father of scientific socialism. The first chapter of *Walden* is "Economy." Ostensibly, it is on the "economy" of Thoreau's household arrangements at the pond—the food, clothing, and shelter encapsulated in the original Greek meaning of the word *economy*—and on living "economically" or sparsely. In fact, a closer look reveals that *Walden,* begun in 1844 (though published in 1854), is at least as much a critique of commercial civilization, of the industrializing society of mid-nineteenth-century America, as it is an encomium of life in the woods.

Like his German counterpart, Thoreau laments the decay of man in a mercantile society, where "the laboring man has not leisure for a true integrity day by day; he cannot afford to sustain the manliest relations to man; his labor would be depreciated in the market." So too, the note of alienation and dehumanization is sounded: the laborer "has no time to be anything but a machine," for "men have become the tool of their tools." As for the basic principle of modern capitalist society, division of labor, Thoreau also disdains it, as when he rhetorically asks, "Where is this division of labor to end? and what object does it finally serve?"[3]

Thus, the two men, Thoreau and Marx, deal with the same subject, the effect of the industrial revolution on man, and share the same critical attitude toward it. Their solutions, however, differ profoundly. Marx recoiled in horror from the accusation of egotism; Thoreau embraces it wholeheartedly, declaring that the correct life consists of securing one's own integrity rather than reforming society. On his very first page, treating of economy, Thoreau announces, "In most books, the I, or first person is omitted; in this it will be retained; that, in respect to egotism, is the main difference." His justification is that "I should not talk so much about myself if there were anybody else whom I knew as well." As a result, where Marx turned primarily to Hegelian dialectics and economic theories, Thoreau claimed to be turning to his own "economic" experiences as the source of solutions to his society's industrial woes.

As part of his "egotism," Thoreau also, unlike Marx, rejects the accumulated "progress" of the past. He does this, first, in relation to the preceding generation: "I have lived some thirty years on this planet, and I have yet to hear the first syllable of valuable or even earnest advice from my seniors." Next, he extends his disdain to historical evolution, which he sees, not as a progressive dialectic à la Hegel, but as a fall from pristine goodness. "I think the fall from the farmer to the operative [i.e., the shift from agriculture to the factory] as great and memorable as that from the man to the farmer." Thoreau's solution, unlike Marx's, is not to move toward a communist society, built on the accumulated, historical capital of the preceding generations, but to return to the primitive, self-sufficient state of the solitary individual.

Before going further, I need to make it very clear that I am dealing here not with Thoreau in the round but mainly as a critic of modern society who, implicitly when not explicitly, is recommending another way of life. From another perspective, one could focus (as most literary scholars have done) on Thoreau as an artist, a writer, who comes to be one by a self-transformation whose vehicle is itself his writing. He goes to Walden Pond to make a new man of himself by producing *Walden*. In such a view, his spiritual experience is real. Inasmuch as we participate in it, it is also real for us.

Such an interpretation places its weight on Thoreau's inner experience, its validity for him. It accords with his "egotism" and his insistence that his mode of living is for himself alone. It may also correspond to our personal need. I believe it naïve, however, to think that this is all that Thoreau intended. Inasmuch as there is an external, public side to Thoreau's experience—his self-transformation is to serve as an inspiration or model for ours and his society's—then there is also an inauthentic quality to it in precisely the terms I spell out. The problem I am addressing is not his spiritual rebirth, or self-therapy by means of what one scholar, Leo Marx, calls his "extravagant idealization of himself"—nor the quality of the literary works that emerge from this regeneration—but the validity of his experience as a social cure.

Thoreau's experience and glorification of solitude is very American: Adam in the New World paradise; the frontiersman in the wilderness. In going to Walden Pond, the young Thoreau claims to have found his true and proper identity. It is a personal solution, one that also claims to be a solution to the social problem of the 1840s. In spite of disclaimers to the contrary, de rigueur for his independent, individualist philosophy—"I would not have any one adopt *my* mode of living on any account; for, beside that before he has fairly learned it I may have found out another for myself, I desire that there may be as many different persons in the world as possible"—it is evident that Thoreau is presenting his life experiences to us as a model of how a man should live (it is noteworthy that there is hardly a word about women).

Lebeaux, in the conclusion of *Young Man Thoreau,* puts it well when he says, "It is this persona, this 'presence'—rather than the historical Thoreau—which has captured the imagination of so many Americans. In writing *Walden,* Thoreau created a myth of personality and experience which helped to sustain him, and which has given inspiration and hope to others."[4] Working out his own personal transformation, I would add, or at least claiming to do so, the author of *Walden* invites us to believe that we too can effect a self-transformation; and, in so doing, transcend our increasingly commercial, industrial culture. By writing of his purported experience, Thoreau creates an "idea," which then has the power to lead other men into similar experiences, or at least the achieving of a similar personal identity.

The fallout for society is less clear. Unlike Marx, Thoreau offers little in the way of a social science. He does offer, however, a *praxis* of sorts: live as he does, independent of other men, free from the division of labor and the ambitions of increased affluence. (In another part of his work, he also recommends the "action" of civil disobedience, which does and did have direct social and reforming consequences; but it too is in the service of his independent mode of life.)

This is the Thoreau most of us know. What if it turns out that the real, historical Thoreau is different from his persona? Should this disclosure in any way affect our judgment of his philosophy and his recommendations about life? Does it make us any less likely to concur with his ideas and make them our own? Should it? These questions take on concrete life in the light of Lebeaux's book, the starting point for my reflections.

According to Lebeaux, young Thoreau was a deeply conflicted individual: with strong feelings about his "failed" father, ambivalent about his dependency feelings towards his mother, tormented by competitive feelings towards his brother, and so on. The interpretation is Eriksonian, filled with references to the life cycle, identity crisis, and the other terms made ubiquitous by the author of *Young Man Luther*.[5] I am not concerned here, however, with this facet of the book but rather with its evidence that, for whatever reasons, Thoreau's account is at variance with his own experiences. He, who "brag[ged]," "as lustily as chanticleer in the morning . . . if only to wake my neighbors up," about his vaunted independence and self-sufficiency, was, in fact, only bragging.[6]

One scholar, Channing, cited by Lebeaux tells us that "some have fancied because he moved to Walden he left his family. He bivouacked there, and really lived at home, where he went every day." Another, Harding, is quoted by Lebeaux:

> Thoreau visited the village, or was visited at Walden, almost every day. Such people as Emerson, the Alcotts, and the children of Concord visited often. Some Concordians, says Harding, "claimed that 'he would have starved, if it had not been that his sisters and mother cooked up pies and doughnuts and sent them to him in a basket.' . . . The Emersons, too, frequently invited him to dinner, as did the Alcotts and the Hosmers. They had all done so before he went to Walden Pond and continued the custom after he left. Rumor had it that every time Mrs. Emerson rang her dinner bell, Thoreau came bounding through the woods and over the fences to be the first in line at the Emerson dinner table."[7]

Of all this, Thoreau admits nothing in *Walden*. He thus misleads us, even if only by omission.

With our eye now altered, we can ourselves return to the book, able to see discrepancies. We can remember that Thoreau himself acknowledges that his tools are borrowed; he is dependent on his neighbors ("It is difficult to begin without borrowing," he confesses).[8] If we know anything outside *Walden* about Thoreau's life, we can reread his statement about living thirty years without hearing anything valuable from his seniors and recall that Thoreau himself acknowledged that his six-week stay with Orestes Brownson in Canton, Massachusetts, in 1836 affected him profoundly, declaring the period "a new era in my life";[9] and even more to the point is his relation to Ralph Waldo Emerson, fourteen years his senior (of another generation), who, starting in 1837–38 became his revered teacher and second father and who, in fact, owned the fourteen acres of woodland bordering Walden Pond where, starting in 1845, Thoreau took up his immortal "independent" existence.

So what? the reader may say to this and other such evidence. Thoreau's message had a validity independent (if I may pun) of whether or not he actually lived the independent life about which he bragged. And so, up to a point, I am inclined to agree. I would argue further, however, that it does matter, in at least one particular and important way. If Thoreau's own "experience" was not as he reported, then it cannot serve as evidence for the livability of his ideas. The ideas may still be "right," but we have no evidential grounds on which to come to that conclusion.

Rather, we may have grounds to believe that we are in the presence of a fantasy, with all the pro and con that may entail. The historical Thoreau, not the chanticleer of *Walden*, actually speaks to us about an adolescent, somewhat delayed, who has no fixed job as understood by ordinary men, no wife, or loved one, or sexual relations of any kind; and no children or other dependents, except for himself; in short, not about a mature adult. *Walden* is, therefore, profoundly misleading as an exemplar of how a real, complete life should be lived.

Let me hasten to add, it is brilliant, powerful, and well worth reading. So is *Robinson Crusoe* (of which it is a modern version). As long as we recognize that it is largely a fantasy and can distinguish it from reality (which, of course, it can nevertheless illuminate), we gain from reading it. It is when we allow it to inspire us, as in the 1960s, to become a hippie, to "drop out" of society, that it may (and I emphasize *may*) be misleading us in a direction and to an identity that we have followed under the false belief that it had already been tested and found valid.

Thoreau, though criticizing industrial society, is speaking to the individual and offering an individual fantasy. Only indirectly, and very indirectly, is he advocating a vision of a new society (actually, a return to an old one) or offering us a social theory by which to reshape ourselves and society. As with Jesus, and our imitation of his life, the inauthenticity of Thoreau's experience would seem to be cause for a reexamination of our commitment to his ideas. If *he* could not authentically live his ideas, why should we assume we can, or that the ideas can, in fact, be so lived at all? It *is* important, consequently, who Thoreau was. Especially telling in this regard is that Thoreau had said that he knew himself best, thus validating his account. In fact, he portrayed not his true self but a fiction. Not knowing even himself well, could he really presume to know authentically about us, the rest of humankind? Or the kind of society in which we should live the good life, on real terms?

With Marx, we have a thinker who goes well beyond Thoreau's efforts, and offers us, overtly, a social theory, a social science, and a vision of the good society. How, in the light of what we have said about Jesus and Thoreau, do we now regard the question of "the importance of being Karl Marx"? To repeat: Does it matter what sort of person the author of the *Communist Manifesto* and *Capital* really was?

On reflection, the analogy of Marx to such figures as Jesus and Thoreau may not be entirely appropriate. In their case, imitation of the life—and thus the life itself—is intrinsic to the doctrine. Marx never proposed himself as a model for his followers or asked them to follow him in this regard. Whether he was a scoundrel or a saint, he would have argued, could in no way affect the validity of his ideas and theories.

His followers seemed to think otherwise. In spite of Marx's attitude toward the role of personalities in history, they have come close to deifying him. The official reminiscences, while allowing for a few human blemishes, paint a picture of a good-natured, good-humored giant, a doting son, husband, and father, whose whole life is unegotistically and selflessly devoted to the cause of revolution and the masses. His picture (along with Engels), blown up, smiles benignly and wisely down on Red Square and other Communist public and private spaces in godlike fashion.

Revolutions, like religions, it seems, need persons to imitate. In the early days of the French Revolution, Robespierre was the figure of Virtue incarnate; then, in the failing days of the Revolution under the Directory, it was Babeuf. His personal character, and the story of his conspiracy and martyrdom, took on legendary features and became an inspiration for the revolutionary underground of the early nineteenth century. Blanqui, his successor, was in the same mold. It was his example rather than his doctrines that attracted youthful followers. As one biographer, Patrick Hutton, puts it, "Blanqui was for his disciples more than a living archive of past revolutionary glories. He was a model of revolutionary asceticism. His followers stood in awe of the patience with which he endured imprisonment for most of his adult life. Those who shared his confinement pointedly comment upon the quasimonastic regimen of work, conversation, and exercise from which he never permitted himself the slightest departure." As Hutton concludes, "His appeal to the youth movement which assumed his name in the latter half of the nineteenth century was in the authenticity of a way of life grounded in moral passion."[10]

Marx never consciously wished for such identification. Nevertheless, his apparent selfless dedication, his sacrifice of comfort and family to the revolutionary cause—the revolutionary ascetic qualities I mentioned earlier—did make him an example to others. Many followers, at least, presumed that the purity of the revolution was somehow connected to the purity of its doctrinal founder. Thus, for years, the Soviet Union suppressed the evidence in its archives as to Marx's adultery with Lenchen, his wife's maid, and the illegitimate child produced therefrom, just as Marx had repressed it during his life. Communists today either try to turn their heads or pooh-pooh this matter as a meaningless piece of scandal, meant to discredit Marx and communism.

Such reaction points to the fact that many people do think it matters. The message, for them, is affected by the nature of the messenger. Is this mere human frailty, which we should disregard, or an intuition to be heeded? Let us press on with our inquiry.

Is it not true that in various areas of human endeavor, such as the natural sciences, the validity of a theory is totally independent of its discoverer's personal attributes? To take one example: is the validity of Einstein's theory of relativity affected one way or another by the fact that he more or less abandoned the children of his first marriage when they were ten and four years old (which he did), or that he was a warm, kind, loving friend to his co-workers and mankind (which he was)?[11] The answer is clearly no. Theories in natural science are verified, or at least not falsified, on other grounds than the scientist's personal life.

We may be interested in the scientist's biography for other reasons. We may be vicariously curious about how he came to be a scientist, what the life of a scientist is really like, and how his creativity came to be developed. Some of us might even believe, in principle, that there might be some connection between his personality and his theories but have no hope of tracing it out. I confess this was my position, until I heard my friend, Gerald Holton, lead a two-day seminar in Stockbridge, Massachusetts, at the suggestion of Erik Erikson, on Albert Einstein and his work. To my amazement, Holton was able to relate traits of Einstein's personality to statements and formulas in the 1905 papers on relativity in a meaningful way. It was almost as if one could see Einstein's characterological thumbprints in the paper itself!

Even in the most recondite papers on physics, then, personality, on this account, does seem to matter, in the limited sense of leaving some discernible trace. I myself am convinced of this fact in the less mathematical field of nineteenth-century biology, where the imprint of Darwin's personality can be found in many places in the theory of evolution by natural selection.[12] Yet even here, the validation of the theory, once created or discovered, stands apart from the life of its progenitor.

Is this the case with Marx and his work? Or is he closer to Jesus and Thoreau, after all? Let us see. Natural science, we are told, is cumulative. As Newton remarked, he stood on the shoulders of giants; it is implied that if he hadn't sighted his theories of optics and gravitation, someone else would have. Indeed, the differential calculus was invented simultaneously by Newton and Leibnitz. Even Darwin found his "double" in Alfred Russel Wallace, who in 1858 independently promulgated the theory of evolution by natural selection. Was Marx, too, we must ask, merely the product of his "climate of opinion" or the state of science at his time and, if he had not come along, replaceable by someone else? In short, the implication of all that we have said about natural science is that personality doesn't matter very much.

The fact is we are now in deep waters. These are highly involved and difficult questions in the philosophy of science. Though the validity of the differential calculus stands apart from its discoverer, those in the know say that the "style" of the two men, Newton and Leibnitz, was very different and had powerful effects on their relative followers and thus the course of mathematics in England and Germany. Though the theory of evolution by natural selection stands or falls on "nonpersonal" evidence, it mattered greatly that it was Charles Darwin, rather than Wallace, who publicly fathered the theory. Wallace, a relatively unknown amateur, would have had his paper buried in some obscure journal; Darwin was a part of the Establishment, to whom attention had to be paid. The whole attendant paraphernalia of social Darwinism (Wallace had socialist tendencies, and was anti-imperialist), eugenics, implications for religion, and the like would have differed.

Nevertheless, though the outriders, so to speak, of theories in natural science may differ, the strong implication is that personality is only accountable for the errors, not the verifiable findings of the scientist. Once the theory is promulgated and propagated, its value is totally independent of the theorist himself. It could be Joe Doaks, instead of Newton or Einstein, who stands as the scientist in back of gravitation or relativity. The phenomenon exists on its own merits, and the personality doesn't affect the validity of the theory developed to account for it.

Science is "impersonal" in these terms. Oddly enough, the endeavor perceived as most opposite to natural science is also read in the same manner. Literature and art are the most personal of all products, but the artist's personality is generally judged to have little to do with the value of his creation. Van Gogh may have cut off his ear to send to a girlfriend and gone insane at the end of his life, but our judgment of the aesthetic worth of his pictures remains, or ought to remain, unaffected by such biographical detail. Do we really care, as we read Byron's poems, that he may have had an incestuous affair with his half-sister?

Matters can, of course, get political. During the First World War, Beethoven and Brahms, as German musicians, were banned from concert halls in the United States. Today, Wagner cannot be performed in Israel. (We might recall that, in science, relativity theory was denounced in Nazi Germany because Einstein was a Jew, with more serious consequences for the German nation than Israel's abstinence from Wagner visited on itself.) Ezra Pound's poetry was attacked because of his association with Fascist Italy. Yet, though occasionally the effort is made to condemn the music or the poetry because of its creator—guilt by association—most of us recognize the difference between an aesthetic and a political judgment. St. Thomas Aquinas's medieval distinction between acts of "doing" and "being"—i.e., deeds, which can be moral or immoral, and products, which are either good or bad aesthetically—still largely holds today (separate from this issue is the moral effect of a work of art, e.g., a drama leading to lascivious or violent behavior).

Where in all of this discussion do we place Karl Marx? He was neither simply a natural scientist nor an artist. Marx thought of himself as a social scientist (although what this meant for him, especially as his thought developed in his later works, was a kind of natural scientist whose area of inquiry was human affairs). His language in the Preface of 1867 to the first German edition of *Capital* testifies to his desired identity: "Intrinsically, it is not a question of the higher or lower degree of development of the social antagonisms that result from the natural laws of capitalist production. It is a question of these laws themselves, of these tendencies working with iron necessity towards inevitable results."[13] In this same spirit, he compared himself to Darwin, claiming to do for social history what the latter had done for natural history.

I cannot follow Marx in this assertion. The problem is that the social sciences are, sui generis, partaking on one side of the humanities and on the other of the sciences. The claim to "science," in the sense of the natural sciences, with their generalizations, lawlike statements, and theories open to experimental testing, is suspect. The attempt, as in physics, to simplify and to subsume more and more partial theories under a more general one runs counter to the reality of the social or human sciences, where ambiguities mount, historical reruns are impossible, the subject matter—the human—is part of the solution, and a key problem is how to deal with "what should be" as well as "what is."

This is not the place finally to decide the nature of the social sciences. For our purposes, I need only hint, as I have, at the way it differs from both the natural sciences and the arts. The fact is that Marx, on one side, is offering us a vision of the way the world ought to be—it is almost a literary vision—at the same time as he declares its realization to be a matter of scientific certainty (i.e., social science). Are the vision and the certainty separable from his personality as, it may be argued, Van Gogh's visionary paintings (or Thoreau's fantasy?) and Einstein's theory of relativity are from theirs?

If Marx were like Einstein, a scientist in a cumulative tradition, we could argue that "scientific socialism" was a necessary discovery, Marx or no Marx. Someone else would have come up with the same theories. After all, similar theories were indeed in the air. A glance at Marx's intellectual ancestry shows how he borrowed from Hegel and Feuerbach, Smith, and the other classical economists and from a whole host of utopian and other socialists. My point is joined exactly here: although the climate of opinion made possible Marx's synthesis, that synthesis was uniquely his. He alone, the particular person, Karl Marx, made possible the fusion we know as Marxism. His very nastiness and combativeness, exemplified in his constant polemics and backbiting comments in his private letters, I am asserting, was necessary to his personal vision, to Marxism.

After Marxism exists, we can say that someone else could have developed it. Marxist theory would exist, just like the theory of gravitation or relativity or evolution by natural selection, independent of its particular progenitor. I do not believe this. No one but Marx could have developed Marxism as we know it. In saying this, I am also implicitly saying that Marx's theories are not "scientific" in the natural science sense.

What about his theories as social science? After all, unlike a Thoreau, Marx does claim to offer us such a science (which we can free from his confusion as to its being equivalent to a natural science). Here we are on different ground. For example, how should we evaluate, or validate, Marx's theory that "history is the history of class struggle"? It seems, as presented in Marx's assertive prose, a persuasive statement, a piece of respectable social science.

In fact, it is historically suspect, to say the least. Class is a nineteenth-century term, referring to economic divisions created by the industrial revolution. It replaces earlier usage of orders, estates, ranks, and so forth (Adam Smith habitually spoke of ranks). It is a useful, nay, essential term in analyzing social stratification in modern industrial society. It is anachronistic, however, to impose it on earlier and other forms of society, where stratification on other than economic grounds—religious, political, ethnic—was more important.[14] It does not particularly help to explain the struggle of Guelphs and Ghibelines in Dante's Florence, the crusading wars of medieval Christians and Muslims, and so on.

Marx's purpose is obviously polemical. The social scientific validity of his "theory" of class struggle is not his major concern. The theory itself is a reflection of Marx's perception of the world and is rooted in his own instinctual needs—we note his obsession with "endless strife" in his early poetry, his emphasis on struggle and strength, and his own combative nature—and his effort to forge an integrated self, which he tried to realize in his struggle for a coherent sense of the world. As a cognitive matter, "class struggle" is less an acute historical generalization than a perceptive awareness of a contemporary situation, shared by many of his contemporaries—one thinks of Disraeli's "two nations" among other such references—but made into a "terrible simplification" (to use Jacob Burckhardt's evocative phrase) by Marx for personal and political reasons. It also becomes prescriptive: strength and struggle is the right way. As such it takes on the quality of self-fulfilling prophecy: although class struggle is not an accurate generalization from the past, it may inspire the proletariat to give life to it as a generalization in the future.

With all this said, the critical reader may still withhold consent from my argument. "You are committing the etiological fallacy," he or she may point out, "of confusing the origin of Marx's theory of the class struggle in his personal nature with the question of its validity." Then, generously, the reader may add, "Your appeal to the historical evidence persuades me that the class struggle theory is poor social science—shallow and limited—but your relating it to Marx's personality is immaterial and unnecessary.

At this point, I ought to rest content. But I am not. Somewhere in these arguments, the intuition of the average person that Marx's character and behavior, as with Jesus' and Thoreau's, does matter is being lost sight of. The reason, I believe, still lies in the confusion between social science and natural science. The former, while it too tries to be as objective as possible (an effort, incidentally, which I strongly favor), is necessarily subjective. It is so, not only in the sense that human beings are involved in formulating the theories but in the more important sense that they are formulating them for other humans to live by.

Philosophy, Nietzsche remarked, as I have noted earlier, is the confession of the philosopher.[15] So, I would assert, is social science. However disguised, it tells us about "what should be" as well as "what is." In Marx, this is especially evident. His social "philosophy," although he repudiates the term, is inextricably mixed with his social "science." His disclaimers aside, he is prescribing the way all persons should live, just as much as, indeed even more so than, was Thoreau. And the way they should live, for example, locked in class struggle, mirrors Marx's own personal needs. He is constructing a new world to replace the one surrounding and conditioning him, one that would be deeply satisfying for a world of Marxes.

At this point, the question becomes one of psychology as much as of sociology. Is Marx's view of human nature sufficiently realistic? Sigmund Freud, for example, thought not. Abstaining from judgment on the details of Marx's investigations into the economic structure of society, Freud did lament the lapse of Marxism into dogma and, more important, questioned its view that "economic motives are the only ones that determine the behaviour of human beings in society." Marxism, Freud added, in abolishing others' illusions, seemed to have developed its own illusion: that Marxism would "in the course of a few generations so alter human nature that people will live together almost without friction in the new order of society, and that they will undertake the duties of work without any compulsions" seemed improbable to Freud.[16]

We do not have to be Freudians to raise the question as to what role aggression, for example, plays in human affairs. Did Marx believe his own aggressive and ambitious "feelings"—see his poem by that name—came only from the economic conditions of society? His own father, Heinrich's, response, subjective as it was, to what he called an "embittered" letter from his son must give us pause:

> Frankly speaking, my dear Karl, I do not like this modern word, which all weaklings use to cloak their feelings when they quarrel with the world because they do not possess, without labour or trouble, well-furnished palaces with vast sums of money and elegant carriages. This embitterment disgusts me and you are the last person from whom I would expect it. What grounds can you have for it? Has not everything smiled on you ever since your cradle? Has not nature endowed you with magnificent talents? Have not your parents lavished affection on you? Have you ever up to now been unable to satisfy your reasonable wishes? And have you not carried away in the most incomprehensible fashion the heart of a girl whom thousands envy you? Yet the first untoward event, the first disappointed wish, evokes embitterment! Is that strength? Is that a manly character?[17]

Marx, in youth and adulthood, is necessarily the first source of his own understanding of human nature and its possibilities. What *was* his own nature? What awareness did he have of his own nature? He was not given to introspection. Did he have at hand a satisfactory psychological science, an "objective," cognitive account of man's mental and emotional processes? It appears not. Did history supply him with an "experimental laboratory," revealing the operations of human nature in a manner that would allow him confidently to generalize about the future? The historical record concerning human nature appears to testify against Marx's hopes. It is at this point, it would appear, that Marx's own nature—his own psychological dynamics and aspirations—combines with the "what should be–what is" problem in social science. Man, as a self-creating, independent creature, Marx seems to be saying, could, by will, impose himself on what is, in spite of the fact that "what is" has its own "necessary" laws.

There is an alternative argument that Marx (or Marxists) could employ. "All right," he could say, "I'm sometimes embittered, aggressive, backbiting, hypocritical, prejudiced—whatever you want to call me—in short, not the sort of person I'd ideally like to be. But that has nothing to do with my projection of how people will be under communism. My undesirable character traits are a result of the conditions and institutions that have shaped me. A different society, and I and everyone else would be entirely different."[18] The response must be, "Of course you would be different, but different doesn't mean perfect; you'd have new human flaws, and these would have untidy consequences for the society as well."

In *The German Idealogy,* Marx had declared, "In revolutionary activity, change of self coincides with change of circumstances."[19] He believed that communism meant not only a just society but a new, redeemed man. Unlike the "driven" Marxes of this world, harmonious and loving humans would be the sole inhabitants of the world to come. It is this faith of Marx's that leads me to claim that the eschatological vision overwhelms his efforts at social science and, within Marxism, distorts and vitiates them. It turns human nature into divine nature.

Marx's hopes and aims were natural and potentially constructive. Dreams and fantasies can be constructive and creative ways of approaching reality if understood as ways *into* reality rather than as mere substitutions *for* reality. It can be psychologically healthy to try to change the world to fit our particular nature, as well as to change ourselves to fit the existing world more satisfactorily. It is understanding of this fact, not condemnation, that needs to be brought to bear on Marx and Marxism. We should try to extract particular and useful pieces of "social science" from Marx's doctrines, yet realizing that this is to be distinguished from embracing his completed system.

In this light, it *does* matter, and powerfully so, who Marx actually was; a different Marx, and we would have a different utopian view of the future. Without his own struggle over the accusation of egotism, there would be a different quality to his views on money, competition, and alienation. Greater self-awareness and introspection on Marx's part would have meant a different sense of human nature and its needs in others—and thus of the sort of society *they* would construct and that *should* be constructed for them.

This is not to say that Marx was not also reflecting powerful forces in his own culture—of course he was, which makes him the great figure of history he is, rather than an obscure eccentric, complaining about his boils. It is only to say that the prism through which these forces were refracted was the person, Karl Marx, as he developed from a youthful poet to a mature revolutionary. The result was *his* vision of "reality," which, like that of a great painter or literary artist's, then imposed itself on millions of people (at least for a while) as also being *their* reality.

# CHAPTER SEVEN

# Jevons's Science and
# His "Second Nature"

$T$HE figure of William Stanley Jevons can symbolize a second "revolution" in the science of economics. Though he did not found a school, and though contemporaries such as Carl Menger, Léon Walras, and Antoine Augustin Cournot were working on similar theories, Jevons, by his single-minded approach to his subject, dramatizes the transformation from the classical economics of Adam Smith, with its emphasis on political economy and the labor theory of value (in fact, Smith waffled and, in one mode, held a cost-of-production theory) to a "pure" economics, emphasizing mathematics and the theory of marginal utility. As Lionel Robbins phrases it, Jevons's great idea was "revolutionary."[1]

Though the great idea is now known as marginal utility, Jevons himself did not use that term (he called it final utility). Value, Jevons insisted, must be given a precise meaning. The value of a commodity is its utility to us, and the utility of an article varies "according as we already possess more or less of the same article."[2] The final degree of utility, which Jevons described as "that function upon which the theory of Economics will be found to turn," is based on the fact that each increment of a commodity possesses less utility than the previous one because this final portion is less urgently desired or needed: a pound of bread per day may be essential; a second, highly desirable though not indispensable; but a third, superfluous.

With this formulation worked out in detail, Jevons stood classical economics on its head. By stating that the objective exchange values of the market originated in the subjective valuations of individuals, he made consumption, not production, the key to economic theory. Jevons replaced the classical labor theory of value with his new marginal utility theory. He attacked both David Ricardo and Thomas Robert Malthus and, by undermining their emphasis on supply factors, seemed to weaken the whole capital-labor class conflict, turning it into one between consumers and producers. Land, labor, and capital became mere abstract factors entering into a price structure determined by subjective desires, not objective "costs."

Jevons's great idea seems simple enough; as stated, even simplistic. But it was revolutionary because it moved economics away from a concern with "natural" prices and a dithering between value in use and value in exchange toward a unified value theory expressed in neutral, merely operational terms. Of equal importance, it is the context in which Jevons embedded his idea that accounts for the claim to a second revolution: economics, for Jevons, was no longer to be political economy but a pure science, mathematical in its nature and expression.[3]

At its highest pitch, Jevons claims for economics the status of an exact science. It will be such, he tells us, when it can base itself on a complete set of statistics. Jevons concludes that "I know not when we shall have a perfect system of statistics, but the want of it is the only insuperable obstacle in the way of making Economics an exact science."[4] Admitting as it does of mathematical analysis and expression, the Theory of Economy, in Jevons's view, bears a "close analogy to the science of Statistical Mechanics, and the Laws of Exchange are found to resemble the Laws of Equilibrium of a lever as determined by the principle of virtual velocities."[5] Adam Smith's vague Newtonian inspiration has given way to exact nineteenth-century mechanical comparison.

Whatever its exact scientific nature, one thing seemed clear: Economics was to be sharply distinguished and set off from what Jevons called the Classical, historical, or poetical studies. Though Jevons admitted that he regarded them "as the most elegant, and interesting," he hastened to add that "possessing no certainty and being unprogressive they could not compare in usefulness with anything sure and progressive."[6] The inference was clear: Economics, as he defined it, in contrast, provided certainty, usefulness, and progressive knowledge.[7]

Yet, on another side, Jevons was inspired by a lofty idealism, a conception of economics as a moral science. Almost in the opening words of his *Theory,* Jevons announces that, though "many persons seem to think that the physical sciences form the proper sphere of mathematical method, and that the moral sciences demand some other method,"[8] he will insist on both the mathematical and moral nature of economics. The theory that allows him to make this claim is utilitarianism, and the intermediate term that links the two aspects of economics is, I suggest, psychology.

The very definition of economics given in the *Theory* is a moral one: "The object of Economics is to maximize happiness by purchasing pleasure, as it were, at the lowest cost of pain."[9] Though stated as an object, we see immediately that economics is implicitly *defined* as that science whose object is to maximize pleasure—and the rest follows. (In a letter of 1858, Jevons writes more neutrally, "*Economy,* scientifically speaking, is a very contracted science; it is in fact a sort of vague mathematics which calculates the causes and effects of man's industry, and shows how it may best be applied.")[10] Jevons bases economics on a "calculus of pleasure and pain." And fully embracing the Benthamite position, he adds, "I have no hesitation in accepting the Utilitarian theory of morals which does uphold the effect upon the happiness of mankind as the criterion of what is right and wrong."[11]

In his *Theory,* Jevons tells us that "in the science of Economics we treat men not as they ought to be, but as they are."[12] He echoes Adam Smith here, but he defines men "as they are" in the terms of Benthamite morals and psychology, and not of Smith's sympathetic psychology. Nevertheless, in both cases, different though their grounding may be, men are being *told* how they should be in the guise of a mere description of how they are. If men will, in fact, behave as they are told they do behave, then the calculus of utility can be brought to bear on their economic actions.

As for Jevons, he certainly envisioned the practice of his science of economics as free from any intrusion of moral value. Its mathematical form blazoned that fact forth for all to see. Jevons's concern was with the *theory* of economics, which, once establishing inductively a few truths—such as "that every person will choose the greater apparent good; that human wants are more or less quickly satiated"[13]—could proceed, deductively, with exact certainty. One result, for example, would be to establish the beneficent results of free trade on a priori, deductive grounds. Jevons was aware that applied economics involved other kinds of problems—collection of data and the like—but dealt with this issue by insisting that economics

> is no more one science than statics, dynamics, the theory of heat, optics, magnetoelectricity, telegraphy, navigation, and photographic chemistry are one science. But as all the physical sciences have their basis more or less obviously in the general principles of mechanics, so all branches and divisions of economic science must be pervaded by certain general principles. It is to the investigation of such principles—to the tracing out of the mechanics of self-interest and utility, that this essay has been devoted.[14]

What cannot fit into Jevons's formal theory, of course, is history. As Jevons confesses in his letters, speaking of Macaulay's *History,* he has no feel for history: "History must no doubt be an excellent and useful subject but my only feelings to it are those of despair."[15] Progress was a different matter. Belief in it was an essential condition for Jevons's work in economics, an indispensable assumption about the direction of economic activity. If Macaulay meant nothing to Jevons, "Buckles [*sic*] History of Civilization in England" was a "most masterly book. . . . Although he may not be correct in all points, it is most clever—and *the* book of the age—Holding Science and Scientific method so high."[16]

Others in Jevons's time were seeking to combine history and economics. The German Historical School, and Jevons's own countrymen, William Cunningham and even Alfred Marshall, were at least entertaining the idea. Jevons, in contrast, felt threatened by history and moved to separate it firmly from economics; hence, to move from political economy to economics. As he wrote,

> instead of converting our present science of economics into an historical science, utterly destroying it in the process, I would perfect and develop what we already possess, and at the same time erect a new branch of social science on an historical foundation. This new branch of science, on which many learned men, such as Richard Jones, De Laveleye, Lavergne, Cliffe Leslie, Sir Henry Maine, Thorold Rogers, have already laboured, is doubtless a portion of what Herbert Spencer calls Sociology, the Science of the Evolution of Social Relations.[17]

Jevons's science of economics was to stand separate from social relations. One feels, in fact, that for Jevons it could only be "scientific" on that condition; whatever "science" there could be in social relations was of a different kind from that involved in the theory of economics. Here, in his new science, Jevons was aiming at a special kind of purity, uncontaminated by the messy reality of humans and their actual history.

The Jevons I have presented so far is the scientific figure, the public Jevons who might figure in a standard history of economic thought. There is another, more private, Jevons. It is the Jevons who writes to his sisters that he has a "second nature within me hidden to the world, yet directing all my behaviour towards the world."[18] It is a Jevons whose own life is a microcosm of the economic behavior he is prescribing for the public world. Taking his own development as prescriptive, he also prescribes it for his favorite sister, Henny, as when he writes,

> I think you do not duly appreciate the comparative importance of *preparation and performance,* or perhaps as I may illustrate it, of *Capital and labour.* You desire to begin and hammer away at once, instead of spending years in acquiring strength and skill and then striking a few blows of immensely greater effect than your unskilled ones however numerous, could

be. We enter here into one of those deeply laid & simple propositions of Economy which I hope some day to work out into a symmetrical & extensive manner hitherto unattempted even by Mills or Adam Smith. It comprehends the whole question of Education and employment of Capital in Industry, and will define the proper relation of *preparation & performance*.[19]

What is right for the Jevons family, I am arguing, is then writ large in the macrocosm of economic science.

Is such an assertion merely a case of the etiological fallacy? Do the origins of Jevons's theories, in his personal experience, have anything to do with their verifiability as public knowledge? In one sense, of course, the answer is no. The theory of marginal utility is either valid in logical terms and in its application to real data, or not. In another sense, however, I am suggesting that the answer is yes. The particles in molecular physics do not have to be told how to behave; human beings, as self-interpreting creatures, do. The "telling" comes, in large part, from the lives of Jevons and his compatriots. The prescribed behavior then becomes a fact that can be "scientifically" described, allowing for a certain inexactness.

How can we "test," or understand, this assertion? It happens that Jevons kept a journal during part of his life. Also, much of his correspondence is available. These two sources, plus his biography, shed light on both his beliefs and their development.

The influence on Jevons of his family—a comparison with Darwin comes quickly to mind—was most important. On both sides, the family was Unitarian. On the paternal side, both grandfather and father were iron merchants and manufacturers; the father, Thomas, claimed to have built the first iron boat to sail on salt water, in 1815. On the maternal side, Jevons's grandfather was a banker as well as a leading citizen of Liverpool. The mother, Mary Anne Roscoe, was a poet, botanist, and general supporter of the arts. At the age of eight, Jevons was given his first lessons in economics, interestingly enough, by his mother.

When Jevons was ten, his mother died. Her loss was a matter of continuing grief to him and may have played a major role in the depressions that descended on him at intervals in his formative years. An older brother experienced a complete breakdown at age eighteen, about the time of the mother's death, and Jevons's favorite sister, Henny, later experienced emotional difficulties, from age thirty on, through the remaining forty years of her life. Thus, an air of tragic mental life and concern with death hung over Jevons's life, impelling him to wrestle with religious and moral questions of the most painful nature.

Effectively, it was the father who played the major role in Jevons's development. Alternatively lecturing his son as to the correct path to take in life, and appealing to him for assistance as a friend, Thomas became the conscience and guide for all of Jevons's life. Thomas preached the need for his son to develop "manly qualities," adding that it was out of "my unalterable love for you and my desire to do and say what may be for your present happiness and your future welfare."[20] Apologizing for his "sermon," Thomas urged his son on to fame, while pressing upon him the importance of leading a moral life, pursuing duty. To arrive at decisions, the father urged "an enumeration of the advantages and disadvantages in the shape of a mathematical sum on paper."[21]

Most of this was standard Unitarian-Utilitarian admonition, in language that was to be echoed in Jevons's later economic formulations. But the father's exhortation to pursue duty and ambition seems to have set up, unknowingly, a special sort of tension in the young Jevons. It was exacerbated by the father's ambivalent persuading—for the father alternately urged and spoke against—Jevons going to Australia as an assayer to help the family financially, thus forcing the seventeen-year-old boy to leave his beloved father and siblings, never again to see his father, who died before Jevons's return five years later. A reader of Jevons's letters gradually gets the impression of a feeling of resentment at the double bind his father had put him in. He never openly expresses it, but we can guess at the depth of his feeling when he refers to his sojourn in Australia as a "sentence of transportation."[22]

All of these psychic pushes and pulls come together for Jevons in his effort to join religion and science, to serve society at the same time as he fulfills his ambitions to be personally successful. In the process, he must come to terms with his fears that he is being merely selfish and self-centered. R. H. Hutton, writing Jevons's obituary notice, observed that "moreover, there was a deep religious feeling at the bottom of his nature which made the materialistic tone of the day as alien to him as all true science . . . was unaffectedly dear to him."[23] This is true; but although materialism did not tempt Jevons, the power of self-interest that presumably lay behind it had a fascination that frightened at the same time as it attracted him.

Jevons begins his journal entries in 1852 by telling himself that the "useful and important" part will be on his "own character prospects, or on religion."[24] He admits to himself, in naive and open fashion and in many entries, his ambitious, and ambivalent, nature. At one point, he writes that "I really cannot believe that success in this world is always to be sacrificed."[25] In another, delightful entry, he confesses that

> I have had a strange habit of lying in bed awake for hours—dreaming in full
> wakefulness, imagining myself in all sorts of positions—always doing
> something very clever & extraordinary but sometimes very good & other
> times quite as bad, in short inventing endless novels with myself as the
> constant hero for them. Many of these dreams were so agreeable that I
> continued or repeated them night after night or recurred to them after
> considerable intervals. One especially in which I was prime minister—far
> the most celebrated that ever was—In others I was a prince, a king—leader
> of armies, people—etc. etc. at other times of brigands, or thieves and
> murderers.[26]

He worried endlessly that he was selfish, a leader of brigands. He notes
sadly at one moment that "I have lost & forgotten all my first feelings &
motives and I find left only a sort of ambitious impulse. It is disagreeable to
me to examine the nature of this impulse for I always find in it so little but
what is selfish & I always used to ground my principles on unselfishness."[27]
What made the whole matter so uncomfortable was that, while religion and
morals urged man to be unselfish, material reality showed him to be all too
selfish, and irredeemably so, by nature. "I regard man," Jevons wrote, "in
reality as essentially selfish, that is as doing everything with a view to gain
enjoyment or avoid pain. This self interest is certainly the main-spring of all
his actions, and I believe that it is beyond a man's nature to act otherwise."[28]

Jevons was wrestling with the impact of evolutionary biological thinking
on religion and morals that tortured so many of his contemporaries, caught
"between two worlds," as Matthew Arnold put it so well. In 1852, seven
years before the publishing of Darwin's great book, Jevons wrote in his
journal that

> I have also had a talk about the *Origin of Species,* or the manner in which
> the innumerable races of animals have been produced. I, as far as I can
> understand at present, firmly believe that all animals have been transformed
> out of one primitive form, by the continued influence for thousands and
> perhaps millions of years of climate, geography, &c, &c. Lyell makes great
> fun of Lamarck's [*sic*] that is of this theory but appears to me not to give
> any good reason against it.[29]

Jevons's guides were Lamarck, and probably Herbert Spencer, and certainly Robert Chambers, whose *Vestiges of Creation* (1844) elicited from
Jevons the remark that he "approve[d] of [it] greatly on the whole."[30] These
pre-Darwinian insights confirmed for Jevons the scientific fact that he could
no longer believe "that we have any 'Moral Sense' altogether separate and of
a different kind from our animal feelings."[31]

Animal feelings meant self-preservation, or the pursuit of self-interest. Yet Jevons could not rest with this "materialistic" conclusion. Our "Moral Sense" had, somehow, to be made higher than that. Jevons's *personal* way out of his dilemma can be followed through his comments on a novel, Bulwer Lytton's *My Novel* (1853). Though a "trashy" work, it provoked Jevons to "serious reflections" on the two characters, Leonard and Randal, "so applicable to one in my circumstances." Jevons then goes on; and I give the long quote because he is really talking about the two souls warring in his own breast.

> Ambition was the characteristic of each, and knowledge or ability was the instrument to which each principally looked to raise himself in the world. From the first every one approves of Leonard's disposition, and equally detests that of Randal; in which really consists the difference. I cannot see that it is in selfishness and unselfishness for each had an equal family affection and beyond that neither could be said to labour with a view to other than their own benefit. It *might* happen too that both should gain equally high stations and to all appearances be equally praiseworthy, still the difference, the direct opposition of characters remains unexplained. I cannot quite understand the exact difference which lies perhaps under the same mystery as *selfishness* does in my mind.
>
> It is that Leonard was prompted & urged on by an inward, perhaps innate sense of the *Good and Great,* an idea which working within him, leads him, without any positive view to his own or others mere happiness & comfort; continually on an upward path to stations of eminence & influence. He looks not to the pleasure of receiving praise for this probably is distasteful and the exercise of power would be merely a burden. But it is in satisfying this natural appetite and feeling himself continually moving in an upward direction that the exquisite happiness of a person like Leonard would consist. Randal Leslie on the other hand has not the slightest appreciation of the meaning of Good or Great; his satisfaction is in continually approaching the same goal of eminence, esteem, & power but for the sake of the mere reward of these: hence he is always ready to take a short cut in which he thinks he will be unobserved though it be by a *dishonourable step*.[32]

Jevons had to accept his "natural appetite." The "upward direction" could be found by placing his selfishness and ambitiousness in the service of others, that is, of society. Exultantly, by 1857 he could declare that "my whole second nature consists of one wish, or one *intention, viz* to be a powerfully good in the world." His goodness would not be directed to individuals as such—Jevons, overcome by shyness, was never very sociable or agreeable in company—but toward humanity at large: "To be *powerfully good,* that is to be good, not towards one or a dozen, or a hundred but towards a nation or the world, is what now absorbs me. But this assumes the possession of the *power*."[33]

The power, for Jevons, would take the form of science, specifically Economics. Earlier he had quoted approvingly Bulwer Lytton's phrase "knowledge is Power."[34] Jevons's "knowledge," I am arguing, both satisfied his need to feel moral and incorporated the tensions exemplified in the conflicting forces surrounding his "second nature." The private Jevons merges into the public Jevons, and he can now write:

> I seem to have more clearly before me by degrees the position to which I
> would aspire. Accepting the progressive triumphs of physical science I
> would aid in the reform of abstract science and in the establishment of
> moral & political sciences. But I would also join science to morals & reli-
> gion. I would try to show that they are not antagonistic.[35]

Jevons could now resume the interests he had manifested somewhat earlier in his life, but in a more scientific form, economics. While a boy in Liverpool, he had become aware of the poverty of most of its inhabitants. At college in London, his eye sharpened by the reading of Dickens, he walked the streets struck by the squalor of the life around him. As early as 1851, he confessed himself interested in "the industrial mechanism of society," and with his father visited the Crystal Palace exhibitions. In that same year, the taking of the census inspired Jevons to attempt a classification of trades. It formed part of an unfinished work that Jevons began in 1856, entitled, "Notes and Researches on Social Statistics, or the Science of Towns . . ." (to the study of London, Jevons added Sydney, as a result of his "transportation" to Australia).

Modeling part of this intended work on Mayhew's great classic description of London and its poor, Jevons proposed that knowledge of the characteristics of these cities would "eventually lead to such knowledge of their nature as shall ensure their improvement, as any scientific knowledge is eventually reduced to practice."[36] The aim of his scientific knowledge was clearly to cure "social ills," as we see from his comment in a chapter called "Social Cesspools of Sydney": "To a person of humane feelings, . . . the sight and acquaintance of social ills, has the same lively, although painful, interest that a rare and terrible bodily disease has to the devoted physician."[37]

The language was very different but the aim similar when Jevons turned his "second nature," his desire to be "powerfully good," fully toward economics with the writing of his first, important papers, "On a General Mathematical Theory of Economy" and on "Commercial Fluctuations," in

1862.[38] In the largest sense, Jevons saw his work as contributing to a full-scale study of Man. As he recorded in a diary entry of 1857, he was proceeding on his "book on Anthropology or the general consideration of Man in the concrete, comprising Political and Social Economy, Moral Philosophy and parts of Ethics and Metaphysics."[39]

Influenced by his views on the "origin of species," as well as by general contemporary opinion, Jevons's anthropology would show man as progressing and improving, toward civilized existence. "It is a great thing is *Progress* and I have adopted that idea as the foundation of my whole philosophical system. It is progress alone which in my opinion constitutes all human happiness."[40] The principal means of progress were economic, and by his studies in that field he wished to show the mechanism by which man improved his condition, achieved happiness, and progressed through the world and time.

Jevons's conception of economics as a part of anthropology was only a momentary vision. In seeking to make economics scientific, Jevons started from assumptions about human behavior that he derived more from psychology, his own and that of his contemporaries, and from metaphysics. Once assumed, Jevons could conveniently forget the basis of his assumptions, and proceed to the equivalent of the equations applying to the equilibrium of the lever, as if man were a lever. And aptly so. For Jevons had prescribed lever-like economic behavior to all men. So behaving, they were sure to progress.

To ensure progress, men must prefer the future to the present. They must save now to invest later. Hence capital. They must incur pain—labor—to inherit distant pleasure. They must improve all around them—land as well as self. For Jevons, these were fundamental facts of economic behavior, independent indeed of human desiring. He had only to look inside himself to know that this was so. "My life," he informs himself and us, "always was, and is now more especially, a laborious one, and I have always looked more to the future than to the enjoyment of the present."[41] He was aware of the conflict between the desire for present gratification and deferment, and wrote plaintively that "I confess I can hardly bear the thought of a solitary life of unrelieved labour. The happiness of marriage may not be the only happiness the only good I aspire to; but am I excluded from the one because I hope for the other. It is at times truly depressing to work for future appreciation only."[42] He believed that one must invest in oneself, just as society had to do, for immediate use was *bad economy*. "To work," he editorialized, "tooth & nail for many years upon yourself alone and with all appearances of doing it selfishly, may be in reality the best means of rendering yourself capable of benefiting others to an extent altogether surpassing what you might have done by working for a longer period with undeveloped strength."[43]

Constant exertion, not relaxation, was required, of man and society. Work was man's pleasure, deferred. As Jevons wrote, "happiness is in the *acquisition* not the *possession* and that which produces the *greatest proportion* of improvement and progresses most is the happiest."[44] Further, it is the *rate* of acquisition or improvement, and thus the activity itself, that counts most: "The *rate of rise*," Jevons wrote pastorally to his younger brother, "or improvement is far more to be considered than the *point actually* attained."[45]

Through such beliefs, enshrined scientifically in his economic theory, Jevons could at last understand and explain the meaning of evil in both the world and himself. Just as he was candid enough to admit his own selfish nature, so he confessed that "evil exists and I see no way of completely reconciling it with any religious theory."[46] Yet, if reconciliation with religious theory was not possible, reconciliation with science could take its place. As he wrote his sister Lucy:

> For some six or seven years past I have been chiefly engaged in learning science and taking the very evident views of things, and the consequence has been to show me *greatness* and wonderful *order or design* in nature, but no *feeling* or actual *good*; on the contrary, we find *evil* or *pain* prevailing everywhere almost equally with pleasure. It is in the human mind (made as we know after the image of God), but particularly in the feelings of love and friendship that I can find any indications of positive *good*. *Evil* is inseparable from *nature,* and no writer has ever explained satisfactorily why evil should exist at all. I can no more understand why it is to be found in material nature; but I discover in man certain properties and feelings which enable him in thought to triumph over evil, and form a conception or rather an expectation of a state free from it, and approaching, therefore, to perfection.[47]

Science, the product of mind, was man's salvation, and the solution to the theodicy problem. A few weeks later Jevons could write his other sister, Henny, about his faith:

> It is a faith in Humanity; in the fact that man was created for happiness. In nature we find an inexplicable mixture of evil. Pain and death may always come to our bodies, and, say what they will, nature cannot therefore be perfect. It is in the mind and nature of man that we find a provision against this. By a thought, a hope, a wish, an intention, or even the remembrance of a thought, a hope, he can rise superior to evils.[48]

Jevons's science, the product of his mind, allowed him to rise superior to death and evil. Economic science brought happiness more mental than material. It would be absurd to "reduce" Jevons's economics to his personal needs; for, within the context of his economic system, his formulations and formulas lead an independent existence; it would be equally absurd, however, to deny the correspondence of the latter, his own existence, with the most fundamental assumptions of his "scientific" work. The "pure" theory of Jevons's economic science emerges from, and is coincidental with, the prescriptions he has given to both himself and mankind as to the necessary path leading to progress and perfection.

# CHAPTER EIGHT

# The Iron Cage
# of Max Weber

$B$Y now, we are all familiar with the effort to use a man's writings to illuminate his personal, psychological development. Erik Erikson's *Young Man Luther* and *Gandhi's Truth* are in this genre, although they go beyond it by also relating their subjects to larger historical events. In each case, a historically important man is analyzed in terms of psychobiography or psychohistory, and his words, so to speak, are used against him. Less frequently is the direction followed by Arthur Mitzman, in which a great thinker's personal, psychological development—in this case, Max Weber's—is used to illuminate the meaning of his theoretical writings.[1] (The movement from the writer's personality to his creations is, of course, more common in literary studies.)

Since Marx, the sociology of knowledge has been recognized as an accepted discipline. We are all alerted to the need to search for the material and social basis of a man's thought. But the "psychology of knowledge," if I may coin the phrase, is only now coming into its own. Under this rubric, we look for the psychological, especially psychoanalytic, basis of a man's conscious thoughts. How do his personal defenses and adaptations affect the way he views the world? What transferences does he bring to his perception of men and events? As usual, Erikson has pioneered in analyzing some of these problems. Moreover, he has also concentrated on the role of the psychohistorical investigator himself, as illustrated by his article "On the Nature of Psycho-Historical Evidence: In Search of Gandhi."[2]

Unlike Erikson, Mitzman does not attempt a theoretical and typological treatment of the methodological problems of the psychology of knowledge, but offers us instead a formal case study of the method in operation. Mitzman's choice of Max Weber is unusually apt, for Weber not only is identified with the thesis of Western civilization's increasing rationality but is intimately related to the concept of value-free research. If Weber can be shown as a man of subterranean passions flawing his rationality and, even more important, undermining his putative value-free work, then the "psychology of knowledge" will indeed have made a telling point. It is largely to this task that Mitzman has addressed himself. He has done it with subtlety and judgment, and, as I shall try to show, with possible conclusions different from the ones to which he comes in the end.

In 1964, the hundredth anniversary of Weber's birth was celebrated. It coincided with the publication of various documents from the *Nachlass* in Eduard Baumgarten's *Max Weber, Werk und Person* (Tübingen, 1964), as well as the appearance of personal memoirs by a number of Weber's close friends. These publications, along with two fundamental earlier works—Marianne Weber's *Max Weber, ein Lebensbild* (Tübingen, 1926) and Weber's early letters, *Jugendbriefe* (Tübingen, 1936)—have made possible the sort of analysis undertaken by Mitzman. The Baumgarten family was especially important to Weber's development; and Hermann Baumgarten, married to the sister of Weber's mother, appeared to have become a model, a substitute father, for young Max. Max's first love was his cousin Emmy, the Baumgartens' daughter. Mitzman has been very fortunate, therefore, in being able to draw on Eduard Baumgarten, who is the son of Max's cousin Fritz, not only through his book but in person, even to the extent of having him scrutinize the present work in detail. Without Eduard Baumgarten, for example, we would not know many intimate details of Weber's life, such as the fact that "he never consummated his marriage" (p. 276) and that between 1911 and 1914 he had a deep personal relationship, perhaps an affair, with a young woman in Heidelberg (p. 277). Indeed, there are still many unpublished letters—including more than a hundred from Weber's correspondence with the young woman—in Baumgarten's possession. What Mitzman makes of these personal details—the sort of details that are beneath the concern and often the contempt of traditional intellectual historians—remains to be seen.

Mitzman uses Friedrich Meinecke's review of the *Lebensbild* in 1927 as a point of departure. According to Meinecke, "in Max Weber himself, we can see an Orestes [to his mother's Iphigenia], when we learn how, out of love for his mother, he intervened ruthlessly against his father and then shortly afterward was shattered by his sudden death." Moreover, according to Meinecke, Weber's opposition to his father mirrored "the historical opposition of two generations" (p. 307). But Meinecke's line of thought remained unfollowed in the following decades, for good reasons, as Mitzman points out: involved family members were still alive, the necessary *Nachlass* was unavailable, and the application of psychoanalytic categories to intellectual biographies was less acceptable than it is now. As a result, instead of Oedipus, or Orestes, Weber was portrayed as a stately German liberal, pursuing his magisterial social science without values, emotions, or the intrusion of his own personality. It was not until Wolfgang Mommsen's penetrating study, *Max Weber und die deutsche Politik* (Tübingen, 1959), that the placid picture of Weber the value-free scientist was shattered and he was shown to be "a prime mover in German liberalism's embracement of imperialism in the mid-90's and a ruthless advocate for most of his career of nationalist *Realpolitik*" (p. 311). With Mommsen having deepened our understanding of Weber as a public figure, Mitzman now sets out, in Meinecke's footsteps, to do the same for the private person, and to show how the two figures coalesce as one personality.

Mitzman's major theses are

1. "Weber's view of the world in the years before 1897 was shaped by his struggle to escape from and finally challenge the dominance in the Weber household of his father, a dominance which he identified subconsciously with the political hegemony of the Junkers over the landworkers in particular and the German people in general" (p. 6).

2. In 1897, aged thirty-three, Weber finally stood up to his father and ordered him out of his house; seven weeks later the father died and Weber gradually succumbed to feelings of guilt, which left him psychically incapacitated until around 1902 and intermittently thereafter.

3. Thus, Weber's "view of the world in the years after 1902 was structured by the lessons he drew, consciously or otherwise, from the agonizing collapse which resulted from this struggle" (pp. 6–7).

4. Weber's Oedipal struggle was representative of that of his generation, who could no longer discharge their aggressive feelings against the aristocracy, because bourgeois politicians (i.e., their fathers) now ruled alongside or in the former's place; thus, "revolt against the generation in power no longer permitted the easy transference of patricidal aggressions to enemies condemned by Reason and History" (p. 9).

As Lewis Coser judiciously remarks in his Preface, Mitzman's account is "suggestive—even though it may not be fully convincing in all its details" (p. vii). Let me take my stand openly. I find Mitzman's book a major contribution—always heuristic, even in its faults—to the comprehension of Weber's work and to the newly emerging field of psychohistory. It supports the view, convincingly, I believe, that intellectual history ungrounded in psychoanalytic understanding tends to be incomplete. One can no longer treat Freud as merely a figure in intellectual history; one must now also apply Freudian insight to intellectual history.

I am, therefore, on Mitzman's side. With this firmly said, I must admit that I find more convincing his relating of Weber's psyche to his writings than I do the larger thesis relating Weber's struggle to the generational conflict of the time. Mitzman may very well be right, but the evidence he offers is too gross, more assertive than demonstrative.[3] For the moment, a book such as *The Wish to Be Free* by Fred Weinstein and Gerald Platt, takes us farther along the road of understanding the movement toward increased autonomy of the sons from the fathers.[4]

In any event, Mitzman's overall conclusion is reflected in his title, *The Iron Cage*. The phrase comes from Weber's *The Protestant Ethic and the Spirit of Capitalism*, which he ends with a warning that the ascetic ethos, freely adopted by the early Puritans and playing such an important role in the development of Western capitalism, may be becoming a deterministic and mechanistic cloak suffocating modern man. As Mitzman reminds us, Weber's phrase is *ein stahlhartes Gehäuse*—literally, a housing hard as steel, or, in Talcott Parsons' translation, an "iron cage."

Now, Weber's writings are filled with references to the "secure homes" German fathers had built for their sons, and it is clear that Weber had a difficult, even traumatic, time breaking free from control by his father's "house." Part of Weber's inheritance—a combined inheritance from his capitalist father and his Calvinist-inclined mother—was undoubtedly the iron cage, the Protestant Ethic as elaborated by Weber himself. On the basis of this background, Mitzman claims that Weber's "discovery that his inherited ethic led to collapse coincided with a similar discovery by his generation and the one following. With the prospects of the political sublimation of repressed instinct brought to an end by the victories of European liberalism between 1860 and 1870, the mortal hostility of the bourgeois superego for libidinal impulse—the psychological underpinning of the Victorian ethic of transcendence—would have to cease or all Europe would become a madhouse" (p. 304).

This claim, as I have suggested, while partly right, is too large. Weber, at the end, did see a danger in Western civilization's becoming an iron cage, and Mitzman offers us a healthy corrective to the prevailing view of Weber as a sort of chamber-of-commerce proponent of modernity and "rationality." There was ambivalence and an enormous creative tension between passion and reason in Weber's life and thought, and it is this that makes him so relevant—increasingly so in the portrait so well painted by Mitzman—for our time. Yet I would claim that Weber's "house" was not Mitzman's "madhouse" and that in the greatest part of his work Weber reaffirmed rationality—which he equated with modernity—more strongly than he might have otherwise because, in fact, he had tested his convictions in the traumas of his own soul.[5] Was it not, rather, the rejection of the "hostility of the bourgeois superego for libidinal impulse"—and, like Freud, I make no claim here for maintenance of the excessive aspects of Victorian morality—that led to the madhouse of Nazism? It was Weber, we must remember, not Stefan George, who opposed the impulsive elements that eventually went into Hitler's National Socialism.

With this friendly disagreement aside, let me now return to Mitzman's analysis of Weber and his writings. We are all accustomed to a "Life and Works" treatment of distinguished thinkers. Mitzman's book is in this tradition—but with a difference: his Life is an inward life, which is then related intimately to the outward works. Weber's ancestors on both sides were Protestants, originally of strong evangelical convictions. His paternal ancestors, however, became capitalists in the linen trade (one thinks of Engels and his similar textile background), although Weber's own father studied law and became a magistrate and eventually a member of the Reichstag. Weber's maternal ancestors included French Calvinists who, emigrating to Geneva and then Frankfurt, accumulated a great deal of wealth while retaining their religiosity. Weber's own father was a typical authoritarian Victorian in his own household, with robust tastes and little inner religion. The mother was a deeply pietistic woman who, although she bore her husband numerous children out of duty, had a manifest distaste for sexual relations. The marriage, needless to say, was filled with tensions.

Weber, the eldest child, inherited and experienced these tensions in overflowing measure. As Mitzman convincingly argues, Weber sought to reconcile, intellectually, the capitalist spirit of his father with the pietist ethos of his mother, strong libidinal impulses with the need for ascetic controls, compulsive work with the notion of a "calling." But underlying the intellectual effort was the personal emotional life of Weber himself. Perhaps we can illustrate this relationship with an example provided by Mitzman, from the sphere of sexuality, which, though trivial in itself, opens up a whole world of meaning.

It begins with a typical Victorian situation: a tutor who makes advances to the daughter in the household. The tutor in this case was Gervinus, the historian, and the girl was Helene Fallenstein, later to be Max Weber's mother (Gervinus, incidentally, was married but childless). As Mitzman tells it, Gervinus, originally a friend of Helene's father, after the latter's death apparently developed "a more than fatherly interest in one of them [the Fallenstein children]. When Helene was sixteen years old, she was forced to repel his advances, an experience which left her with a permanent distaste for sensual passion" (p. 19).

Fleeing from Gervinus, who next tried to marry her to a student of his, she went to live with her sister Ida in Berlin. Ida was married to the liberal historian Hermann Baumgarten, and it was his friend and political colleague, Max Weber, Sr., whom Helene married two years later.

Now, Mitzman himself does not make the comparison, but one cannot help thinking of the case presented to us by Freud as "Dora." Dora, too, as we recall, recoiled from the advances of an older friend of the family, with traumatic results. The case was incredibly complicated, but one aspect of Freud's analysis shows that part of Dora's conscious revulsion was because of the very strength of the positive attraction, which she felt had to be fought off savagely. Is there any reason not to assume a similar ambivalence on the part of Helene Weber?

In any case, the traumatic episode appears to have left her with a lasting distaste for sexual passion. This attitude was clearly conveyed to her son Max, and we can be sure that it played a role in his own relations to his wife, Marianne. Thus, as promised earlier, the personal detail—Weber's inability to consummate his marriage—spurned by traditional intellectual historians, takes on added resonance and, as we shall also show later, "intellectual" significance. Before that demonstration, however, a few more comments about the "tutor episode."

There is a curious, inverted, almost compulsive repetition of this episode in Helene's later life. This time it is she who insists on keeping a tutor for her younger son in the household, against the strong opposition of her husband. Needless to say, there is no hint of the sexual; the tutor, a Herr Voigt, is a highly spiritual young theologian. Nevertheless, Max Weber, Sr., felt threatened by the presence of the young tutor in his household, who was taking his wife away from him "spiritually," and ordered him dismissed. In the words of Marianne Weber, Helene felt this "as unjust to him [the tutor] as well as to her son; it was a long time before she got over it." On this, Mitzman perceptively comments: "It may have taken her eldest son even longer. Thirty-one years later he wrote of Herr Voigt's dismissal: 'The nasty correspondence which resulted from it at the time completely estranged me too from papa'" (p. 46).

What I am suggesting now is that the tutor affair was overdetermined. Trivial in itself, it obviously called forth overreactions on the part of those involved. I have tried to suggest why for Helene and Max Weber, Sr. That Max Weber thirty-one years later would still remember it as completely estranging him from his father is also striking. As Mitzman reminds us, it was a turning point in Weber's growing loathing for his father and "a deep sympathy for his maltreated mother" (p. 47). What was at stake was the authoritarianism of a father whom Weber could no longer respect, and the dismissal of the tutor struck at Weber's own autonomy as much as at the mother, with whom at this point in life he was increasingly becoming identified.

Weber's parental identifications were in constant change and turmoil. Originally a shy and reserved young boy, at the time of going off to university, aged eighteen, he experimented with being like the father. At the university to study law, as his father had done, Weber quickly became a typical beer-drinking, fraternity-dueling German student (one thinks of Karl Marx's comparable experience). He changed physically, from a quiet, thin boy to a boisterous, full-bodied man. Helene Weber was dismayed at the change in her beloved son and did not hesitate to display her displeasure. In a well-known story, as Mitzman retells it, "on his return from Heidelberg, she greeted his bloated, saber-scarred face with a resounding smack" (p. 24).

Why? The picture we have of German fathers always stresses their authoritarianism,[6] and Mitzman supports this view. Yet one must not underestimate the similar role of the mothers. Though expressing it differently from the father, Helene Weber exercised an enormous moral authoritarianism over the young Max. Her piety formed part of Weber's demanding superego, curtailing and limiting his instinctual needs. It was his mother's "influence that kept Max Weber chaste in his Strassburg student days" (p. 33). Worse, it was the mother who set him against his father, and thus against a most important part of himself. In fact, it was Helene Weber who commanded the impossible, psychologically, of her son: to obey God, the Father, and to rebel against his own, real father (cf. pp. 93–94).

At first, in this turn of his psyche, Weber heeded his mother. He began to despise his father as a philistine and as an authoritarian with clay feet (for in the political arena, Weber now saw his father as prostrating himself supinely before Prussian authoritarianism; once again a comparison with

Marx's life history is in order). His father's "house" now became for Weber a "house of servitude"—to use a phrase from one of Weber's writings in 1906.[7] It also became a question of who would "rule in the house"; and as any Freudian knows, the "house" also symbolizes the mother. Unable to drive out his father, Weber became desperate to gain his own freedom and financial independence and to leave; yet his feelings were probably ambivalent, for he did not make the break until 1894, aged thirty!

In 1887, the father had driven the tutor out of the house, symbolically asserting his authority over young Max as well. Surely, that is the real significance of the episode. Ten years later, in 1897, it was the son's turn. Married to Marianne, and a precociously successful academician at Heidelberg, Weber invited his mother to visit him. The father insisted on coming along and on determining the time and duration of her stay. Mitzman summarizes what happened: "When the son saw his father arrive with his mother, the pent-up anger of a decade finally burst forth: such tyranny might still go on in Charlottenburg, but in Max Weber's own house, in his mother's childhood city [Heidelberg], it must stop. If, in 1887, his father had forced Herr Voigt, a spiritual son of Helene Weber if there ever was one, out of his house, now, in excellent conscience, the son by blood would pay him back . . . the old man must leave. The old man did leave, and his wife spent a few guilt-ridden weeks with her son and daughter-in-law" (p. 150).

Max, Jr., had finally done what his mother had asked of him: rebelled against the father. He had separated his parents. Seven weeks later, Max, Sr., estranged from his wife, died suddenly of a stomach hemorrhage. At first, Weber showed no signs of remorse or guilt. In a short while, however, he began to exhibit unusual irritability and nervous exhaustion. A year later, about the anniversary of his father's death—and the way in which Mitzman establishes the correspondence of the dates is a lovely bit of detective work—Weber was overcome by sleeplessness and "functional disturbances." What followed was a complete nervous breakdown, involving an inability to sustain his academic or any other duties. Weber's almost total incapacitation, as we have already noted, lasted until about 1902, reappearing thereafter intermittently and influencing the rest of his life and career.

The doctors, according to the custom of the times, diagnosed the cause of Weber's breakdown as overwork. Two years later, in 1900, a relatively unknown neuropathologist, Sigmund Freud, published his *Interpretation of Dreams,* which advanced a different diagnosis for cases such as Max Weber's. In a preface written a few years after the original publication, Freud commented, apropos of a portion of his own dream material, that the most important event in a man's life was the death of his father. Later, he wrote the paper "Mourning and Melancholia," in which he analyzed the sort of delayed reaction found in Weber's case. The overall diagnosis that Freud would have offered for his contemporary Weber was, of course, a classical Oedipal conflict.

Upon his gradual recovery in 1902, Weber inched his way back to scholarly work. Now he began to reject identification with his mother as well as his father and to search for his own creative synthesis. On one side, he became interested in Marx's explanation of the nature and origin of capitalism. On another side, he manifested an interest in Russian culture, especially Tolstoy, and its challenge to the values of rational and rationalized society. He also involved himself in the George-Kreis, with its glorification of instinct and impulse. In an extraordinary corpus of work—again, one thinks of Darwin, who, intensely neurasthenic, able to work only for two or three hours a day, turned out a staggering intellectual production—Weber sought to comprehend the elements of the ancient and modern world and to integrate his comprehension in a true social science.

According to Mitzman, Weber moved intellectually "from asceticism and toward admiration for aristocratic and mystical modes of charisma" (p. 287). His affair with the young lady started about the same time, 1911, and paralleled in its anti-Victorian nature Weber's new intellectual commitments (cf. 287–288). For the rest of his life, Weber's creative intellectual ambivalence and his personal experience of emotion tended to run together. The putative proponent of Western rationalism had come, by the end of his life in 1920, to see and acknowledge the darker hues of existence as well.

Such is part of Mitzman's argument. I have not done justice to his depiction of Weber's life, for the argumentation and detailed knowledge that Mitzman brings to his task needs to be encountered by the reader directly. Nor have I indicated that Mitzman is well aware that his hero, or antihero, did not exist in a historical vacuum. Mitzman reminds us of the predicament of liberals in Bismarckian Germany, where, successful in their quest for unification and nationalism, they were not allowed to share power with the man who had pushed through to their aims, though by means they had not intended. He sketches for us, too, the nature of Germany as a "modernizing" society and the problems of bureaucratization and democracy concomitant with this development. It is in this context that he analyzes the development of Weber's life. Overall, there is no doubt that by his study and depiction of Weber's inner and outer life, Mitzman has enormously deepened our knowledge of the man.

But what of the work? Weber's earlier contemporary, Nietzsche, perceived a crucial aspect of the general relation between a man's life and work when he said: "Most of the conscious thinking of a philosopher is secretly guided by his instinct and forced along certain lines. Even behind logic, and its apparent sovereignty of development stand value judgments, or, to speak more plainly, physiological demands for preserving a certain type of life."[8] Specifically, for Weber, we can see some of his "instincts" and "value judgments" at work in his "conscious thinking" about the East Elbian Question, treated by Mitzman under the heading "Assault on the Junker Hegemony."

Between 1892 and 1895, Weber analyzed the changing economic and social conditions of the German East, and especially the exodus of German peasants from the East Elbian region and their replacement by Slavic agricultural workers. This analysis foreshadows all of his later work. I shall try to summarize Weber's main points. First, worldwide changes in the marketplace—in this case, the grain market—were leading the Junkers toward capitalistic agricultural production. To maximize their profits, that is, in following economic rationality, the Junkers turned from traditional semi-feudal labor to wage contracts on their estates and to securing tariff protection in the country at large by exercising their political power. The result was paradoxical: ardent patriots, the Junkers were driving semi-independent Germans off their lands and colonizing the East with Slavic workers; vocal anticapitalists, the Junkers were behaving as badly as the most crass capitalist parvenu.

Weber did not rest content with rational economic analysis. He saw that the economic developments he had analyzed rested on deep psychological foundations. The Junkers were pushed to exploit their holdings more efficiently in order to keep up with the rising standard of living of the urban bourgeoisie (i.e., men like Weber's father), in short, to maintain their status, or "honored" position. The German workers, in turn, were psychologically unable to accept the wage contract system, because it violated their need for personal independence, their growing desire for autonomy from Junker patriarchal control. As Mitzman summarizes it: "The key forces in bringing about this change were not, as Marx might have put it, the development of the forces of production, but psychological motives among both rulers and ruled" (p. 79).

For Weber, the entire development he had described was a disaster. An ardent nationalist, Weber saw Germany being potentially dismembered in the East. A proud liberal bourgeois, he saw his father's generation of middle-class politicians aping the Junker way of life and kowtowing to Junker political domination. Above all, Weber wished economic development to be

subordinated to *true* rational control—not the hitherto unintended consequences of seeming economic rationalism—and for Weber this meant
*Staatsraison,* that is, rational political control; or such, at least, is my interpretation. It was to this end, I believe, that he worked all of his life to create
a true social science. Thus, Weber's intense German nationalism, which we
may see as a blemish, was an essential motive for his work.

What were some of the other personal motives? Mitzman suggests, and
I agree with him, that there was a powerful identification with the German
workers' desire for independence and autonomy. As Weber himself put it,
"*Psychological* factors of overwhelming power lead both to the flight into
the cities and to the disorganization of this labor constitution [*sic*]" (p. 101).
Weber saw the workers' "psychological factors" as mirroring his own desire
to escape from his father's patriarchal domination. I would also argue that
Weber was fighting his own temptation to succumb, as his father before
him, to the Junker value system and its assumed social superiority. We have
already seen his trial identification with these values in his life at the university. His mother's smack recalled him to his own Calvinist inheritance and
to a more authentic part of himself. At this point, I suggest, Weber perceived
and demonstrated the falseness and weakness—the clay feet—of Junker
patriarchalism, and thus of his father's own model.

Weber's personal motives did not determine his findings. They combined with his intellectual developments, his legal and philosophical thinking, and helped supply some of the passion animating his rational analysis.
Reinhard Bendix, summarizing Weber's early studies as pointing to all of
his later work on the sociology of religion, comments from a purely intellectual point of view:

> His disenchantment with the world in which he lived led him to a search of
> the past for the origin of the values he prized. As an individualist Weber
> sought to recover the historical sources of the individualism that prompted
> the farm workers to prefer the uncertainty of seasonal labor to the security
> of personal subservience. As a member of the middle class he inquired into
> the sources of the collectivism and rationality that prompted English and
> Hanseatic stockbrokers to impose an ethic of trade upon themselves—a
> practice that stood in marked contrast to the aping of aristocratic ways
> among his compatriots.[9]

What Mitzman has done is to supply the unconscious factor to the conscious equation of Weber's work offered us by Bendix.

The breakdown of 1898 dissolved the synthesis worked out in the East
Elbian Question. With his gradual recovery after 1902, Weber laboriously
set to work to reintegrate himself and the world, but this time on deeper

foundations. In 1903, he began work on the "Protestant Ethic," and this led him to a full-scale sociology of religion, and, in fact, to a complete sociology of the modern world. Mitzman summarizes the general dynamics involved when he says:

> Weber was able to gauge out of his superego and examine critically the commandment of unceasing labor that had been lodged there. Thus, by identifying the work ethic of his mother's Calvinist ancestry as a device which formerly gave evidence of divine grace but now served only as a "housing hard as steel," Weber was focusing his intellect on his own experience in order both to liberate himself from it and to interpret the history of the modern world; he was perceiving the historical dimension of his personal dilemma. (pp. 173-174)

In turn, Mitzman takes the fundamental concepts of Weberian sociology—for example, charisma and bureaucracy, class and status, asceticism and mysticism, rationalism and magic—and seeks to offer an insight into the "personal dilemma" underlying these notions. I have tried to give a hint as to how he proceeds, by drawing on the example of East Elbia. For the full picture, the reader must again go directly to Mitzman's book.

Mitzman, however, disregards large aspects of Weber's life and works that might have deepened and broadened the picture offered to us. For example, we are told almost nothing about Weber's sibling relationships, yet these must have been of great significance in affecting his attitudes to other men and women (e.g., sisters as affecting his propensity to fall in love with his cousins). A few lines are given to Weber's brother Alfred, an important scholar in his own right, but the relationship is not followed out satisfactorily. In short, Weber's father and mother have been allowed to overdominate the scene, without allowing for the psychologically mediating effect of siblings. (If Mitzman was unable to obtain information in this matter, then we should have been so informed.)

Similarly, Weber's experience in the army is almost completely neglected. Gerth and Mills tell us in their brief introduction to *From Max Weber* that he adjusted to the boredom of military life "by having his fill of alcohol in the evening and going through the military routine the next day in the daze of a moderate hang-over."[10] With Mitzman's gift for analysis, I would have expected him to make more of Weber's youthful encounter with stupefying military bureaucratic authority. And then, what of Weber's 1904 visit to the United States? Since Weber drew so many of his examples and so much of his understanding of modernity from the American model, further examination of this personal and intellectual experience would have been useful. Indeed, the intellectual aspects of Weber's encounter with America are short-changed, as well as, on the other side, an account of Weber's contribution to economic history.[11]

Now Mitzman could respond that he was not trying to present a complete psychological-intellectual analysis of Weber but only to select certain aspects of the man and his works to illustrate certain theses. This is a perfectly legitimate position, and I suspect it is the one Mitzman would quite properly take. Let me press on then with broader, more methodological considerations. As is well known, the leading theorist and practitioner of psychohistory is Erik H. Erikson. Do his ideas figure in Mitzman's treatment? The only reference to Erikson is a footnote (p. 4), noting his ego-psychology as a branch of post-Freudian theory. Fine; but one wonders why Mitzman does not think it worthwhile to make more use of Erikson's analysis of the role of the psychohistorian himself, remarked upon earlier, in studying the sources and persons involved with his subject? Thus, in *Gandhi's Truth,* Erikson subjects himself, and his transferences to Gandhi and the information about Gandhi, to a searching analysis. Only then does he start on Gandhi per se.

How might this apply to Mitzman's work? In the first instance, one would have wished Mitzman to be more self-conscious about his use of Marianne Weber's *Lebensbild*. Surely, before we can evaluate her revelations, we need to understand *her* more thoroughly as a person. More critical still, of course, is the question of Mitzman's own psyche, his own transferences and values (psychically and intellectually). How does *he* feel about parent figures, political authority, technological and scientific society, value-free research? Where are *his* sympathies involved in the pressing social and economic problems of today? How conscious is he of his own psychic processes, as they affect his work?

For example, Mitzman concludes at one point that "the visible danger in *fin de siècle* Europe was by no means a wildly destructive mass breakthrough of the irrational, but the contrary: the permanent victory over human spontaneity and autonomy of the machine, that harsh, material quintessence of the nineteenth-century superego" (pp. 251–252). This sounds very present-minded, where those in favor of a radical "aesthetic revolution"—to use the phrase of Herbert Marcuse—see no danger of a "breakthrough of the irrational" but only the terrible pressure of a "rational," mechanized, and thus alienating society. Surely, the danger, then and now, is of *both* kinds. To speak first of *fin de siècle* Europe: was virulent racism not a "visible danger" to those with eyes to see? Was Freud not reacting to the political irrationality he saw around him when he took up a Le Bon-like conservatism in the face of the "mob"? Mitzman mentions Carl E. Schorske's article, "Politics and the Psyche in Fin de Siècle Vienna: Schnitzler and Hofmannsthal,"[12] but he does not seem to reckon with Schorske's comment on a novel by Schnitzler: it "shows that instinct has in fact been let loose in the sphere of politics, parliament has become a mere theatre through which the masses are manipulated, sexuality has become liberated from the moral code which contained it" (p. 938).

To pass to another sort of criticism, there is always the temptation to "reduce" thought to the unconscious impulses, to forget that we must seek a *correspondence* of various levels of the human psyche. Occasionally, it seems to me, Mitzman gives way to this temptation, as when he comments apropos of Weber's work on the East Elbian Question: "the most superficial of these realms of consciousness [Mitzman is discussing four such realms] is Weber's broad, scholarly analysis of the social and economic changes occurring in the relationship between Junker landlord and peasant in the German East" (p. 75). Why the word "superficial"? One of its definitions, of course, is simply "on the surface." Another, however, is "not profound; shallow." By his use of a semipejorative word, Mitzman risks the sort of implicit reductionism that lurks in psychohistory.

Perhaps I can come to grips more fully with my major caveat to Mitzman's work by a discussion of value-free inquiry. Clearly, the context for both Mitzman's and my views is the debate on the subject between so-called radicals and liberals. Such a debate, for example, forms the core of the interesting book by Hugh Stretton, *The Political Sciences*,[13] whose thesis is that the social scientist must work by a principle of selection that necessarily involves his values: result, value-free inquiry is impossible and undesirable. Stretton concludes by demanding a clear commitment to values (in his case, activist values).

Like Stretton, Mitzman places the subject of value-free inquiry at the very beginning of his book. His first words in his introduction are

Max Weber's shadow falls long over the intellectual life of our era. His insistence that a value-free methodology is indispensable to the scientific analysis of society dominates contemporary sociology, often paralyzing the scholar's human commitment and justifying his remoteness and irrelevance. Further, the Weberian vision of modern society as subject to an inexorable rationalization of human activity, and of the modern mind as necessarily disenchanted when it fully comprehends this inexorability, places before us the bleak vistas of universal bureaucratization, the death of art and impulse, the suffocation of instinct . . . our options are far more open than his, our values are more fluid, and our youth determined to wrest control over their fate from impersonal bureaucracies. At the heart of Weber's vision lies *only* the truth of his epoch, his country and his station, the truth of a bourgeois scholar in Imperial Germany . . . developed under agonizing personal pressures, themselves exerted and maintained by the dilemmas of family, social milieu and historical position. [p. 3; my italics]

The "personal pressures," as Mitzman has explained, came from Weber's parents, threatening Weber with unassimilable differences. According to Mitzman, "Weber's justification for not taking sides in his parents' quarrels—i.e., for not making a value judgment of them—was, basically, that their notions were set in such different worlds that it was impossible, knowing both, to judge either" (p. 60). Thus, Mitzman concludes: "Weber's methodological pre-supposition of a rigid separation between the spheres of logical analysis and value judgment serves the critical function of maintaining an equally rigid separation between his attitudes toward his mother on the one hand and his father on the other" (p. 61; cf. pp. 169–170). Such, then, is Mitzman's etiological explanation of Weber's value-free inquiry.

Now, Mitzman, I suspect, is largely correct in his etiology. However, does the origin of a position in "personal pressures" vitiate its correctness? Is Darwin's theory of evolution any less scientific because we can show how its originator's neurasthenic condition helped him stumble toward it? As I tried to show in Chapter 6, these questions are extremely complicated, especially in the area of the social sciences. In regard to Weber, I believe, we find a borderline case.

What, in fact, is Weber's theory of value-free inquiry? Gerth and Mills, in my view, take us closer to an understanding of Weber's position than does Mitzman. Discussing Weber's reaction to William Ellery Channing, who made a deep impression on him, they state: "Characteristically, Weber does not enter into a theological dispute about the Sermon on the Mount; he keeps at a distance from Channing by locating his perspective in the social and historical situation; he tries thereby to 'understand' and, at the same time, he relativizes Channing's position." Thus, Weber went beyond ethical absolutism. As he wrote in one of his letters: "The matter does not appear to me to be so desperate if one does not ask too exclusively (as the Baumgartens, now as often, do): 'Who is morally right and who is morally wrong?' But if one rather asks: 'Given the existing conflict, how can I solve it with the least internal and external damage for all concerned?'"[14]

Weber was a true social ecologist. By that I mean he constantly tried to understand the secondary, the unintended, consequences of actions and motives. That was what social science was about. His analysis of the East Elbian Question, as we have seen, was couched in these terms. Weber's social science was operational science, *Realpolitik* in the best sense of the term, where one recognizes the necessary means to a given end and at least envisions the consequences of these means in systematic fashion.

Whence come the ends, the ultimate values? Weber did not ignore this question; he confronted it first and then put it to one side. In "Science as a Vocation," Weber quoted Tolstoy to the effect that "science is meaningless because it gives no answer to our question, the only question important for us: 'What shall we do and how shall we live?'" Weber's answer is mild and thoughtful:

> That science does not give an answer to this is indisputable. The only ques-
> tion that remains is the sense in which science gives "no" answer, and whether
> or not science might yet be of some use to the one who puts the question
> correctly. Today one usually speaks of science as "free from presupposi-
> tion." Is there such a thing? It depends upon what one understands thereby.
> All scientific work presupposes that the rules of logic and method are valid;
> these are general foundations of our orientation in the world; and, at least
> for our special question, these presupposes that what is yielded by scientific
> work is important in the sense that it is "worth being known." In this,
> obviously, are contained all our problems. For this presupposition cannot
> be proved by scientific means. It can only be *interpreted* with reference to
> its ultimate meaning, which we must reject or accept according to our ul-
> timate position toward life.[15]

Elsewhere, in *Wirtschaft und Gesellschaft,* Weber went a bit further on the subject of meaning, declaring:

> "Meaning" may be of two kinds. The term may refer first to the actual
> existing meaning in the given concrete case of a particular actor, or to the
> average or approximate meaning attributable to a given plurality of actors;
> or secondly to the theoretically conceived *pure type* [i.e., ideal type] of
> subjective meaning attributed to the hypothetical actor or actors in a given
> type of action. In no case does it refer to an objectively "correct" meaning
> or one which is "true" in some metaphysical sense. It is this which dis-
> tinguishes the empirical sciences of action, such as sociology and history,
> from the dogmatic disciplines in that area, such as jurisprudence, logic,
> ethics, and esthetics, which seek to ascertain the "true" and "valid" mean-
> ings associated with the objects of their investigation.[16]

It is a travesty of Weber to claim that he himself was not an openly committed man, a true activist. One may not like his imperialist or nation-alist leanings, but one cannot deny his strenuous public advocacy of these positions. Moreover, it is not for nothing that his journal was called the *Archiv für Sozialwissenschaft und Sozialpolitik,* and I stress the last part of the title. Equally, it would be foolish to contend that, in fact, Weber's activist values did not color and perhaps warp his value-free inquiries. What he sets before us is an ideal type, from which he himself, understandably, often fell short.

Weber's ideal was the construction of the "empirical sciences of action." One can understand, for example, the connection of the Protestant Ethic, or other religious injunctions, with the spirit of capitalism *only* if one seeks to understand the values of the actors of the time without passing "dogmatic" judgment on them. Thus, Weber announced that "the question of the relative values of the cultures which are compared here will not receive a single word," and, more specifically, "in such a study, it may at once be definitely stated, no attempt is made to evaluate the ideas of the Reformation in any sense, whether it concern their social or their religious worth."[17] What Weber has done—and it is of enormous importance—is to take the historicist position and stand it on its head; that is, to place its relativist value position in the service of universalizing social science. I cannot stress the point just made too strongly. In short, Weber's value-freedom is a purely heuristic necessity; to understand unintended consequences, one must first abstain from judging actors.

Thus, to achieve knowledge, an empirical science of action, one must start from a value-free position *as defined by Weber.* Next, *insofar as one is a scholar* one must then offer one's findings objectively to students. Weber detested a Treitschke, who used the scholarly podium as a forum for political propaganda. Equally, he scorned those students who "crave a leader and not a teacher."[18] Weber's claim was that

> you can take this or that position when concerned with a problem of value.
> . . . *If* you take such a stand, then, according to scientific experience, you
> have to use such and such a *means* in order to carry out your conviction
> practically. Now, these means are perhaps such that you believe you must
> reject them. Then you simply must choose between the end and the inevita-
> ble means. Does the end "justify" the means? Or does it not? The teacher
> can confront you with the necessity of this choice. He cannot do more, so
> long as he wishes to remain a teacher and not to become a demagogue. He
> can, of course, also tell you that if you want such and such an end, then you
> must take into the bargain the subsidiary consequences which according to
> all experience will occur.[19]

Weber pronounced these words in 1918. To the very end of his life, he held fast to rationality. He knew, as Mitzman has so well shown us, the possible price to be paid: disenchantment of the world, the loss of some kinds of meaning. He also realized that excessive rationality, in the perverted form of overmechanization of life, could lead to an "iron cage." Weber, however, like Freud, was a rational stoic. In the face of such dangers, he did not lose faith in man's effort at rationality. What was needed, he believed, was more and better rationality: a making intended what was before unintended (or to use the Freudian idiom, making conscious what was unconscious). Today, with rationality itself rather than its abuses under attack, Weber's call to attention to the "subsidiary consequences" of seeking a particular end seems especially pertinent.

Of, course, much of Weber's achievement is "only the truth of his epoch," as Mitzman says, but because he tried so desperately to transcend his own limitations, his theories and concepts are frequently "truths" for our time as well. Weber's insights into charisma and status, the Protestant Ethic, and the Spirit of Capitalism may indeed be grounded in the fact that he was "a bourgeois scholar in Imperial Germany," but they reach out far beyond that narrow social terrain.

There is, in fact, a paradox in Mitzman's treatment of Weber. For Mitzman calls upon Freud, a "bourgeois physician in Imperial Austria" (my phrase), to treat Weber, on the assumption that Freud's "truths" transcended his particular setting. Then why not Weber's? In fact, what Mitzman himself has done is to strip away much of the dross surrounding Weber's work and allow us thereby to see what remains of transpersonal worth. In short, by adding psychology of knowledge to sociology of knowledge, Mitzman has helped to "free" Weber's work of its personal limitations and, so to speak, has placed before us an "ideal type" of Weberian sociology.

Weber's theories, then, have not been "reduced" to his psychic hang-ups. They have been lifted out of them. Or rather, Weber's theories have been placed in creative tension with his "agonizing personal pressures." Intentionally or unintentionally, Mitzman has given us a Weber, not larger or smaller than life, but truer to life.

# The Examination
## of Political
## Leadership

# Prolegomena
# to Psychohistory

SOME books, by their very success, illuminate the end of a road. Such a book is Victor Wolfenstein's *The Revolutionary Personality.*[1] It is the best exemplification of Harold Lasswell's famous dictum—political men displace their private motives onto public objects—enunciated years ago in *Psychopathology and Politics,* that we are likely to have for a long time. Its analyses of Lenin, Trotsky, and Gandhi are very Freudian, and very good—much, much better than the Freud–Bullitt analysis of Woodrow Wilson. Yet its successes (unlike the Freud–Bullitt fiasco) cast into bold and useful relief the failures and limitations of the orthodox Freudian–Lasswellian approach, an approach that earlier dominated so much of the work in history, political science, and psychoanalysis. Rather than a pointer to despair, the book directs our attention to other possibilities in the emerging field of psychohistorical inquiry.

Wolfenstein's primary aim is "to generate a set of useful psycho-political propositions about revolutionary involvement and leadership." This takes the form of an effort to work out the model of a "revolutionary personality." The basic psychological inspiration is Freud (mediated through Wolfenstein's distinguished aunt, Dr. Martha Wolfenstein, which gives an authenticity and professional insight to the analyses missing from the work of less lucky social scientists). The application of Freud's findings to politics, he acknowledges to have been best done by Lasswell and Erik Erikson.

Wolfenstein's method is to develop his notion of a "revolutionary personality" from three life histories: Lenin, Trotsky, and Gandhi. Repeatedly, we are told that Wolfenstein is only erecting "hypotheses" on these case studies, which other empirical studies will confirm or disconfirm. Wolfenstein's hypotheses are as follows. The "revolutionary personality" is a man who "had an unusually ambivalent relationship with his father." Two more conditions, however, are necessary to turn him into a revolutionary: "The conflict with paternal authority must be alive and unresolvable in the family context as adolescence draws to a close" (the father has just died, or the son leaves the family); and "there must exist a political context in terms of which the conflict can be expressed." This last is made more specific by Wolfenstein's shrewd observation that the precipitant factor emerges when "established political authority acts with unexpected aggressiveness towards the potential revolutionist" (e.g., executing Lenin's brother, imprisoning Trotsky). This may sound like naive Freudianism but as worked out, it is most soberly and persuasively handled. Whether Wolfenstein is using a "fair sample" is, of course, another matter.

What of Erikson in all of this? Wolfenstein does make substantial outward gestures to Erikson's theory of psychogenetic development stages, trying to apply them to his three revolutionaries. At the end of this effort, Wolfenstein concludes that there are no common characteristics to be derived from Erikson for the model of a "revolutionary personality." We are left, then, with the shared conditions. And I, for one, find the spirit of Erikson's work almost entirely missing. I am not persuaded that Wolfenstein has made the Eriksonian interpretation, with its essential stress on the correspondence of somatic, ego, and social process, central to his analysis. Wolfenstein wishes a model of a "revolutionary personality," and not Erikson's complex description and analysis of what Erikson calls "a convergence in all three processes."

At the core of Erikson's theory is his emphasis on the interaction between the individual and the group (family and society). In each of his stages of development, he centers attention on three processes: the somatic, or biologically given; the individual's ego mastery; and the social context (in *Young Man Luther,* for example, involving such elements as level of technology, communication system, problem of territorial or national identity, social structure, marginality, and so forth). Erikson sees these three processes as corresponding processes, in which each one interacts with the others. As a gross example, an infant born crippled (somatic) will have difficulty learning to walk at the appropriate age level and thus have a problem of "autonomy" (ego mastery), complicated or made easier by the way in which his society treats its cripples—e.g., as a product of the Devil, remediable physical affliction, etc. (social context). The three processes run both together and forward in all of Erikson's stages of development—for which he has such polarity names as basic trust or mistrust (Freud's oral stage), autonomy or shame (anal), initiative or guilt (genital), and so forth. (For the full scheme, see *Childhood and Society,* 1963).

Wolfenstein's application of the above to his three figures is roughly as follows. Lenin was basically mistrustful, least shameful, and least guilty; Trotsky and Gandhi were both trustful in the earliest stage, and both are placed on the shame and guilt side of the development spectrum, with Gandhi nearer the end. During the "identity crisis" of the adolescence period, to put it in crude summary terms, Lenin was most successful in identifying with a strong father, Trotsky was ambivalent, and Gandhi tended to identify with the mother. In short, Erikson here is only frosting (though very good frosting) on the Freudian-Lasswellian cake.

Within his own terms, however, Wolfenstein offers us generally excellent analyses. Thus, discussing the change of name from Bronstein to Trotsky, which occurred during an escape from prison, Wolfenstein points out:

> He chose Trotsky—the name of one of his jailors in Odessa. In this simple act he revealed that ambivalence which was to be so injurious to his political fortunes. Just as he had posed as a Marxist when fighting off submission to Marxism [described previously], so now he (so to speak) posed as his jailor when trying to escape from captivity. Trotsky's fatal flaw was this indecisiveness about submitting or fighting, as shown in this case by his identification with aggressive authority. He did not call himself Lenin, a name innocent of political connotations or Stalin, a name connoting steel and hardness, but Trotsky, a name which embodied the very authority against which he was to fight.

As an instance of how to articulate the Lasswellian "private-motives-to-public-agencies" mechanism, I cite admiringly Wolfenstein's analysis of Gandhi's increasing shift to a feminine identification, culminating in a vow to renounce sexual intercourse (in Gandhi's thirty-sixth year), which is then given a political dimension:

> With the vow [to embrace *satyagraha,* usually translated as "nonviolence"] a link was established between the private and the public aspects of his life. Just as a vow had marked his dedication to sexual renunciation, so the September vow [to *satyagraha*] sanctified his role in politics and made clear to him what the course of Indian action must be: feminine (that is, non-

violent) resistance must be used against the oppression of British masculine authority.

Wolfenstein writes with a minimum of psychological jargon, yet he does not go to the opposite extreme and underinterpret his material. With a sure grasp of the historical and political background of his personalities, he avoids the incredible gaucheries and gaps perpetrated by Freud–Bullitt on Wilson. Everyone interested in or working on Lenin, Trotsky, or Gandhi (though one must note Wolfenstein's bravery in venturing into a psychological analysis of Gandhi on the eve of Erikson's own writing on that subject) is in Wolfenstein's debt for what he does and the way he does it. Nevertheless, with an apology to Wolfenstein, who has rightly written the book he wanted to write, I consider some of the book's limitations and some of the possibilities and problems for psychohistorical inquiry.

Any work of psychohistorical inquiry, just like any work in history or political science, has been open to certain types of sniping. Is a minor error of induction from the data more serious in psychohistorical inquiry than elsewhere? We are told, presumably on the basis of his sister Anna's description, that as a boy Lenin's "whole aspect . . . was jovial, humorous, mischievous, self-confident, aggressive. . . . [He] was noisy and boisterous, a player of practical jokes, an inveterate tease, quick of repartee, sharp of tongue." Immediately after this description, Wolfenstein states that "Vladimir thus appears to have been a somewhat shy boy." If no grandiose "hypotheses" are built on such flimsy induction from the evidence (and Wolfenstein doesn't build out from this one), then I do not think the temptation of anti-Freudian historians to discredit the whole approach can be taken seriously; general historians can be faulted all too readily and often on this score for them to throw the first stone.

What of the more serious problem, of making tentative but tendentious statements based on insubstantial and scratchy evidence? (Wolfenstein admits this readily in the case of Lenin: "The interpretation of Lenin's development . . . has been highly speculative." For example, Wolfenstein analyzes the effect of the extended absences from home, as part of his job, of Lenin's father. Such an absence we are told

> *tends* to create feelings of insecurity and mistrust. . . . It *must* have had a strange effect on young Lenin's mind. . . . The loving, temperate attention of his mother *undoubtedly* provided a stiff leavening of stability . . . but

130

the pattern of alternating great attention and prolonged absence [of the father] . . . *probably* produced strongly ambivalent feelings. . . . These feelings were *probably* further intensified . . . the high moral rectitude of the father *undoubtedly* resulted in an unusually demanding superego for the son. [my italics]

Such language arouses our strongest doubts. Nevertheless, I would be the last to deny the usefulness of "speculation" in psychohistory, and history generally; it must never be confused, however, with sound (or as sound as the historian can get) induction from the evidence. In psychohistorical inquiry, as in all historical inquiry, it is *probably* a good idea to abstain as much as possible from the overemphatic extrapolatory voice.

In addition to the problems of false extrapolation and overassertive extrapolation from the written evidence, there is the key problem of possible false interpretation of the material. Even if one accepts the purely Freudian approach, can one be sure of a particular analysis? Let me give an example at some length. Wolfenstein quotes a wonderful passage, stuffed with psychological images, from Trotsky's autobiography. In it, Trotsky gives one of the classic descriptions—reminding us of similar ones concerning Hitler—of the demagogue's relations to the mass of listeners:

> I spoke from out of a warm cavern of human bodies. . . . At times it seemed as if I felt, with my lips, the stern inquisitiveness of this crowd that had merged into a single whole. Then all the arguments and words thought out in advance would break and recede under the imperative pressure of sympathy, and other words, other arguments, utterly unexpected by the orator but needed by these people, would emerge in full array from my subconsciousness. On such occasions I felt as if I were listening to the speaker from the outside, trying to keep pace with his ideas, afraid that, like a somnambulist, he might fall off the edge of the roof at the sound of my conscious reasoning. Such was the Modern Circus [the hall in which Trotsky was speaking]. . . . The infants were peacefully sucking the breasts from which approving or threatening shouts were coming. The whole crowd was like that, like infants clinging with their dry lips to the nipples of the revolution. Leaving the Modern Circus was even more difficult than entering it. . . . In a semi-consciousness of exhaustion, I would float on countless arms above the heads of the people, to reach the exit. . . . Then some gate would open, suck me in, and close after me.

Wolfenstein's interpretation, in part, is as follows: Trotsky, he says, "de-

131

scribes his actions in peculiarly passive tones"; the effect of the crowd on Trotsky is to break down "the tight controls of consciousness, the inhibiting forces of guilt"; "the crowd in terms of personal contact is analogous to the inevitable forces of history in terms of ideology and abstraction, in each case a benevolent force carrying him safely forward"; and "Trotsky feels himself to be the mother of the revolution, nursing it as the mothers in his audience are nursing their children. He unconsciously views himself as a better mother to his revolutionary children than his mother was to him."

Now, some of this is suggestive, especially the comments on the effect of crowds. On the question of Trotsky's being the "mother of the revolution, nursing it," I offer an alternative interpretation. Surely, it is Trotsky whose oral needs are being satisfied and who is being nurtured and sustained by the crowd and the revolution. "I felt, with *my* lips, the . . . crowd," he tells us first. Then he identifies with the crowd—"I felt as if I were listening to the speaker from *the outside*"—and only then talks of the crowd as being "like infants clinging with their dry lips to the nipples of the revolution." The crowd's "new-found unity" can be interpreted as Trotsky's unity with the nurturing mother, and a gate opening to "suck me in" translated as the child's well-known desire for incorporation with the mother through the nipple. To back this up, we have the knowledge that Trotsky suffered from "chronic catarrh" of the stomach, indicative of early feeding problems, and Trotsky's own admission, in reference to his reading habits, that he was always afraid he would not get enough. "I swallowed books, fearful that my entire life would not be long enough. . . . My reading was nervous, impatient and unsystematic."

The reader need not choose between Wolfenstein and me. I pose this instance simply to make vivid the general problem. The solution to the problem, of course, is that the interpretation of any one passage must be based on a host of other, similar passages and on the resultant picture of the personality and its dynamics that the "analyst" erects on this basis. The difference between the clinician and the psychohistorian is that the former can recheck his "diagnosis" with the living patient, while the latter must do so against further published data. (Later, I shall try to show that there are gains and losses on both sides.) Both ought to place their interpretation of the individual against a wider social context: for example, what are the characteristics of Russian feeding habits, of Russian toilet-training, and so forth (Wolfenstein does not even mention, if only to dismiss, the existing literature on these subjects). For the clinician this is generally intuitive; for the psychohistorian it must be by a sort of psychological and anthropological "distancing" from his own preconceptions, obtained by studying the works on these subjects by other scholars.

The problem of rival psychoanalytic interpretations, however, is a key problem because it treads heavily on the historian's wariness as to preparation in psychoanalytic theory. How is one to know about "oral" needs? about guilt? about passivity? Must the historian be analyzed, or become a candidate at a psychoanalytic training institute (assuming the time, the money, *and* admission)?[2] There is, as yet, no simple answer to all of these questions. One thing, I think, can be said with certainty. Merely going through a personal analysis does not turn one into a psychohistorian. One can cite the renowned historian Lewis Namier as an instance, for he is often cited as one who went through analysis, tried to apply it to history (see, for example, his *Charles Townshend* [1959]), and admitted a large measure of failure. While psycho-historical inquiry can undoubtedly be widened by personal experience of psychoanalysis—as Freud said, "There is knowing, and knowing [i.e., rationally, and emotionally]"—it is, in fact, an intellectual discipline that must be created out of very different materials from the merely personal.

Without entering further into this question here, we can return to the original point concerning rival interpretations and conclude that, in any case, historians (or political scientists) are faced with a similar problem in all their work. Their main task, in fact, is to decide whether the interpretation of a particular document or event is in accord with the rest of the "evidence" and with the general picture that they have constructed from the evidence. In short, the terms of psychohistory may be new, but the charge to the historian is the same: to pass judgment on the totality of the evidence.[3]

The danger of the *sort* of Freudian analysis of the Trotsky passage—both Wolfenstein's and mine—is that it may lead one into psychological reductionism. It can become a closed game, as in the Freud–Bullitt *Wilson,* where Wilson is reduced to his oral, anal, and genital aspects, divorced from the social context, and made into a purely pathological clinical specimen. Wolfenstein, for example, is well aware of this danger:

> My interest has been quite exclusively in the motivations of the subjects and certain emotional capabilities related to these. As a result I have been forced to forgo any systematic analysis of the men's cognitive characteristics and of the more broad-scale social psychological and sociological aspects of revolutionary behaviour. . . . Hopefully, I have not created a procrustean bed of psychological reductionism, in which there is no room for analysis of other aspects of the revolutionary process.

Yet, in spite of Wolfenstein's consciousness of the danger, and his own wide historical knowledge of the "other aspects of the revolutionary process," his Freudian–Lasswellian approach either tumbles him into the reductionist abyss or leaves him constantly teetering on the edge. Indeed, as I said at the beginning, the power of *The Revolutionary Personality* is that its very success in using the Freudian–Lasswellian method pushes that method to its limits, highlighting for us its built-in weaknesses. It demonstrates, conclusively I believe, that an interest "exclusively in the motivations of the subjects," detached from an integral and corresponding analysis of the other, social–historical aspects of behavior is an exhausted mine.

One quotation from Wolfenstein illustrates the danger. "Although much experience comes between the first year of life and full adulthood, there should be indications in that first year of what the adult will be like and *therefore* of what his political behaviour will be like" (my italics). For instance, on the basis of Lenin's basic mistrust ("highly speculative," as we have seen), Wolfenstein asserts that "his adult behaviour should be characterized by attempts to make his environment less risky, both by keeping the initiative himself and by creating structures which would leave him less exposed. Thus we would seem to have here one root of his later creation of an organization subject to his directives alone." Wolfenstein may, in fact, be right; but the jump from Lenin's first year to the creation of the tight-knit Bolshevik party is breathtaking. And the "therefore" leading to political behavior covers over the problem with an assertion rather than a demonstration from the evidence.

That "therefore" is the crux of Lasswell's "Private Motives, Public Agencies" (if I may paraphrase Mandeville's "Private Evils, Public Benefits" adage). Lasswell's work is a brilliant, pioneering effort to translate Freudian clinical psychology into political psychology. Freud himself, of course, prepared the way, first with *Totem and Taboo* (1912–13) and then with such works as *Group Psychology and the Analysis of the Ego* (1921), and *Civilization and its Discontents* (1930).[4] But like Freud's own "psychohistorical" work (especially the Woodrow Wilson book), Lasswell's is outdated. As yet, there has been little demonstration that we can move confidently from personality studies to political behavior. The first major effort in this direction, the *Authoritarian Personality* (1950) studies (the model for Wolfenstein's effort, though he is analyzing dead subjects through historical materials instead of live ones by depth interviews and questionnaires), was not reassuring as Edward Shils and others pointed out.[5] Some sort of connection obviously exists, but we cannot understand the connection merely as an abstract generalization, divorced from an exhaustive analysis of the concrete political condition.[6]

Does the fault lie in the effort to construct a "revolutionary personality" consistent, so to speak, for all revolutionists? In yearning for a "model," rather than for the analysis of limited and time-bound situations in the hope of producing "limited generalizations"? For example, why does Wolfenstein choose Lenin, Trotsky, and Gandhi in an effort to derive hypotheses? Would not Stalin have been a better choice to fill out the triumvirate, avoiding the problem of a new and different social context provoked by Gandhi and offering us at least a "Bolshevik revolutionary personality" with which to begin? And if one were serious about constructing a "revolutionary personality" per se, would not a choice from a number of revolutions— perhaps Cromwell in the Puritan, Washington in the American, Robespierre in the French—be methodologically more useful? Wolfenstein, of course, can answer that he expects others to undertake such studies. But this is to beg the question. The wider option might immediately have shown that revolutions themselves are different—is the Indian "revolution," in fact, of the same order as the Russian Revolution?—and require different revolutionary personalities to lead them.

One of the most astute students of comparative revolutions, Chalmers Johnson, has put the challenge directly: "The aspect of psychological studies of revolution that we do not find useful is the misinformed generalization of micro data without reference to a macro model—namely, the derivation of revolution from psychological studies of individual revolutionaries. . . . Psychological data on revolutionaries must be related to the social system."[7] If Johnson is right, as I believe he is, then the effort to study motivations separate from social context, leaving the latter to be "filled in" by others, may be from the beginning methodologically ill-conceived.[8]

Wolfenstein himself knows this. Thus, for example, commenting on Gandhi's increasing turn to a feminine identity, Wolfenstein remarks,

> In any case, for many Indians, and for Gandhi as he grew older, the British model of masculinity, with its martial ideals and emphasis on physical courage, was a discomforting one. In fact, it was as alien to the major stream of traditional Hindu ideals to act out one's manhood in British terms as it was difficult for Gandhi to think of himself as a man at all. This "fit" was to be one of the essential aspects of Gandhi's success in Indian

revolutionary politics, just as Lenin's ready assumption of a paternal role was to aid him greatly in his revolutionary struggle.

The "fit" is what allows us to move from the micro to the macro model, from the individual to the collective psychology and back again. This movement seems most fruitfully handled in terms of the relation of leader and led.[9] We need to ask questions such as: Are the reasons the leader is ready to lead similar to or different from the reasons followers are ready to follow? Can we treat the led as one category, or do we need to differentiate between immediate disciples and general supporters? between different groups of supporters? What is the communication system used by the leader, and how does it relate to the technological structure of the society? Are the psychological qualities that make a revolutionary leader the same as those that allow that leader to take power? to institutionalize the revolution? to provide for a successor? To answer such questions is to move away from the exclusive concentration on individual motivations and to set them in the necessary social framework. It is to go from "models" to "historical complexity."

I suspect that one reason for the passion of some political scientists for a model of a revolutionary personality, or other political actor, is the desire to be able to predict. Thus, on another front, James David Barber (of Duke University) studied various American presidents in an effort to establish a "style" of leadership, revolving around active–passive categories.[10] On this basis, he sought to forecast the performance of a future Coolidge or a Hoover as president. Like Wolfenstein, Barber was better in his particular analyses, illuminating the specific, historical performances of American presidents, than he was in setting up his model.

The moral, I believe, is clear. Psychohistorical inquiry requires profound and careful attention to the analysis, in this case, of individual personalities interacting with the historical context that shapes and is shaped by them. It errs, as in Freud–Bullitt, when it "reduces" its political figures to pathological specimens. It goes astray, as in Wolfenstein, when it "inflates" them too quickly to "personality types" (revolutionary or authoritarian).[11] And it jumps into the void, as with the Lasswellian formula, when it seeks to move unilaterally from the private actor to the public arena, without analyzing the complex and changing interaction of the two, as well as the intermediary actors between them.

The problems of psychohistorical inquiry are largely the problems of historical inquiry in general. Both aim primarily at the understanding of human behavior in its "historical" dimension. Both run the danger of making false extrapolations and overextrapolations from the data, and of misinterpreting evidence by poor judgment as to its relation to the "totality" of evidence. The psychohistorian runs the additional danger of reducing or overreducing materials to the psychological dimension; but so do the economic historian, the military historian, and so forth. Naturally, the psychohistorian uniquely needs to have a good working knowledge of psychology, specifically psychoanalysis, *as it relates* to historical interests. Nevertheless, the overall problem of the validity and usefulness of psychohistorical inquiry falls under well-established rubrics in the philosophy of history.

Methodological problems remain, and these are the interesting ones: specifically, the validity of analyzing past figures; the validation and verification of such an analysis; the use of traditional materials, such as autobiographies; and the use and development of "new" materials, that is, materials relating to subjects that have too often been overlooked or neglected.

It is frequently asserted that psychohistory is impossible because its subjects are beyond the reach of the analyst, that is, they are dead, or, if living, unavailable for actual analysis. If the aim is therapy, this is undoubtedly true. If the aim is psychoanalytic understanding of a personality, then surely it depends on the amount of material extant; where there is little or no pertinent material, psychohistorical inquiry obviously ought not to be attempted. (Incidentally, it might be remarked that a patient who will not speak or go to an analyst is also a hopeless enterprise—a not unfamiliar clinical experience.) As the political scientist Alexander George has pointed out, the clinician's ability to question a patient is limited to the patient's response; that is, there is almost no way of verifying the patient's picture of the self and the surrounding world. All the clinical analyst can have, more or less, is "psychic reality" as presented by the patient.[12] The psychohistorian, on the other hand, if lucky, will have a mass of relevant material: family, friends, and enemies. The result is a check and double check on the psychohistorian's interpretation of the general character pattern of a subject, from outside sources. Moreover, interested in psychohistorical understanding, not therapy, the historian will usually not be concerned with certain kinds of intimate data that might be missing from the written record. In terms of validity, then, there is no reason to abandon hope for psychohistory: quite the opposite.

As for validation and verification of a particular analysis, this is immeasurably aided by a special aspect of psychoanalysis itself: the phenomenon of overdetermination. The problem of determinism in psychoanalysis is a point that bothers unsympathetic critics of psychoanalysis. Freud insisted that strict determinism prevailed in respect of psychic acts; there are no "accidents." For example, "free association," the basis of dream analysis and of therapy, is "free" only in the sense that it is not hampered by the censorship of "logical," "rational" thought and mores. It is not, however, undetermined. In fact, free association, like almost all of the other processes in psychoanalysis, is *overdetermined*. Indeed, it is the latter phenomenon— the fact that the same word or symbol refers to many elements in the unconscious thought process, on the one hand, and that the single unconscious drive or pattern of behavior will manifest itself in innumerable different conscious manifestations, on the other hand—that warrants the historian in the use of the evidence. Because the psychological phenomena are overdetermined, the evidence can be abundant and self-confirming.[13] When this fact is placed next to the one made above, of the frequent existence of outside observations—by family or friends—we find ourselves quite comfortably ensconced with the historian's traditional task of reconciling and interpreting conflicting and confirming evidence. The only difference in psychohistory is that the interpretation and confirmation of evidence must be done in terms of informed awareness as to the meaning and application of psychoanalytic theory. But then, what would one expect?

# CHAPTER TEN

# The Hidden
# Khomeini

AYATOLLAH Ruhollah Khomeini is now dead. The revolution he led into power over a decade ago is still running its course. Its future outcome is not clear, though sooner or later (and probably sooner) we can expect a more moderate, even "Thermodorean" reaction. One thing is, however, clear. Khomeini's legacy will live on in one form or another in Iran, and his impact on world history, in terms of his Islamic revolution, will engage the attention of historians for decades to come. As with Lenin's and Mao's, his revolution bears the unique imprint of his ideas and personality.

What was the Ayatollah Khomeini like, and how were his ideas and personality related?* Bearing in mind some of what I have said in the preceding chapter, I will use a psychohistorical approach in seeking to comprehend this mysterious and frightening figure, who even in death held such a grip on his followers as to cause millions of them to surge into the streets of Tehran at his funeral and to tear at his coffin for shreds of his shroud.

Other approaches have not always shed much light on him. Ayatollah Ruhollah Khomeini was called a madman by George Meany and an outlaw by James Reston; such terms are emotionally rewarding but bring little understanding. Andrew Young saw Khomeini as a saint, and Richard Falk, a distinguished professor of international relations, regarded him as a worthy visionary; the naïveté of such views was soon apparent.

Khomeini was puzzling in part because there was so much myth surrounding the reality. Much of that myth was created by Khomeini and

---

*My analysis of Khomeini was originally written and published in 1979, just as he was entering upon power. A decade later, it seems to hold up, or so I have been assured by Iranian scholars. So encouraged, I have left it as it was, adding only a few paragraphs and a few minor changes.

his followers. That myth was often as important—and revealing—as the reality.

One part of the myth was that Khomeini was a rigid adherent to principle, a fanatic who never stooped to dissimulation, compromise, or, worse, opportunistic political action. Khomeini was a fanatic adherent to his religious principles, but he was *also* a past master of dissimulation who hid his true intentions even from many of those surrounding him. He manipulated others, dividing to conquer, while allowing still others to believe that they were manipulating him. The soft-spoken, emotionless Khomeini, as seen on TV, was matched by a Khomeini filled with tremendous anger and resentment. The ayatollah who denied any ambition hid a man—a revolutionary ascetic with grandiose traits that would tempt a clinician to label him a classic narcissist.

Khomeini was seen as the leader of an Iranian nationalist revolution; he was that, but the revolution he wished to lead was his own "hidden" one, an Islamic world uprising. That aim was part of his grandiosity, which sat together in odd juxtaposition with his shrewdness in bending the daily events of the Iranian revolution to his larger purpose. Khomeini's revolution was for export. Whether as supreme guide of Iran or martyr to Islam, Khomeini served the same purpose: the spread of *his* personal revolution.

These are large generalities. Now I must offer the evidence and analysis in back of them. Khomeini the myth and Khomeini the man must be disentangled, in full recognition that the myth, as we shall see, was incorporated by Khomeini himself into his identity as a man who becomes a prophet for his people.

Khomeini was a real man, with a real life. In his own words, "I cry, I laugh, I suffer. Do you think I'm not a human being?" He was raised in a real family. But behind that real family stands a mythic family, which had as much "reality" for Khomeini as his own father and mother. It is a particular version of what Freud has called "a family romance."

The real family starts with Khomeini's great-grandfather on his father's side, who in the nineteenth century left the area of Khorasan in the northeastern part of Iran for India, presumably Kashmir, where Khomeini's grandfather was born. At some point, this grandfather returned to Iran and settled in Khomein, 180 miles south of Tehran. His son Mostafavi had three sons and one daughter, at least (*Time* magazine claimed six children in all), the youngest being Ruhollah, now known as the Ayatollah Khomeini. The mother's background is not known, a sign to Iranians that her family was of no great social significance.

What in all this is important psychologically? It is Khomeini's "Indian" roots. Indians are not well respected in Iran; yet the leader of Iranian nationalism was suspected by many of having an original Indian identity, through his grandfather. One of Khomeini's brothers, the middle one, who died in 1976, affirmed his Indian roots by taking Hindi as his required family name. The oldest brother took the name Pasandideh. Khomeini had earlier taken the name Mostafa, after his father, though the people of Qum chose to call him Khomeini, as coming from that town. When Khomeini wrote poetry in his early twenties, however, he took the Indian pseudonym Hindi.

Outwardly, Khomeini was a totally assimilated Iranian. Some of the rumors about his "really" being "Indian" were spread by SAVAK (the shah's dreaded secret police) to discredit him. Even pro-Khomeini Iranians tell stories about Khomeini's being Indian, and say that in fact he was *born* in India (contrary to fact). At the Shia colleges in Lucknow, India, some students speak of him as originally from Kashmir and therefore Indian. Popular perception dimly senses there is something unusual about Khomeini's origin. We can speculate that at some level of his being, Khomeini the man also knew that he was different.

Other "nationalist" leaders have also had an identity partly outside the dominant ethnic strain. Napoleon was a Corsican who came to embody French nationalism. Hitler, the Austrian, did the same for German nationalism. Erik Erikson has made us familiar with the outsider who can stress "sameness" more convincingly for others.

The next thing to note is that Khomeini's father was killed when Khomeini was very young. The accounts vary wildly: The father was killed by bandits, or by the mayor of the town; Khomeini was still not born, or he was seven years old. The facts seem to be that his father was killed by a local landowner in a dispute over land or water when Khomeini was between three and six months old. As the myths take over, the story is told that the landowner was the agent of Reza Shah, hence Khomeini's undying hatred of the Pahlevi dynasty. This is a case of an elegant theory stumbling over an inconvenient fact: Reza Shah did not come to power until the 1920s, and Khomeini was born around 1900.

What is certain is that Khomeini grew up without a father. He was raised by his mother, though some claim it was by a strong aunt, and others postulate some male relations of the mother in the background. A source close to Khomeini tells us of a "caretaker," a woman who took care of him as a young child and whom he liked and still remembers. The mother, meanwhile, sought justice—and retribution. In a brave move for a woman of those days, she went to the nearby town of Arak to plead her case, finally securing the execution of her husband's murderer. (Another account has her going to Tehran and securing the removal of the governor.) Khomeini, the close source says, has talked about being sad that he was not raised by his father.

The themes, if not the exact facts, are clear: a father unjustly killed, his son deprived of his rightful possessions (i.e., his father and perhaps land), the need to seek justice, and obstinacy, in the pursuit of that justice, finally rewarded. Such are the symbolic overtones of Khomeini's family and early life.

At this point, a connection must be made with another family—the family of the prophet Mohammed, as perceived by the Shiite Muslims. Mohammed, without having male children, adopted Ali and raised him as his son. On Mohammed's death, Ali was to succeed him but was cheated out of his inheritance by the "wicked" Abu-Bakr, Mohammed's father-in-law, who became the first caliph. Ali, who bided his time, was finally elected the fourth caliph but was challenged by Muawiyah and eventually assassinated. Muawiyah had promised to let Ali's sons succeed him, but he broke his promise and named his own son, Yezid, as his successor. It was Yezid who caused the death of Ali's second son, Husein, in a story marked by betrayal, injustice, and martyrdom. Husein's true successors, however, were the Imams, who succeeded in the line until the twelfth, who is said, as a young boy, to have gone into "occultation"—that is, hiding—when his father died (in 872 A.D.). The twelfth Imam, according to Shiite belief, is not dead and will reappear.

This story is of intense seriousness and meaning to Shiite Muslims. It exists as a present reality in their lives, flaming forth anew in the sacred celebration of the month of Moharram, when the passion plays reenact the battle of Karbala, where Husein is betrayed and killed. It speaks of present, as well as past, injustice, deceit, violation of family rights, heroism, and martyrdom. It obliterates time, especially in the ritual reenactment of Husein's death on Ashura, the tenth day, when a procession of young men in black flagellate themselves in representation of the repentance of those who abandoned Ali's son Husein.

I believe that Khomeini secretly identified his own family with Mohammed's and, in the ways of the psyche, with *both* Ali and Husein. It was his "family romance." Ali, too, had been orphaned, like Khomeini. Ali, the father of Husein, is unjustly killed, as is his son. The twelfth Imam also loses his father at a young age, yet the Imams persist, ultimately to triumph. What counts is not logic or one-to-one overlap but the symbolic, or psychological, continuity between the themes of that family history and Khomeini's own. As a "seyyed," he claimed direct family descent from the prophet, as do many other Iranians. Khomeini, with his particular life history, claimed this with a peculiar intensity.

Obviously, numerous Iranians today believe the same. Some hailed him as the twelfth Imam returned, and though this was blasphemy to other ayatollahs, Khomeini did not discourage his followers from doing so.

We know almost nothing about the period from his formative years through adolescence; it is as though Khomeini had been in occultation, like the young Imam. Apparently, Khomeini's early studies were with his older brother; then, at age fifteen or sixteen, he went off to Arak, fifteen miles from Khomein, to study with Yazid Ha'iri, a famous and widely respected theologian. When Ha'iri moved to Qum (approximately thirty-five miles from Arak) about two years later to establish an institute in Islamic jurisprudence, Khomeini moved with him. Until Ha'iri's death in the 1930s, Khomeini remained as his student, while also teaching at the school's lower level. It is Ha'iri who seems to have served as a substitute father for the young Khomeini, though Khomeini was to break with his teacher's politically passive doctrines later on. (It is noteworthy that the Ayatollahs Shariat-Madari, who emerged briefly as a rival to Khomeini, and Gopayeghani were also classmates of Khomeini's under Ha'iri.) Around late 1928, according to my sources, Khomeini married the daughter of another, older student of Ha'iri's, the Ayatollah Thaquafi, and at about the same time made the pilgrimage to Mecca that allowed him to include "Haj" in his name. The son of Yazdi Ha'iri, Mehdi Ha'iri, later became one of Khomeini's students, then his assistant, and now an illustrious professor of philosophy. Khomeini's oldest son subsequently married Mehdi Ha'iri's niece.

Clerical intermarriages are common and important in Iran. They establish a network of power and communication in a country where family is still of the utmost importance, especially in politics and religion. Though stories circulated that Khomeini had two wives, he has certainly had only one of long duration, and by her he had six children. His oldest son, Mostafi, died mysteriously a few years ago, at the age of forty-nine; most Iranians believe that he was killed by SAVAK. Khomeini *may* have believed this; when pressed, he shrugged off the question and declared, "It is the will of God." His second son, Ahmed, about thirty-seven, assisted his father from the beginning and now, after his father's death, has become one of the major leaders of the revolution. One son-in-law (Eshraghi) and his father were both religious leaders in Qum. Another son-in-law, named Arabi, served in the Bazargan administration. Even the oldest son of Khomeini's deceased son Mostafi was pressed into service, being sent on a mission to Lebanon. Revolution and government are a family affair in more ways than one in Iran.

For most of his mature years, Khomeini was a teacher of religion. His special subjects were "philosophical." He was described as the only distinguished Iranian philosopher of existentialism. Sources confide that privately Khomeini was an exponent of Sufi-like mysticism—a suspect subject among the clergy in Iran, who are uneasy about the courting of mystic experience. He was also a follower of Aristotelian logic.

Most critical for our interests was Khomeini's mysticism. It had political as well as philosophical importance. According to Mehdi Ha'iri, Khomeini's former assistant, it was Khomeini's mystical convictions that gave him his appearance of tranquillity in the face of disturbing events. When his infant daughter drowned years ago, Khomeini, though he loved his child deeply, betrayed no emotion, neither sorrow nor turmoil.

In Sufi mysticism, there is a kind of journey, from earth to heaven and from heaven back to earth. In ascending the first ladder, the self is elevated to God; the descending ladder, however, returns one to community. At this point, every characteristic of God is one's own, and such a mystic may rightfully come down to manage and rule the community. He is rightfully the leader because he leads by the power of God and is identical with both Him and the community He has created.

Such religious beliefs enforced Khomeini's sense that he was qualified to lead Islam and, incidentally, Iran. Khomeini's mysticism armed him in the face of danger and strengthened his willingness to suffer hardship and to face martyrdom. To these convictions, Khomeini eventually added a theological position: Against almost all of the other major ayatollahs, he insisted that Islam meant complete and immediate involvement of religion in politics and that no compromise could be tolerated with the shah. By acting on these beliefs, especially in 1963, Khomeini became the symbol around which the forces in Iran pressing for revolution could gather.

Sigmund Freud, as I noted earlier, has described great leaders as having "few libidinal ties"; such individuals, loving only themselves, appear detached from normal human emotions. I suggest that this be conceptualized in terms of "displaced libido," where love is shifted away from persons onto an abstraction—the People, the Revolution, Humanity—which is all-perfect and can never disappoint. This permits what I call the "revolutionary ascetic" to break all normal emotional ties in the name of the cause; he can now send his best friend to the guillotine.

How does Khomeini look in the light of this notion? Because of his simple habits of life, his frugal eating habits, he was frequently described in the press as ascetic. Was he, however, a "revolutionary ascetic"? Certain facts appear to weigh against such a judgment. Khomeini was happily married and had six children whom he loved. He was described as often gay and joking in the bosom of his family. He was certainly not ascetic in the sense of withdrawing from the world, like St. Simeon in the desert; his interpretation of Islam demanded complete involvement in politics. Moreover, asceticism in Islamic culture must be viewed in its own terms. *Zohd*—asceticism—does not mean a turning away from the world but a refusal to be captured by materialistic concerns. Sexuality, too, is not a matter of puritanical repression but a matter of socially sanctioned sensuality. It is only sex outside of that situation that is regarded as sinful.

With all this said, there are a number of facts that do point to Khomeini as a revolutionary ascetic. His personal ascetic qualities—the plainness of his life, his disinterest in material things, his disdain for sensuality—allowed him to symbolize properly the opposition to the corrupt, impure, and overly sensual image of the shah and his regime. Khomeini's traits permitted both him and his followers a satisfying "splitting" between cleanliness and impurity, spirituality and sensuality, goodness and evil. Such a split took symbolic form as a conflict between Khomeini and the shah, with the West, and especially America, taking on the shah's "satanic" role after his fall.

As for displaced libido, there is also a good deal of evidence. In his book *Islamic Government,* derived from lectures delivered in Iraq in the 1960s or early 1970s (the authenticity of this book has been questioned, but Khomeini refused to repudiate it), Khomeini tells us bluntly that the "amir of the faithful," referring to Ali, "must not pay attention to emotions." Khomeini then gives specific examples of the necessary qualities in the correct ruler: "The nation's leader and amir deterred his brother, Aqil, and heated an iron with which to punish him so that he may not covet the monies of the Moslems. He censured his daughter when she borrowed a necklace from the treasury and said: 'Were you not . . . guaranteed you would be the first hashimite woman to have her hand cut off.'" More personally, Khomeini stated of his opponents, "If they had taken my son, my baby Ahmed, and killed him I would not have said a word." Khomeini's mystical beliefs joined displaced libido in a powerful curtailment of personal feeling.

Khomeini's libido, I suggest, was displaced onto the abstraction "Islam." In its name all else can be sacrificed. Talking to Oriana Fallaci, he spoke of "Islam, which contains everything . . . includes everything . . . is everything." It was "perfect," "pure." Khomeini portrayed himself as merely the "servant" of Islam, utterly selfless in his devotion. He had no personal ambition or desire for power. He conceived of himself, like the Imam he described in *Islamic Government,* as "not running after the governorship, nor was he fond of it." He did confess to enjoying the "love" of his followers who sing his praises, because in praising him they are really only praising the revolution against the shah and thus praising Islam.

But something more is involved. I sense, and clinical evidence suggests, that beneath Khomeini's control of feeling lay hidden ambition and rage of monumental proportions. It is what fueled his defiance of the shah. It is what animated his hatred of the West and America. Its source is unknown, but one could talk of "narcissistic rage," some devastating injury to sense of self, and self-esteem, in Khomeini's early life, perhaps relating to the loss, through murder, of his own father. We feel in all of Khomeini's utterances the hatred that lies on the other side of love.

One specific sign of the rage and hatred was Khomeini's intolerance. The Western press made a special point of his anti-Semitism, though Khomeini and many Iranians denied the charge and say that he was anti-Israeli or anti-Zionist, not anti-Jewish. In Khomeini's defense, one can say that there were many reality factors in his anti-Israelism: The Israelis, following *realpolitik* rather than human rights, did help train SAVAK, and Iranian Jews undoubtedly did supply Israel with general information. Being anti-Israeli, then, was not a crime for Khomeini. Did it become anti-Semitism? Islam preaches tolerance of Jews (and Christians), and Khomeini quoted Ali on the need to give Jews justice, even against Muslims. Khomeini assured Tehran Jews of his protection if they obeyed the laws, and he meant it.

The problem was that Khomeini was ambivalent. His religion told him one thing, but his passions another. He confused Jews and Israelis. He was a demagogue who insisted that Iranian soldiers, even under the shah's orders, could not have shot Muslims on Black Friday; it had to have been Israeli soldiers sent to do the deed. Khomeini mouthed phrases in support of the idea of a Jewish conspiracy controlling Western capitalism. In *Islamic Government,* he described the burning of Al Aksa Mosque as a "Zionist crime" (it was set on fire by a demented Australian). No wonder that Khomeini was prepared to believe that the seizure of the Grand Mosque at Mecca was an American-Zionist-Jewish plot! Still, Khomeini's anti-Semitic feelings must be seen in perspective. He hated others more. Thus, though Jews and Christians were suspect, Bahais were guilty by definition and not to be tolerated at all.

Khomeini was also an excessively suspicious person. He was convinced that plots, conspiracies, and treacheries abounded; the stories of Ali and Husein confirmed for him and for other Shiite Iranians, the reality of his beliefs. (Again, one must emphasize that there were some realities behind Khomeini's suspicions; after all, the American CIA did conspire to bring back the shah in 1953.) In the interview with Fallaci, he claimed that both the Kurdish uprising and the leftist opposition to him in Iran were of American contrivance. They were "taking advantage of our tolerance" to subvert and destroy us, he declared.

So too, the theme of poisoning was omnipresent in Khomeini. He talked of how "the agents of colonialism . . . have injected their poisons into the people's minds and ethics until they corrupted them" with their "sick ideas." He spoke of Western music as "poisoning" Iranian youth. He characterized America as a "corrupt germ" that needs to be driven out of history and Iran. Like other Shiites, Khomeini was convinced that Hasan, Husein's older brother, died of poisoning rather than, as Sunnis believe, of consumption; indeed, he believed that all Imams except the twelfth have been poisoned by an outside, corrupting hand, else how could they have died?

Such a notion can be connected to fears of ritual pollution, such as by menstruation, etc. It is clearly connected to notions of corruption, and these, in turn, lead to the theme of outside invasion. Viewed in these terms, Khomeini is a "carrier" of cultural suspicions.

These notions of poisoning, corruption, and invasion lead to another important theme: the inner-outer dichotomy. Iranians feel keenly that the inner is good, whereas evil is from outside. Thus, houses traditionally have a drab exterior, while within, protected by high walls, a garden and warm family life exist. Women, inwardly good and innocent, must be hidden behind a veil, protecting them from the corrupting glances of the outside world.

Iranians are very ambivalent on this dichotomy, admiring and accepting what is called *zirangī* (cleverness or wiliness) as well as integrity and simplicity of thought and action. This is one source of the deep-seated Iranian feeling of mistrust: Recognizing a desire for *zirangī* in themselves, they fear it in others. It is a fear tinged with admiration. Support for dissimulation and deception comes both from Iranian culture and, more important, Islamic religion. Shiism alone among the major religions explicitly allows and encourages believers, for their own protection and that of the survival of the faith, to conceal their beliefs.

Khomeini, however, while admitting in principle the need for dissimulation to preserve the true religion under certain circumstances, insisted that the present times cry out for an end to dissimulation, to compromise, to a willingness to work with the enemy. Instead, they call for an outright declaration of Islamic intransigence. "Dissimulation," Khomeini stated, "was legislated to preserve one's life or others' from damage on subsidiary issues of the laws. But if Islam in its entirety is in danger, then there is no room for dissimulation and silence." Khomeini created and reinforced the image of himself as a rigid stickler for principle who did not dissemble or stoop to opportunism.

The record showed otherwise. Khomeini erected a myth that accorded with the needs and wishes of his followers. The reality was that Khomeini was a consummate opportunist, dissembling and hiding his true intentions all along, as befits an Imam emerging from occultation. In gaining control of the revolution, he altered positions rapidly, supported and repudiated individuals, and seized every opportunity that came his way to grasp at power. First agreeing to meet Prime Minister Bakhtiar in January 1979, he abruptly changed his mind and rebuffed the peace overtures. In February, Karim Sanjabi, the seventy-four-year-old leader of the National Front who had allied himself with Khomeini, let it be known that he had a clear agreement with Khomeini that the task of the provisional government was to prepare Iran for fuller democracy. In March, Khomeini appeared to order Iranian women to wear the chador; under pressure, he backed off and said he meant it was a "duty" for Muslim women to wear chadors, not an "order." In April, Khomeini allowed that, instead of being merely the "guide" of the revolution, he intended to be its "strong man," directing the government himself. By June, Hassan Nazih, chief of the National Iranian Oil Company, overtly recognized Khomeini's shifting stances in a letter that said,

> Today, we find your leadership is not what it used to be. . . . When you returned to Iran, you said, "I'm a clergyman," meaning "Not I nor the clergy, no one can claim the governorship of the country." . . . Today we find any order you issue is carried out with lightning speed without regard to the above principle. Today, you not only personally interfere directly in the affairs of the country but also that of foreign countries.

Nazih's awakening came too late. As Bazargan was to lament, "the trouble is that something unforeseeable happened after the revolution. What happened was that the clergy supplanted us and succeeded in taking over the country."

Of course, Bazargan meant Khomeini. Bazargan should have read, and believed, Khomeini when he said in *Islamic Government,* "The just jurisprudents must wait for opportunities and must exploit them to form and organize a wise government intended to carry out God's order."

Khomeini was a past master at seizing the moment. He moved quickly at each moment of crisis to amass more power: When the Kurds arose, Khomeini appointed himself commander of the army; when Bazargan met with Brzezinski in Algiers, Khomeini forced him out as prime minister; when America permitted the shah to enter the country for medical reasons, Khomeini instantly saw that it was an Allah-given opportunity to rally the country behind him again in the face of gathering opposition to his one-man rule, and, using the hostages as the occasion, to press both for the ratification of his new Islamic constitution and, more astoundingly, toward the goal of an Islamic revolution.

In moving toward both his Iranian and Islamic revolutions, Khomeini dissembled and dissimulated in the spirit of his revered predecessor, Ali. There is a lovely story about Ali that "reveals" the true path. Firuz, the murderer of the caliph Omar, Ali's enemy, ran out of a building and past where Ali happened to be sitting outside, and as Firuz ran past, Ali rose and changed his seat. When pursuers came to Ali, they asked if he had seen Firuz. Ali replied, "As long as I have been sitting on this spot, I did not see him." (I owe this story to Professor Michael Fischer of Harvard University.) In the name of the cause, to preserve and expand Islam, such *zirangī* thoughts and actions are not only permitted, but are required of Khomeini by himself and by his religion.

In this spirit, Khomeini led and misled the factions opposed to the shah into thinking that he was leading their revolution, while all along he was aiming at his own. The extraordinary thing was that, like Hitler in *Mein Kampf,* Khomeini openly spoke about his "hidden" intentions, for example, in *Islamic Government,* only to have his competitors or opponents not take him seriously. As a result, he captured Iran for his own "occulted" revolution.

In his important book, *Leadership,* James MacGregor Burns postulates that the only acceptable notion of leadership is moral. The leader, especially, seeks to lift both himself and his followers to a higher moral stage. Khomeini, similarly, enforced a high standard of Islamic morality upon himself, and he certainly sought to lead his followers to a purer, more moral life.

But Khomeini did not only lead; he also misled. The revolution he had in mind was not just an Iranian revolution but an Islamic one. The "Indian" Khomeini, in the figurative sense, sought his true identity and destiny in a worldwide Islamic mission. Symbolic of his feelings was the comment he made when he returned from fifteen years of exile to Iran and was asked how he felt: "Nothing" was his reply. Mystical in part, Khomeini's laconic "nothing" also reflected his lack of Iranian nationalism. He inhabited another terrain, one that transcends any earthly boundaries.

I have pictured a Khomeini whose "true" family is the prophet's and who identifies himself with Ali and Husein, a Khomeini who shares in the age-old feelings of betrayal, injustice, and oppression embodied in that family history, who projects an image of steadfast adherence to principle. But there is the other Khomeini, who in fact dissimulates and behaves opportunistically in the name of Allah, whose outer calm and control are belied by underlying rage and hostility, which find an outlet in "anti" feelings of great vehemence.

We must add to this picture one last piece of analysis. It is of a Khomeini who alternates between a sense of himself as a grandiose and humiliated figure. On one side, we have the Khomeini who shares in the total perfection of Islam. "Islam," he lectures, "has laws and regulations to raise perfect and virtuous human beings." In itself, Islam contains everything. It must necessarily spread over the whole world. On the other side, we have the Khomeini who feels inferior to a West that can put a man on the moon but who consoles himself that Islam "alone" possesses the "morals and laws" necessary to man's true existence; who feels that without Islam and its controls "social chaos, corruption, and ideological and moral deviation would prevail"; who idealizes a past when "Islam was the ruler" and "justice was dispensed," and laments a present characterized by the "humiliation and insult" involved in borrowing from the West.

These traits—the alternating but overlapping senses of grandiosity and humiliation—fit the classic definition of a narcissistic personality. And these feelings of Khomeini's corresponded with those of a large number of Iranians, who were therefore prepared to follow him to the end. Narcissism, in the form of self-love and large ambition, can be a healthy, normal part of development, indeed a requisite for the sense that one can do great things in the world. In its more malign, overextended form, it can become unreal grandiosity, megalomania, a reaching for inhuman perfection.

Khomeini's grandiose and idealizing tendencies impelled him to his "hidden" revolution. His goal was to have the Iranian revolution become the seedbed of a worldwide Islamic revolution. That revolution is timeless. Almost two decades ago, Khomeini spoke of the Koran as "teachings that are intended for *all* peoples in *all* ages and in *all* countries and must be implemented and followed until the day of resurrection" (my italics). Islamic government must be aimed everywhere, first by propaganda, then by all other means. This was Khomeini's "plot," which he then projected onto the Jews and their foreign supporters, who "seek to snare Islam and pave the way for Jews to dominate this entire world."

Khomeini's own grandiose design for the world was not intended to be an idle threat. He reminded his followers that "the Shiite sect started from the zero point. When the prophet laid down the foundation of the succession, he was met with derision and ridicule." Khomeini was prepared for no less. But he was also prepared to wait and suffer for vindication. The personal note was strong when he said, "Great men plan for future generations and are not saddened [not] to see the effects of their plans. . . . Such men do not feel despair even in the humiliation of captivity and in the bowels of prisons."

Khomeini believed he would, through Islam, conquer the world at some point in time. Myth and reality would then become one, and Khomeini would, symbolically and psychologically, enjoy total allness. Alternatively, Khomeini and his supporters would become martyrs, overcome temporarily by their enemies, as were Ali and Husein. Khomeini courted in martyrdom his self-destruction, a form of nothingness, as the other side of his search for all-ness.

Khomeini's actions and thoughts started or widened fissions in the international scene whose results are still incalculable. The tragedy is that it is all occurring in the name of an Iranian revolution whose original aims were largely justified and whose leader, Khomeini, at first embodied and proclaimed many laudable moral aims. In reaching or overreaching to "perfection," however, Khomeini led the way to a kind of perdition for his people—and others.

The torture and murder of opponents of the regime, the spread of terrorism to other parts of the world, the Iran–Iraq war with its numerous casualties, these are only some of the "Satanic" consequences of Khomeini's personality. They linger on, personified in his death sentence on Salman Rushdie, author of *The Satanic Verses*. How ironic that Khomeini, in the last few months of his life, wrote a highly erotic, Sufi-like mystical poem, as one of his last utterances, thus reestablishing continuity with the youth who in his early twenties also wrote heretical poetry! The currents ran deep but continuous in Khomeini's life and now do the same in the Islamic revolution, which lives on after him.

> *I have become imprisoned, O beloved, by the mole on your lip!*
> *I saw your ailing eyes and became ill through love.*
> *Delivered from self, I beat the drum of "I am the Real!"*
> *Like Hallaj, I became a customer for the top of the gallows.*
> *Heartache for the beloved has thrown so many sparks into my soul*
> *That I have been driven to despair and become the talk of the bazaar!*
> *Open the door of the tavern and let us go there day and night,*
> *For I am sick and tired of the mosque and seminary.*
> *I have torn off the garb of asceticism and hypocrisy,*
> *Putting on the cloak of the tavern-haunting shaykh and becoming aware.*
> *The city preacher has so tormented me with his advice*
> *That I have sought aid from the breath of the wine-drenched profligate.*
> *Leave me alone to remember the idol-temple,*
> *I who have been awakened by the hand of the tavern's idol.*

# CHAPTER ELEVEN

# Orwell inside
# the Whale

$I$N an age that has seen the Bolshevik Revolution, the Nazi revolution, and, most recently, the Islamic revolution, *1984,* the novel, looms over us as a kind of Frankenstein creation—an image of a monstrous society. Orwell's book is a modern Gothic, whose power over us is puzzling and disturbing. Are we to take it as a forecast of a real future, or an extrapolation of paranoid fears? The carefully crafted literary product of a gifted writer, or the compulsive working out of an author's personal fantasies? A novel or a political tract? Or what mixture of all of these elements?

In a letter of 26 December 1948 to the man who was writing the jacket blurb, extolling the book as "a thriller mixed up with a love story," Orwell protested, "I didn't intend it to be primarily that. What it is really meant to do is to discuss the implications of dividing the world up into 'Zones of influence' (I thought of it in 1944 as a result of the Teheran Conference), and in addition to indicate by parodying them the intellectual implications of totalitarianism."[1] A year and a half later, he declared,

> I do not believe that the kind of society I describe necessarily *will* arrive, but
> I believe (allowing of course for the fact that the book is a satire) that some-
> thing resembling it *could* arrive. I believe also that totalitarian ideas have
> taken root in the minds of intellectuals everywhere, and I have tried to draw
> these ideas out to their logical consequences. The scene of the book is laid
> in Britain in order to emphasize that the English-speaking races are not
> innately better than anyone else and that totalitarianism, *if not fought
> against,* could triumph anywhere.[2]

And in between these statements, he stated more succinctly, "My new book is a Utopia in the form of a novel. I ballsed it up rather."[3]

Orwell's intentions are, obviously, convoluted; I shall seek to understand what the book is most fundamentally about, and why it exercises such a power over us, by evaluating both its novelistic and political intentions and its location in literary and philosophical discourse. I shall argue that, ultimately, Orwell the political actionist falls into pessimism and passivity; such a fall reveals his final personal and political message, which places him, in his own words, "inside the whale." Orwell's politics were actually the politics of despair. He shared what he described as "the essential thing" in Jonathan Swift—the latter's "inability to believe that life—ordinary life on the solid earth, and not some rationalised, deodorised version of it—could be made worth living."[4]

Almost 150 years ago, in 1840, in *Democracy in America*, Alexis de Tocqueville described what he saw at the outcome of the preordained tendency toward equality: the "Tutelary State." It would be a new "despotism," an "immense, protective power" covering "the whole of social life with a network of petty, complicated rules that are both minute and uniform." It "does not break men's will, but softens, bends and guides it . . . is not at all tyrannical, but it hinders, restrains, enervates, stifles and stultifies so much that in the end each nation is not more than a flock of timid and hardworking animals with the government as its shepherd." In his chilling vision, Tocqueville sees "an innumerable multitude of men, alike and equal, constantly circling around in pursuit of the petty and banal pleasures with which they glut their souls. Each one of them, withdrawn into himself, is almost unaware of the fate of the rest."[5]

Liberty, Equality, and Fraternity: these were the catchwords and concerns of political discourse of the French Revolution and its aftermath. By Tocqueville's time, the worry was whether they would lead to a new form of despotism. Moving toward the twentieth century, the concern takes on slightly new phrasing and nuances. People now argue more in terms of whether freedom and happiness are compatible and ask whether modern science and technology, while bringing us a satisfying hedonistic life, are also leading us to a cold, rational, and totalitarian society.

A certain amount of this debate is conducted in the genre form of utopias and dystopias. Before Orwell, Eugene Zamiatin had written *We* (1924), and Aldous Huxley had published *Brave New World* (1932). Huxley, in a sense, solved the dilemma of freedom and happiness by making human nature a matter of scientific production: humans would be happy as a result of eugenics, conditioning, and drugs and have no desire for vague metaphysical freedom. The "Savage" is a misfit, who, wishing to be "free" to be unhappy, pays the price by taking his own life. Earlier, Zamiatin had written about "a mathematically faultless happiness"[6] in a new "paradise" and the way in which, for one of its "numbers," it became oppressive. Orwell, who reviewed *We* and was deeply influenced by it, preferred it to Huxley's work because Zamiatin, as Orwell put it, had a deeper insight into the recesses of "human sacrifice" and "cruelty as an end in itself."

Orwell not only borrowed heavily from both Zamiatin and Huxley but, as is well known, was also much influenced by other contemporaries, such as James Burnham and his *Managerial Revolution* (1940). In this book, which Orwell reviewed, Burnham had written about three great super-states, about the necessity of fraud to rule the masses, and about an irresistible drift to totalitarianism, with capitalism doomed and socialism a dream. These and similar features are readily identifiable in *1984*.

Further back in time is Jonathan Swift. Swift attracted Orwell mainly by his "ultimate despair" and his "sincere loathing" mixed with "morbid fascination" toward the human body. *Gulliver's Travels*, moreover, was a dystopia for Orwell, who writes that Swift had foreseen the "spy-haunted 'police state' with its endless heresy hunts and treason trials."[7]

It is clear that, in the best sense of the term, Orwell in 1984 was intensely derivative. He worked within a well-defined discursive tradition, drawing on it for his harmonic resonances. He thus gave novelistic form to a nagging fantasy—as well as a partial reality?—of modern man. His subject is the same as that of much dystopic literature and political discourse, ranging from Tocqueville to Zamiatin and Huxley and to books such as Eric Fromm's *Escape from Freedom* and heavier tomes of political philosophy. Drawing on the earlier sources and dealing with the same concerns, Orwell operates on our nervous system at the point where politics and literature intersect, penetrating our imaginations as much as our cognitive processes. He has taken up the possibilities of modern science and technology and applied them to the everyday details of political life: the TV that allows Big Brother's eye to be everywhere, the atomic bomb that perpetuates a state of constant warfare but prevents it from being all-out and conclusive, the psychological conditioning that modifies behavior. He has given a contemporary "mundane" reality to the abstract freedom–happiness argument.

*1984* is a literary work of a very peculiar nature: a political tract in the form of a novel, drawing on a tradition of utopias and dystopias at the same time as on realism. One needs to speak here of Orwell's Dickensian realism. Orwell's long essay of 1939 on Dickens bears sustained reading. Of all authors, I believe, Dickens, so admired by Orwell, is closest to him in literary spirit, if not in political stance (although even here the affinities are striking). In Orwell's case, the concrete realism of style matches perfectly his political content. His politics, in the end, come down to a simple assertion of the need for decency and commonplace happiness.

There is a paradox here, however: simple happiness is what the proles of *1984* are given by the Party. Thus, it might appear that Orwell and the Party have the same ends in view. One might rescue the author from such an odious comparison by pointing out that Orwell strove for happiness with decency; the Party's goals did not include the latter.

As a political analyst, Orwell leaves me unimpressed—political analysis is, in fact, not what he is really about. He could not have thought much about his subject when he wrote, "I don't believe that capitalism, as against feudalism, improved the actual quality of human life."[8] Nor, though a Socialist, was he much of a theoretician. He did grasp the essence, as when he went on to say, "And I don't believe that Socialism *in itself* need work any real improvement either."[9] One could not fob Orwell off with capitalized words.

His own "Socialist" credo was summed up in his statement that "I think it is vitally necessary to do something towards equalising incomes, abolishing class privilege and setting free the subject peoples [i.e., the colonies]." He added, "The thing that frightens me about the modern intelligentsia is their inability to see that human society must be based on common decency, whatever the political and economic forms may be."[10] Elsewhere, he summed up his feelings "that our job is to make life worth living, which is the only earth we have."[11] The search for perfection leads one astray, in fact, to *1984*. Orwell, abandoning the search, accepts the human condition with all of its weaknesses and ordinariness.

It is these attitudes—a reverence for ordinary human life, a belief in decency, and a desire to rectify injustice—that give positive meaning to Orwell's position. It is his awareness of how language is being perverted, how history is being falsified, and how his fellow modern intellectuals, especially of the left, are succumbing to the fallacy of perfection and forgetting the "essential thing" that fills Orwell with fear. It led him to write *1984*, a satire on totalitarianism, which is also a powerful "human" novel because of Orwell's concrete style and his concern for human decency.

Many commentators have noted Orwell's allusion in *1984* to Dostoevsky's Grand Inquisitor. Winston, the hero, paraphrases that classic statement of the freedom–happiness dilemma, thinking it is what O'Brien, representing the Party, will want as justification of his rule: that the Party "sought power because men in the mass were frail, cowardly creatures who could not endure liberation or face the truth, and must be ruled over and systematically deceived by others who were stronger than themselves. That the choice for mankind lay between freedom and happiness, and that, for the great bulk of mankind, happiness was better."[12]

To Winston's astonishment and discomfort, O'Brien disdains such a political theodicy. No, he says, "The Party seeks power entirely for its own sake. We are not interested in the good of others; we are interested solely in power" (p. 217). Why? One reason is that power defeats death; by utterly submitting to the Party, the individual, otherwise doomed to death, merges with the immortal Party. Power over matter as well as mind is thus what the Party offers, or so O'Brien appears to be saying.

Another reason plays on the old Utilitarian pleasure–pain calculus. "Obedience is not enough," O'Brien lectures Winston. "Unless he is suffering, how can you be sure that he is obeying your will and not his own. Power is in inflicting pain and humiliation." The pleasure–pain principle has become inverted. "It is the exact opposite," O'Brien continues, "of the stupid hedonistic Utopias that the old reformers imagined" (p. 220). Dystopia has become the pursuit of pain inflicted on others.

Ten years before *1984*, Orwell was worrying about the subject of power as an end in itself, exercised by an elite without self-deception. Reviewing Bertrand Russell's *Power,* Orwell wrote: "It is quite easy to imagine a state in which the ruling caste deceive their followers without deceiving themselves. Dare anyone be sure that something of the kind is not coming into existence already?"[13] To his claimed insight about the nature of power, Orwell attached his fear of thought control. By employing psychological conditioning, the rulers could make their populace believe and confess anything. "It is quite possible," Orwell continues, "that we are descending into an age in which two and two will make five when the Leader says so."

Readers of *1984* will remember how Winston is brought to acknowledge that "two and two make five." There is an irony here. At the beginning of the nineteenth century, the French thinker Vicomte de Bonald had justified the rule of the Catholic church on the grounds that there were moral truths as certain as scientific ones. Would one tolerate mere "opinion" in science—the example Bonald used was that "two and two make four"—and allow for wrong answers? Then why in moral science, where the answers are just as sure and known to the custodians of the science? On this basis, Bonald heralded a social science, before Auguste Comte, on which a stable society could find its footing. Orwell, in his and our world of absurdity, transforms the mathematical example into its opposite: "Anything could be true. The so-called laws of nature were nonsense" (p. 229). Or so, in a totalitarian society, people could be led to believe.

Orwell, it must be repeated, is operating within a well-recognized tradition. Put more positively, it is because he draws so heavily on literary and political tradition that he works his effect so successfully, sometimes subliminally, on us. Thus, the prison scene at the end echoes Bentham's Panopticion. "'Smith!' yelled the voice from the television screen. '6079 Smith W! Uncover your face. No faces covered in the cells'" (p. 193). Bentham, that prime source of the freedom–happiness, pleasure–pain debate, wrote of his scheme for a penitentiary.

> It is obvious that the more constantly the persons to be inspected are under the eyes of the persons who should inspect them, the more perfectly will the purpose of the establishment have been attained. Ideal perfection, if that were the object, would require that each person should actually be in that predicament, during every instant of time. This being impossible, the next thing to be wished for is that, at every instant, seeing reason to believe as much, and not being able to satisfy himself to the contrary, he should *conceive* himself to be so.[14]

We are already in the world of Orwell's telescreens and Big Brother.

We should also note that Orwell's world has indeed become a prison enlarged. In the early nineteenth century, as Michael Ignatieff has so brilliantly shown in his book *A Just Measure of Pain,* bourgeois reformers such as John Howard introduced the modern penitentiary, with its reduction of its inmates to numbers, wearing identical uniforms, under constant supervision, and "converted" to repentance. In an extraordinarily prescient statement, a prison chaplain, the Reverend W. L. Clay, wrote in his memoirs of 1869,

> . . . a few months in the solitary cell renders a prisoner strangely impressible. The chaplain can then make the brawny navvy cry like a child; he can work on his feelings in almost any way he pleases; he can, so to speak, photograph his thoughts, wishes and opinions on his patient's mind, and fill his mouth with his own phrases and language.[15]

If Bentham and his followers spoke of constant supervision and "reform" of the personality, we know it was Pavlov and his disciples who gave scientific form to their desires. Whether called behavioral modification or operant conditioning, Pavlovian psychology seemed to hold out the possibility of molding human beings and their minds into any shape wanted. The reality of "brainwashing," or "thought control" looms before us. There is an extensive literature on how real and successful these practices actually are. I do not want to get off onto that track but rather to stay with Orwell and pursue its meaning to him, whether as fantasy or fact.

The question posed by Bentham and Pavlov, in the final analysis, concerns human nature. As Erich Fromm in his Afterword to *1984* phrases it, "the question is . . . can human nature be changed in such a way that man will forget his longing for freedom, for dignity, for integrity, for love—that is to say, can man forget that he is human?" (p. 260). O'Brien thinks he has the answer: "We create human nature. Men are infinitely malleable" (p. 222). Was this also Orwell's view? In 1939, reviewing a book on Soviet rule, Orwell notes that the author, "as a liberal . . . takes it for granted that the 'spirit of freedom' is bound to revive sooner or later." But will it? "The terrifying thing," Orwell concluded, "about the modern dictatorships is that they are something entirely unprecedented. . . . Mass-suggestion is a science of the last twenty years, and we do not yet know how successful it will be."[16]

By the time of writing *1984* Orwell seems prepared to concede that humanity cannot stand against the new forces working on its nature. Winston will have been the last human being; his rebellion has finally been crushed. At one time, Orwell's working title for the book had been *The Last Man in Europe,* echoing thereby one of Mary Shelley's titles, *The Last Man* (1826), a story of the destruction of the human race. In *1984,* O'Brien says to Winston, "You are the last man," meaning the last futile attempt to guard the human spirit from being crushed by mechanical conditioning. The Frankensteins of *1984* have come into complete power, creating and destroying human beings with one and the same pressing of a lever.

In explaining "Why I Write," Orwell listed four motives: sheer egoism, aesthetic enthusiasm, historical impulse, and political purpose. "I am a person," he tells us, "in whom the first three motives would outweigh the fourth."[17] If we wish to understand Orwell's intentions in writing *1984,* we must pay attention not only to his specific statements about *1984* but to his general attitudes to his craft. His self-image was as a novelist rather than as a political writer. His concern was with human "memories," as well as historical ones.

Yet most of his writing is about politics of one kind or another. The conundrum is solved when we realize that Orwell believes that "all art is propaganda" (p. 448). He explains further what he means when he says, "Every writer, especially every novelist, *has* a message."[18] Overtly, Orwell's message is self-announced in his statement "Every line of serious work that I have written since 1936 has been written, directly or indirectly, *against* totalitarianism and *for* democratic Socialism."[19] That may be, but I want to suggest that there is another, more fundamental message in Orwell, which constantly threatens to join his overt one and awakens in us, his readers, a sense of unease.

Orwell's fundamental message, I believe, is passivity. It is what I shall call his Jonah identification, his desire to be "Inside the Whale." In his essay by that name on Henry Miller, he credits him with embracing "a very widespread fantasy": wishing to be inside the whale. "For the fact is," Orwell goes on, "that being inside a whale is a very comfortable cozy, homelike thought. . . . The whale's belly is simply a womb big enough for an adult. . . . Short of being dead, it is the final, unsurpassable stage of irresponsibility." As Orwell concludes, the person giving way to his fantasy "has performed the essential Jonah act of allowing himself to be swallowed, remaining passive, *accepting*."[20]

"Nonsense!" the reader will expostulate. Orwell passive! Why, he volunteered to fight in Spain, was wounded, and then spent the rest of his life, as he tells us, combating totalitarianism with his writings. And so he did. What I am saying is that, in the end, his impulse to passivity overcame his combativeness and became the dominant political message.

The evidence is in *1984* and other writings (such as "Inside the Whale"). What is the ending of *1984*? It is Winston, passive and defeated at the end: "It was all right, everything was all right, the struggle was finished. He had won the victory over himself. He loved Big Brother" (p. 245). This ending is foreshadowed earlier in the book when Winston becomes fascinated with a glass paperweight. Orwell writes that for Winston, "it was as though the surface of the glass had been the arch of the sky, enclosing a tiny world with its atmosphere complete. He had the feeling that he could get inside it, that in fact he was inside it." The critic Murray Sperber calls the paperweight a "crucial metaphor" and interprets this to symbolize the enclosed world that Winston and Julia tried to create for themselves in their retreat at Charrington's.[21] I am suggesting that the wider ramifications of the metaphor lead us "inside the whale," and to passivity.

What could possibly be the roots of this underlying attitude? Orwell reveals himself autobiographically in his account of his schooldays, "Such,

Such Were the Joys" (1947), as well as in "Why I Write" (1946). The latter paints a picture of a man who sees himself as a bit of a failure, whose identity is broken, and whose personality is on the edge of dissociation, who has a natural hatred of authority, a morbid preoccupation with isolation and solitude, whose sense of injustice compels him to political writing. The former depicts a child who suffered keenly at an English public school from social snobbery, frequent canings, feelings of loneliness, and general unhappiness. He felt acutely, as he confesses to us, the sense of "being locked up not only in a hostile world but in a world of good and evil where the rules were such that it was actually not possible for me to keep them," and had "learned early . . . that one can do wrong against one's will, and before long I also learned that one can do wrong without ever discovering what one has done or why it was wrong."[22] He also learned that school life consisted of the "triumph of the strong over the weak," with the strong "dominating them, bullying them, making them suffer pain, making them look foolish. . . . Life was hierarchical and whatever happened was right."[23] As for what was taught, "the greatest outrage of all was the teaching of history. . . . History was a series of unrelated, unintelligible but—in some way that was never explained to us—important facts with resounding phrases tied to them."[24] Worst of all, the brutal methods of education— conditioning, he would call it later—worked successfully on its victims.

Given this autobiographical background—Orwell, in fact, was always cautious about revealing himself—*1984* can be read as a projection of personal fears onto the political world. Murray Sperber, among others, has explored the psychological structure of Orwell and *1984* to good effect.[25] A large part of the power of *1984* over us is that Orwell has made us share his childhood fears and fantasies, which, as it turns out, have become the partial realities of our public life. Orwell's creative art has turned this "fit" into a powerful cognitive statement and not just an expression of personal hysteria or paranoia.

Nevertheless, in the face of realities, Orwell's stance is basically one of pessimism and passivity. Orwell admired both Swift and Miller, in part, for their pessimism. His own bleakness is revealed when he says, in one of his reviews, ours "is an age in which every *positive* attitude has turned out a failure. . . . The only 'ism' that has justified itself is pessimism."[26] He draws the connection to passivity when he remarks à propos of Henry Miller, "Seemingly there is nothing left but quietism . . . Get inside the whale—or rather, admit that you are inside the world (for you *are,* of course). Give yourself over to the world-process, stop fighting against it or pretending that you control it."[27]

*This* is the message of *1984*. Orwell was a man committed to human decency, to the ordinary, humdrum pleasures of life that made for happiness. His prosaic, ordinary writing style reflects his attachment to the concrete realities of life. He was also a man, however, whose inner life had been violated, both by his personal childhood experiences and by the traumatic public events of his time. In the face of such betrayal of his being, he *accepted* the forces of evil, and counseled passivity: writing about the First World War, he said, "The truth is that in 1917, there was nothing that a thinking and sensitive person could do, except to remain human, if possible."[28] It was the same in 1944 and in 1984.

*1984,* as a novel, is expressive of Orwell's fantasies—and ours—as much as or more than of history or political realities. Yet it builds convincingly on the debates and philosophical arguments over history and politics. Although it operates effectively on us on a number of levels—love story, thriller, and dystopia—in the end the disparate elements become the source of its failure as a great work of literature. Instead of Dostoevsky's Grand Inquisitor, Orwell offers us a Grandiose Commissar. Describing the modern period as he knew it, Orwell wrote of it as "a scenic railway ending in a torture-chamber."[29] In the last analysis, then, *1984* is a kind of Gothic political work, a nightmare of the past—Orwell's personal and our historical one—rather than a dream, even a bad dream, of the future.

# The Case of
the USA

# The Iron of
# Melancholy

"RELIGIOUS insanity," Tocqueville wrote in *Democracy in America,* "is very common in the United States." More specifically, he noted the "strange melancholy" that haunted Americans, awakening in them "disgust at life . . . in the midst of calm and easy circumstances."[1] The great Frenchman was writing in 1840, but melancholy was a Puritan complaint, going back to the earliest settlers in the 1620s and reaching forward to their descendants, physical or spiritual, in twentieth-century America.

John Owen King takes up Tocqueville's observation anew in his book *The Iron of Melancholy,*[2] tracing the way melancholy figured in the Puritan conversion experience and then became a component of Victorian neurosis. Along the way, he pays special attention to such figures as John Bunyan, Jonathan Edwards, the elder Henry James, William James, Josiah Royce, and James Jackson Putnam. More is involved: King connects conversion with work and works, and both of these with Max Weber and the "iron cage" of industrial civilization. It is all linked together by the elder James reading Jonathan Edwards, Max Weber being inspired in his writing of *The Protestant Ethic and the Spirit of Capitalism* by William James, and all four men being classic depressives.

*The Iron of Melancholy,* a title derived from James's *Varieties of Religious Experience,* is a tortuous and difficult book. One senses that beneath the analysis lies a deep personal experience of the author. For example, King notes the obsessional nature of Weber's footnotes—a "malignant growth," Weber confessed—and the way Weber's writing "expresses a need for such mastery that at times his words evolve into a private, almost magical or totemic language" (p. 316), comments that could be applied to King's own writing. This makes for an indefinable, subjective note, hard to sift out. With this said, the book is an important work—perhaps a major one—impressive in the way it wrestles with its subject, and well worth the hard work its reading entails. It has much to say to those who work in history, psychology, religion, sociology, and literary studies. The book operates significantly on many levels. It is, first of all, a reexamination of the literature on the Puritan self, a kind of study in national character. It is, next, an exercise in structuralist analysis, as well as psychoanalysis, counterposing Foucault to Erikson and Freud; at the end, we need to evaluate structuralism and to question the universality in time and space of psychological categories. And, last, it is a rather sibylline statement about the "disenchanted" world of Weberian rationalism: our present "sick society."

Americans have been uniquely concerned with the "self" from the beginning. The genre of autobiography flowered about the same time we created ourselves as a new nation but drew upon the earlier mode of religious confession. Scholars such as Perry Miller, Edmund Morgan, Sacvan Bercovitch, and Philip Greven have sought to understand and depict the American "character," "self," or "temperament."[3] There is an "anxiety" to the inquiry, which mirrors the anxiety present in the materials.

King begins his inquiry with attention to the obviously obsessional and compulsive aspects of the Puritan confessions. Greven, for example, sees the obsessional personality as a creation of evangelical child-rearing techniques. Others emphasize the neurotic quality of the recorded experiences. To a twentieth-century Freudian, such behavior borders on the abnormal. Is this a judgment that applies accurately to seventeenth-century accounts? King seeks his answer by looking at the confessions as *literary* expressions, not as statements of case histories. "The present book," he informs us, "is not attempting to find reflected in various texts the fact of pathology, but rather the expression of pathology" (p. 7). The texts are a way in which the Puritans *organized* their psychological-religious experiences and gave *meaning* to otherwise chaotic lives. Quoting Mikhail Bakhtin, King declares that "it is not experience that organizes expression, but the other way around— *expression organizes experience*" (p. 7). Expanding this idea, he insists that textual expressions can, in fact, create a person's character. By making sense out of our lives, texts also "make" our lives.

Melancholy then becomes a form of discourse, rather than an evidence of pathology. (I might add that the act of confession—the endless statements about being a sinner, a worm in the eye of God, a heap of offal—can take on a limited therapeutic quality of its own, though one runs the risk of being mired in the self-indulgence of such confessions.) In King's eyes, melancholy is the consequence of the Puritan psychomachia, or war in one's soul, which imitates the temptations experienced by Christ and becomes the necessary path to one's salvation. True conversion requires melancholy as a sign of religious health, not of personal abnormality. In such conversion experiences, there were acknowledged "steps"—the initial awakening to a conviction of sin; then battle joined with the devil's temptations, which might last for years; the experience of melancholy; and then, one hopes, the promise of salvation. The convert is a "pilgrim" passing through the valley of melancholy to a new kingdom.

Others might see the person experiencing such depressive trauma as mad, or at least damned. Nonevangelicals in seventeenth-century England saw the precisians in exactly these terms. John Winthrop, for example, at Cambridge University, was a perfect representative of obsessional or compulsive behavior and admitted that his neighbors thought him harebrained. In his own eyes, however, his "madnesse" was in ever having left the true fellowship of Christ. Once in the New World, Winthrop and his fellow precisians, though they still exhibited the same "symptoms," were no longer abnormal; instead, they acted according to the collective norm.

As King points out, the melancholics did not consider their behavior abnormal at all, in the sense that it had to be hidden. (A comparison with modern-day psychoanalytic patients might be in order here.) Most important they saw themselves at "work," rather than seeking salvation by "works"; melancholy was hard work, public work, a testing and travail necessary for self-redemption. Alienated from God, and thus from one's true self, one had to work one's passage back to God—and oneself.

By the end of the nineteenth century, King asserts, "the meaning attached to obsessional ideation had [become] precisely reversed." Now, a horrid thought was not a sign and a step to salvation but rather a possible indication of insanity. "The Puritan's case of conscience has transformed itself into the Victorian's neurological 'case'" (p. 10). Having established the healthy meaning of the Puritan sick soul, King spends the rest of his book tracing the shift in meaning to its end in Victorian neurosis. The reader should see for himself how this is done through King's analysis of men such as William James, James Jackson Putnam, and the others I have mentioned earlier.

King reminds us of, or introduces us to, the fact that texts are cultural products as well as personal ones, and they shape the way we personally experience life. As cultural products, texts stand within a tradition. We are what we are because of historical experiences, embodied in memories, shaping our perception of our personal experiences—and thus ourselves. King applies this awareness, in detail, to his subject. No one approaching

167

the subject of Puritan melancholy should be able henceforth to ignore King's valuable insights. The informing principle of his *Iron of Melancholy* is structuralism and especially the work of Michel Foucault. In fact, King's book can be seen as an equivalent, using American materials and a much denser analysis, of Foucault's *Madness and Civilization,* where the movement from premodern madness as a sign of God's presence to the nineteenth- and twentieth-century conception of it as psychosis is traced. King explicitly praises Foucault for centering a history of thought on "the arrangements that persons make between words and things" (p. 301). Texts are not to be viewed as "reflecting" some actual fact but are to be approached structurally (p. 342). By this, King intends to search for a "deeper structure, an innateness not to be rooted in time. . . . There exists instead a form, the re-expression of a significant pattern, a way that Americans for over three centuries have had for seeing, for putting together the meaning of their lives, for choosing, in a sense, their neurosis" (p. 330).

What are we to make of all this? Structuralism is obviously in fashion; it also recalls us to important truths. Indeed, King finds it before Foucault in both William James and Max Weber. "Thus James held," he tells us, "that like any act of signification, words did other than reflect or translate experience; they made the stuff of experience, the matter, for example, of religious conversion" (p. 94). And Weber, seeking to understand the words of Jeremiah, realized that, as King puts it, "the interpreter's production of meaning can itself become significant, rather than the interpreter's use of a particular sign" (p. 307).

Adherence to structuralism per se means a special vocabulary: reference to sign, signifier, and the "other" are de rigueur. It generally means an obscure prose, as if deep necessarily entailed dense. It seems too bad that the structuralist insights—whose validity I have often acknowledged on other grounds—so often require structuralist expression.

Well, so be it. A more substantive problem lies in structuralism's dismissal of all but mind. According to King, "Neither economy nor society, but a nation's particular psychology, propels history" (p. 81). Personally, I prefer, if necessary, Weber's "the interests of society are the great rails on which humanity moves, but the ideas [I would add passions as well] throw the switches."[4] Like psychoanalysis in its worst hubris—I think of Freud's unfortunate assertion that history is nothing but the conflict of id, ego, and superego, played out on a wider stage—structuralism can go too far, reducing everything to textual expression. The life of the psyche goes on as if no real life—Indian captivities, the American Revolution, the Civil War, the later industrial expansion—existed outside it, which offers us another reality to be considered besides the psychic one. Too often, structuralists pay a heavy price for introducing us to the "realities" of mythic space and time. King, by his unnecessarily provocative structuralism, seems to fall into this mode. Alas.

The issue can be joined more fully if we extended the discussion to psychoanalysis. King informs us in the acknowledgments that his original conception was to "locate Erikson's place in American thought" and that "his [Erikson's] motifs run throughout this book." I suspect that King sees himself as taking Eriksonian psychoanalysis a step further, to structuralism, and building on Erikson's theme that the experiences of a great reformer like Luther are to be viewed as evidences, not of pathology, but of strivings to selfhood. Let us perform a thought experiment. A Puritan, Cotton Mather, enters a psychoanalyst's (Erikson's?) office. How would Mather and his confessions be judged? A tangle of issues immediately arises. King's point is that what today would be considered neurosis was in the seventeenth century considered a socially validated path to salvation. The fact of Mather's melancholia—his incessant musings upon death; his strange dejections; temptations to atheism, blasphemy, and suicide; and violent pollutions that forced him to lie with his mouth tasting the dust of his study's floor, to take a few of King's list of symptoms—is not at issue. What is at issue is what it "means."

I am persuaded that King is initially right, that for Mather his confessional trials were self-interpreted as a cultural requirement. He shared the prevailing myth of the Puritans. Is Mather's text and reading, however, the only reality? Outside of Puritan culture, in his own time and ours, there were and are those who would judge him highly abnormal. His own immediate culture not only judged him normal but placed him at its head and deferred to *his* judgments. After all, Mather's melancholia, so to speak, had results: the Salem witchcraft hysteria, for one.

Mather posed as a scientist of the mind. A member of the Royal Society, he aligned himself with such "Great Names" as Mr. Glanvil and Dr. More, and proclaimed, "Go then, my little Book, as a lackey to the more elaborate Essayes of those learned men. Go tell Mankind, that there are Devils and Witches." He, who had studied medicine for a while, made much of how "Skilful Physicians were consulted" in the witchcraft case, how he, Mather, aided in a "Repetition of the Experiment," and how skeptical he was and careful to test his findings.[5] There were those at the time who saw another reality. They spoke of witchcraft as "but an illusion of crasie imagination,"[6] and appealed to a different scientific reality than Mather's. What I am trying to suggest is that there was more than one cultural reality in seventeenth-century America, and while we must understand Mather's choice, we must also make our own in understanding him.

The question really becomes one of why the Puritans, more or less alone, as a collective, first took up publishing melancholic confessions, which then became a form and structure for others. The question, of course, must go back to Luther and his particular "reading" of the world and its potential chaos, a reading that made sense for him, joining the inner and outer world in a meaningful manner, and then became a way for other people to see the world. It is a historical question, not just a structuralist one; and Erikson is careful to point to the political, technological, theological, and other cultural factors—and the ego and superego elements—surrounding this particular cultural development.

Puritan theology or culture, in turn, imposed an impossible burden, or double bind, on some people (others merely went through the motions). It asked them to believe in a God who, if not mad, was malignant. How could an infinitely good God condemn people to be sinners? On this simple, logical absurdity, brilliant men like Mather were forced to break their spirits, give assent to logical gymnastics about predestination and free will, and feel enormously depraved and guilty for bad thoughts. For the bad thoughts were there, as Mather confessed. It never occurred to him, however, that when he described the bewitched children in Salem as "discomposed" at a religious exercise—"If there were any Discourse of God, or Christ, or any of the things which are not seen and are eternal, they would be cast into intolerable Anguishes. . . . All Praying to God, and Reading of his word, would occasion a very terrible Vexation to them: they would then stop their own Ears with their own Hands; and roar, and shriek; and holla, to drown the Voice of the Devotion"[7]—he was describing his own case. An absurd world calls forth absurd behavior.

The cause of his melancholia, it must be admitted, also carried its own possible cure. Confessions of "Anguishes" became institutionalized as public matters, and the working through them a form of therapy. I see no reason, however, why the structuralist interpretation requires us to ignore others, such as Greven's more psychoanalytic one. What King does, valuably, is to remind us that "confessions" all take place in a cultural context, and we must listen with the "third ear" attuned to what the language means on a number of levels. (An Iranian psychoanalyst, temporarily in this country, diagnosed as hallucinating a student who, coming out of the rain for his appointment, spoke of "its raining cats and dogs outside.")

I am suggesting that structuralism and its interpretation must themselves be brought to the bar of reality, as best we can know it. I am aware that all reality is a matter, at one level, of perception and paradigm. Nevertheless, the historian is not at liberty to dismiss the deepest, most scientific reality we can obtain in favor solely of texts and minds. Mather's melancholia was not merely a matter of a culturally validated path to salvation, though it was this; it was also the travail of a very sick-minded man, who managed to remain functional in society by erecting elaborate defenses of an irrational nature, which depended on an irrational cultural system to support them.

Freudian psychoanalysis, with all its faults and limitations, is a better, more *realistic* way of understanding and dealing with the phenomenon of melancholia than were earlier Puritan interpretations. There is a nice irony in the fact that women, excluded from Puritan public confession, played the leading role in the development of psychoanalysis. It was hysteria, not obsessional neurosis, that displayed itself in the reigning "myth of passivity," namely Victorian conversion symptoms, and first served as the new paradigm for psychological explanation.[8] After hysteria, Freud went on to obsessional thoughts and compulsive acts, and to an analysis of melancholy.

I expected the last chapter of King's book to be on Freud; after all, the subtitle ends with "Victorian Neurosis." Indeed, the penultimate chapter is on James Jackson Putnam, whom King calls the first practicing psychoanalyst in America, whose conversion to Freudian doctrines occurred after he was sixty years old (confirmed later by a six-hour analysis by Freud in Vienna). There is an additional nicety in that Putnam was a direct descendant of the Thomas Putnam who, with his family, was an accuser in the Salem witchcraft trials two hundred years earlier.[9] Whom the gods wish to cure, they first make mad! Instead of Freud, however, King writes his last chapter on Max Weber. The line leading from Henry James, Sr., through his son William, and then through Royce and Putnam suddenly turns to a consideration of work as an industrial activity, not as a salvationist experience or therapeutic labor. The argument is as follows. Weber himself experienced severe melancholy, indeed a complete breakdown for a three- or four-year period; part of his recovery involved a visit to America, where he met William James, read his lectures, *The Varieties of Religious Experience,* and then, returning to Germany in 1904, completed his essay "The Protestant Ethic and the Spirit of Capitalism." In this essay, according to King, Weber embodied his own obsessional traits and identified them, correctly, as the core character of capitalism. For Weber, the rational compulsion of modern society had become an "iron cage." For King, the "iron of melancholy," a meaningful religious experience, had become the prison house of a sterile, sick society, encased in its own "iron cage" (ironically, Bunyan had also used this phrase, though with a different intention.)[10]

In dealing with Weber's own character, King evokes the aid of Arthur Mitzman, whom he calls "Weber's finest psychological interpreter" (p. 311). As I have argued in Chapter 8, in his book *The Iron Cage: An Historical Interpretation of Max Weber* (1969), Mitzman gives a most interesting reading of Weber, emphasizing his oedipal and generational struggle, as well as his Calvinist tensions; King pays attention only to the latter aspect. He reads Weber as a victim of his habits of labor in a "disenchanted" world, who realized that his own compulsion and alienation is an ethic, whereas for Freud it is a character type.

While King's concluding analysis is ingenious, I am not fully persuaded by it. That is, I accept King's overall transition from the Puritan conscience, to Victorian neurosis, to Freud. I also accept the idea that the Puritan "worldly asceticism," in the form of the Protestant ethic, is congenial to capitalism and that Weber's theory is a useful one. Is capitalism the cause of Weber's melancholy, however, as puritanism appears to have been the cause of Mather's and others' melancholy? King hardly discusses the issue, settling for a kind of "sick society" metaphor. In dealing with the Puritans, King offers a "thick description," to use Clifford Geertz's term; in dealing, not so much with Victorian neurosis as with modern society, King's description is "thin." The turn to Weber, rather than Freud, while immensely suggestive, has not really worked out, or been fully worked out.

I hope that I have stressed sufficiently the author's contribution, mediated through structuralism, to a deeper reading of Puritan melancholy and conversion experience. In indicating my points of divergence and my questions, I am paying tribute to a book that has been profoundly felt and thought about by its author. No less is demanded of the reader, in a worthwhile act of hard work, both scholarly and spiritually.

# CHAPTER THIRTEEN

# Crèvecoeur's
# New World

$A$ LITTLE more than two hundred years ago, just as the thirteen colonies were emerging victorious from their War of Independence, *Letters from an American Farmer* appeared in print.

Published first in London and followed quickly by editions in Dublin, Belfast, Leipzig, Berlin, and Paris, the book was addressed to "a friend in England." It described the customs, manners, work habits, and "modes of thinking" of Nantucket fishermen, backwoods frontiersmen, and Carolina slaveholders, as well as the people in the New World whom the author knew best—the small farmers and freeholders of New York and Pennsylvania.

The volume, twelve letters, or chapters, in all, was widely read in Europe, serving, as one scholar recently put it, "as a report on the application of the liberal and humane doctrines of the Enlightenment to a functioning society." But the book's persistence as a minor classic in Europe and the United States may be largely credited to Letter III with its lavish (and highly quotable) description of the American as "a new man, who acts upon new principles." Such phrases as "melting pot" and "new man," derived from the *Letters,* have become part of the American mythology.

More recently scholars have recognized the *Letters'* considerable merit as social commentary—as acute in many ways as Alexis de Tocqueville's better-known *Democracy in America* (1835 and 1840). Yet the special significance of *Letters* derives in part from the ambiguities that troubled the author himself. The title page named him as J. Hector St. John and further identified him simply as "A Farmer in Pennsylvania." The larger story is a bit more complicated: Born in France, baptized Michel-Guillaume-Jean de Crèvecoeur, the author had immigrated, by way of Britain and Canada, to the northern English colonies in 1759. Curiously, he made no mention of his mixed heritage or uncertain identity, though it is precisely these elements that give the *Letters* its special interest. For Crèvecoeur was not simply describing a nation of "other" people, as Tocqueville later did; he was also attempting to make sense of himself—as an *American*.

Crèvecoeur was born in 1735, in Caen, Normandy; his father was a member of the lesser nobility. Sent to a Jesuit college for schooling, Crèvecoeur later remembered being treated harshly and living in a "dark and chilly garret." At age nineteen, he was shipped off to England, possibly because of a quarrel with his father, to live with relatives. There he proceeded to learn English and to fall in love with the daughter of a Salisbury businessman. The death of his fiancée prompted him to sail for Canada in 1755, where he enlisted as a cadet in the French militia.

Endowed with mathematical abilities, he served as a surveyor and cartographer, growing acquainted with both the North American landscape and its inhabitants. Three years later, he secured a commission as a second lieutenant in the regular French army. In the last battle of Quebec, September 1759, trying to help save New France from the British, he was wounded.

At this point, a mystery clouds Crèvecoeur's life. One month later, in October, he was forced by fellow officers to resign from his regiment. We have no idea of the reason. Had Crèvecoeur, cited earlier for bravery, somehow disgraced himself in the Quebec battle or after it? In any case, he sold his commission, and, boarding a Royal Navy ship, arrived in New York City on December 16, 1759. Crèvecoeur, the Frenchman, now adopted the name J. Hector St. John, and a new American was born.

Americans, almost uniquely, are a hyphenated people. To a remarkable degree, we are still German-Americans, or Italian-Americans, or what have you, dragging our other-than-American past behind us. Crèvecoeur was more than ordinarily divided. First of all, as a Franco-American (and appropriately he named his first daughter America-Francés), he was never sure which half dominated. Though he spoke of himself sometimes as "a good Frenchman and a good American," on most occasions he either emphasized his New York colonial citizenship (obtained in 1765–66) or reverted to his natal claim. Though he wrote in the *Letters,* "the American ought therefore to love this country much better than that wherein either he or his forefathers were born," he became a French consul in 1783, an action sufficient to make the American statesman Gouverneur Morris feel he had abrogated his American citizenship. About this time, moreover, Crèvecoeur wrote to the Duke de La Rochefoucault, calling himself "a Frenchman."

Besides a confused *national* identity, Crèvecoeur wrestled with a provincial one: Never fully settling on any one claim, he kept calling himself, variously, a Pennsylvanian or a New Yorker (he had his farm in that colony) or a Vermonter. (Ethan Allen, in 1787, arranged for Crèvecoeur and his three children to be declared naturalized citizens of the Green Mountain state; St. Johnsbury, Vermont, was named after Crèvecoeur.)

To complicate matters further, he even flirted with an Indian identity. In Letter XII, the last of the collection, Crèvecoeur fantasized about leaving his farm in New York, menaced as it was by the Indians under British command, and fleeing to a friendly tribe of Indians, among whom he and his entire family would take up life as full tribal members. In his *Voyage* (1801), a book he published after the *Letters*, he stated on the title page that the author was "un membre adoptif de la nation Onéida" (an adopted member of the Oneida nation); his Indian name was Cahio-Harra.

The ambivalent qualities that emerged in Crèvecoeur's life and work have usually been neglected. His praises of the "American" are cited by students of American literature who have read no more than the lyric passages from Letter III, so often reprinted in anthologies.

*"He* is an American," Crèvecoeur wrote, "who, leaving behind him all his ancient prejudices and manners, receives new ones from the new mode of life he has embraced, the new government he obeys, and the new rank he holds. . . . Here individuals of all nations are melted into a new race of men, whose labours and posterity will one day cause great changes in the world."

Thus, few readers know that his view of the frontiersman (whose life, he believed, led to moral degeneration) anteceded and influenced James Fenimore Cooper's "Leatherstocking" portrayals or that his description of the whalers in Nantucket, including their opium-using housewives, is a worthy prelude to that given in Herman Melville's *Moby Dick.*

Crèvecoeur's private ambivalence aside, his experiences were, for an American, typically broad and varied. After his arrival in the colonies, he traveled, worked (as a surveyor or farmer), and lived in different parts of Pennsylvania and New York. In 1769, he married a Yonkers woman, Mehitable Tippet, and settled down on a farm in Orange County, New York, about 35 miles northwest of Manhattan. During the 1770s, Crèvecoeur led the life of a prosperous American farmer, writing most (if not all) of his *Letters,* as well as occasional articles critical of British taxation. Yet when the war broke out, Crèvecoeur sided with the Tories and soon felt himself forced to flee, along with his oldest son but without his wife and two other children, to New York City, then to England, and ultimately, in 1781, to his native France. He returned to America as a French consul in 1783, only to learn that his wife had died the year before; he finally retired to France in 1790.

It was probably Crèvecoeur's private allegiance to his own class, the aristocracy, and his fear of the unruly rabble that drove him, albeit with reluctance and mixed feelings, to the Loyalist side during the War of Independence. Yet, in his *Letters,* Crèvecoeur went to great lengths to stress his own simple, rustic qualities. He insisted that he was "neither a philosopher, politician, divine, nor naturalist, but a simple farmer."

In fact, he was a relatively sophisticated student of French Enlightenment thought and something of all of the above. In one area, religion, he was misled by the anticlericalism of the Enlightenment into predicting that the children of Americans would "grow up less zealous and more indifferent in matters of religion than their parents. The foolish vanity, or rather the fury of making Proselytes, is unknown here."

Crèvecoeur dedicated the *Letters* to the Abbé de Raynal (a minor Enlightenment thinker), whose own work on North America, *Histoire Philosophique* (1770), helped inspire a favorable view of the New World.

The cultural baggage Crèvecoeur brought with him also included, significantly, an admiration of Jean-Jacques Rousseau. Here, too, we have a highly ambivalent figure, partly *of* the Enlightenment and partly *opposed* to it. In any case, Crèvecoeur echoed many attitudes found in the writings of the "Citizen of Geneva": a tendency to romanticize nature, an eager willingness to shed tears, and a stress on the virtues of sincerity and the language and feelings of the heart.

Firsthand experience delivered Crèvecoeur from any idolization of the "noble savage." Nevertheless, he too recognized and mythologized some of the good qualities of the Indians, even as he noted their lack of strict morals and self-discipline.

Crèvecoeur, a cultivated European, wished, like Rousseau, to shed his overcivilized veneer in order to become a new man. Although he wanted to know what that new man would be like as an American, he also posed a larger question: What might any new man be? More to the point, what *should* he be?

Behind the philosophical question was Crèvecoeur's own unrelenting quest for an identity. Like a religious convert, he sought to become a new man, for that was the only way Crèvecoeur believed he could become a fully human being. We sense the personal note when he writes of how the newcomer to America "begins to feel the effect of a sort of resurrection; hitherto he had not lived, but simply vegetated; he now feels himself a new man, because he is treated as such." A few pages later, he repeats, "for the first time in his life [he] counts for something; for hitherto he has been a cypher."

Crèvecoeur was willing to take on a new life in any setting, French or American, as long as it promised to answer the question, what is *this* man? What gives Crèvecoeur and his writing a historical as well as a personal dimension is that in the course of seeking his definition he offered one to all others who would wish to find theirs by calling themselves Americans, however mixed their cultural origins.

The new American was one who had left Europe and its old authority relations. He was an immigrant. He became an American, dipping himself in a melting pot and emerging with his "past" behind him.

On many points, Crèvecoeur defined America's virtues as the obverse of Europe's ancient vices: "the severity of taxes, the injustice of laws, the tyranny of the rich, and the oppressive avarice of the church," these are all absent for the American. The American is "free"—"possessing freedom of action, freedom of thoughts"—free of the weight of European institutions. The new home is "the general asylum of the world," welcoming to its shores the poor and oppressed of the old continent.

Crèvecoeur claimed to be interested only in the present and the future. He mocked those who were absorbed in viewing ruins and who went to Italy for that purpose; how much more interesting was a civilization emerging, how satisfying the observation of "the humble rudiments and embryos of societies." In America, one could contemplate "the very beginnings and out-lines of human society, which can be traced no where now but in this part of the world."

Nevertheless, here too Crèvecoeur was ambivalent. In his youth he had been interested in artifacts of the past—old worm-eaten furniture, tapestries, and portraits. And in Letter XII, he wrote of an America that was itself in ruins as a result of the Revolutionary War. He was compulsively interested in the ruins, rather than in the glowing future. Before that, however, in the first three letters, he offered an idyllic picture of America, free from the ancient curses of Europe. "Here," he lyricized, "we have had no war to desolate our fields [ignoring the convulsions starting in 1776!]: our religion does not oppress the cultivators: we are strangers to those feudal institutions which have enslaved so many."

Unburdened by these negative influences, America enjoys a number of benefits and blessings: "Here nature opens her broad lap to receive the perpetual accession of new comers, and to supply them with food"; "We are a people of cultivators, scattered over an immense territory . . . united by the silken bonds of mild government, without dreading their power, because they are equitable. We are all animated with the spirit of an industry which is unfettered and unrestrained because each person works for himself"; and "Here man is free as he ought to be." Rousseau could ask for little more.

This is the Crèvecoeur who figures in the anthologies. It is the Crèvecoeur who was writing for Europeans, not Americans, trying to impress them with the wisdom of the choice he and others were making in settling in the New World. It is the Crèvecoeur who was reacting to Constantin-François Volney (the French author of a famous work on ruins), who had just written a widely cited book belittling America and its inhabitants, native and colonial. It is also the Crèvecoeur who was challenging the view of Georges-Louis Buffon and other Frenchmen who saw American flora and fauna as degenerative species, weaker than their European counterparts. Crèvecoeur described the way in which the "plentitude" of both geographic and social space transformed Europeans into Americans: The European "no sooner breathes our air than he forms schemes, and embarks on designs he would never have thought of in his own country."

Crèvecoeur offered an "environmental" explanation of the American and his goodness. "Men are like plants," he announced in Montesquieu-like tones, "the goodness and flavor of the fruit proceeds from the peculiar soil and exposition in which they grow. We are nothing but what we derive from the air we breathe, the climate we inhabit, the government we obey, the system of religion we profess, and the nature of our employment." Nurture, then, is more important than nature in the case of human beings.

As a good eighteenth-century advocate of the primacy of agriculture (one thinks both of the "Physiocrats," who believed land was the source of all wealth, and of Jefferson), Crèvecoeur often tended to emphasize the shaping force of the land. He was, after all, a farmer, and he appears to have said that tilling the soil produces healthy results in men.[1] At other times, he seems to have put the stress on government, as when he claimed that barren

Nantucket "seems to have been inhabited merely to prove what mankind can do when happily governed."

Essentially, however, Crèvecoeur's praise was reserved for the cultivated and the "middle way." His utterly unromantic view of the frontiersman, or "back settlers" makes this clear. "The chase," he tells us, "renders them ferocious, gloomy, and unsociable." Their mode of life produces "a strange sort of lawless profligacy." Their children "grow up a mongrel breed, half civilized, half savage." Such "degeneracy" hardly accords with Frederick Jackson Turner's picture of the frontier as the regenerative source for American democracy.

Crèvecoeur preferred another setting: Between the struggle with the sea and the hazards of the frontier lies the stable state of agriculture. It is the happy man, he wrote, who can "inhabit the middle settlements, by far the most numerous," where "the simple cultivation of the earth purifies them."[2]

Alas, Crèvecoeur's optimism disconcertingly declines as we move further into the *Letters*. His metaphor for man changes from plant to animal. Though he began by treating man the animal as possessed by instinct, which is good, he ended by focusing on the bad side of the passions. Man, Crèvecoeur came to see, is quarrelsome, cruel, and power-hungry. He is, in short, potentially bestial, and on the frontier he relapses into barbarism.

A dark shadow falls over the later letters, in which Crèvecoeur penned a description of Charlestown, South Carolina, its aristocrats given over to foolish pleasures and supported by an exploitative slave system. The end of Letter IX presents a harrowing scene: Crèvecoeur comes across a Negro slave, hanging from a tree in a cage, birds pecking out his eyes and insects eating his rotting flesh. His crime: killing the overseer of the plantation. As Crèvecoeur's host explains to him, "The laws of self-preservation rendered such executions necessary."

Increasingly, as the *Letters* progressed, Crèvecoeur went back and forth between shocking instances of cruelty and suffering in man and nature in America—there is an extraordinary account of two snakes battling one another—and depictions of occasional "benignity" (as in the portrait of the botanist John Bartram).

All falls apart by Letter XII. War had come to Crèvecoeur's idyllic farm. He and his family were threatened by British-led Indians and had to flee. The Revolutionary War for Crèvecoeur, as we know, did not open the way for the pursuit of happiness but instead ended his bucolic contentment. "America," for our "American Farmer," was now in ruins.

Crèvecoeur's only salvation was an imaginative retreat. He would take his family and escape to some "good" Indians, where they would be sheltered from the storm. He was aware that in becoming "A Frontier Man"—the title of his letter—he ran the risk of degenerating into bestiality. But he imagined that he would, in fact, help civilize the Indians and help prevent his children from adopting their ways. The severe divisions within Crèvecoeur are striking in this final fantasy. We witness a terrible transformation, as the American dream becomes a nightmare. In the end, Crèvecoeur was overwhelmed by a riven sense of identity and the loss of a stable world.

Ironically, Crèvecoeur's claim to be describing the reality of America and Americans has generally been taken by critics at face value. The claim, in fact, is valid, but not precisely in the way he asserted.

Crèvecoeur's intent was, at least in part, philosophical; and the English publishers were right when they saw through his project for a third book, to be titled *Journey through Northern Pennsylvania and the State of New York*. Writes Julia Post Mitchell, an early biographer: "When they learned that this was not an actual journey, in reality undertaken by the author, but rather a philosophical description of America, their interest cooled, and the plan had to be abandoned."

The importance of Crèvecoeur's *Letters* lay in its message to Americans and to those outside who wished to know about this strange new world. His *was* an "actual journey," but it was also a *mythical* one through a largely psychological landscape. In writing his account of *this* journey, Crèvecoeur helped create the myth of what it was to be an American, and that myth, in turn, helped shape reality. He also suggested the ambivalences, as well as the darker aspects, of the American character.

In his own ambivalence and his painful search for identity, Crèvecoeur was one prototype of the new "American," especially the American writer. He mirrored and prophesied for us the polarities—what Erik Erikson calls the "counterpointing of opposite potentialities"—that still partly define us as a nation two hundred years after *Letters* was first published.

# CHAPTER FOURTEEN

# Leadership in the American Revolution: The Psychological Dimension

IN my own definition of psychohistory, the "history" is at least as important as the "psycho." In earlier, more confident days, psychoanalysts could parachute into the historical field, do a fairly quick psychobiography, secure in the belief that intrapsychic processes were relatively insulated from external historical factors, and emerge triumphantly with the scalps, if not the heads, of their famous subjects, need I say, now nicely "shrunk." Alas, ego-psychological developments have destroyed such halcyon possibilities. One needs now to know as much about the political, social, economic, and intellectual conflicts of the time as about the Oedipal conflicts of the individual.

In discussing the psychological dimension of leadership in the American Revolution, for example, the first problem is to identify the leaders. Not being a historian of the American Revolution but one concerned with the comparative history of revolutions and with the general psychological dimensions of history, I was first struck by the absence of what I shall call "elite" studies. Objective statistical analyses of the kind done, say, in the Hoover Institute studies of Communist or Nazi leadership cadres seem to be missing in the American field, as do Lasswellian-type analyses of political agitators, administrators, and propagandists. Dankwart A. Rustow's brilliant review essay "The Study of Elites," published in *World Politics,* mentions books on the Turkish and Ceylonese elites, but there is nothing remotely comparable on Americans.[1]

Now I am not saying that there are no studies of American leaders in the Revolutionary period that use data on education, economic standing, literacy, social background, and the like. As far as I can see, there is a plethora of these. It is simply that for better or for worse—it may indeed be for better, as a glance at Rustow's article may show—they are not put in the same form as the comparative elite studies that I have in mind.[2]

It may be that a democratic revolution does not sit readily with elite studies (it is doubtful if Communist revolutionaries analyze themselves in these terms, either). Or more likely, the concept of the elite as a social classification emerges only after a society based on orders and ranks breaks into class and elite stratifications as the result of a revolution such as that of 1776 or 1789. Or most likely of all, one can effectively do elite studies only where there is a nationwide party, as with the Communists or Nazis, or a national parliament, or at least national politics involved in the revolution.

Thus, the absence of conventional behavioristic elite studies, while it complicates our task of identifying the leaders, points attention to the actual factors conditioning the exercise of leadership during the American Revolution. For my own satisfaction at least, I have had to ask what were the political and social contexts in which potential leaders might emerge and what tasks did they face.

The most striking fact for me is that the American is an extraordinarily complicated and untidy revolution. It is not a "national" revolution like the English or French, where local and provincial issues, although important, are not paramount. Events in England in 1640 took place in the context of a sovereign Parliament; those in France in 1789, of an Estates General, summoned by the king and in Paris. There is simply no equivalent of parliamentary London or monarchical Paris in America, though there were good-sized cities such as Philadelphia, which ranked among the four or five largest English-speaking cities in the British Empire. Hence, there is no national revolution as in England but a confused series of colonial or provincial ones, with the leaders in 1763 not the same as those in 1776, and no urban revolution as in France, where a Robespierre could emerge as master of the masses.

The overriding demand on American leaders then, was that they be able to work toward unity of effort, if not unification itself. (In fact, the British seemed the foremost leaders in this effort, inadvertently bringing the colonies together by such measures as the Stamp Act.) Yet such leaders could exert a unifying influence only by working up through local leadership and by reflecting colonial interests and slow-paced colonial responses to the need for unity. As Sydnor puts it in his *Gentlemen Freeholders,* "in exercising its vast electoral power the Assembly seldom chose a man who had not served in the Assembly, and it usually chose from its present membership.

All of the first ten governors of the State of Virginia, of the seven Virginia signers of the Declaration of Independence, and of the five Virginia delegates to the Federal Constitutional Convention had been members of the Assembly except Edmund Randolph."[3] Thus, most leadership resulted initially from appealing to one's fellow members of the elite. Whatever the correct argument over the role of the mob in the American Revolution, it is clear that leaders were not trying to appeal to them, except in local instances. Not demagoguery but, at most, oratory in a house of burgesses was the skill generally demanded. Addressing a highly literate people of relatively homogeneous race and religion, not consciously divided into class, the leader could earn his way by a well-penned pamphlet or declaration, or even a treatise. While the situation might vary widely—one is struck by the different kinds of leaders and followers in, say, Virginia and Massachusetts, where internal conflict and habits of deference were different—the variation is about a common theme. Gradually, out of planters and lawyers a new generation of leaders emerged, conditioned by the need to slowly espouse independence—no one could be a leader for long who hung back from his followers—and, even more gradually, to press for unity and eventually unification. Only with the emergence of national forums—the Stamp Act Congress first and then the various Continental Congresses—could these new leaders, however, find the appropriate institution within which to function effectively and to exercise the qualities required of them by the structural demands imposed by the forces we have so briefly analyzed.[4]

It is in this context that we can try to talk about the psychological aspect of leadership in the American Revolution. Although we do not have at our disposal an objectively delineated elite, we do have long compendiums of minor local leaders and even a clearly agreed upon group of major leaders: Washington, Jefferson, Madison, John Adams, Samuel Adams, Benjamin Franklin—their names seem to appear on everyone's list.[5] Here, surely, is at least a subjective list, fit material for psychological statements. Can we not generalize from them as to the psychological dimension of leadership in the American Revolution?

The first question to ask is: were the "great leaders," as I shall call them, "charismatic," to use a word bordering on the sociological and the psychological? *Charisma*, as is well known, is a term linked to the name of Max Weber; it is also an extraordinarily ambiguous term. In Weber's sociology, it is one of the three concepts by which to analyze the ways in which authority is legitimized: traditional authority, such as that associated with hereditary monarchs and those others who have always, so to speak, held it; rational–legal authority, obeyed because it is sanctioned by the system of rules under which the leader has won and holds office; and charismatic authority, based on faith in the exceptional personal qualities of the leader. According to Weber, where patterns of traditional and rational–legal authority have broken down, a charismatic situation arises in which authority must be self-made. The analysis is complicated by the fact that we also talk about charisma as a personality trait. For clearly, although Weber's first two categories are situational, his last seems to imply a psychological as well as situational demand. Hence we hear people speak, for example, of Franklin Delano Roosevelt as a charismatic leader when obviously he achieved authority by rational–legal means, although endowed with much personal attractiveness and charm.

Was the situation in America in the 1770s charismatic? It seems to me the answer is no. By and large, the leaders were chosen by rational–legal means, though these were amended so as to eliminate the traditional authority of the king and his appointees. Such a view, incidentally, coincides with the conviction that the American Revolution was not particularly a social revolution, as my readings confirm for me. It follows, almost by default, then, that the leaders of the American Revolution would not be charismatic, and I believe this to be the case. Thus I think that Seymour Martin Lipset points in a misleading direction when he says in *The First New Nation* that "the early American Republic, like many of the new nations, was legitimized by *charisma*. We tend to forget today that, in his time, George Washington was idolized as much as many of the contemporary leaders of new states."[6] So was Franco idolized in Spain, as was Stalin in the Soviet Union. But neither is to be considered charismatic for that reason. The truth about George Washington and his role is more adequately expressed by an early writer, Henry T. Tuckerman, who in his *Essays, Biographical and Critical* (1857) remarked: "If we may borrow a metaphor from natural philosophy, it was not by magnetism, so much as by gravitation, that [George Washington's] moral authority was established."[7] In short, neither Washington nor any of the other great leaders was a charismatic personality, nor were they even operating in a truly charismatic situation.

There is a second question to be asked. In my study of various revolutions I became struck with the frequency with which a number of prominent revolutionaries—though not all, by any means—exhibited strong traits of what I have come to call "revolutionary asceticism." As Eric Hobsbawm puts the matter, "There is . . . a persistent affinity between revolutions and puritanism. I can think of no well-established organized revolutionary movement or regime which has not developed marked puritanical doctrines. . . . The libertarian . . . component of revolutionary movements, though sometimes strong or even dominant at the actual moment of liberation, has never been able to resist the puritan. The Robespierres always win out over the Dantons."[8] In pursuing this line of thought, I came to combine a notion of Weber's with a notion of Freud's. Weber, of course, had taken the cluster of traits—self-denial, self-discipline, and so forth—associated with the term *ascetic* and traditionally placed in the service of religion and traced their evolution into worldly asceticism, where they were placed in the service of economic, that is, capitalistic, activity. I have tried to appropriate this idea and to apply it in developing an understanding of how and why asceticism has also come increasingly to be employed in the service of revolutionary activity. Alongside of this idea, however, I have tried to place one of Freud's. In his *Group Psychology and the Analysis of the Ego,* Freud spoke, as I have noted before, of the leader with "few libidinal ties." Such a leader, as Freud tells us, "loved no one but himself, or other people only in so far as they served his needs. To objects his ego gave away no more than was barely necessary. . . . the members of a group stand in need of the illusion that they are equally and justly loved by their leader; but the leader himself need love no one else, he may be of a masterful nature, absolutely narcissistic, self-confident and independent."[9] This is the sort of leader, in fact, who can deny the normal bonds of friendship, feeling, and affection and eliminate all human considerations in the name of devotion to the revolution. A Robespierre can send his friends Desmoulins and Danton to the guillotine without a shred of compunction. A Lenin can refuse to listen to Beethoven's *Appassionata* sonata because it may weaken his revolutionary fervor. Taken together, the virtual absence of libidinal ties—or more properly expressed, the existence of displaced libido—and the salient presence of traditional ascetic traits make for what I have called the "revolutionary ascetic."

Psychologically, such character traits are functional for the revolutionary. They allow him readily to break ties with the past, with family, and with existing authority, and to do so in the face of threats of poverty, torture, and deprivation of various sorts. His ascetic traits appeal to followers, who seek an obviously uncorrupt and disinterested leader. His denial of tender feelings, or at least their displacement, permits him not only to stay at meetings and congresses when others have long since gone home to their families but also, and less trivially, to face exile or prison. And so forth.

Now the fascinating thing for me is that, in spite of its strong Puritan background, what I am calling revolutionary asceticism is conspicuously absent in the American Revolution. Hobsbawm is wrong when he says that no well-established organized revolutionary movement, to use his terms, is without a puritanism to which it succumbs. Unless I am badly mistaken, there is simply no important counterpart to a Robespierre or a Lenin, the prototypes par excellence of the revolutionary ascetic, in the American Revolution. Washington, for example, is no more a revolutionary ascetic than he is a charismatic personality.

Why is this so? The answer, I believe, confirms certain judgments about the American Revolution. To make my point, however, I must return briefly to my thesis about the revolutionary ascetic. It is my contention that the traits of traditional asceticism and displaced libido became increasingly functional in the service of revolutionary activity with the following developments: (1) the emergence of revolution as a profession, a lifetime career, as exemplified first in the early nineteenth century by Blanqui and Buonarroti and later by Bakunin, Marx, Lenin, Castro, Mao Tse-tung, and so forth; (2) the achievement of modernization by means of a revolution, where private ascetic capitalism was insufficient and only a party or state form of Weber-like asceticism could take its place; and (3) the need for either anti-feudal or colonial revolutions, where the desire for a new identity called for violent rejection of the past and a sharp break with former ties of loyalty. Where these conditions obtained, leaders who were revolutionary ascetics held high cards. The situation favored their kind of personality, and their kind of personality further shaped the situation.

This was not the case with the American Revolution. Although primarily of the colonial revolutionary type, in my view, it was not modernizing in intent, not rejecting of its own past, and not made by professional revolutionaries. Although it was a war of independence, it was not one of liberation of the type associated with colonial revolutions of this century, for America had never been conquered by a foreign power and culture. As Louis Hartz argued, there was no feudal or ancient regime to be rejected, and as Wesley Frank Craven shows in *The Legend of the Founding Fathers,* the colonialists appealed to their own history as support for what they saw as a continued and legitimate assertion of right.[10] Thus, there was no need—indeed, no room—for revolutionary ascetic leaders. Instead, the colonists had two models before them of what a leader should be like: one, from the Puritan tradition, of a Moses type who would lead his people through the difficulties and dangers of the wilderness, as Cotton Mather claimed John Winthrop had done at the beginning; and the other, from the

Roman inspiration, of a Cincinnatus who combined military prowess with agrarian virtue. The composite is hardly the model of a modern revolutionary ascetic.

Why, however, with so strong a Puritan ethos in the country was there no Puritan army, no Cromwell? Part of the answer is that the American Revolution took place not in the seventeenth century but in an enlightened eighteenth century. Another part is that the Puritan ethos did not need revolutionary efforts to help it modernize the country, a process that was taking place under private auspices, by society rather than the state. True, the Puritan ethic was invoked, as Edmund S. Morgan has told us, in support of nonconsumption and nonimportation. Frugality was also seen as "renewing ancestral virtues" and as the basis of freedom and independence.[11] As Morgan also informs us, however, the austerity campaign was not supported by the very merchants whose ethos it was but whose commercial interests paradoxically pulled them in another direction. So too, the fear of corruption in Puritan provincial America, as Richard L. Bushman has described it, might have been expected to produce revolutionary ascetic consequences. Certainly there was a residue of the fear that power would corrupt—reflected in the writings of James Madison, among others—but it led to restraints on leaders rather than to grants of greater power to incorruptibles such as Robespierre. In provincial America, as Bushman informs us, "There is precious little evidence that the legislature was corrupted in the towns where the deputies were chosen or in the capital where patronage was dispensed."[12] Only when, as in England, political corruption was seen by Americans as subverting liberty and not just serving avarice did it become a real psychological threat. Even then, however, it did not give birth to revolutionary ascetic leaders.

So far, we have been circling warily around the edges of the psychological dimension of leadership in the Revolution. "The American Revolution: The Ideology and Psychology of National Liberation," by Edwin G. Burrows and Michael Wallace, helps us get closer to the center of our inquiry. It is a natural extension, it seems to me, of the ideological–idealist interpretation of the revolution so brilliantly expounded by Bernard Bailyn, who, I might add, has done penetrating psychological profiles on Jefferson and John Adams.[13] As one of Bailyn's pupils, Gordon Wood, remarks, "We must . . . eventually dissolve the distinction between conscious and unconscious motives, between the Revolutionaries' stated intentions and their supposedly hidden needs and desires, a dissolution that involves somehow relating beliefs and ideas to the social world in which they operate."[14] This is almost a definition of psychohistory.

The Burrows–Wallace theses can be simply put, though such a summary does not indicate the wealth of detail and subtlety of their interpretation. According to these authors, Revolutionary leaders were faced with the need to break former dependency ties—in short, to assert independence—while dissipating the anxiety of Americans that they were not yet fit or mature enough for such a break. This break was effected in the general context of a challenge to patriarchal authority in the English, and indeed the European, world, as symbolized in Locke's polemic against Filmer in the *First Treatise on Government*. One result is the surprising frequency with which the polemical literature on both sides was filled with allusions to father, mother, and sons (not unexpectedly, allusions to daughters are notably absent) and their relations to one another. For Burrows and Wallace, these are collective symbols, not Oedipal images. In any case, England as a protective paternal and nurturant maternal image is rapidly perceived as changing to a threatening parent, wishing to kill its child. The child's response is a terrible sense of betrayal, leading to paranoid accusations of conspiracy and of being attacked first. At the end, Burrows and Wallace conclude that the real issue "appeared to be not so much economic grievances [such as "restrictions on colonial manufactures and arbitrary taxation of colonial commerce"] as symbols of humiliation and degradation." So provoked, the rebels were able to feel justified in the release of anger against the parental figure, eventually sanctioned by the Revolutionary ideology, which also "pointed it toward the ultimate goal of independence."[15] In their conclusion they link their psychology with Bailyn's ideology—Bailyn had pointed ahead to this link when he described the ideology of the American Revolution as the "radical idealization and rationalization of the previous century and a half of American experience."[16]

Basically, I think Burrows and Wallace have the picture right. Let me therefore put a gloss on it. What we have here, in fact, is the particular American version of the necessary break in ties of affection that we discussed earlier in terms of the revolutionary ascetic, only in this case the tie is with a father–mother image rather than with the past of a feudal or ancient regime or with a foreign cultural overlay. This peculiar American version of breaking affective ties befits the particular kind of colonial revolution that we have described it as being.

The first thing is to refine Burrows and Wallace's use of paternal and maternal images. They are really not interchangeable. As I read the numerous quotes, the father is the true authority figure; he is embodied in George III, "father" of the country and empire. When the father's authority is seen as unjustly exercised, the sons have a right to reject it. As "Sons of Liberty," they struggle with the father and become in turn "Founding Fathers" in their own right. And what a happy coincidence for the psychohistorian that George III gives way to another George as father of his country. In fact, it is worth noting that the authority is pluralized, for there is not just one American father, as in most other, similar revolutions, but a number of them. The Founding Father, in reality, is a male peer group.

Were there any demographic and family changes in eighteenth-century America that coincided with this psychological shift? It is here that the work of John Demos, Philip Greven, and others becomes so important. As Burrows and Wallace sum up the matter, patriarchal authority in the colonial American family was in a pronounced state of disintegration. By the early nineteenth century Tocqueville could assert that "as soon as the young American approaches manhood, the ties of filial obedience are relaxed day by day." Was this relaxation of authority the result of struggle? Tocqueville assures us otherwise. "It would be an error," he says, "to suppose that this is preceded by a domestic struggle in which the son has obtained by a sort of moral violence the liberty that his father refused him. The same habits, the same principles, which impel the one to assert his independence predispose the other to consider the use of that independence as an incontestable right."[17] In short, the fathers cannot deny to the sons the same right they had asserted for themselves.

Now if Tocqueville is right, Americans experienced a different development at the end of the eighteenth century from that which their peers in Europe were undergoing. There, father–son conflict raged in increasingly open and violent terms. What Tocqueville calls "a sort of moral violence" is later labeled by Freud as "an Oedipal conflict" and is obvious in Diderot's *Rameau's Nephew,* John Stuart Mill's "Mental Crisis," Turgenev's *Fathers and Sons,* and numerous other accounts, both fictional and true. Was America really exempt from such struggle? Did the American Revolution traumatically solve the problem once and for all, energized by a concurrent evolution (rather than revolution) in domestic relations, an evolution strengthened in the future? I do not know. Burrows and Wallace, in a footnote, mention Francis Hopkinson's *A Pretty Story,* published in Philadelphia in 1774, which tells of "sons contesting their parents' administration of the family properties," and also cite Freneau's poem "To the Americans."[18] Only a further search of the literature can tell us what the true state of affairs was in this area.

One thing we know for sure: the "son" in this case, America, was growing lustily. Between 1700 and 1760, the population of America went from 223,000 whites and 28,000 blacks to 1,268,000 whites and 326,000 blacks. What is more to the point, if we can extrapolate from other data, actual sons and daughters were extremely numerous proportionately to the general population. Thus, in France, for example, there were 64.9 youths aged 15–29 for every 100 persons 30 years and over in 1776. The proportion of young people dropped steadily from that point on: by 1870–71 there were 50.3 youths per 100 persons in the over-30 group and by 1964, only 38.0. We can assume a comparable profile for America. Figures for the eighteenth century are lacking, but in 1870–71 the corresponding U.S. ratio was 86.4 per 100, reflecting a massive immigration of predominantly young people, and by 1965 it had dropped to 45.4; thus, we have levels generally similar to those in France, though not over the exact same time period.[19] In any event, it seems clear that sons were relatively strong in numbers in America at the time of the Revolution.

Connected with this sense of strength was the feeling of also being "purer." Whereas English leadership and authority were increasingly perceived as sinking into corruption, enervating luxury, and indeed effeminacy, the American sons prided themselves on their purity, manliness, and virility—all seen to be interconnected. As soon as the king showed himself as exercising his withering authority "unjustly," the sons could turn against him as a tyrant to be fought with righteous anger. Even in the fight, however, psychologically the sons needed still to identify with the parental figure, and this they did by establishing the fact that they were merely reaffirming the rights of freeborn Englishmen. They rejected the image of the bad father and appealed to that of the good father, thereby mitigating any sense of guilt and sin they might feel at opposing patriarchal authority in the person of the king.

The image of the mother is much more complicated. The paternal king symbolizes authority, whereas maternal England, the mother country, symbolizes nurturance. This "tender mother," as James Otis called her, generously gave her breast to her young offspring. The images are frequently oral, with much talk of suckling. So too, the mother country is seen as protecting the sibling colonies from squabbling among themselves. The feelings aroused are obviously quite different from those connected with paternal authority. Then suddenly, just as the father's authority had been perceived as unjust, the mother's nurturance is seen as being taken away. If anything, the reaction is far more violent. For John Adams, the mother country had become like Lady Macbeth, capable of plucking her nipple from America's boneless gums and dashing the brains out. He used the image in "A Dissertation on the Canon and Feudal Law" of 1765 and was sufficiently impressed, or compelled, by it to use it again in a letter of 1818 to Hezekiah Niles, where he stated that when the colonies found Britain to be "a cruel Beldam, willing like Lady Macbeth, to 'dash their brains out,' it is no wonder their filial affections ceased and were changed into indignation and horror."[20] One feels an especially personal element in Adams's usage, but it was in tune with others of his time. The former "tender mother" is now seen by Richard Henry Lee, for example, as a "step-mother," an "oppressive step-dame."[21] Worse, she is also "an old abandoned prostitute," refined in the "arts of debauchery."[22] Such violent language makes one think of Freud's theories about the child's split of the maternal image into the pure, protective mother, devoid of sexual aspects, and the fallen, violated prostitute. America in the 1770s seems to have swung violently from the overidealized image to the other, negative one. Was the split deeply rooted in the American psyche of the time, waiting to be exploited?

In any case, the breaking of affective ties with both parental images was now complete. One consequence was that the sons had become "new men" in a "Novus Ordo." It is interesting, however, to compare Crèvecoeur's new man with, say, the new man of the nineteenth-century Russian revolutionist Chernyshevsky, whose novel *What Is to Be Done?* had such enormous influence on Lenin. Chernyshevsky's new man was hard, self-controlled, and devoid of natural human feelings—the perfect revolutionary ascetic. Crèvecoeur's new man, as we all know, was one "who acts upon new principles; he must therefore entertain new ideas, and form new opinions. From involuntary idleness, servile dependence, penury, and useless labor, he has passed to toils of a very different nature, rewarded by ample subsistence.—This is an American."[23] In short, with independence came a renewal of nurturance—"ample subsistence"—but this time also independence from the mother.

Such new men are self-made men, and it is no accident that Flexner heads the very first section of his three-volume biography of Washington "A Self-Made Man."[24] There is an interesting confirmation of this attitude toward mothers in Erikson's essay "Reflections on the American Identity." There, discussing "Momism" and noting the existence of countless case histories of patients whose mothers were either cold and rejecting or hyperpossessive and overprotective—again the split—Erikson comments that "behind a fragmentary 'oedipus complex,' then, appears the deep-seated sense of having been abandoned and let down by the mother, which is the silent complaint behind schizoid withdrawal. . . . But wherever our methods permit us to look deeper, we find at the bottom of it all the conviction, the moral self-accusation, that it was *the child who abandoned the mother* because he had been in such a hurry to become independent."[25] Erikson, of course, was not thinking of the American Revolution and the paternal–maternal images that concern us here. Yet there is a kind of uncanny feeling provoked in us by the coincident views, suggesting that much of our national character was annealed at the time of the Revolution. For this process to occur, the original elements had already to be present, in a way I can only guess at. In any case, independence was asserted from the mother and her nurturance at that time, as the sons stood now as free men. As for the father, his authority was assimilated by the sons as a whole, who were basically able to identify with him by seeing their revolution as a reassertion of existing ancestral rights.

In all of this a price had to be paid. Let me address myself briefly to a few parts of the inheritance. One is the terrible sense of betrayal that gathers strength in the Revolutionary period and waxes as the "paranoid style" in American life, so well described by Richard Hofstadter and others. It is intimately connected with the belief in a "conspiracy," wherein all acts of the parent country, however innocent, are interpreted as being part of a plot. A caution is necessary here, however: conspiracy fears are part of almost all revolutions—one thinks of the French Revolution's "Great Fear"—and therefore one must try to sift out what is special about them in the American Revolution. I believe that the particularity of the American case lies in its connection with the sense of parental betrayal as we have outlined it.

From a psychological viewpoint, one may also look for evidences of fear of body loss or injury, as analyzed in the case of children, for example, by Melanie Klein. Thus, Dickinson characteristically speaks of the colonists as "torn from the body, to which we are united by religion, liberty, . . . we must bleed at every vein."[26] In this area, too, we shall seek evidences of a fear of "poisoning," for example, of the "body politic." One would also expect data in terms of what child psychologists call "separation anxiety," the fears manifested by a young child when the parent leaves him. These, however, are all recondite subjects, and one would have to be very careful in translating psychoanalytic concepts into true psychohistorical work.

The evidence is firmer on a second issue: the sense of being attacked first. The accusations are numerous that it is the father who has first taken up the cudgel against the child. A most interesting analysis of the "American military experience," by John Shy, argues that against a background of seventeenth-century colonial anxiety, insecurity, and violence the Americans saw the Indians as striking first and unexpectedly.[27] An outside observer, alas, sees the reality as being one of Americans projecting their aggressive impulses—in fact, they are the true invaders—onto the Indians as a way of effacing the guilt they might otherwise feel in themselves. In any case, Shy sees the Americans as developing a characteristic style of dealing with such a threat: not by means of a specialized, professional army but rather through military potential in terms of the great mass of people. "With great strength," he tells us, "but weak defenses, the colonies experienced warfare less in terms of protection, of somehow insulating society against external violence (as was increasingly true of European warfare), than in terms of retribution, of retaliating against violence already committed."[28] This belief, or style, was confirmed by the French and Indian Wars, where the attack seemed to come now not so much from the Indian per se as from unsuspected European wars, erupting mysteriously on the American continent; the belief is made a hardened conviction by the events of the 1770s. Thereafter, as Shy shows, Americans interpreted all of their future military experiences in terms of being innocent, passive people who were suddenly and unexpectedly attacked. Once again, I suspect, this general pattern is especially connected to the feelings associated with the break in affective ties with the "parent" country.

Overwhelmingly, in all of the issues we have looked at, the symbolism of father, mother, and son seems paramount. These are the inner springs underneath the conscious assertions of constitutional right, economic grievances, and ultimately independence. Whatever their roots in American family life and experience, however vaguely and tenuously they manifest themselves, the feelings attached to this symbolism provide the psychological context in which leadership must exert itself. The leader of 1776 had to be strong enough to break the ties of affection with the parent country and to inspire others with the confidence that they too could sustain the shock. He had to offer a trustworthy substitute for the old authority—the image of a son who had become a Founding Father. He had also to provide promise of nurturance to take the place of that formerly provided by the mother country. He needed to assuage feelings of parricidal guilt by justifying the filial release of anger and resentment. He had to inspire confidence that, though unjustly and unexpectedly attacked, he would persevere until the unprepared military potential could be mobilized to overcome the enemy. Above all, he had to unify all of these feelings into a new continental synthesis, expressed consciously in a new ideology and imaged forth for all to see in the person of a "new man": the American.

In 1776, no one man emerged to be "the leader." Instead, as remarked earlier, sons grew up to become Founding Fathers, a development certainly conformant with the existence of sibling colonies. Thus, only detailed analyses of all Founding Fathers could offer the evidence as to how each, out of the experiences of his own personal life, was able to contribute to the psychological synthesis of leadership in the American Revolution. Among them, however, one was primus inter pares: George Washington. Above all the others, he symbolized the new "father of his country" who stood for unity of action against the authoritarian king and the no longer nurturant mother country.

It must be said right off that any effort at an Eriksonian life history of Washington will confront major difficulties. In his studies of Luther and Gandhi, Erikson analyzed primarily religious figures who only secondarily became involved with political revolutions. In his terms, by having first solved their own identity problems, they were able to offer a solution to the identity crisis of large numbers of people and, in the process, to become "second fathers" to their followers. Now this sounds helpful to us in our study of the American Revolution. Whatever the Puritan aspect of America, however, it was within an Enlightenment context of nonreligious or even antireligious belief that a leader such as Washington developed (though he was an Anglican by form). There was no crisis of faith, no challenge to authority in a religious guise. Thus, to provide salvation for an individual or a group was not one of the demands made on a potential leader. Instead, military endurance and continental unity were required. A better model for the study of Washington is therefore probably provided by Mustapha Kemal Pasha of Turkey, strange as it sounds, than by Luther or Gandhi.

The next difficulty is that Washington was simply not an introspective man. Though he left letters and diaries that now fill more than forty volumes, he revealed little of his personal feelings in them—indeed, as we shall see, a major component of his personality was coldness and reserve. Unlike Gandhi, he wrote no autobiography. Unlike Luther, he did not table-talk with disciples. How are we to get inside this man? Is there all that much inside to be gotten at? There seems no identity crisis, no trauma to have lent drama to his inner development. Thus, as Marcus Cunliffe suggests, "his personality baffles because it presents the mystery of no mystery."[29]

Yet he did have a personality. Consequently, out of his life experiences, let us draw not a life-historical sketch—an impossibility here, if not at any time—but four or five themes that relate to psychological dynamics operating at large, which Burrows and Wallace have pointed us toward. The first theme we notice is the omnipresence of parental and sibling loss. It runs through Washington's whole family history. His father, Augustine, lost his own father at age three and then his mother at seven. George's mother, Mary, also lost her father at three and then her mother at twelve. Hence, both grew up in the tutelage of stepparents or guardians. This, then, was George Washington's grandparental heritage, so to speak. George himself lost his father at age eleven. Before this, a sibling—a half-sister—had died when he was three and another sister had died in infancy when he was about eight.

Now, to say that such family losses were characteristic of the times is merely to indicate how resonating would be George's personal experience (although we must also realize that, as a result, such loss would have a somewhat different quality from what it has today). The problem would still be one of how to deal with the death fears and wishes, the anxiety at separation—incidentally, the family uprooted itself three times before George was seven—and the mourning and melancholy occasioned by these removals. I suggest that we view the emotions aroused by this problem under the term *threat of abandonment*. For a child to counter such a threat, I believe, would mean generally having to learn early to deny close affective ties, to be willing to see them broken where they existed, and to mature early into feelings of independence.

Such traits in a mature Washington, as leader of his people, would correspond fittingly with the needs of the situation in the 1770s. A glimpse of this fact is what may have led Cunliffe to describe Washington as "a sort of splendid foundling at the head of a foundling nation."[30] In some ways, Washington had never known—or at least felt he had never known—a proper father. As Freeman tells us apropos of the death of George's father, "He had seen little of his father and in later life he was to remember only that his sire had been tall, fair of complexion, well proportioned and fond of children."[31] This paucity of memory—extraordinary if we remember that George was eleven years old when his father died—suggests a possible major blocking of feeling toward the father, allowing later disengagement from another parental image without undue rancor.

Our second theme is incipiently Oedipal. George's mother was twenty-three when she married his father, who was thirty-seven at the time. In classic Freudian terms, little children often wonder how a young mother can be married to an almost grandfatherly type. Did young George so wonder? This would be especially likely, since a half-brother, Lawrence, aged twenty, returned from school in England in 1737, when George was at the ripe Oedipal age of five. Freud himself had assumed that his own mother at twenty-one should more rightfully sleep with his half-brother of about twenty than with his "old" father of forty-one.

Somehow, however, I doubt if things worked so classically for young George. The evidence, of course, one way or another, is nonexistent. What we do know is that George dealt with whatever Oedipal feelings were present by regarding his half-brother Lawrence as a kind of second father. When the latter married within two months of Augustine's death, George made his half-brother's house his own second home, adding parental regard for Lawrence's father-in-law, William Fairfax, to that for his brother. In addition, he treated William Fairfax's son, another George, as an equal or less, though the young man was several years his senior. It was the future wife of George Fairfax, Sally Cary, with whom Washington was to fall deeply in love only a few years later, when she was eighteen and he was sixteen. It is difficult to believe that, in the realm of the unconscious, George Washington was completely untouched by the Oedipal aspects of this relationship. The whole subject, however, is far too tortuous and unclear to do anything more than note it as in some way a background for Washington's feelings about parental and sibling symbolism shaping British and colonial relations. Only in terms of the substitute father figure, Lawrence, are we on sure grounds. By identifying with him rather than with his real father, George Washington came to shape his identity as a military man—Lawrence held a regular commission in the British army—the role in which he most obviously offered leadership to the American Revolution.

We must say one further word about George Washington's mother, Mary. All observers agree that she was a demanding and "majestic" woman. She opposed her son's military ambitions and appears not to have approved of his successes. In fact, she seems to have constantly depreciated his achievements. In psychological terms, one would expect real hurt to young George's self-esteem and therefore a constant need to prove himself. Here, indeed, we may find the root of his driving ambition, noted by all who have written of him. His mother's lack of confirming love seems to have reaffirmed the need for self-reliance and the absence of strong affective ties we have postulated earlier as being laid down by what we called the threat of abandonment. Washington turned "cold." As one later observer commented in 1784, "I could never be on familiar terms with the General—a man so cold, so cautious"; another a few years later noted that "there seemed to me to skulk somewhat of a repulsive coldness . . . under a courteous demeanor."[32] Rejected by his mother, Washington avoided deep intimacy with others. Although he certainly did not become a misogynist—indeed, he married a widow with two children and always prized his domesticity—he did not marry for love. Able, however, to reject his own mother, he could also lead his fellow Americans into a war that rejected, and expelled from the ancestral house, the mother country, England.

My last theme concerns Washington's sense of betrayal at not being accepted at his true worth and given a correct rank in the regular British army. Having identified himself with Lawrence, George nursed expectations of similar treatment. When his deeply held hopes were disappointed, Washington became bitterly resentful—it appeared that the British army was rejecting his military ambition, just as his mother was doing. Indeed, in the years 1753–58, one senses a touch of what many of his biographers describe as paranoiac suspicion in the young Washington, as he sought preferment by every route and seemed to imagine it blocked by plots and conspiracies against him. Only in 1775, after what we can view as an unusual kind of Eriksonian "moratorium" of seventeen years, in which he came successfully to terms with himself, was Washington able to return maturely and independently to his first ambition, with what momentous results we all know.

My reflections on Washington are not even the shadow of a life history. I hope they are suggestive, however, even if perhaps occasionally wrong in their specifics, of the sort of questions one might wish to ask about the personal lives of the leaders of the American Revolution. The next question, of course, would be how the themes of their life histories relate to the psychological themes sounded forth by large numbers of fellow colonists, in pamphlets and books, letters and diaries. In fact, it is in the conjunction of these two sets of inquiries that we shall find the best answer to the overall question: what is the psychological dimension of leadership in the American Revolution? Only thus shall we come to know the Founding Fathers in the deepest aspect of their great creative effort.

# CHAPTER FIFTEEN

# A Psychohistorical Inquiry: The "Real" Richard Nixon

POLITICAL leaders have both a public and a private "face," image, identity, or self—however one might want to express it. As I shall argue in the next chapter, although the public image is what counts politically, in fact the two often merge, with the private affecting the public and vice versa. How exactly this works, and to what degree, will vary, of course, in particular cases.

Richard Nixon, regarded in this light, is a particularly fascinating case.* He himself had a difficult time establishing what was real about his self, often falling into denial bordering on mendacity. In spite of his considerable gifts, he often had a hard time recognizing who was the "real Nixon." The public had an equally difficult time. When Richard Nixon became the thirty-seventh president of the United States, friends and foes alike conceded that they did not know who the "real" Nixon was and how he might be expected to behave. Typical of innumerable comments was Tom Wicker's: "In fact, the career and personality of Richard Nixon defy confident analysis, and what he will do in the White House is by no means easy to divine."

Wicker, of course, was right. Yet the power of the American president is

---

*This is basically what I wrote and published back in 1970. While a great deal of new data has become available (for example, see Fawn Brodie, *Richard Nixon: The Shaping of His Character* [New York, 1981]), my analysis has, I believe, been confirmed by the events of Watergate and the materials on Nixon that have appeared since then. I have not attempted an updating, therefore, aside from verifying a few facts and episodes, believing that there is a gain in leaving the chapter as an illustration of a particular way, a stage, of practicing psychohistory. As Part V will show, if I were to attempt the task anew I would do it in more Kohutian and cultural terms.

such that "analysis" of his "personality" was requisite and justified. Insofar as his personality could and did affect his decisions and actions, it was incumbent upon us to seek the best possible understanding of his character. Most commentators, however, flitted like moths around this subject; thus, as Richard H. Rovere correctly points out, "Nixon's leanings, we know, are mostly conservative. But a politician is not a tree that must incline as the twig was bent a long while back." Having said this, Rovere then unconsciously undercut his own observation by remarking that "to my mind, the greatest and most distressing revelation of this period has been the President's political ineptitude . . . some *kind of perversity* [my italics] or some failure of calculation seems to make everything go wrong."[1]

Without taking "perversity" too seriously and abandoning Rovere's ambivalence, we can ask: what was the interplay between Nixon's fundamental character traits—the way in which the twig was bent for the *young boy*—and the demands of his situation as a *politician?* To answer the first part of this question, our main preoccupation here, I have been arguing that we can usefully turn to the body of theory and fact that concentrates most deeply on this problem: psychoanalysis. In its classic form, of course, psychoanalysis is oriented to clinical data about a patient in therapy. It is necessary, therefore, to bypass orthodox psychoanalysis and to approach a political subject who is *not* a patient in therapy in terms of the new discipline, variously described as psychohistory or psychological history. Such an approach emphasizes strengths and abilities, creative and adaptive powers, as much as if not more than the usual difficulties pictured in psychotherapy.[2]

Many people are deeply suspicious of psychoanalysis as applied to political figures. And rightly so. There have been some egregious instances of how not to go about this task. For example, the "questionnaire" concerning Barry Goldwater, addressed to the members of the American Psychiatric Association during the 1964 campaign and eliciting a majority response as to his psychological "unfitness" for the position of president, is a model of irresponsibility. "Treating" Goldwater as if he were a patient, but without the slightest clinical evidence for their conclusions, many psychiatrists simply voted their political prejudices rather than exhibiting their professional competences.

Freud himself, alas, as I have noted in earlier chapters, has contributed to the discrediting of psychological history. His book, in collaboration with William Bullitt, on Woodrow Wilson is a sad exemplar.[3] However one may excuse Freud—he was an old man at the time, morally indebted to Bullitt for helping to rescue his family from the Nazis—and however much one stresses that Bullitt, in fact, wrote the bulk of the book, the stain on psychological history, though undeserved, is indelible. At the end, all one can say is that the book is more psychopathology, and bad psychopathology, than psychohistory and treat it as a warning example.

In addition, the effort to cast doubt on Richard Nixon's mental stability by vague accusations that he visited a psychotherapist in the late 1950s itself indirectly cast doubt on psychological history. The initial hush-hush handling of the facts showed how sensitive, *politically,* might be the effort at understanding, *psychoanalytically,* a political candidate. Without involving ourselves too deeply in Drew Pearson's allegation that Nixon was in therapy for approximately 4½ years, we can side with the opinion of one observer that, if the fact were true, "I feel more hopeful about his presidency. When a man has the inner strength to seek competent professional help in finding out more about himself, looks for a way to grow as an individual, tries to improve himself in his own eyes, wants to do something real and constructive about himself as a person . . . then he's on the right track."[4]

In any case, let us put the negative examples aside. Psychohistory does have some positive work to exhibit. Thus, to counterbalance the Freud–Bullitt *Woodrow Wilson* we can point to the sound and penetrating work of Alexander and Juliette George, *Woodrow Wilson and Colonel House,* which grounds its psychoanalytic insights in solid professional data, giving us a most revealing picture of Wilson, the man and the politician.[5] Erik H. Erikson's contributions in his *Young Man Luther* and his book on Mahatma Gandhi, are pioneering efforts to interrelate psychological processes with the political and social currents in which a given individual finds himself or herself and self-identity.[6] Indeed, Erikson's "identity crisis" has become one of the clichés of our current language. Thus, a psychohistorical study of Richard Nixon had some valid inspirations upon which to draw.

At the beginning of the 1968 campaign, I became convinced of the importance of a broad psychohistorical study of the future president. Indeed, it seemed to me of sufficient importance to warrant an interruption of my own work, on a very different subject, in order to form a "team" to undertake the presidential project. What more significant task than to seek greater understanding of the way in which one of the most powerful men in the world might approach his power and position?

It may be of interest to explain what happened to this original plan, which was interdisciplinary in terms of both the people involved and the fields. I sounded out five or six outstanding scholars—other historians, political scientists, and psychoanalysts—on their willingness to serve on a "team" inquiry into the psychodynamics of our next president. (This was after both Nixon and Humphrey had been nominated but before the election, and we intended simply to study *whoever* won.) Each of us, using an individual set of theories, was to write up an analysis of the president; then we would try to reach a group portrait. Moreover, we would try to secure alternative "scenarios" of the major problems and events that might confront the president and "predict," as best we could, how we thought that he would act in the face of such pressures and opportunities. In order not to have our work misused for political purposes, it was *not* to be made public until *after* the president's term of office. Then, we would compare our analysis and predictions with how things had turned out and in that light review our successes and failures of theory. Predominantly, then, the project was heuristic.

The estimated funding was small, only $15,000 to $20,000. We approached a number of foundations and agencies, and their response was uniform: The proposed project was a most interesting, imaginative, and important one, we were told, but it was politically inadvisable for the particular foundations to which we were applying to be involved in such a study.

I mention this background for the light it sheds on the difficulties of doing one kind of interdisciplinary work, psychohistory, in relation to living figures, and not primarily to criticize the reactions of the foundations. (In their place, I might have returned the same answer.) Having read a certain amount of material on Richard Nixon for the proposal of the project, and thought about it, however, I was loath to discard my work completely. Perhaps, I thought, a sketch might inspire others to further effort. Thus, I prepared a psychological sketch of the thirty-seventh president, Richard Nixon, informed by an awareness of psychohistorical theory and practice—and a good deal of humility on the subject as well.

The first thing that struck an observer at the time was the paucity of information on Nixon. For a man who has been as long and as prominently in politics as he has, the lacunae are impressive. A major library, for example, Widener Library at Harvard University, had only nine or ten items in its catalogue, and of these only a few were of any consequence. *Nixon, A*

*Political Portrait,* by Earl Mazo and Stephen Hess, was the 1968 rewrite of Mazo's original book of 1959. It was put out, with the 1968 presidential campaign in mind, by two Nixon partisans (Hess served as a writer on Nixon's staff, and Mazo was a former *New York Herald Tribune* reporter), with a serious attempt, however, to be nonpartisan. It was certainly one of the indispensable sources, at the time, for any data on Nixon's personal life. Nixon's own *Six Crises* (published in 1962, and republished with a new preface in 1968) was the one piece of sustained self-revelation that we had in 1968.[7]

Those early books often raised more questions than they answered and raised no questions where they should. For example, during the war Nixon worked as a lawyer in the OPA for six months. According to Mazo and Hess, "Nixon's six months as a minor government bureaucrat shattered some of his illusions and reshaped a bit of his political philosophy."[8] Entering a "liberal," he emerged a "conservative." What happened during those six months? The experience sounds very important, semitraumatic, yet we were told almost nothing of the personal aspects of this "conversion" episode. The "team" project that I mentioned earlier would have delved into such matters. I, perforce, had to work only with the existing materials.[9]

The second thing that struck an observer was the opaqueness, the non-revealing quality of Nixon's life and writings. Thus, the claim on the back cover of the 1968 paperback edition that "Crisis Shapes and Reveals a Man's Character" might be true as a generalization, but required sharp examination in this case. Throughout, there was an extraordinary lack of affect about Nixon, and this was not dissipated by the occasional outbreak, such as the 1962 press conference following his gubernatorial defeat. If Nixon did visit a psychoanalyst, then I suspect the going must have been very tough for the doctor. Nixon's opaque quality thus became a subject for investigation, and pointed our attention to the time when the young Nixon must have "switched off" his emotions (or was he born with the tendency?). In any case, part of the problem labeled "the real Nixon" was rooted in his lack of affect. It certainly added to the difficulties of our psychohistorical analysis.

One last preliminary comment. An analyst treating a patient must deal not only with the latter's transferences—the displacement onto him of the patient's feelings toward previous figures—but with his or her own countertransferences. No less is demanded of the psychohistorian.[10] The general problem of the historian's own bias and involvement with the materials is lifted to another level (or rather, brought to another depth) in psychohistory. But psychohistory has the virtue of compelling one to look as consciously as possible at one's own feelings, as well as at the feelings of one's subject. It was in this spirit that I then sought an understanding of Richard Nixon.

A true psychobiography would approach Nixon chronologically, seeking to study his personal development in the context of the changing times. Another approach would deal with themes or patterns discernible throughout Nixon's life; and it was this approach that I took, attending to Nixon's chronological personal development when possible.

Both theme and chronology indicated that Nixon's family upbringing should be our first topic. According to Mazo and Hess, "his family intimates see Richard Nixon as a composite of his father, mother and grandmother" (M-H, 15). We needed, however, to see how this "composite" was formed and interrelated. Nixon's own account of his grandmother is that she "set the standards for the whole family. Honesty, hard work, do your best at all times—humanitarian ideals. She was always taking care of every tramp that came along the road, just like my own mother, too. She had strong feelings about pacifism and very strong feelings on civil liberties. She probably affected me in that respect" (M-H, 16).

Nixon's mother, Hannah Milhous, was much like his grandmother, a pious Quaker and a strong hard-worker. Clearly, it is from her (and his grandmother) that Nixon seems to have acquired the traits of the Protestant Ethic that have predominated so forcefully in his makeup. As Nixon's brother Donald recalls, "Dick always planned things out. He didn't do things accidentally . . . he had more of Mother's traits than the rest of us" (M-H, 18).

Richard Nixon was the second son, born January 9, 1913, to Hannah Milhous Nixon. His brother Harold was born four years before him and after Richard came Donald in 1914, Arthur in 1918, and Edward in 1930. What effect did these siblings have on Richard, and on his relations to his mother? The Mazo–Hess account gave us only the following data, without interpretation. The oldest boy, Harold, contracted tuberculosis. Mrs. Nixon took him to Arizona in hopes of a cure and stayed there for two years. The rest of the family stayed in California, with the boys and their father taking turns at preparing the meals. "It was a period of extreme hardship for the whole family." Meanwhile, we are told, "Arthur, the fourth son, became seriously ill, and a week or so later died of tubercular meningitis. He was seven." Worse was to come, for Harold, returned from Arizona, was not cured. One morning, after Richard had driven Harold to town and back home and then headed off for school, a message came to him: "Come home. Your brother has died" (M-H, 16–17).

How old was Richard when his mother "deserted" him? If Arthur was seven or so at the time, Richard was about twelve or thirteen. What effect did these "traumatic" events, "desertion" and death, have on him? We can only speculate. First there is the strong possibility that he unconsciously perceived his beloved mother's leaving him for two years as a "betrayal." Consciously, he obviously understood the necessity.[11] If I am right about the unconscious feeling of "betrayal," this might affect his later attitudes on the subject of "traitors" in high places, preparing him emotionally for such a belief. Whatever the effect, we can be sure of one thing: his mother's absence for two years must have had a crucial impact on the young Richard. (I suspect it turned him back to his father, but more of this later.) We can also postulate that the birth of his brother Donald, only a little over a year after Richard's birth, must also have been perceived as "taking" his mother away from him, thus laying the first seeds of his feelings of the precariousness of life and love. Of course, this perception must have been balanced by the loving concern for all of her children that the hardworking, admirable Mrs. Nixon seems to have exhibited.[12]

What of the death of Harold and of Arthur? We can speculate on at least two effects. The first is the arousal of strong unconscious guilt feelings. It would be only natural that Richard, the second son, would have rivalrous feelings toward the earlier sibling and an unconscious desire to "replace" him (especially in the affection of the mother); all of this, of course, would be accompanied by feelings of love toward his brother. The death of his brother would awaken all of the feelings of "survivor guilt" so well described by analysts, such as Robert Lifton.[13] It is not at all clear, however, how Nixon coped with his ambivalent feelings. It was a subject that would arise again, when we examined Nixon's relationship with President Eisenhower.

The second effect would be to arouse in him the threat and fear of death. We were told by Mazo–Hess that Nixon narrowly escaped death, at age three, in an accident that has left him with a still-existent "ugly scar" (hidden, physically, "by hair always parted on the right"). They continued, "Nixon has always been susceptible to illnesses of one kind or another since that childhood experience. When he was four he nearly died of pneumonia" (M-H, 13). More than most children, then, we can assume a death anxiety in Nixon, accentuated by the actual death of his brother Harold and compounded by the death of his brother Arthur. It may be, therefore, that

Nixon's need for "crises" was partly motivated by the need to confront his own death fears, repeatedly and constantly.

The paucity of our information left us only with these speculations: a possible sense of betrayal by the beloved mother, guilt over death wishes, and anxiety over death fears. Out of these feelings, Richard Nixon could draw either strengths or weaknesses, or both.

What of his father? Here the picture seems even more complicated. Francis (Frank) Nixon seems to have been a good man in a family dominated by strong women. In spite of his efforts, however, he seems also to have been a "failure," who drifted from enterprise to enterprise: the American who did not "make it rich." Frank Nixon, we are told, first emigrated to Whittier, California, for reasons of health, having suffered severe frostbite while running an open trolley in Columbus, Ohio. When he met Hannah Milhous in 1908 in southern California, he was still the motorman of a trolley. Since grandmother Milhous, we are told, had "a big house on the boulevard," we can assume that Frank Nixon had married above his station. In any case, he tried to improve himself. Speculating that Whittier would grow rapidly, he opened a gasoline station in 1922, moving, in fact, from nearby Yorba Linda, where Richard was born, to Whittier proper; in Yorba Linda, Frank Nixon had planted a lemon grove that failed. He also converted an abandoned meetinghouse nearby into a general store (where Richard worked at the counter and pumped gas). In none of these enterprises did he seem to have great success. As one commentator puts it, the elder Nixon was "a rolling stone and man of many jobs."

My theory is that Richard Nixon, who was so like his mother in her traits of hard work and persistence, eventually turned those traits to use in terms of an *identification* with the father. In this identification, he also sought to redeem his father by being successful. I suspect the full identification took place shortly after what I have called the mother's "betrayal," around age twelve or thirteen, when young Richard would have been moving into the swift currents of feelings that we call the reawakened Oedipus complex. All in all, he seems to have navigated these currents with relative success, being able to "let go" of his mother and to take on the role of his father. There was, of course, a price to be paid psychically, if not outwardly. For one thing, he must always have been haunted by the sense that he too might fail.

What is the evidence in back of such an early speculation? Mazo and Hess tell us how Richard's father served as inspiration for his decision to become a lawyer and to go into politics. Incensed by the Teapot Dome Scandal, Frank Nixon "became increasingly livid over each new disclosure in the sensational theft of government oil reserves through the connivance of principles [*sic*] in President Harding's administration. His diatribes against 'crooked politicians' and 'crooked lawyers' dominated the family conversation for weeks and provoked twelve-year-old Richard to abandon the romance of railroading for a more idealized road to greatness. His mother was the first to be told of the decision. She recalls that the boy declared 'I will be an old-fashioned kind of lawyer, a lawyer who can't be bought.' Donald, the third Nixon boy and Richard's junior by two years, believes his brother 'made up his mind to political life then and there, whether he realized it or not'" (M-H, 11). We can also see that the father's diatribes against "crooked politicians" corresponded closely to the mature Richard Nixon's attacks on "corruption." In Watergate, later, Nixon was to reject his father's judgment, possibly in a vain effort, as it turned out, to avoid his father's pattern of failure.

More revealing than the Mazo–Hess account were Richard Nixon's own statements in *Six Crises*. Noting that "the last thing my mother, a devout Quaker, wanted me to do was go into the *warfare of politics*" (my italics),[14] Nixon explains that there were "two major reasons for my competitive drive." One was economic (the necessity to win a scholarship in order to go to college), the other personal:

> The personal factor was contributed by my father. Because of illness in his family he had had to leave school after only six years of formal education. Never a day went by when he did not tell me and my four brothers how fortunate we were to be able to go to school. I was determined not to let him down. My biggest thrill in those years was to see the light in his eyes when I brought home a good report card. He loved the excitement and the battles of political life. During the two years he was bedridden before his death (which came just at the start of the 1956 campaign) his one request of me was that I send him the *Congressional Record*. He used to read it daily, cover-to-cover, something I never had the patience to do. I have often thought that with his fierce competitive drive and his intense interest in political issues, he might have been more successful than I in political life had he had the opportunity to continue his education. [N, 318]

In many ways, this was perhaps the most revealing of the rare revelations of Richard Nixon in *Six Crises*. We have honest affect. Let us analyze it. "I was determined not to let him down." Here we have Nixon redeeming his unsuccessful father. There are also strong guilt feelings in this account. The father awakens guilt in his sons by telling them how fortunate they are to have what he did *not* have: education. Yet Richard could overcome this guilt (and the resentment he must have felt at the accusation), as well as the natural guilt at doing better than his father, by offering excuses for the latter's failure. Frank Nixon had had to leave school because of family illness, and *this* had kept him from being successful. Moreover, Nixon concludes that *if* his father had had the same educational opportunities as he, Richard, his fierce competitive "drive and interest" in political issues would have made him even more successful than the future president of the United States. Hence, Nixon was not really displacing and exceeding his father—the dangerous fantasied Oedipal victory—but, by identification with him, merely doing in his person what his father would have accomplished, given the opportunities. As a result, Nixon could, with a good heart, follow his father, forsaking his mother in this crucial matter, into the "warfare of politics."

Hannah Milhous, a dedicated Quaker, was strongly pacifist. Her psychological dominance over her husband manifested itself here too, it would seem, when he gave up his forebears' "Bible-pounding" Methodism and, once married, embraced her faith. The children then were all raised as Quakers, and this fact had great influence in Richard Nixon's life. His attitudes toward political "warfare" and feelings about aggressive impulses were obviously influenced by his religious background (and this will require special study in itself later). So were many of his friendships and personal relations.

Initially, Nixon was most influenced by his mother's version of Quakerism, presumably akin in its idealism and pacifism to that found among Philadelphia Quakers. Gradually, it appears, he swung over to his father's watered-down version, which corresponded much more to the "informality and emotionalism" of the frontier Quakerism generally to be found in California.[15] In this form, it was hardly distinguishable from a sort of fundamentalism. Interestingly enough, Nixon definitely cast his lot with his father's reversion to "Bible-pounding" in a conversion episode at which his mother was not present. As Nixon tells it, "I remember vividly the day just after I entered high school, when my father took me and my two brothers to Los Angeles to attend the great revival meetings being held there by the Chicago evangelist, Dr. Paul Rader. We joined hundreds of others that night in making our personal commitments to Christ and Christian service."[16]

It is also interesting to note that Nixon revealed this episode (unmentioned by Mazo and Hess) in the November 1962 issue of Billy Graham's monthly magazine *Decision,* thus showing that his fundamentalist "commitment" still held. Such a commitment would drastically color not only Nixon's emotional life but his cognitive beliefs. That Billy Graham was Nixon's first preacher in the White House, that he preached at the funeral of Nixon's mother, Hannah, in 1967 (had she changed her views? would she have approved?), that Nixon was one of his original sponsors in 1965 for his New York rally, and that Nixon appeared at a number of Graham rallies, including the grand finale of his last New York "crusade" are all facts that support the contention.

Yet Nixon, in general, did not wear his religion on his sleeve. Although we are told that as a boy "he and his family attended one form of service or another four times on Sunday and several times during the week" (M-H, 17), the mature Nixon did not attend church regularly. Religion, if we judge by his account in *Six Crises,* seems not to have played a role, except as a general ethical inspiration, during his crucial encounters. In short, outwardly, Nixon is not a deeply religious man.[17]

What was the inward significance of his religious training and convictions? We have almost no data here; what little we had allowed us to postulate that a significant attitude toward authority (along with the ambivalence to aggressive impulses mentioned earlier) emerged from Nixon's religious background.

Our clue comes from his relationship with and approval of Billy Graham. Graham's views on "authority" were apparent in such quotations as "Man rebelled against God, and so he was separated from God by sin" and "The human race was made for the control of God, and young people are made for the control of their parents"; and in his statement, made to an organization of Protestant policemen in New York, paraphrasing a section from Romans 13 on the obligation to submit to authority (and substituting the word "policeman" for "authorities"): "the Bible teaches that the policeman is an agent and servant of God, and the authority that he has is given to him not only by the city and the state but is given to him by Almighty God."[18]

I am not suggesting that Nixon and Graham are totally alike, although there are a number of unusual similarities in their background. Both came from deeply religious families, with the mother being most devout; both had fathers (Graham's, incidentally, though named William Franklin Graham, Sr., was also known as Frank) who had less education and "breeding" than their wives and sons; both had "conversion" episodes in their high school years, and so on. The key difference seems to be that Billy Graham strenuously rebelled in his early years and then, in adolescence, gave in *completely* to "God the Father." Nixon neither rebelled nor, as a result, bowed so totally before authority. It seems, in fact, that he never questioned it. (Or has all of the data on his rebellion simply been passed over in silence?)

One curious line in the Mazo–Hess account further related to this problem of attitude toward authority. "Richard," they tell us, "took his spankings without a whimper" (M-H, 10). I would certainly have passed by this line without a second thought—after all, parents were less inhibited about physical punishment in Nixon's generation—except for my attention being drawn to the role of whippings in Graham's life. Autobiographical information about Graham is filled with stories of the harsh whippings given him by his father. "If I broke a rule," Graham reports, "believe me, Father never hesitated. Off came his belt. Mother preferred a long hickory switch. I had literally hundreds of whippings until I was thirteen or fourteen."[19] Billy Graham's powerful spirit, and physique, ultimately buckled to the "rightness" of punishing authority. What of Nixon? Was he at any time a rebellious child who needed repeated spankings? Who exercised this "authority," his father or mother? Until what age? The impression we are given is that Nixon's "tussle" with authority was never, at any point, traumatic. He simply accepted the structure of things as they were. But we cannot be sure. There is general agreement that the father, Frank Nixon, was given to fits of anger and irritability, and spanked his sons. Whether Hannah also spanked them is unclear, though doing so would seem out of character for her. Whether his father actually whipped Richard is also unclear, as the following passages from Kornitzer indicate: "Frank's rigid and uncompromising attitude, not only toward politics but toward life in general, made life hard for his family. 'He would not hesitate using the strap or rod on the boys when they did wrong,' Hannah says, 'although I don't remember that he ever spanked Richard.'" When asked directly, Richard Nixon told Kornitzer, "'Dad played no favorites with us . . . when you got into mischief, you had to be pretty convincing to avoid punishment. . . . He had a hot temper, and I learned early that the only way to deal with him was to abide by the rules he laid down. Otherwise, I would probably have felt the touch of a ruler or the strap as my brothers did.'"[20]

In any event, I am suggesting that Nixon's Quaker–fundamentalist religious background is undoubtedly important in explaining his attitude toward authority, though it must be placed in the context of his family's general mode of upbringing. While the picture is shadowy, we seem to see the outlines of a fairly placid development, with an easy and unrebellious identification with the father, and thus with authority.[21]

Nixon's Quakerism also figured, dramatically, in the Hiss case, which first brought him to prominence. Nixon became convinced that Chambers was telling the truth when the following incident occurred, as told to us in *Six Crises*. "I happened to mention the fact," Nixon tells us (but without telling us why he mentioned this particular fact),

> that I was a member of the Society of Friends. He said that he and his family attended the Friend's meeting in Westminster. He recalled that Mrs. Hiss, at the time he knew her, also had been a Friend.
>
> Then his eyes lit up, he snapped his fingers, and he said, "That reminds me of something. Priscilla often used the plain speech in talking to Alger at home."
>
> I knew from personal experience that my mother never used the plain speech in public but did use it in talking with her sisters and her mother in the privacy of our home. Again I recognized that someone else who knew Priscilla Hiss could have informed Chambers of this habit of hers. But the way he told me about it, rather than what he said, again gave me an intuitive feeling that he was speaking from first-hand rather than second-hand knowledge. [N, 24]

The coincidence of so many Quakers in the Hiss case is rather extraordinary, given the comparative rarity of Quakers in the United States. I cannot help suspecting that part of the intensity of Nixon's involvement in the case was a partial identification with Chambers, against Alger Hiss, the insolent representative of the Eastern Establishment. Thus, Nixon described Chambers as "a thoughtful introspective man, careful with his words, speaking with what sounded like the ring of truth" (N, 3–4); and "like most men of quality, he made a deeper impression personally than he did in public" (N, 32). This sounds much like Nixon's vision of himself. In any event, in defending Chambers's "truthfulness," Nixon was attesting to his own belief in his Quaker past—and thus his own "truthfulness."

The setting in which family and religion exercised their influence on Nixon was rural and Californian. The attraction of the big city and the East became the counterpull to his life, and throughout, I believe, he manifested great ambivalence. In this, he mirrored the attitude of many of his fellow Americans.

The farming village in which Nixon was born, Yorba Linda, was about thirty miles inland from Los Angeles. Whittier, where he moved at about nine, was thirteen miles from Los Angeles. By 1937, when Nixon returned to Whittier to practice law, it had become a suburb of Los Angeles, with a population of about 25,000. As Mazo and Hess tell it, at that time "Nixon confided to a few intimates that he aimed sooner or later to get into a big city law practice" (M-H, 31).

Nixon's goal was not simply a "big city law practice"; it was, really, an Eastern city law practice. After graduation from Duke Law School, Nixon and two fellow seniors went job-hunting in New York. "They applied at practically all the well-known law offices," we are told. Nixon's "highest hope was to find a place with Sullivan and Cromwell, of which John Foster Dulles was a senior partner. Nixon recalls that he was attracted more by the 'thick, luxurious carpets and the fine oak paneling' of the Sullivan and Cromwell reception room than by the possibility of being a low-echelon associate of Dulles, however. 'If they had given me a job,' he said in 1958, 'I'm sure I would have been there today, a corporation lawyer instead of Vice-President'" (M-H, 22).

Nixon's two friends landed New York jobs, one with a distinguished law firm and the other with a large oil corporation. "Nixon got only an 'iffy' response from the Donovan firm" (M-H, 22). Then, after waiting for an FBI job that did not materialize, Nixon returned to Whittier to practice law. Nixon, clearly, had not made it on his first try. Psychologically, he must have perceived himself as, like his father, a failure. There was, therefore, much to atone for when he finally succeeded in his initial ambition, to be a big corporation lawyer, and took his place in 1963 as a senior partner in the Wall Street firm of Mudge, Stern. Ironically, it was only through his second choice, politics, that Nixon realized his boyhood dream.

Rural versus urban—this has been a perennial tension in American political life. As for Nixon, he was a "farm boy" who made good in the city. Yet the values that he started with and that are strongest in him are rural values (especially Protestant), and it is those that he brought into confrontation with his urban desires. We saw this ambivalence (it reminds one, in many ways, of Henry Ford's) in Nixon's Presidential Acceptance Speech of 1968, when he said, "I see a day when life in rural America attracts people to the country, rather than driving them away" (N, xiv).

So too, Nixon is a "Westerner," who finally made good up to a point in the East. (How good he was and how careful to hew to the pattern, we see in Nixon's sending his daughters to Finch and to Smith College and presenting them to society in a debutante ball, as well as in his own joining of prestigious New York men's clubs, such as the Metropolitan and the Links.)

Yet ambivalence about the Eastern Establishment undoubtedly ran deep in Nixon (as it did in Eisenhower). Some of this feeling must have been present in the encounter with Hiss, who was everything Nixon was not: in Nixon's own words, Hiss "had come from a fine family, had made an outstanding record at Johns Hopkins and Harvard Law, had been honored by being selected for the staff of a great justice of the Supreme Court" (N, 19), and so forth. Hiss, the embodiment of Eastern values, treated Nixon, the thirty-five-year-old freshman Congressman, like dirt. Nixon's chapter on the Hiss case is filled with statements about Hiss, such as "His manner was coldly courteous and, at times, almost condescending" (N, 7); "He was rather insolent toward me" (M-H, 48); and "his manner and tone were insulting in the extreme" (M-H, 52). If I am right that there was a partial identification with his fellow "failed" Quaker, Chambers, then the scorned Nixon's feelings must have been doubly outraged by the patrician Hiss. Obviously, Nixon had straightforward legal and political reasons for attacking Hiss as he did; I am only suggesting here that the passion and tenaciousness came from deeper sources.

There is a strange irony in the fact that, in the end, Nixon was rejected by his own state of California, in his traumatic 1962 defeat for governor (and largely on the grounds that he had deserted California and its interests for larger, more Eastern-oriented spheres). Only after finally succeeding in the East was he able to mount his winning campaign of 1968 for president.

To understand Nixon fully, one would need carefully to analyze the turbulent currents of Californian life, values, and politics. Its mixed Republican–Democratic politics, its evangelical setting in Los Angeles, its extremes of right-wing Birchites and left-wing Bohemians, all of this and more have shaped Nixon's perceptions and feelings.[22] Thus, in many ways, he is a "typical" southern Californian, only with a heightened ambivalence toward the Eastern Establishment.

One wonders, therefore, at the significance of Nixon's acquisition, as president, of a luxurious house in San Clemente, California. In that heavily Birchite county, in the exclusive Cyprus Shore community, Nixon bought himself a ten-room house and five acres for $340,000. Had he, figuratively speaking, returned "home," successful? It is interesting to note that his new house was only four miles away from his favorite restaurant at San Juan Capistrano where, we were told, "he dines at least once each time he comes here. It is a setting that evokes memories for the president and First Lady who dined there during their dating days thirty years ago." It is interesting, too, that there was a railroad track along the beach, below the house, "on which six trains pass daily between Los Angeles to San Diego to the South."[23] Did it remind the president of his boyhood dreams, associated with the Santa Fe Railroad line that ran past his house in Yorba Linda? As Mazo and Hess describe it, "Long freight trains rumbled past at all hours. The Nixon homestead shook and the throbbing stirred in Richard visions of faraway places" (M-H, 10).

Having gone far, Nixon could now afford to return home. Yet his comparable house in Key Biscayne, Florida, checked our thesis here and reminded us that Nixon still retained his ambivalence about the East. Part of his political strength and appeal, one suspected, was that he is a composite of the American dream, or at least the middle-class dream, about East and West. In Nixon the two met, even if they did not necessarily fuse psychologically.

Let us return now to the young Nixon. What strengths and weaknesses, of body and spirit, did he bring to his "socialization" process? The picture we are given is of a boy prone to illness and physically rather clumsy. Not only had he been vulnerable to illnesses since infancy, nearly dying of pneumonia when he was four, but in addition, "during his senior year at high school he had a severe attack of undulant fever. . . . He was absent much of that school year" (M-H, 10). He tended to "motion" sickness; he had hay fever; and he was constantly afraid of getting fat.

Once in college, Nixon worked hard to make the football team—unsuccessfully. "A classmate," Mazo and Hess tell us, "recalled that Dick had two left feet. He couldn't coordinate." At mealtime he was "too tensed up" to eat (M-H, 18-19). His wife, Pat Nixon, reminiscing about their courtship, remarked: "We liked to do active things like sports of different kinds. We were taking up ice skating, the artificial ice rinks had just opened up and it was the gay thing to do. But it was awful for Dick. He almost broke his head two or three times, but he still kept going" (M-H, 30).

Nixon seems to have made up in persistence and drive what he lacked in native ability. It was almost a classic case of compensation for inferiority, if we choose to use the Adlerian notion (especially as it has been taken up by Harold Lasswell[24]). Quiet, shy, Nixon became a source of inspiration to others. He seems to have been well liked by everybody. He became an "organizer" and a "doer": he helped form a new fraternity at Whittier College and was elected president of his freshman class; as a junior he organized dances and was active in student government and debate, and so on in the typical pattern of "campus leaders." As Pat Nixon recalled, "He was always president of some group . . . so I knew that he would be successful in whatever he undertook" (M-H, 30).

Nixon's real ability was verbal. He was a debater at Whittier, and this became his primary skill as a politician. Not very good at physical "warfare," he could release his aggressive feelings successfully in oratory. Another strength was the use of caution and planning. Lacking spontaneous coordination and the ability to react properly without thought, Nixon turned his weaknesses into strengths. As numerous observers have testified, Nixon "always played it cautious" (M-H, 33). This trait was combined with the decision to succeed where his father had drifted and failed, and we saw the result in the comment of a wartime friend that Nixon "was one guy who knew where he was going. Most of us had big, grandiose schemes. Dick's plans were concise, concrete and specific" (M-H, 33).

Thus, the mature Nixon compensated for the physical awkwardness and the propensity to sickness of the young Nixon by careful planning and reliance on verbal and organizing skills. In times of crisis, as he admitted on numerous occasions, he experienced all of the physical symptoms of tension: edginess, short temper, inability to eat and to sleep (N, 115). Were these symptoms especially prominent in Nixon, building on his earlier stresses and strains? Or are they normal to anyone in time of crisis? In any case, as Nixon tells us in *Six Crises,* he learned, painstakingly, to cope with his tensions and, as he sees it, to use them as a source of strength. The pattern throughout was constant: weakness and failure turned into strength and success by dint of sheer persistence and hard work. Later, after the devastating rejection in his loss of the presidency, he would seek to reestablish his reputation as a statesman through books and a judicious public role.

The other outstanding trait of the young Nixon was that he was a daydreamer. It sits in rather odd combination with the hard worker; but there it is as a persistent theme in Nixon's life, probably accounting for much of his reputation as an introspective thinker. Young Nixon, we are informed by Mazo and Hess, "preferred daydreams to anything else on earth" (M-H, 10). His constant daydream as a child concerned traveling to far-off places. Even more specifically, he dreamed of becoming "a railroad man." Was this a heightened and successful version of his father's experience as a motorman? In any case, Nixon held onto this dream, in spite of his mother's wishes that he become a musician or a preacher, practically until he was in high school. Then, as we have seen, inspired by his father's diatribes against competitive politicians, he switched to the ambition of becoming a lawyer-politician.

Still, the dream sequence persisted. Even as a successful politician, vice-president of the United States, Nixon played with a daydream, though this time in terms of a denial:

> I suppose this would make a better story if I could fit the facts of my life into the Great American Legend as to how presidential candidates are born and made.
>
> The legend goes something like this. A mother takes a child on her knees. She senses by looking into his eyes that there is something truly extraordinary about him. She says to herself and perhaps even to him, "You, son, are going to be President some day." From that time on, he is tapped for greatness. He talks before he walks. He reads a thousand words a minute. He is bored by school because he is so much smarter than his teachers. He prepares himself for leadership by taking courses in public speaking and political science. He drives ever upward, calculating every step of the way until he reaches his and—less importantly—the nation's destiny by becoming President of the United States.
>
> So goes the legend. The truth in my case is not stranger than fiction perhaps—but it may be more believable. [N, 317]

Nixon's dream of becoming a railroad engineer was "not because of any interest in engines (I have no mechanical aptitude whatever)," he tells us, but because he wanted "to travel and see the United States and the world" (N, 317). When he changed his daydream to lawyer-politician—"I will be an old fashioned kind of lawyer, a lawyer who can't be bought," he fantasied at age twelve—the "Great American Legend" was the dream he should have had but did not.

It was however, the dream that came true for Nixon. There is an extraordinary passage in his Acceptance Speech of 1968 to the Republican Convention, where Nixon links his own dream life to the Great American Dream. It is worth quoting the whole passage. First, he talks of all children:

> Tonight, I see the face of a child.
>
> He lives in a great city. He is black. He is white. He is Mexican, Italian, Polish. None of this matters. What does matter is that he is an American child.
>
> That child is more important than any politician's promise. He is America. He is a poet, a scientist, a great teacher, a proud craftsman. He is everything we have ever hoped to be and everything we dare to dream to be.
>
> He sleeps the sleep of childhood and dreams its dreams. Yet when he awakens, he awakens to a living nightmare of poverty, neglect and despair.

He fails in school.

He ends up on welfare.

For him the American system is one that feeds his stomach and starves his soul. It breaks his heart. And in the end it may take his life on some distant battlefield.

To millions of children in this rich land, this is their prospect for the future. [N, xv]

Then Nixon talks of himself.

I see another child.

He hears the train go by at night and dreams of faraway places he would like to go.

It seems like an impossible dream.

But he is helped on his journey through life.

A father who had to go to work before he finished the sixth grade, sacrificed everything so that his sons could go to college.

A gentle, Quaker mother, with a passionate concern for peace, quietly wept when he went to war but understood why he had to go.

A great teacher, a remarkable football coach, an inspirational minister encouraged him on his way.

A courageous wife and loyal children stood by him in victory and defeat.

In his chosen profession of politics, first scores, then hundreds, then thousands, and finally millions worked for his success.

Tonight he stands before you—nominated for President of the United States.

You can see why I believe so deeply in the American Dream.

For most of us the American Revolution has been won; the American Dream has come true. [N, xv–xvi]

At the end, Nixon exhorts his listeners, "I ask you to help me make that dream come true for millions to whom it is an impossible dream today. This is the cause in which we enlist tonight" (N, xvi). There is, in fact, a dream-like quality to the whole passage. Nixon had just been made his party's candidate with the support of Southern politicians, such as Senators John Tower and Strom Thurmond, and was about to select Spiro Agnew of Maryland as his vice-president; yet he holds out the American Dream of everyone a potential president to a "black" child, too. He speaks of his Quaker mother, with a passionate concern for *peace,* and then employs the military term *enlist.* He talks of the American Revolution to a party that dreads revolution of any sort. The sacrificial father, the weeping mother, the land of equal opportunity, they are all there in a dream landscape of Amer-

216

ica. One can only assume that Nixon's daydreams became a dominant means by which he perceived selected aspects of reality.[25]

On the way to becoming a successful lawyer-politician, Nixon claims to have started as a "liberal" and ended as a "conservative." According to Mazo and Hess, "Nixon classified himself as 'liberal' in college, 'but not a flaming liberal.' Like many law students of that period, his public heroes were Justice Brandeis, Cardozo and Hughes" (M-H, 22). Once in Washington, D.C., however, working for the OPA, Nixon apparently experienced a "conversion" (though Nixon's immediate superior recalls he was "very quiet, self-effacing, conservative" [M-H, 32], from the beginning). Nixon's own account is as follows:

> "I came out of college more liberal than I am today, more liberal in the sense that I thought it was possible for government to do more than I later found it was practical to do. . . . I became greatly disillusioned about bureaucracy and about what the government could do because I saw the terrible paper work that people had to go through. I also saw the mediocrity of so many civil servants. And for the first time when I was in OPA I also saw that there were people in government who were not satisfied merely with interpreting the regulations, enforcing the law that Congress passed, but who actually had a passion to get business and used their government jobs to that end. There were of course some of the remnants of the old, violent New Deal crowd. They set me to thinking a lot at that point." In the OPA, Nixon said, he learned first-hand how "political appointees at the top feathered their nests with all kinds of overlapping and empire building." [M-H, 32]

How can we explain what happened? On the most obvious level, Nixon had come to identify the "corrupt politicians" of his father's wrath with the "old, violent New Deal crowd." Is there anything more to this episode? Further research will probably help answer this question. At the time I suggested a psychological line of inquiry to use in relation to future information. It emerged from a consideration by a psychologist, Lawrence F. Schiff, of a number of case studies of what he calls "Dynamic Young Fogies—Rebels on the Right." Schiff studies the conversion to conservatism as it occurs at adolescence, and sets up two categories: where the conversion occurs (1) immediately following puberty (between twelve and seventeen) and (2) in late adolescence (beyond seventeen).

Of this second category, I quote Schiff:

> The late converts—whom I call "the obedient rebels"—were the ones most representative of campus conservative activists. Typically they were from homes very much concerned with high status and achievement. In almost all cases their early experiences were dominated by a determined parent, or parents, with detailed and ambitious expectations for their children. All but one were eldest or only sons and the burden of parental ambition fell on them. The obedient rebels (at least in the early years and again after conversion) were usually considered the "good boys" of their families.
>
> Each "rebelled"—sometimes because he felt he could not live up to or realize himself under such pressure—or departed to some degree from the path set out for him. But the revolt was not without peril. Suddenly he would be horrified to discover (on the campus, in the armed services, or among the lower-classes) that he was surrounded by "radicalism," "immorality," or personal hardship—something for which his comfortable background had not prepared him. He would reject the new environment totally and become converted to a conservatism not much different from the one he had left in the first place—but which, superficially at least, he had accepted on his own initiative and conviction.
>
> Psychologically, in essence, his conversion was a reaction to the threat of genuine personality change—which allows great creative possibilities, but also involves dangers. In effect he had come to the pit of change, looked down into it, and turned back, rejecting all alternatives beyond the reaffirmation of obedience.[26]

Did something conformable to this pattern happen to Nixon in Washington, D.C.? Do we recognize a familiar note in Schiff's account of one of his case studies: "Herron's conversion took place while he was stationed abroad in the Navy. Disturbed by the 'slothfulness' and 'self-indulgent habits' of the local citizenry, he had a sudden realization of 'the consequences of not subscribing to a strict moral code.'"[27] Is this where any potential "rebellion" against authority became grounded and harmless in the case of Nixon? All we can now say with certainty is that Nixon experienced some sort of significant reassertion of conservative beliefs while in the big city of Washington, D.C.

We are used to anthropologists studying the courtship patterns of small societies; surely, with even more justification, psychologists ought to study the courtship pattern of individuals. Above all, a man's marriage tells us much about him, as well as helping to shape what he will be in the future. Thus, Richard Nixon's courtship and marriage to Pat Ryan reveal more than might appear at first glance.

Before he met his future wife, we are told, Nixon had neither time nor money to be a ladies' man. According to Mazo and Hess, "He dated the daughter of the local police chief steadily before going east to law school [if only *her* memoirs were available], and at Duke he attended occasional dances as a stag" (M-H, 26).[28] Once back in Whittier, as a struggling lawyer, he attended a tryout for a Little Theatre play. There he met Catherine Patricia Thelma Ryan, a new schoolteacher of commercial subjects.

Pat Ryan, two months younger than Nixon, had been born in Plymouth, Nevada. Her father was a miner, who moved his family to California (about eighteen miles from Los Angeles) and took up farming. Everyone in the family worked together, and the picture we have of their life then is a very pleasant one. When Pat was twelve, her mother died, and the young girl took on the responsibility for the house. Her father died five years later. Graduating from high school, Pat worked in the local bank for a year, went East with relatives for a year or so (working during that time in a hospital near New York), and returned to Los Angeles to attend the University of Southern California. To earn money, she took bit parts in movies, though her real love was the field of merchandising. More money in a teaching job unexpectedly caused her to shift vocation and to come to Whittier. A friend trying out for a Little Theatre play persuaded her to come along. Here occurred her "fated" meeting with Richard Nixon.

That very night Nixon proposed. Mazo and Hess report Pat as saying, "I thought he was nuts or something. I guess I just looked at him. I couldn't imagine anyone ever saying anything like that so suddenly. Now that I know Dick much better I can't imagine that he would ever say that, because he is very much the opposite, he's more reserved" (M-H, 27). Though she admired him from the beginning, she was in no mood to settle down; she had visions of travel, she tells us. But Richard Nixon persisted. We have already seen how he was prepared to break his neck ice skating. He took up dancing. While Pat kept dating, Nixon gave up all other dates (no real sacrifice on his part). We are given the extraordinary information by Mazo and Hess that "he hung around dutifully even when she had other dates and would drive her to Los Angeles if she was to meet someone there, and wait around to take her home" (M-H, 29) (what did her other swains think of that?). Finally, in the spring of 1940, Pat said yes and they were married on June 21, 1940.

What is the significance and meaning of Nixon's courtship? The first thing to notice is his unusual impulsive behavior: proposing to Pat Ryan on their first meeting. It seems, as it did later to Pat, "out of character." I suspect that it was not, that it just appears impulsive and out of character. Given the general pattern of Nixon's behavior—cautious, planned, and contrived—we are on better ground postulating his proposal to Pat not as an impulsive exception but as part of a "plan," even though perhaps an unconscious one, as to the girl he wished to marry. We have already seen his propensity to daydream. I suspect plan and dream came together in the person of Pat Ryan, and Nixon acted accordingly, with complete deliberation. Persistence did the rest.

The second thing to notice about his conquest of Pat Ryan is that it was his first real success. At about the time of meeting Pat, Nixon had helped set up the Citra-Frost Co. to market frozen orange juice, which, apparently through no fault of his, folded after a year and a half. Earlier, as we have seen, he had failed to secure a job in an Eastern law firm. Failure to have won Pat Ryan would have been a tremendous blow on top of the others; success undoubtedly gave him a great uplift. As Freud has remarked (and I paraphrase), "To win the girl of one's dream is to have the feeling that all of nature is on one's side."

Moreover, and this is the third point to notice, Pat Nixon undoubtedly brought Nixon real strength. In the pattern of his own parents, in fact, she seemed the stronger of the two. Loyally, she stood by him through failure and success. Patiently, she worked in his campaigns. There is some evidence that she would have preferred some other life than the political—the attack on the Nixons, culminating in the "Checkers speech" of 1952, especially seems to have soured her, and she even prevailed upon Nixon to write out a decision to retire from politics after his term as vice-president ended in 1957 and to pack this note into his wallet—but always she followed where he led. Yet even Nixon admitted that she was the more decisive and stronger of the two. It was Pat who insisted, in the 1952 fund controversy, that Nixon could not resign under fire. Three minutes before he was to make his famous talk, Nixon tells us, he turned to Pat and said, "'I just don't think I can go through with this one.' 'Of course you can,' she said, with the firmness and confidence in her voice that I so desperately needed" (N, 120). In the campaign of 1960, Nixon informs us that "her physical stamina had been even greater than mine. In the long hand-shaking sessions, it was I, rather than she, who would first have to ask for a break in the line" (N, 404). In Caracas and in Moscow, Pat Nixon showed similar sangfroid and decisiveness.

Thus, in marrying Pat, Nixon gained great strength, both in her and in the affirmation of his own possibilities for success that lay in her acquiescence in his persistence and determination. Moreover, insofar as Pat would embody some of the qualities of his mother (and we assume a certain amount of transference here, as in all such relations), it also meant approval and acceptance of his decision to enter the "warfare of politics."

Before we leave the years of Nixon's youthful and young manhood character formation and enter into a consideration of his political patterns of behavior and belief, we need to look briefly at another element in his makeup: acting. Nixon's career as an actor began at Whittier College. We are told that he collaborated in writing his fraternity's first play, a "shocker" entitled *The Trysting Place* and was its director and male lead. And we already know that he met Pat Ryan at a Little Theatre tryout. Such facts make us look twice at the picture of Nixon as a shy, introspective boy.

There is a most interesting comment on his acting ability made by one of his Whittier teachers, on seeing Nixon weeping on Senator Knowland's shoulder after the Checker speech: "'I taught him how to cry,' said Dr. Upton, 'in a play by John Drinkwater called *Bird in Hand*. He tried conscientiously at rehearsals, and he'd get a pretty good lump in his throat and that was all. But on the evenings of performance tears just ran right out of his eyes. It was beautifully done, those tears'" (M-H, 19).[29]

Nixon obviously learned his lesson well, and in later life he rose to the occasions. For a "strong" man, it is strange how often he breaks down in tears. Thus, we are told that on the evening of his Checkers speech, "when a 'Have Faith' message was handed him from his mother, Nixon stepped into a vacant room to hide his tears" (M-H, 109) (how, one wonders, was this observed?). After his speech itself—one of the most sentimental political speeches in all of American history, embarrassing even to many of Nixon's partisans—"when he reached the dressing room, Nixon turned away from his friends and let loose the tears he had been holding back" (M-H, 120). When Eisenhower put his arm around Nixon, "Nixon turned his head to the window and tried to keep back the tears" (M-H, 123). Nixon explained his various effusions by saying that he cried because he had exhausted all of his "emotional reserve" (N, 132). In the Introduction to *Six Crises,* he claims that "I have found leaders are subject to all the human frailties. . . . Sometimes even strong men will cry" (N, xxvii).[30]

Nixon is right in his analysis of leaders. But the words of Dr. Upton, "It was beautifully done, those tears," cast a strange light on Nixon's Rousseau-like performances. Certainly, Nixon himself felt he was an authority on when other people were acting, and this "intuition" on his part seems to play an important role in much of his political activity. For example, he frequently talked about the Hiss case as if it were a sort of stage play, a momentous soap opera. The stage itself is set for the Hiss-Chambers confrontation at the Commodore Hotel in New York. Nixon even remembers the "decor": "The living room was decorated with Audubon prints," and, he concludes, "We then proceeded to set up the room" (M-H, 51–52).

The "actors" play out their roles. In an earlier interview, Nixon tells how he became convinced that Chambers was telling the truth: "His [Chambers'] voice broke and there was a pause of at least 15 to 20 seconds during which he attempted to gain control of his emotions before he could proceed. This one incident was to have a considerable bearing upon my own attitude toward him because I did not feel that it was an *act*. . . . On the contrary, I felt he indicated deep sincerity and honesty" (M-H, 45–46; my italics). Hiss, on the contrary, now comes through as a ham actor: "I felt he had *put on a show* when he was shown a picture of Chambers . . . his statement 'This might look like you, Mr. Chairman,' seemed to me to be *overacted*" (M-H, 48; my italics). According to Nixon, this hearing "showed the committee the *real* Hiss because, except for a few minutes at the beginning and . . . end . . . he *acted* the part of a liar who had been caught, rather than the part of the outraged innocent man, which he had so successfully portrayed before then" (M-H, 52; my italics).

Nixon's own "performances" were obviously far more professional. After his emotional Checkers speech, he received a phone call from Darryl Zanuck, the Hollywood producer: "The most tremendous performance I've ever seen" was the comment of this professional (M-H, 120). Now one does not have to equate Nixon with Hiss—I, for one, have no doubt that Nixon was "clear" of the corruption charges leveled against him, while the evidence against Hiss was very strong—to realize that Nixon's training in acting must have stood him in good stead during his performance. Nixon seemed to have sensed this himself, when he remarked in disgust about the televised Army–McCarthy hearings: "I prefer professionals to amateur actors" (M-H, 137–138).

Even in the international arena, with foreign-language-speaking politicians, Nixon felt he could distinguish between acting and sincerity. Speaking of Khrushchev's reaction to the Captive Nations Resolution, asking for prayer for the liberating of "enslaved people," passed by Congress just before Nixon's trip, he said, "I was sure that he was going through an *act*— that he was using the resolution as a pretext for taking the offensive against me" (N, 271; my italics). Nixon also told of speaking to Zhukov about the behavior of the Soviet police and crowds: "'Mr. Zhukov,' I said, 'this little game you've been playing with me through your planted hecklers for the past few days has not been going well with the press, and in my opinion it is backfiring even among your own people. You underestimate their intelligence. They aren't dumb. They know when somebody is acting and when it is the real thing—particularly when the acts have been so amateurish'" (N, 299–300).

Constantly, then, Nixon was concerned with acting. At one point, he informs us that, during the 1960 campaign, his problem was to hold the Republican vote (the minority party) and then persuade 5–6 million Democrats to leave their own candidate and vote Republican. "I recognized that I could accomplish this only as President Eisenhower had—by *acting* [Nixon means this in the sense of "action," but the other meaning inheres in it] and speaking not just as a Republican partisan but as a representative of all the people. My trips to Caracas and Moscow had provided an opportunity for me to appear in this *role*" (N, 326; my italics). Nixon's highest praise for the campaigning of his wife, Pat, is that she was "a good trouper" (N, 137).

Of course, all American politicians must play many "roles," and "act" many parts. Moreover, Nixon's own Thespian experiences may have given him greater empathy for the "acts" of the Hisses and Khrushchevs whom he encountered on the political stage. However, Nixon's empathy may also carry a good deal of projection with it. The one thing we can be sure of is that Nixon's attitude to acting is more significant and more conscious than that of most politicians. It does give rise, in fact, to a suspicion that the "real" Richard Nixon may by now have been lost in the variety of "roles" in which he had acted. As with other professional actors, the man becomes his roles—and that is his character.

With this postulated, one would then have to add that Nixon's acting probably served extremely important political functions. A leader must communicate effectively with his followers: Nixon obviously "reached" through the new medium of television a large segment of the American population, especially the middle class. His ability to play a role lent itself to the pragmatic politics so typical of America; Nixon, unlike Sir Thomas More, was, in fact, a "man for all seasons." Thus, whatever ideological commitments inhered in Nixon's personality development, they were severely tempered by his devotion to "acting."

A word must also be said of a close cousin of Nixon's acting abilities: his skill as a debater. As with his acting experience, this, too, seems to have started in college. It first became politically important for Nixon in his 1946 Congressional campaign against the incumbent Jerry Voorhis. In all, the two men had five debates, and, according to Mazo and Hess, Nixon believed "the turning point for him, as the underdog, was the first debate. 'It was tough,' Nixon says. 'I was the challenger, and he was the experienced incumbent. Once that debate was over, I was on my way to eventual victory'" (M-H, 39).

In the light of this debate, we must look at his more famous debates with John F. Kennedy in the 1960 election. Why did Nixon, then, so to speak, in Voorhis's position as an "incumbent," agree to debate the relatively unknown Kennedy? "'He [Nixon] had no reason to help build up an audience for Kennedy,' Sorenson wrote" (M-H, 234). The explanation Nixon gave— that the other people wanted the debates—is weak. Mazo and Hess grasp the truth when they write:

> But there seems to us to be another, perhaps overpowering, reason why Nixon chose to debate, namely, *he was convinced he could win.* Nixon's whole career led him to this conclusion—he had been elected to Congress by outdebating his opponent in 1946; he had stayed on the ticket in 1952 by his effective use of television; he reached his highest popularity after the "Kitchen Debate" with Khrushchev in 1959. Now by combining debating and television he could impress millions of Democrats and independents (whom he could not otherwise reach) and put the election on ice. [M-H, 234–235]

Clearly, Nixon believed intensely in his own verbal and acting skills. He had built much of his political career on it. How, then, could he consider for a moment that he would "lose" with his own choice of weapons to Kennedy?

I believe another reason is that Nixon is the sort of person who constantly has to test himself, in order to quiet his self-doubts and the continuous threat of failure. In the *Six Crises* he offers us his reason for accepting the Kennedy debates. "Had I refused the challenge, I would have opened myself to the charge that I was *afraid* to defend the Administration's and my own record" (N, 348; my italics). It is interesting, too, to note that in his unnecessary and disastrous press conference after his 1962 gubernatorial defeat, Nixon placed his relations with the press on an agonistic basis, saying, "You've had an opportunity to attack me and I think I've given as good as I've taken. I have welcomed the opportunity *to test wits with you*" (M-H, 281–282; my italics). Thus, in his formal debates, as well as reports and encounters, Nixon could give way to his aggressive impulses at the same time as he was testing himself. Making full use of his verbal and acting skills in debate provided a wonderful release, with an extremely high chance of a successful outcome. It is no wonder that Nixon fancied himself as a debater and a performer.

What was the content of Nixon's political debates? His reputation, as we know, was based on his "anti-Communist" positions, and these need now to be examined. We must start with a paradox: Though Nixon came, as a congressman, from an isolationist district, he quickly showed himself an internationalist in orientation. Thus, he worked on the Herter Committee, whose report led to the Marshall Plan, and considered this the most important service of his congressional career. From the very beginning of his political life, Nixon showed his inclination toward the Eastern Establishment and its internationalist position.

But Nixon gave it a very special twist, combining it with a Western fundamentalist attack on communism. In vehemently attacking communism, Nixon was defending Americanism. Indeed, one could then define the latter by the former action. It allowed for the luxury of polarizing feelings, so that total hate could flow out to the enemy and total love to one's "own" people. Yet, as we shall see at the end, there is a certain strange identification with the "enemy," the "Devil," which must be strenuously denied.

We must remember throughout this discussion, however, the context in which Nixon operated. The late 1940s saw the beginning of the cold war. Although *domestic* communism was not an issue in the 1948 election, it became one thereafter and was linked, by Nixon and others, with the sensitive theme of corruption—in the fund controversy, for example, Nixon defended himself by saying, "I was warned that if I continued to attack the Communists and crooks in this [Truman's] Government, they would continue to smear me" (M-H, 103). After 1948, threats of recession, the outbreak of the Korean War, and all of the other Russo-American developments supplied the background of fear in which anticommunism flourished. Nixon was merely a "typical" American in much of his position.

Nixon's anticommunism first publicly manifested itself in his debates with Congressman Voorhis. Nixon attacked him as a front-man for the "Communist-dominated PAC" and suggested that he was one of those "lip-service Americans . . . who front for un-American elements, wittingly, or otherwise, by advocating increasing federal controls over the lives of the people" (M-H, 39, 40). (Here, incidentally, we see a trace of Nixon's OPA "conversion" experience, now linked to anticommunism.) In opposition to Voorhis's "un-Americanism," Nixon resorted to the sentimental promise "to preserve our sacred heritage in the name of my buddies and your loved ones, who died that these might endure." One wonders whether Nixon believed his own statement following his victory: "Our campaign was a very honest debate on the issues" (M-H, 40, 41).

225

In any case, the pattern of Nixon's "warfare of politics" was set. He tried to narrow his senatorial campaign of 1950, against Mrs. Helen Gahagan Douglas, to one issue, "simply the choice between freedom and state socialism" (M-H, 65) and implied that the latter also meant pro-Russian communism. Nixon, of course, pictured himself as the warrior preserving the American way of life. It was a rough campaign, and, on top of the Voorhis contest, left Nixon with the image of "Tricky Dicky," a rabid anti-Communist who did not hesitate to use the same tactics of smear and simplification that he accused the Communists of using. Indeed, one wonders if mammoth projection were not at work in Nixon. Was he in fact defending against his own evil impulses by imputing them all to some other?

Did Nixon believe in what he said, or was his anticommunism largely a matter of practical politics, a convenient way to win? One suspects a good deal of both. In any case, there was strong personal feeling in Nixon's view of the "enemy." On his Latin American trip in 1958, he talked of the "Communist bully" (N, 223) and described his reaction to the Caracas attack on him as "a feeling of *absolute hatred* for the rough Communist agitators who were driving children to this irrational state" (N, 235; my italics). He further talked about "the ruthlessness and determination, the fanaticism of the enemy that we face. That was what I saw in the faces of the mob. *This is really Communism as it is*" (M-H, 177; my italics).

One cannot help asking what Nixon actually knew about Marxism. (Should we take seriously his comment that "I do not presume to be an expert, and only the experts on Communism, who are sprouting up all over the landscape these days, have single, simple solutions for the problem" [N, 311], even though Nixon then betrayed his own words by offering rather simple solutions to, and simplifications of, communism?) Did he ever, then or later, meet any of the leading Marxist theoreticians of Latin America? Did he ever think of comparing lynch mobs in the North American South with the Caracas mob he faced, and realize that one cannot characterize a whole political setting by such incidents, or if one can, that both must be characterized equally? Nixon's view of communism, of course, was primarily "dramatic" and thus did not allow for such subtleties. His attitude toward communism is best shown when, in relation to the Hiss case and the meeting in the Commodore Hotel, he told his television audience, "Let me describe the room for you, because it is here that you can see the Communist conspiracy in action . . . twisting and turning and squirming . . . evading and avoiding" (M-H, 59).

Nixon could not, at least in this stage of his life, envision communism as anything *but* mob action and individual conspiracy. Can we, however, place this attitude in a larger context? Social scientists have tried to isolate the characteristics of what they have called an "authoritarian personality," and to analyze the belief system of a hater, such as Adolf Hitler.[31] It is worth looking at Nixon's anticommunism in such terms. What are the images that he used? Whatever the reality (and there was certainly some), the extreme concentration on this aspect of communism bears traces of paranoid fear. For Nixon, communism is also an "infection," which can reach almost everyone. It is like the plague, hidden and unsuspected but capable of striking anyone. As Nixon said of Chambers and Hiss, "They were both idealists. Yet, here are two men of this quality who became infected with Communism, infected with it to the degree that they were willing to run the risk, as they did, of disgrace in order to serve the Communist conspiracy. The fact that this could happen to them shows the potential threat that Communism presents among people of this type throughout the world" (M-H, 62).

Communism, of course, could correctly be described as "aggressive international Communism . . . on the loose in the world," "an insidious evil." It was engaged in "infiltration of the American government" (N, 2, 3, 4). Nixon's only objection to Joe McCarthy's question, "Why worry about being fair when you are shooting rats?" was that you must shoot straight because wild shooting means some of the rats will get away (M-H, 137). (And rats carry plague, and plague means infection.) The adjective "Communist" is different, but the images of infection and conspiracy are images similar to those used by many in Nazi Germany to describe the international and domestic "influence" of the Jews.[32]

How much of the paranoiac fears that some members of the Nazi movement defended against by these projections and displacements of their own impulses onto the Jews was shared by the early Nixon (though, needless to say, not against the Jews) is a question to be decided only by the prior decision as to how much of his rhetoric was motivated "purely" by political factors. We saw Nixon, who constantly smeared *his* political opponents, accusing his enemies—Communists and crooks—of smearing him. So too, we wonder about his accusation that his Democratic opponents are "a group of ruthless, cynical seekers after power" (M-H, 66). The pattern of projection in Nixon ran strong, at least in the early years.[33]

Yet we must balance this knowledge with the knowledge that Nixon began to have a different view of communism, based on his visit to Moscow and his encounters with *Russian* Communists, and later, with Chinese Communists. While he still insisted that "the Communist threat is indivisible . . . universal" (N, 312), by 1968 he was prepared to say that "the

Communists are a very pragmatic people" (M-H, 312). This is an especially interesting statement in the light of Nixon's concluding remark in the Mazo–Hess biography, based on an interview with him on May 5, 1968: "I'm a pragmatist with some deep principles that never change" (M-H, 316).

The solution to the puzzle of how Nixon could have such "extreme" feelings about communism, as exemplified above, and yet cordon them off by his pragmatism is explained to a large extent, I believe, by his subordination of feeling to what he perceives to be the "national interest." Nixon was constantly involving the good of his party (usually identified with the good of his country) and the good of mankind as a justification for his own activities. In the Hiss case, he told us that "more important by far than the fate of the [House Un-American Activities] Committee the national interest required that this investigation go forward" (N, 15). (In the light of my thesis that Nixon partly identified with Chambers, it is interesting to note Nixon's analysis of Chambers's motives: "He had come forward out of necessity, he said, as a kind of duty to warn his country of the scope, strength and danger of the Communist conspiracy in the United States. It would be a great pity if the nation continued to look upon this case as simply a clash of personalities between Hiss and himself. Much more was at stake than what happened to either of them as individuals. Turning to me, he said with great feeling, 'This is what you must get the country to realize'" [N, 24].) The claim widens further in his writing, when Nixon says, "It [the Hiss case] involved the security of the whole nation and the cause of free men everywhere" (N, 40). Similarly, in discussing the fund case in 1952 and his decision to stay on as Eisenhower's vice-president, Nixon claims that "most important of all, I believe that what I did would affect the future of my country and the cause of peace and freedom for the world" (N, 102).

Is this hyperbole mere rhetoric, or did Nixon sincerely believe what he said? I have no doubt whatever that the latter interpretation is correct. Like most politicians, only more so, Nixon believed in his mission and identified his own self and fortunes with the success of his country. It was part of the secret of *his* political success, since total belief in the self is a means by which politicians convince others to believe in them.

We can see Nixon's sublime belief in the identification of his own interests with the national interest, and indeed the interests of all mankind, in his comments, such as the following: "The Hiss case was the first major crisis of my political life . . . [it was] not only an acute personal crisis but . . . a vivid case study of the continuing crisis [i.e., communism] of our times" (N, 12); "While my meeting with Khrushchev might be a personal crisis for me, I recognized that in perspective it was only one episode in the

228

continuing crisis that Mr. Khrushchev and his Communist colleagues are determined to perpetuate through our lifetime" (N, 264); "I recognized the obvious strategy of the Soviets to probe for any weakness that might be within me, not unlike their international strategy of probing for soft spots around the world" (N, 298); "I believe in the American dream, because I have seen it come true in my own life" (N, 344), already quoted.

Thus, the "crises" of Richard Nixon took on a vastly more important character than the merely personal, though his "crisis syndrome" is of crucial significance for Nixon himself. Nixon's one sustained piece of writing is his own *Six Crises*. Throughout that book, he is obsessed with the problem of "crisis." Nixon's crisis, however, was far from the psychologist's or psychohistorian's concern with "identity crisis"; for Nixon, it is not a question of "finding" himself, but of "testing" his already formed self. The orientation is largely to public events.

Nixon's own initial definition of "crisis" has always been rather lame. "Life for everyone is a series of crises," he informs us. "A doctor performing a critically difficult operation involving life and death, a lawyer trying an important case, an athlete playing in a championship contest, a salesman competing for a big order, a worker applying for a job or a promotion, an actor on the first night of a new play, an author writing a book—all these situations involve crises for the individuals concerned" (N, 12). Nixon raises the significance of crisis, however, when he continues, "Only when I ran for Congress in 1946 did the meaning of crisis take on sharply expanded dimensions" (N, 13). At this point, Nixon jumps personal crises to the hyperbolic level we have discussed before, where, for example, his fund crisis became critical to the national interest. In neither of his definitions did he rise above the ordinary, to the sort of real national crisis embodied in one of Nixon's own inspirations: Tom Paine's pamphlet of 1776, *The American Crisis,* with its famous line, "These are the times that try men's souls" (N, xvii).

Nixon's own account of how he came to write his *Six Crises* is worth recounting in full, especially since the book itself is one of our main "autobiographical" sources. "Shortly after the election [1960]," he informs us,

> I had the honor of sitting by Mrs. Eisenhower at a White House dinner. I told her that one of the reasons I had decided against writing a book was my belief that only the President could write the story of his Administration and that, by comparison, any other account would be incomplete and unin-

teresting. She answered, "But there are exciting events like your trips to South America and to Russia which only you can tell, and I think people would be interested in reading your account of what really happened."

In April, I visited President Kennedy for the first time since he had taken office. When I told him I was considering the possibility of joining the "literary" ranks, of which he himself is so distinguished a member, he expressed the thought that every public man should write a book at some time in his life, both for the mental discipline and because it tends to elevate him in popular esteem to the respected status of an "intellectual." [N, xxiii]

The reference to Kennedy is particularly interesting. Throughout their political careers, one has the feeling that Nixon was measuring and testing himself against this self-assured scion of Eastern wealth and position. The famous television debate was undoubtedly partly motivated by a desire to best Kennedy personally. Moreover, Kennedy was a war hero who had shown remarkable personal courage. It is no accident, then, that Nixon wished to match Kennedy's *Profiles in Courage* with his own *Six Crises*. He would prove there not only that he had pretensions to being an "intellectual," but that he, too, like Kennedy, had courage.

"The one who had the greatest influence on my decision," he continues, "was Adela Rogers St. Johns. From the time I entered public life, as a Congressman in 1947, she has been a close friend and adviser. Through the years she has insisted that I should take time off to write a book. Until January 20, 1961, I could always plead that I was too busy" (N, xxiii–xxiv). The defeat of 1960 left Nixon with time, and when Mrs. St. Johns sent Ken McCormick of Doubleday and Company to see him, Nixon was receptive.

> The night before McCormick arrived, I tried to jot down some ideas which might form a basis for discussion. I decided that what particularly distinguished my career from that of other public figures was that I had the good (or bad) fortune to be the central figure in several crisis situations with dimensions far beyond personal consideration. I made notes covering a dozen such situations and then selected six of them—the chapter headings of this book—for presentation to McCormick. He approved the concept, told me how easy and enjoyable I would find writing a book to be, and finally convinced me that I should undertake the venture. [N, xxiv]

At no point did Nixon see his "venture" as an aid in coming to understand himself: "I still did not believe I had reached the point in life for memoir-writing" (N, xxiii).[34]

In the introduction, Nixon makes his gesture toward intellectuality. He does so with an air of humility: "I do not presume to suggest that this is a scholarly treatise on conduct in crisis. The experts will have to judge what contribution my observations may make to a better understanding of that intriguing and vitally important subject" (N, xxiv–xxv). Nixon then proceeds to offer some generalizations on the topic. There are two points of particular concern to us.

The first is Nixon's conviction that crisis behavior is primarily a "learned" action, and thus available to him. "These attributes [quickness, smartness, boldness] are for the most part acquired and not inherited. . . . Confidence in crisis depends in great part on adequacy of preparation—where preparation is possible" (N, xxvi, xxvii). Thus, Nixon's pattern of careful planning and caution works even in the area of personal courage.

The second is even more revealing. Over and over again, Nixon repeats his main insight about crisis: it is the *aftermath,* not the crisis itself, that is critical for him. At one stage of the Hiss account, he remarks:

> The next morning I learned a fundamental rule of conduct in crises. The point of greatest danger is not in preparing to meet the crisis or fighting the battle; it occurs after the crisis of battle is over, regardless of whether it has resulted in victory or defeat. The individual is spent physically, emotionally, and mentally. He lets down. Then if he is confronted with another battle, even a minor skirmish, he is prone to drop his guard and to err in his judgment. [N, 40]

In this particular case, what Nixon means is that he went "soft" on Priscilla Hiss,

> I subconsciously reacted to the fact that she was a woman, and that the simple rules of courtesy applied. She played her part with superb skill. When I asked her to take the oath to tell the truth, she inquired demurely if she could "affirm" rather than "swear." Subtly, she was reminding me of our common Quaker background. . . . She succeeded completely in convincing me that she was nervous and frightened, and I did not press her further. I should have remembered that Chambers had described her as, if anything, a more fanatical Communist than Hiss. I could have made a devastating record had I also remembered that even a woman who happens to be a Quaker and then turns to Communism must be a Communist first and a Quaker second. But I dropped the ball and was responsible for not exploiting what could have been a second break-through in the case. [N, 40–41]

(It is worth noting, incidentally, Nixon's awareness that Mrs. Hiss was playing on their common Quaker background, a fact he has admitted for himself vis-à-vis Chambers; it is also worth noting his imagery of the football game—"I dropped the ball.")

Nixon then hyperbolizes the personal to the political interest.

I was never to make that same error again. In the years ahead I would never forget that where the battle against Communism is concerned, victories are never final so long as the Communists are still able to fight. There is never a time when it is safe to relax or let down. When you have won one battle is the time you should step up your effort to win another—until final victory is achieved. [N, 41]

Since we are interested mainly in the personal aspect, Nixon's most important remark comes when he says, "I experienced a sense of let down which is difficult to describe or *even to understand*" (N, 39–40; my italics). Can we understand what happened better than Nixon himself?

We must ask what function crisis performed for Nixon. On the public or political level, as he perceived it, the successful handling of what he calls a crisis enhances a leader in the eyes of his followers. For example, the Caracas "crisis" boosted Nixon's popularity greatly. As he put it, "In June 1958, just one month after my return from South America, the Gallup Poll showed me leading Adlai Stevenson for the first time, and running neck-and-neck against John F. Kennedy. It was the high point of my political popularity up to that time" (N, 249). Nixon's generalization is that "it is the crisis, itself, more than the merits of the engagement which rallies people to a leader. Moreover, when the leader handles the crisis with success, the public support he receives is even greater" (N, 248).

It ought not to surprise us that Nixon projects some of his own attitudes, in this area as in others, onto the Communists. At the head of the chapter on Khrushchev, he informs us that "Communism creates and uses crisis as a weapon" (N, 253). In the body of the chapter, Nixon elaborates: "They [Communists] use crisis as a weapon, as a tactic in their all-front, all-out struggle" (N, 313).

As we know, Nixon defines a leader as one able to act in a crisis. He also stresses the fact that a leader without crisis is almost a contraction in terms. For example, as he remarks about Eisenhower, he "demonstrated a trait that I believe all great leaders have in common: they thrive on challenge; they are at their best when the going is hardest. When life is routine, they become bored; when they have no challenge, they tend to wither and die or to go to seed" (N, 181–182). One of Nixon's concluding remarks to his chapter on the campaign of 1960 was even more revealing: "But probably the greatest magnet of all is that those who have known great crisis—its challenge and tension, its victory and defeat—can never become adjusted to a more leisurely and orderly pace. They have drunk too deeply of the stuff which really makes life exciting and worth living to be satisfied with the froth" (N, 461). In the light of all of the foregoing, can one help but conclude that Nixon, like the Communists, "uses crisis as a weapon, as a tactic" and would so create and use it in the future, when "tactics" called for it?

The above gives us the "public" dimension of Nixon's crisis. We need to go deeper, however, to try to understand his "let down" feeling. A fuller understanding depends on looking at "crisis" in relation to decisiveness. The latter is obviously a serious problem for Nixon. In discussing Eisenhower's heart attack, Nixon makes two revealing statements:

> This was far different from any other crisis I had faced in my life and had to be handled differently. I had always believed in meeting a crisis head-on. The difficult period is reaching a decision, but once that has been done, the carrying-out of the decision is easier than the making of it. In meeting any crisis in life, one must either fight or run away. But one must do something. Not knowing how to act or not being able to act is what tears your inside out. [N, 152]

A few pages later, he reiterates: "For me . . . this period continued to be one which drained my emotional as well as physical energies, for it was, above all, a period of indecision" (N, 166).

Interestingly enough, Nixon accused Stevenson of being "a man plagued with indecision who could speak beautifully but could not act decisively" (N, 102). As for Eisenhower, Nixon had ambivalent feelings he was hard put to suppress. For example, Nixon says that "what had happened during the past week had not shaken my faith in Eisenhower. If, as some of my associates thought, he appeared to be indecisive, I put the blame not on him but on his lack of experience in political welfare" (N, 102). Further on, he declares emphatically:

> Eisenhower was a man of decision. As General Walter Bedell Smith had pointed out in his book, *Eisenhower's Six Great Decisions* [another inspiration for Nixon's *Six Crises*?], he never did anything rashly. Sometimes he took more time to decide an issue than some of his eager lieutenants thought necessary, but invariably, when the line was drawn and the lonely responsibility for making the right decision rested solely with him, he came up with the right answer. [N, 116]

After his television program about the fund, Nixon said to Eisenhower, "If you think I should stay on or get off, I think you should say so either way. The great trouble here is the indecision" (N, 106).

Nixon, however, had to wrestle not only with the problem of indecisiveness, his own and others (his constant attention to this problem is an indication of its importance for him), but with the problem of holding fast to a decision once taken. We have already noted his "decision" to retire from politics after his term as vice-president ended in 1957, a decision reinforced by being put on paper and tucked into his wallet—and then repudiated promptly in 1960. Earlier, in 1956, during the "Dump Nixon" movement, we are told that "on a Wednesday he told two or three friends he would call a press conference the next day to make an announcement of retirement from public life" (M-H, 146); naturally, he was talked out of this "decision." The high spot in this pattern was his 1962 "retirement" speech to the press (after his gubernatorial defeat), and then his Lazarus-like resurrection in 1968. Clearly, the really decisive member of the Nixon family was Pat.

Plagued with the torments of decision and indecision in a "crisis" situation, we can begin to see why Nixon felt "let down" after his emotional fight was over. Nevertheless, I believe that there is an even more important reason, and this is related to Nixon's attitudes about aggression. My thesis here is that Nixon has enormously ambivalent feelings, probably dating back to his mother's injunctions, about the release of hostile emotions, and consequently experiences strong, though unconscious, feelings of guilt after their release. Moreover, because of the tremendous effort of control needed to fight effectively and to harden himself for a struggle (*which does not come naturally to him,* even though events and his party have cast him in this role) and because of his constant personal need to "test" himself, Nixon runs the danger of going "soft." This moment of weakness is, then, additionally threatening to him.

What is the evidence for this combined thesis? One of Nixon's most revealing comments is when he says:

> the most difficult period in one of these incidents is not in handling the situation at the time. The difficult task is with your reactions after it is all over. I get a real let down after one of these issues. Then I begin to think of what bums they are. You also get the sense that you licked them . . . though they really poured it on. Then you try to catch yourself . . . in statements and actions . . . to be a generous winner, if you have won. [M-H, 183]

Here, again, we have the use of the term "let down." If one's opponents are "bums," then one is clearly justified in fighting them without quarter. But the guilt sets in, and one catches oneself and tries to be a generous winner. To sum up, before the fight there is the agony of indecision: whether or not to release the aggressive impulses. Then there is the blessed release. "As I had learned in the Hiss case," Nixon says typically, "the period of indecision, of necessary soul-searching was the hardest. Now the emotions, the drive, the intense desire to act and speak decisively which I had kept bottled up inside myself could be released and directed to the single target of winning a victory" (N, 103). In short, there is the fight, followed by letdown, guilt, and self-justification.

Nixon alternated between denial of aggressive intent and glorification of the hard struggle. Typically, he identified himself with the nation, and denied for both any aggressive desires. He tells us that "Khrushchev does not need to be convinced of our good intentions. He knows we are not aggressors and do not threaten the security of the Soviet Union" (N, 260). Again, "It was my belief that Khrushchev knew that our intentions were peaceful" (N, 263). The fact that Khrushchev, and the Russians, might remember the American intervention in the Russian Civil War, the American willingness, in part, to have Germany invade Russia, the American ring of nuclear bases around Russia, and so forth was all written off by Nixon as merely an "act" on Khrushchev's part. In this denial of his own aggressive intent, and a refusal to recognize his opponent's real fears of it, Nixon seemed at one with much of America's self-image at the time.

Yet, while denying aggressive intent, Nixon could glorify fighting and the hard masculine qualities necessary for it. Nixon could compare Khrushchev and Eisenhower in an interesting conjunction of adjectives: "Men like you and President Eisenhower," he told Khrushchev, are "tough, reasonable men who are not soft or frightened" (M-H, 199). Nixon spoke in praise of the average Russian: "There was a steel-like quality, a cold determination, a tough, amoral ruthlessness which somehow had been instilled into every one of them" (N, 304). Nixon constantly asked himself, "How did we stack up against the kind of fanatically dedicated men I had seen in the past ten days?" (N, 305). We can see how Nixon wished to answer this question for himself, as well as for the American people, in the following, most revealing, comment about his career in New York after the 1962 defeat:

> "New York is very cold and very ruthless and very exciting, and, therefore, an interesting place to live," he observed to Robert J. Donovan of the Los Angeles *Times*. "It has many great disadvantages but also many advantages. The main thing, it is a place where you can't slow down—a fast track. Any person tends to vegetate unless he is moving on a fast track. New York is a very challenging place to live. You have to bone up to keep alive in the competition here." [M-H, 285]

Such a statement must be placed in the context of Nixon's parental models: the mother who did not wish him to enter the "warfare of politics" and the father with "his fierce competitive drive." Is it any wonder that Nixon had a problem making the decision to fight, to release *his* competitive drive, and that he felt a letdown after the semiforbidden impulses had been unleashed? Yet, having indicated Nixon's ambivalence in this matter, we must conclude with the observation that Nixon did indeed gain strength from his difficulties. Like his Russian foes, he learned to "steel" himself and to reject the softer, debilitating, and feminine impulses that threatened him so fearfully—for the simple reason that they were so strongly contained within him. Once again, out of "weakness," Nixon can be said to have drawn "strength."[35]

There is one particular crisis in Nixon's life that we must briefly discuss a bit further. It is a continuous crisis, involving his relationship to President Eisenhower, which unfolded in terms of half of Nixon's six crises in his book: "The Fund," "The Heart Attack," and "The Campaign of 1960." Much of Nixon's mature life, in his first years in national politics circled about Eisenhower: it was Eisenhower who picked him out of obscurity to be his running mate in 1952, almost dumped him in the Fund controversy that erupted then, allowed a "Dump Nixon" movement to spread in 1956, almost presented Nixon with the presidency itself because of his heart attacks in 1955 and 1957, and played an ambiguous role in Nixon's own campaign for president in 1960. On a more intimate level, the two families were united by the marriage of Ike's grandson David to Nixon's daughter Julie. On the deepest personal level, Eisenhower presented Nixon with a crisis of feeling, involving emotions about Ike as a father figure, to whom death wishes as both father and president became attached. These, we need hardly add, would be on the unconscious level.

The evidence for Eisenhower as the father figure is strong. At one point, discussing the fund, Nixon says of Eisenhower's attitude, "I must admit that it made me feel like the little boy caught with jam on his face" (N, 98). Further on, he says that "Chotiner [his adviser], particularly, insisted that I not allow myself to be put in the position of going to Eisenhower like a little boy to be taken to the woodshed, properly punished, and then restored to a place of dignity" (N, 129) (and we, of course, remember Nixon's possible "spankings" at home). On a slightly different note, Eisenhower is a commanding authority figure, and Nixon remarks that "despite his great capacity for friendliness, he also had a quality of reserve which, at least subconsciously, tended to make a visitor feel like a junior officer coming in to see the commanding General" (N, 81). Given Nixon's feelings of "little boy" and "junior officer" (Nixon was, in fact, a lieutenant commander at the end of the Second World War), we can understand better his tears when, in 1952, Eisenhower, the "father," finally accepted him back on the team:

> "General, you didn't need to come out to the airport," was all I could think to say.
>
> "Why not?" he said, with a broad grin, "you're my boy."
>
> We walked to the head of the ramp, posed for photographers, and then rode together to the Wheeling stadium. I was still so surprised by his unexpected gesture of coming to meet me that I found myself riding on his right as the car pulled away from the airport. I apologized for what I, with my Navy training, knew was an inexcusable breach of political as well as military protocol, and tried to change places with him. He put his hand on my shoulder and said, "Forget it. No one will know the difference with all the excitement out there." [N, 131]

No one "out there" might know, but Nixon "knew" inwardly that he had usurped Eisenhower's place and fulfilled a forbidden, though perfectly natural, wish. Nixon would have had to be inhuman not to have mixed feelings toward the man who placed him one heartbeat away from the highest office in the land. The fact that Nixon behaved with exemplary restraint during Ike's incapacity suggests nothing besides shrewd political judgment on the conscious level and tremendous ambivalence on the unconscious level. Death wishes are generally compounded of many parts: love for the potential victim and anticipation of great loss, secret satisfaction at his removal, guilt for this suppressed feeling, and the gladness one experiences at surviving him. Nixon's reaction, for example, to the news of Eisenhower's heart attack shows, first, denial and, then, numbing. According to Mazo and Hess, he reacted as follows when told of Eisenhower's condition:

> "My God!" Nixon whispered hoarsely. He caught his breath, then proceeded to tell Hagerty that heart attacks are not necessarily serious any more, that victims frequently recover completely.
>
> "I don't see how I could describe those first few minutes except as a complete shock," he recalls. "I remember going into my living room and sitting down in a chair and not saying anything or really thinking of anything for at least five or ten minutes. For quite a while I didn't even think to tell Pat, who was upstairs."
>
> The numbness receded gradually. Nixon went back to the telephone and called Deputy Attorney General William P. Rogers. [M-H, 159]

The alternating love–hate relationship really put Nixon through the emotional wringer. First, Eisenhower had taken Nixon for his chosen heir by picking him for vice-president in 1952. Then, he had shown no faith in his choice and seemed willing to drop him before the Checkers speech. Worse, he awakened all of Nixon's problems about indecision, compounded by the fact that Nixon had to inhibit almost all of his aggressive feelings toward Eisenhower. We can see how strong these were by Nixon's one outbreak, when Eisenhower stated that he did not think that he, Eisenhower, should make the decision about Nixon staying on the ticket. According to Mazo and Hess, "At this Nixon stiffened and said sternly, 'There comes a time in a man's life when he has to fish or cut bait.' (Actually, his words were stronger.)" (M-H, 110). We can certainly guess at Eisenhower's reaction to such a statement (possibly anal in the actual words) coming from his "junior officer." One can speculate that his enthusiasm for his "boy" Nixon was always tempered by the memory of that phrase.[36]

Shortly thereafter Eisenhower took Nixon back into his good graces, and the praise pushed Nixon all the way over to the other side of his feelings. After the Checkers speech, we are told, Eisenhower said that "as a 'warrior,' he had never seen 'courage' to surpass that shown by Nixon . . . and in a showdown fight he preferred 'one courageous, honest man' at his side to 'a whole boxcar full of pussy-footers'" (M-H, 121). It must have been music to Nixon's ears, in view of his concern for courage and his desire to be a warrior in politics, according to his father's inspiration.

But Nixon's emotional ordeals with Eisenhower were far from over. The heart attack imposed the next strain. There is an unsuspected psychological aspect to the story Nixon tells about Ike's grandson: "David, the President's oldest and favorite grandchild, provided a pleasant interlude when he came into the room. Hagerty introduced me as 'the Vice President of the United States.' David took a second look and said, 'The Vice President, wow!' Then he turned to his grandfather and said, 'Ike, I didn't know there were two Presidents'" (N, 167). Obviously, there was room for only one president, and as soon as Eisenhower recovered he resumed the full powers of his office. At that point, he expressed no appreciation to Nixon for being the second president. As Nixon remarks, "He had also spoken or written to me personally of his appreciation after each of my trips abroad. But after this most difficult assignment of all—treading the tightrope during his convalescence from the heart attack—there was no personal thank you" (N, 162). That Nixon was hurt is clear, even though he quickly adds, "Nor was one needed or expected. After all, we both recognized that I had only done what a Vice President should do when the President is ill" (N, 163). (If that is so, why does Nixon mention it?)

Anguish over the 1956 vice-president nomination was even greater. We are told that "one of [Nixon's friends] who suffered through the whole emotional ordeal with Nixon said Eisenhower's reluctance to come out flatly and ask Nixon to be his running mate was 'one of the greatest hurts of his [Nixon's] career'" (M-H, 145). Nixon explains it as follows:

> I considered it improper for me to indicate my desires until his plans, which were paramount, were made clear. I couldn't say: "Look, Mr. President, I want to run." He never put the question to me in quite the right way for that response. If he said, "Dick, I want you to be the (vice presidential) candidate, if you want to be," I would have accepted, thanked him, and that would have been that. [N, 171–172]

Further, Nixon writes:

> It seemed to me that it was like the fund controversy all over again. But *then* Eisenhower had not known me well and had every justification for not making a decision with regard to keeping me on the ticket until all the facts were in. *Now,* he had had an opportunity to evaluate my work over the past three years, and particularly during the period after the heart attack. If he still felt, under these circumstances, that he wanted me on the ticket only if I insisted on seeking the post, I concluded he should have someone else in whom he had more confidence as his running mate. [N, 176]

Nixon even goes so far in this mood as to make an indirect accusation: "Letters and calls flooded my office charging that the President was being 'ungrateful,' particularly in view of my conduct during the period since his heart attack" (N, 176).

The extraordinary thing is that, after all this, Nixon finally takes upon himself the blame for what happened. Eisenhower, the father figure, can do no wrong. After finally making the decision—a decision Eisenhower would not make—to ask Eisenhower to keep him on the ticket, Nixon concludes with a roundabout admission of his *own* failure:

> And so ended the personal crisis involved in my decision to be a candidate for Vice President in 1956. In retrospect, it was a minor crisis, for the outcome really never was in doubt. Yet it was part of the much more serious heart attack crisis for me—the aftermath when my guard was down. I would otherwise not have been as sensitive about Eisenhower's attitude toward my candidacy and would have resolved the situation myself much sooner. The significance, at least for me, once again was that the most dangerous period of a crisis is not the preparation or the battle itself, but the aftermath when one's normal reaction, after having mobilized all one's emotions and physical resources to fight the battle, is to relax. If you can-

not take the time off to let your system relax and recharge normally, then you must be alert to the fact that your temper will be short and your judgment less acute than normally. During the trying months when the President had lain ill, I had expended my energies not only in a heavier work schedule but in treading a tightrope of political diplomacy. Then, before I could recover my equilibrium, I found myself on political tenterhooks and I reacted with less than my best judgment. [N, 178]

There was one last twinge of the filial nerve. In 1960, Nixon was at last about to be his own man, running for the presidency himself. At this point, Eisenhower, advertently or inadvertently, made a major blooper. Asked at a presidential press conference on August 24 "to give us an example of a major idea of his [Nixon's] that you adopted," he replied, "If you give me a week, I might think of one" (M-H, 238). Mazo and Hess make a weak attempt to explain this away. Then, they continue:

> Eisenhower's failure to speak out for his Vice President during September and October caused more raised eyebrows. One psychological explanation, propounded by Theodore White and others, was that Nixon was rebelling against Ike, the father-figure—"the Nixon people," wrote White, "and Nixon himself, who had been treated like boys for so many years by the Eisenhower people, now apparently itched to operate on their own." [M-H, 239]

The plot thickens. At an October 31 White House luncheon to plan Eisenhower's participation in Nixon's campaign, we are told:

> The lunch started on a note of high optimism. Eisenhower, in a bouncy mood, declared he now was a soldier in the ranks, ready and willing to undertake any assignment the new commander (Nixon) proposed. Hall cheerfully acknowledged that was the kind of news he hoped to hear. Others chimed in. The country would be reassured and its morale lifted by a dramatic display of the Ike and Dick team fighting shoulder-to-shoulder, as always, suggested one strategist. Another stated the people everywhere were aching to show they still liked Ike, and thus the projected Eisenhower tour would stun the "commentators and politicians" who so fervently wanted the Eisenhower–Nixon administration repudiated. Finally campaign director Hall took from his briefcase the carefully prepared plan for intensive Eisenhower campaigning and proposed, with a chuckle, that "we get down to business" in order to uphold the reputation for political sagacity of all those around the table who had just made victory predictions. But as Hall proceeded to review the projected Eisenhower itinerary, Nixon asked if he might interrupt. Quietly, he expressed gratitude for all Eisenhower already had done in his behalf, said he believed the American people were well aware of his role as the President's associate and deputy

for eight years and the continuing closeness of the Eisenhower–Nixon team, and suggested the President now could be most helpful by concentrating during the remaining campaign days on a couple of previously scheduled appearances and an election-eve broadcast to the nation. As virtually everyone in the room gasped, Nixon added that he had given considerable thought to the idea of a massive politicking drive by Eisenhower and concluded it might not be proper for the President. Nixon said he and all his associates appreciated beyond words Eisenhower's willingness to barnstorm the country for the Nixon–Lodge ticket, especially since no one knew better than the President how exhausting that sort of intensive campaigning would be. It was difficult to resist Eisenhower's offer, Nixon concluded, but on reflection he felt (and hoped) the President and his other friends in the room would appreciate Nixon's decision. [M-H, 239–240]

This time, Mazo and Hess expect us to believe that it was a telephone call the night before from Mrs. Eisenhower and a talk that morning with General Snyder, Eisenhower's physician, cautioning Nixon about the strain on Eisenhower's health of a vigorous campaign, that made Nixon indulge in his strange behavior. Without doubting the facts (though it would be interesting to check them), in order to accept this interpretation we would have to put aside all of Snyder's previous advice that a vigorous life and schedule for Eisenhower was the best possible medicine, and Eisenhower's failure to speak out for Nixon *before* October 31 and the luncheon meeting. In any case, given Nixon's feelings about being the "junior officer," Eisenhower's "soldier in the ranks" offer must have awakened strange, disturbing feelings in Nixon, and the memory of the inept "give me a week" response must have left him with some trepidation as to how Eisenhower might behave in his "lowly" role.

There is little need for further speculation. Nixon's victory, on his own, in 1968 undoubtedly was a successful achievement of the position of primacy, without the replacement of the father implicit in the 1960 campaign. There was, also, no need for death wishes—or fears. In this sense, I believe, we do have a "new Nixon," released from old emotions. I suspect that part of his nomination of the unknown Spiro Agnew was a replaying, in reversal, of his own nomination from obscurity by Eisenhower. The assignment of Agnew to the "low road" of hatchet man, while Nixon strolled along the "high road," offers some confirmation of this hypothesis. Although Mazo and Hess do not tell us when Nixon's father died, other sources indicate the date as 1956. In any case, Nixon was no longer Eisenhower's or anybody else's "little boy." We can postulate that he had passed through this "crisis" in his life—in this unsuspected sense, an "identity crisis"—and finally come to maturity.

What is Nixon's own image of himself? His first self-image is that he is a "big," a "great" man. In the introduction to *Six Crises,* he says, "We often hear it said that truly 'big' men are at their best in handling big affairs, and that they falter and fail when confronted with petty irritations—with crises which are, in other words, essentially personal." A few paragraphs further on, Nixon comments: "No one really knows what he is capable of until he is tested to the full by events over which he may have no control. That is why this book is an account not of great men but rather of great events—and how one man responded to them" (N, xxvi). Nixon's "great events" include the Fund controversy, Eisenhower's heart attacks, the visit to Caracas, and his encounter with Khrushchev—hardly events that will figure large in future history books—yet implicit is his belief that, having handled these "big affairs" well, he is a "big" man.

Nixon made an explicit comparison of himself, during the 1960 campaign, with a great president, Abraham Lincoln, and suggested that the great events confronting him, Nixon, are even greater than those of 1860: "One hundred years ago, in this very city, Abraham Lincoln was nominated for President. . . . The question then was freedom for the slaves and survival of the nation. The question now is freedom for all mankind and the survival of civilization" (M-H, 228). The hyperbole, as to the survival of civilization, is partly the usual political rhetoric, but partly a reflection of Nixon's self-confidence, a vital ingredient for any politician.

Overwhelmingly, what emerges from a reading of Nixon's own writings, as well as the Mazo–Hess biography, is Nixon's ability to think well of himself, to believe he is always acting fairly, and to deny to himself almost any of his nasty, aggressive feelings. For example, he makes one statement, demonstrating considerable psychological insight, but then fails to see its applicability to himself. "From considerable experience in observing witnesses on the stand," he tells us, "I had learned that those who are lying or *trying to cover up something* generally make a common mistake—they tend to overact, to overstate their case" (N, 8; my italics). And this comes from the man who could say about his vicious campaign against Voorhis, "Our campaign was a very honest debate on the issues." This is the same Nixon who could say throughout the 1940s, 1950s, and early 1960s that communism was indivisible and monolithic, and then say, without blushing, in a 1968 interview that "I don't see the Communist world as one world. I see the shades of gray. I see it as a multicolor thing" (M-H, 316). So too, Nixon, who used the smear against Voorhis, Mrs. Douglas, and Adlai Stevenson could complain about a *New York Post* story insinuating wrongdoing in a Nixon political fund, and say innocently, "After all, I had come into this

1952 campaign well prepared, I thought, for any political smear that could be directed at me. After what my opponents had thrown at me in my campaigns for the House and Senate, and after the almost unbelievably vicious assaults I had survived during the Hiss case, I thought I had been through the worst" (N, 85–86). Nixon, one of the most pragmatic and expedient of politicians—witness his 1968 alliance with the Southern politicians, such as Strom Thurmond—could sincerely state:

> My philosophy has always been: don't lean with the wind. Don't do what is politically expedient. Do what your instinct tells you is right. Public opinion polls are useful if a politician uses them only to learn approximately what the people are thinking, so that he can talk to them more intelligently. The politician who sways with the polls is not worth his pay. And I believe the people eventually catch up with the man who merely tells them what he thinks they want to hear. [N, 152]

And Nixon, who appointed Agnew as his running mate in 1968, could state in 1961, when writing *Six Crises,* that the vice-president should be selected as a real deputy, able to be president if necessary: "This being true," he informs us, "it will also bolster the new political trend of selecting capable men as vice presidential nominees, men to whom the presidential nominee would be willing to turn over his duties during a period of disability, rather than the selection of men solely on geographical, factional, or party appeasement considerations" (N, 194). One can argue that changing circumstances make for changing views, and Nixon merely adapted, as in his views on communism, to reality. I cannot accept this explanation. Nixon's ability to believe in the rightness, and *total* rightness, of whatever he is saying at the moment is so pervasive and so in tune with what is expedient that I see no grounds for believing in any real change of principles or perception of reality. For example, Nixon really believed what he said in the 1960 campaign:

> On this and every other issue, the admonition I gave to some of those who had a tendency to let their eagerness to appeal to voters overrule their judgment on the substance of issues went something like this: "We must always assume that we are going to win this election. And I do not want to say anything or do anything during the campaign that I will not be able to live with as President." [N, 359–360]

The aftermath of 1968, as well as the pattern of Nixon's political life before, shows us otherwise (as, for example, with Nixon's espousal of black capitalism). The high point in this double talk came when Nixon described his last television debate with Kennedy, in 1960, and the Cuban issue. According to Nixon, Kennedy accused the Republicans of do-nothingism, and advocated aid to rebel forces in Cuba, *knowing* (he had been briefed) that the CIA had been training Cuban exiles to invade Cuba. Nixon explained how he rose to this crisis:

> What could I do? One course would be simply to state that what Kennedy was advocating as a new policy was already being done, had been adopted as a policy as a result of my direct support, and that Kennedy was endangering the security of the whole operation by his public statement. But this would be, for me, an utterly irresponsible act: it would disclose a secret operation and completely destroy its effectiveness.
>
> There was only one thing I could do. The covert operation had to be protected at all costs. I must not even suggest by implication that the United States was rendering aid to rebel forces in and out of Cuba. In fact, I must go to the other extreme: I must attack the Kennedy proposal to provide such aid as wrong and irresponsible because it would violate our treaty commitments. [N, 382]

Then came the climax; Nixon said in the debate:

> "I think that Senator Kennedy's policies and recommendations for the handling of the Castro regime are probably the most dangerously irresponsible recommendations that he's made during the course of this campaign."
>
> But I could not say why. Instead, I took this tack:
>
> ". . . if we were to follow that recommendation . . . we would lose all of our friends in Latin America, we would probably be condemned in the United Nations, and we would not accomplish our objective. . . . It would be an open invitation for Mr. Khrushchev . . . to come into Latin America and to engage us in what would be a civil war and possibly even worse than that." [N, 382–383]

How, one wonders, could Nixon *possibly* say this, knowing even better than Kennedy that this was *exactly* what America intended to do? And, having said this, how could he then expect us to believe him when he claimed, "I do not want to say anything or do anything during the campaign that I will not be able to live with as President."

This, however, is the same self-righteous Nixon who told Khrushchev that America is completely nonaggressive and spelled out "in detail that the United States had fought in two great world wars and had never exacted any territorial gains or reparations and that the United States had no designs on world conquest" (N, 302). Okinawa, for example, would presumably be unknown to Nixon, who served in the United States Navy in the Pacific. Of course, when Khrushchev says that "the Soviet Union wanted to live in peace and friendship—but was fully prepared to protect itself in war" (N, 273), we are expected to treat this as complete, conscious fabrication.

Fundamentally, Nixon is an uncritical man. Thus, we are told by Mazo and Hess that Nixon "never shared the belief of some in the Eisenhower administration that 'Communism to McCarthy was a racket.' Nixon felt that the Senator 'believed what he was doing very deeply'" (M-H, 132). (Yet Nixon knew that McCarthy had exhibited no knowledge of, or antipathy toward, communism before his West Virginia "numbers" speech.) Similarly, Nixon mentioned that the House Un-American Activities Committee

> had been widely condemned as a "Red-bating" group, habitually unfair and irresponsible, whose investigations had failed to lead to a single conviction of anyone against whom charges had been made at its hearings. It was, the critics said, doing more of a disservice to the country because of its abridgement of civil liberties than any alleged services it might be rendering in uncovering Communist subversives. [N, 14]

But at no point did he admit the justice of the charges.

The uncritical Nixon, however, saw himself in a very different light from the one I have cast on him. For example, he commented about his performance in his first television debate with Kennedy:

> I had concentrated too much on substance and not enough on appearance. I should have remembered that "a picture is worth a thousand words." I would be the first to recognize that I have many weaknesses as a political candidate, but one of my strengths is that I try to be my own severest critic. [N, 367]

Obviously, Nixon's concept of criticism is in no way related to my use of the term.

In general, Nixon's basic vision of himself is as a high-principled, fair-minded man (of greatness), who is constantly being unfairly attacked and smeared by his opponents (mainly Communists and crooks) and who is his own severest critic. Much of this self-image, we must admit, corresponds to the image of self-righteousness projected by America as a whole; and this correspondence is undoubtedly a part of Nixon's political success.[37]

To explore that kind of correspondence further, one has to turn more steadfastly to the study of the led. In the next two chapters, I shall suggest how one might undertake this task systematically, especially in terms of what I call "the American Psyche." Having done this, we might then want to return to Nixon and consider again how his vision of his own drives and desires matched that of his country.

I would conclude by stressing Nixon's belief in his own goodness and morality. Un-self-consciously, he quotes in *Six Crises* the faith in him expressed by Whittaker Chambers. "Almost from the first day we met (think, it is already 12 years ago)," Chambers wrote to him, "I sensed in you some quality, deep-going, difficult to identify in the world's glib way, but good, and meaningful for you and multitudes of others" (N, 460). This is the same Nixon, however, who seems always to *act* in an amoral way and who constantly asserts, for example, that "American foreign policy must always be directed by the security interests of the United States and not by some vague concept of 'world public opinion'" (M-H, 253). Granted that there is some truth to this latter remark, one must question whether "world public opinion" does not point to a morality, or immorality, that can lie hidden in a nation's, or an individual's, pursuit of power (under the name of protection and self-defense) and should also be taken into account in formulating policy.

In short, I am suggesting that there is a "blindness" to his own drives and desires—and those of America—exhibited by Richard Nixon. If we have difficulty in discovering the "real" Nixon, I believe that he has even greater difficulty. Socrates counsels that "know thyself" is the right adage for a successful philosopher. Should a politician also "know himself"? Time, and events, alone will tell us whether Nixon correctly "analyzed" his American Dream, or whether a deeper interpretation would be better for the health and well-being of America and the world.

# Toward a
# Group Psychology

# Leader and Led, Individual and Group

WHY a psychohistorical study of leadership? What does it add to so-called pure historical (i.e., nonpsychohistorical) studies of the subject? We must not take the answer for granted. A look at the work of, say, John Maynard Keynes or Edmund Wilson, gives one pause. In his *Economic Consequences of Peace,* for example, Keynes offers a brilliant sketch of Woodrow Wilson, which anticipates much of the insight of Alexander and Juliette George's classic *Woodrow Wilson and Colonel House* and does so by what we can designate as "literary" means. Edmund Wilson, in *Patriotic Gore,* goes even further, and paints large-scale portraits of a Lincoln, a Harriet Beecher Stowe, a Justice Holmes, a General Ulysses Grant, which are filled with psychological insights, though embedded in general matter, in a general fashion.[1]

It is not enough to say that John Maynard Keynes and Edmund Wilson were "influenced" by Freud. We must simply concede that their studies are psychologically revealing, although not formally psychoanalytic or psychohistorical. In their own right they have value. What, then, is the special value of formal or explicit psychohistory, if any? The answer, I believe, is that psychohistory (1) calls our attention systematically to data generally overlooked by most historians; (2) looks at this data in terms of psychological theories, which are connected to clinical data and to continuous, systematic conceptualization, that is, tries in a manner similar to, say, economics, to be more "scientific" than an intuitive or commonsense approach;[2] and (3) attempts to establish a body of work and of scholars in this subfield of history that generates, even demands, a continuing, systematic critique of such work. Such a critique will bring the requisite theories to bear on the newly "discovered" data, that is, data either new or newly meaningful to historians.

What psychohistory lamentably loses in elegance, it gains in the systematic, continuous examination and evaluation of data and theory by a significant number of scholars. It becomes a continuing scholarly enterprise, rather than, primarily, an individual artistic creation, wonderful as the latter is. Different temperaments will favor one or the other mode of work; only a narrow fanatical temperament would try to exorcise either venture of the human mind seeking to understand itself and its workings.

Until recently, psychohistorical inquiry into leadership has proceeded under two major inspirations, one favored by political scientists and the other by historians. They both hark back to Freud. The first, as remarked upon earlier, takes its real psychological inspiration from Alfred Adler and has as its pioneering figure Harold Lasswell. In the second, one person, Erik Erikson, may be said to play the roles of both inspirer and applier.

Adler was a natural figure to attract political scientists. His concern with power, the pivot of political thought, and his theory of compensation for low self-esteem and sense of inferiority appealed to Lasswell, who elaborated it, as we have seen, into his celebrated formula of the political actor displacing private motives onto the public arena and then rationalizing them in the form of public benefits. The other side of Lasswell's work was an attempt to establish a typology of political types—administrators, agitators, activists, and such—and their typical psychology.

These efforts resulted in some useful and provocative work.[3] There were, and are, problems, however. Lasswell seemed to imply—if not make explicit in a title such as *Politics and Psychopathology*—that the drive was pathological. Thus, the political leader was seen as a kind of patient, exposed to a reductionist interpretation. He was treated in a sort of psychological vacuum, where it was not made clear why he aimed at compensation in the political field—power—rather than, say, sublimation in the artistic field. What is more, he was analyzed in more or less of a political vacuum, with little attention to the public, whose "benefits" he was rationalizing and to whom he was appealing.[4]

What the Lasswellians have done, they have generally done well. And until now, those working in "personality and politics" studies have been content to try to deepen and extend their efforts. It is no affront to such work to suggest that the systematic, continuing nature of psychohistory to which I alluded earlier, pushes toward a building on and transforming of what has been done. One form this has taken is, for example, Robert C.

Tucker's reexamination of the theory used by the Georges and his conse-
quent criticism of their assumption that the power drive of would-be leaders
is derived from low self-esteem.[5] Tucker appeals to data showing that many
power-seeking leaders appear to be expansive personalities with high self-
esteem, and he resolves the apparent dilemma by suggesting an alternative
theory to Adler's, in this case Karen Horney's concept of the "idealized self"
and her recognition that high *and* low estimates of the self can co-exist.
Tucker obviously is trying to sharpen and extend the psychological theory
underlying the study of leadership, but neither has he moved further in this
particular piece of work toward a concern with the "led" or "group" part of
the leadership relation.

If political scientists have tended to an Adlerian/Lasswellian orientation, historians have tended to draw inspiration from Erikson. Erikson,
whom I have discussed earlier in a different context, offered both a new
theoretical inspiration—his ego psychology and life-cycle conceptions—
and an application of his theories to actual historical materials—his Luther
and Gandhi books—and has showed the aspiring historian how the job
could actually be done.[6] Studying religious leaders who became political
leaders, he closed the gap between the two kinds of leadership, both politically and psychologically. He also paid attention to the role of ego ideals—a
natural part of his ego psychology—and emphasized the relation both of it
and of identity to ideology.

Erikson was well aware of the leader–led problem. Hence, his famous
formulation, that in solving a personal psychological dilemma the great
leader was solving the self-same dilemma (e.g., a conflict concerning authority) experienced by large numbers of people, for whom it was a political
as well as a psychological matter. Erikson sought to give a little more
psychological substance to the "rational" analysis of "public benefits"—the
desires for reform and strong leadership—of Lasswellians. Yet the psychological side of the led, or the group, was still merely being adumbrated, not
analyzed, and the interrelatedness of the leader and led was assumed, not
probed.

Can we go beyond the Lasswellian and Eriksonian efforts, and the
others that have grown up alongside them, while still forming part of the
same general forest of thought? Is a new planting, or at least grafting,
possible?

The first thing to be said is that the "leader" as such does not exist; that is, there is no "leader" for all peoples and all seasons.[7] A potential leader must find the right circumstances and the right group to lead. Without the French Revolution, a Robespierre would at best have been a minor footnote in a provincial history of Arras. Without the outbreak of the American Civil War, Ulysses Grant would have been a failed army officer, rusticating in his family's leather business. On a less dramatic level, Walter Lippmann illustrates the needed correspondence between the leader and circumstances when he remarks apropos of two possible relationships in the 1920 presidential election that Frank Lowden could lead the Democratic Party as its candidate if the public continued its quiescent, anticharismatic feelings, and William McAdoo could head it if the public gave him the correct leads, which he could then seize upon and promote effectively.[8]

The next thing of note is that the leader does not exist, fully formed, before the encounter with the group he is to lead. The leader discovers a self, forms and takes on an identity as a particular kind of leader, in the course of interacting with the chosen group. The leader also finds a public style, which may be quite separate from a private style. It is a creative encounter. A perceptive journalist, Henry Fairlie, has grasped this point well. He tells us:

> No political journalist who has followed such opponents as Winston Churchill and Aneurin Bevan, Charles deGaulle and Gaston Deferre, on the stump in great campaigns, can doubt that the interaction between candidate and crowd is of supreme importance to the candidate. It is out of this communion between the candidate and the crowd that the national leader is born; and nothing will replace it.[9]

The ambition may already be there, but it is vague and undirected. It takes on specific shape in the encounter. Speaking of American presidents, Fairlie makes the general point when he goes on:

> A great politician, when he seeks the highest political office, must fit his ambition to the hour. He must become necessary; known to himself, and seen by the people, to be so. It is not his personal identity which he must discover, but his political identity which he must establish.[10]

In discovering, or creating his own political identity, the great leader also creates a political identity for the followers; that is, the leader makes them into a group, however amorphous in actual structure. This explains why, with great frequency, the leader-to-be appeals to previously unpolitical people and brings them into the political arena. A Robespierre draws to him the sansculottes; a Hitler, the nonvoting, lower-middle-class German; a

Mao Tse-tung, the Chinese peasants. Thus, leadership is a creative act, which, psychologically grounded, brings forth a political identity for both the leader and the led.

Of course, the leader also has a personal identity. Up to now psycho-history, as we have noted, has concentrated on this aspect of the problem. It is in this vein that even Heinz Kohut, in his "Creativeness, Charisma, Group Psychology," initially looks at the matter. Speaking of the artist's creativeness, but having in mind the politician's as well, Kohut says:

> In other words, we are dealing either (a) with the wish of a self, which feels enfeebled during a period of creativity, to retain its cohesion by expanding temporarily into the psychic structure of others, by finding itself in others, or to be confirmed by the admiration of others (resembling one of the varieties of a mirror transference), or (b) with the need to obtain strength from an idealized object (resembling an idealizing transference). Thus relationships which are established during creative periods do not predominantly involve the revival of a figure from the (oedipal) past which derives its transference significance primarily from the fact that it is still the target of the love and hate of the great man's childhood.[11]

I will have more to say about Kohut's path-breaking work, but for present purposes I want simply to point out that the discussion at this point—Kohut himself will go beyond it—is still mainly in terms of personal identity. Kohut's insight here is that the leader may better be understood in terms of psychology of the self than of classical Freudian theory; but that self is still being viewed primarily from the "personal" side. The challenge now is to probe the "political identity" side more fully.

To do this, we must look more closely at the "led" or the "group." Unfortunately, we do not have a satisfactory theory of group psychology. Small-group theory, such as Bion's and others, will not do; the historian is mainly interested in large-scale, relatively unstructured mass movements—generally political or religious—grasped or called into being by a leader in particular historic circumstances and in the creative act we have been outlining. We need, therefore, to construct a satisfactory group psychology for ourselves.

Let us begin by postulating that there is a "psychic repository" or culture on which the potential leader can draw. We can conceive of this repository as embodying recurrent themes, ideals, values, fantasies, imagery, symbols, myths, and legends. A fuller exposition would need to sort these out. Such materials tend to be timeless, though their relation to historic events is always changing.[12] They embody elements in tension with one another. These elements in tension can be conceived of as ambivalences, but it is perhaps more fruitful to think of them as positive and negative images, in the manner employed by Erikson as he explored the polarities in American life and culture.[13]

Now, the study of themes and myths is the stock in trade of intellectual and cultural historians. I am willing to settle for Henry Nash Smith's definition of what is involved here: "collective representations" (i.e., not the work of a single mind), "images" expressing collective desires and imposing coherence on the varied data of experience, with the image itself fusing concept and emotion into one intellectual construction.[14]

Our task is not to discover all of this work anew but to use it for psychohistorical purposes. Freud appealed to myths and legends for inspiration and confirmation of his clinical insights; we must appeal to them as our primary data. We can do so by bringing them into relation with the leader, for it is he or she who helps activate this repository, who captures and uses the emotions within it. The leader, in short, serves as a catalyst to our further understanding.

The culture, with its polarities, embodies and expresses the "splits" of what may be called the national or religious psyche; or perhaps group self is better. Analysis of this culture, in static terms, is often called national character studies. Such a culture is subject to dialectical swings, which mirror the splits, only now revealed over time. This is the stuff of history. To take America as an example, Jefferson had spoken of the dialogue of mind and heart. Such a "split" between the rational and the emotional from the beginning has been a major theme of our history. Made dynamic, it takes on specific dimensions, for example, in the movement surrounding Emerson and the transcendentalists, as in the comment that "the American Romantic movement was . . . another of those periodic upsurges of feelings, of a yearning for emotional fulfillment that have regularly counted the periodic cultural control of rationalistic and scientific mind."[15]

It is obvious that this same split, and others like it, can be found in many, if not all, other cultures. The point is that such "eternal" themes take on specific form in particular national cultures, with specific emphasis and ambiances, in terms of specific myths, valuations, fantasies, and the like. Each group, then, has a repository that, though it necessarily resembles all others—just as each individual's psyche embodies universal traits—is unique.

What will be activated in that repository is a result, to a large extent, of circumstances and of leaders who create themselves and the group. One leader, for example, can utilize free-floating discontent at the breakdown of values, or a narcissistic desire for enhanced self-worth and inclusion, in a movement aimed at venting itself at scapegoats. Another can do so in a movement of constructive social protest. Robert Tucker, writing about Stalin's use of the Russian past, actual and mythical, especially concerning Ivan the Terrible, remarked: "Patterns out of a nation's distant past do not rise again simply because they were there. But they can do so if a leader with great power finds them instructive for present policy and acts upon them as precedent."[16] We need to generalize this remark and apply it to the psychic repository, which includes all of the timeless elements of myth, legend, and so on, as well as the historical deposits of a people's recent experiences.

Circumstances will conspire to make certain features of the repository readily available to the would-be leader. The leader will energize these features, sifting out of the population at large the specific group of people who will help define the leadership, while themselves being defined as a group in the process. The elements used by the leader will be a selection from the polarities available in the repository.

Almost always, leadership will be defined in opposition to that of prior leadership, as well as playing on cultural themes from the repository. To take the American example, a John F. Kennedy will embody the image of a vigorous president succeeding a desultory Eisenhower—both images, incidentally, are partly mythical; a Jimmy Carter will stress his own ordinariness and truthfulness—call me "Jimmy" and "I will never lie to you"—in opposition to Nixon's imperial claims and prevarications.[17] In the largest sense, the leaders set themselves and their followers apart from a negative image, and they create a positive image partly by that very fact—that which they are contrary to—and by activating certain themes, images, and myths in the repository that have lain more or less dormant for a time.

So far, we have been talking in general terms about political identity—the creation of self, individual, and group—that takes place in the interaction of leader and led. I wish now to talk briefly about image, in the sense not so much of leaders making use of available images in the repository, but of making and projecting one of themselves. It is the matter of how a leader is perceived, rather than what the leader may actually be, though there is a relation between the two. Recall Peter Sellers in the movie *Being There*, for example. In *The Revolutionary Ascetic*, I have argued that a revolutionary ascetic has a functional advantage because of his traits; also suggested is that even a reputation for such traits gives a revolutionary leader a functional advantage in many circumstances.[18] The image has an importance connected to, but separable from, identity, with *political* identity necessarily combining the two.

We know that images can be largely created and manipulated, as long as they don't too drastically affront reality. Later, I will refer to attitudinal polling. Here, I want to make two separate points. The first is that the image is not simply something external to the leader's true self. It is essential and intrinsic to the leader's own political identity. The leader, in addition to actually organizing a political or religious movement (i.e., a reality role) *becomes* an image, a symbol, and as such, symbolizes the aspirations of the followers, and symbolizes, too, a means of allaying and defending against their fears and despairs. As an image, or symbol, the leader brings to a focus all of their feelings, "binding" them and these feelings to the leader's own self. If the leader disappears from the scene, these feelings are set loose again, available for other, competing leaders to try and refocus in a new combination.

The second point is that image is the way in which a leader's contemporaries perceive him or her; it is a vital part of the relationship and not a fraudulent or misleading picture. When psychohistorians go in search of the "inner man," as in most life histories, they run the risk of opening up a real gulf between our understanding of the person and of how contemporaries perceived that person. As D. A. Hamer argues in his article "Gladstone: The Making of a Political Myth":

> The work of discovering "the man himself" tends to diminish our ability to understand how and why he mattered, what it was about him that made him important, perhaps an object of veneration or of detestation, in the eyes of his contemporaries. We see him through a very different medium, and we may dismiss what they said he was or represented as myth, worthy only to be discarded once we, as historians, have discovered the "truth" about the man and his motivations and aims.[19]

Most critics of psychohistory focus on reductionism as the great danger. I am suggesting that an equally great danger may be misunderstanding the reality of the leader–led relation. The leader unavoidably takes on many of the aspects of a "cult" figure. It is the image, not the squirmy "inner self" that leads followers. Moreover, as we have noted, the leader becomes, in part, the actuality of that image, finding the self defined by what develops between the leader and the group. As Hamer suggests, a leader such as Gladstone has to make his conduct conform to his myth if he is to maintain the connection to his followers.[20] The public style encroaches more and more on the private self, until, given the dramatic, even histrionic, nature of political leaders such as Gladstone, the two begin to merge. Life history, if it emphasizes only the "secret," "real" person and ignores image, misses the central identity, which is both political and personal, and thus, misses reality itself.

What role does ideology play in the leader–led relation? Let us conceive of ideology as an effort to tie together, in a putatively logical and rational manner, as a belief system, a bundle of emotions selected from the psychic repository. It is a secular version of a religious system, a contrived imitation of myths and legends. It can persist after the leader's death, as in Leninism. The ideology is presumed, often, to be impersonal; once in place, it may serve as an "operational code," a total system directing one's thoughts and actions.

In an article, "Thoughts on a Theory of Collective Action: Language, Affect and Ideology in Revolution," Gerald Platt advances a number of interesting theses.[21] He attacks what he calls "Categorical Analysis," which assumes that "some *predispositional* category, i.e., a subjective psychological state or an objective social position somehow compels [revolutionary] participation." Instead, Platt, using the experience of the Nazi Revolution and the English Civil War, recalls our attention to the facts: there was neither homogeneity of motive nor class among the supporters, nor indeed, opponents in the two events. For example, both the English Royalists and Parliamentarians were dominated by aristocrats.[22] Platt also asserts that ideologies, and their language, "are not *causes* of action, but rather modes through which action is made subjectively meaningful." It is not clear to me why ideologies cannot also be thought of in causal terms, inspiring people to action; in fact, a little further on Platt explains that, for example, exploitation of labor, discrimination of persons, and the like are "so experienced because the interpretive rules embedded in ideology inform its adherents that participative activities in the world should be ascribed with such meanings." It would seem to follow that once meaning is given to some actions, it could then serve as motive to further actions. In any case, Platt adds that "ideology is the mechanism by which diverse populations are bound together."

Let me add to Platt's useful formulations the role of the leader. Ideology is imaged forth for the group in the shape of a particular leader. Most populations, in fact, have a hard time understanding and identifying with an ideology, which, as Napoleon well knew, was the construction of intellectuals. As John Kifner says, reporting on the Iranian revolution:

The tendency to embody political thought in a single personality rather than articulate its ideology is a strong Persian tradition. This charismatic style is apparent in the universal use of faces on posters and is a large part of Ayatollah Ruhollah Khomeini's political strength.[23]

Even Lenin knew to speak to the Russian peasants about "Bread, Land, and Peace," and not about Marxist–Leninist ideology, which he reserved for Bolshevik theologians. Like Khomeini, Lenin, by his image and his personal qualities, exemplified the ideology and thus bound together the diverse population of followers. As James Fallows comments about a lesser leader, Barry Goldwater, he is a man "who exemplifies a creed in the nature of his personality" rather than in his thought.[24]

Without underestimating the role of ideology, we can stress the role of the leader as well. Writing about "Why America Loved Theodore Roosevelt: Or Charisma Is in the Eyes of the Beholders,"[25] Kathleen Dalton notes that "America loved Theodore Roosevelt because he tapped an emotional wellspring in the culture. He reached the people on more than rational grounds." As a true leader, a hero, he defined "a culture's aspirations and hopes." I am suggesting that out of the repository of the culture, a leader, such as Lenin or Theodore Roosevelt, selects a number of elements, parts of the polarities, and images them forth, partly in the form of what may be called an ideology, but mainly in the shape of the leader's own person.

One other aspect of the leader–led relation needs to be highlighted. It is the role of organization. Some leaders are rhetorical and ideological in their genius and leave organizational skills to others; a surprising number of the great leaders—a Lenin, a Mao—combine all of the abilities in themselves.

My concern, however, is not with a particular leader's organizational skill, or lack of it, but with the psychological functions fulfilled for the led by the organizational structure. I take my example from the Methodist organization created by John Wesley, who exhibited a special talent in this area. Wesley appealed mainly to the lower middle class in Great Britain, at a time of acute disruption to society at the end of the eighteenth century, caused by the changes associated with the terms commercial and industrial revolution and eventually exacerbated by the democratic upheavals of the American and French revolutions. The unfeeling rigidity of the Established Church offered no religious solace for those cast afloat from old moorings of value or institution.

Into this breach, Wesley stepped. He created not only a new religious "ideology" but a new organization, the Methodist "society," which provided an enormous psychological support for its members. As Robert L. Moore says,

> In his movement he had created and formalized a hierarchy of status and prestige which provided opportunities for upward mobility for those without access to the accepted channels of a traditional society. The lowliest member of the societies could, by membership alone, be a part of a religious elite.[26]

Erikson had spoken of the great leader solving other people's problems in solving his own. We see here the mechanism by which, in part, this solution takes place—though the articulation is very different from what Erikson had in mind. Speaking of Wesley, Moore goes on,

> In making possible the realization of his own special destiny he had given birth to an institution through which many of the dispossessed were able to find an alternative which promised hope and a role which offered a chance for personal development.[27]

"Personal development" is the key concept. Eighteenth-century British "industrial" culture—part of the psychic repository—preached the virtues of success, social mobility, and self-help. Methodism instructed its adherents how to progress up the ladder of spiritual success, a disciplined progress that then assured commercial success and, most important, provided an organizational framework in which that mobility could be exercised and rewarded. A personal development, which would have been blocked by the religious and social elitism of the established world, was now fostered in a new setting.[28] A leader, Wesley, creating a new organization, the Methodist church, provided the led with the inspiration and means to become new men and new women. Together, leader and led formed out of an emergent group a movement, which then became organized and institutionalized.

Whether a Wesleyan class, society, or conference, all being grouped into the Methodist church, or a Bolshevik cell, network, or movement being gathered into a Communist party, we are confronted with the same phenomenon: organizations that, through the roles they provide, offer the possibility, operationally, of realizing ego ideals.[29] The organization, in short, provides an opportunity for personal development that is a critical part of the creative encounter of the leader and the led.

Up to now, I have been seeking to make a number of general points: mainly, I have contended that the "next" "next assignment" for psychohistorians, to take up again William Langer's lesson,[30] is to look in detail at leader–led relations, rather than at the leader more or less in isolation; and at political identity, as I have defined it, rather than at personal identity. This means recognizing that the leader and led both define themselves, and find their selves, in the course of special circumstances and in a creative encounter. In the process, a selection is made from the available psychic repository, the shared culture. Ideology codifies and freezes this selection, but it is made real and alive to the led through the leader's image. The organization created by the leader allows for the personal development of the followers.

These are all fine and true points, I believe. But they are also very theoretical. The problem is to make them operative in detailed, historical examples; that, of course, is the actual next assignment. I cannot undertake to do that now, but I would like to attempt two final things: (1) to examine briefly the theory of narcissism and the psychology of the self in the light of the leader–led problem, and (2) to make a few suggestions as to the kind of future empirical work that should be undertaken.

In the symposium sponsored by the Group for the Use of Psychology in History, in 1974, Heinz Kohut commented:

> In the setting of history narcissistic aspirations, hurts to one's pride, injuries to one's prestige needs, interferences with conscious, pre-conscious, or unconscious fantasies of one's own greatness, distinctness of one's own efficacy and power, of one's specialness, of the specialness of the group that one identifies with, are important motivations for group behavior. The refined study of these types of motivations will go a long way toward adding a new dimension to the other data which historians utilize in describing historical events.[31]

The task, of course, is to use narcissistic theory to join the leader and the led. A brief glimpse at some of Kohut's work offers us a number of leads. In *The Analysis of the Self* (1971), Kohut develops his leading ideas concerning the grandiose self and the idealized parent image, while remaining in the bounds of classical Freudian libidinal theory and giving little formal attention to aggression.[32] With these concepts firmly in hand, as I read him, Kohut then turned to larger issues and contexts, with major implications for history and psychohistory. His article "Thoughts on Narcissism and Narcissistic Rage" (1973)[33] deals with the effect of a narcissistic injury on the fictional hero of Kleist's story "Michael Kohlhaas" but is then extrapolated to groups. In my interpretation of Kohut's effort, he sees groups cohering, in part, around a shared concept of the grandiose self, for example, national prestige, and an idealized parental image, for example, religion and its values. Injury to these, the blocking of the individual's sense of self-realization in their terms, that is, a loss of faith in them, can lead to a devastating sense of failure—and to rage. For Kohut, much of Germany's post-1918 history can be understood in the light of this theme.

Here we are on the borderline where leader and led meet. Hitler is Kohut's prime example of a leader exploiting narcissistic injury, in this case, Germany's. Thus, in *The Restoration of the Self* (1977), Kohut mentions Kleist's "Michael Kohlhaas" again as an example of severe chronic narcissistic rage, and adds that "Hitler's followers with their vengeful destructiveness constitute a historic example in the realm of group psychology."[34] With the article on narcissistic rage and the *Restoration* book, Kohut has repaired his earlier omission of aggression. Further, he has elaborated a full-blown, independent psychology of the self, putting to one side Freud's classical drive theory.

Until recently, according to Kohut, drive theory, with its conflict model, was appropriate to a time when the dominant threat to modern Western man was "unresolvable inner conflict" brought on by "emotional over-closeness between parents and children" as well as between the parents themselves.[35] The centrality, for example, of the Oedipal conflict follows naturally. Today, however, family relations are not close but distant; the danger is not over- but understimulation. Thus, historic change commands a new theory to deal with the new facts, and Kohut responds with his psychology of the self. Now the central problem becomes the threat of a disintegrating self, marked by "severe fragmentation, serious loss of initiative, profound drop in self-esteem [and], sense of utter meaninglessness."[36] The threat holds equally for individual and group, and again we can see the suggested lines relating the leader and the led.

During the period 1966–1976, Kohut was mulling over the ideas contained in his article "Creativeness, Charisma, Group Psychology." Earlier, in *Restoration,* Kohut had wisely pointed out the healthy aspects of the grandiose and idealizing tendencies, the usefulness, say, of a fantasy of being supported by an omnipotent, godlike figure, a fantasy often held by great religious or political figures. In the "Creativeness" article, he reminds us in an important footnote that many creative people, looked at in terms of psychopathology, "would have to be counted among the narcissistic personality disorders."[37] But psychopathic diagnosis is not Kohut's intent, nor ours. Having set up a typology of charismatic and messianic personalities, with the former identified with the grandiose self and the latter with the idealized superego, he insists that the elucidation of the personality of the charismatic and messianic person, and of the psychological basis of the intense relationship which the followers of such a person establish with him, is an important task for the depth psychologist who, with the tools of psychoanalysis, attempts to investigate group processes and their effect on the dynamics of history.[38]

Continuing, he suggests that "in addition to the study of historical figures, the psychoanalytic historian must also undertake the study of historical processes, of the dynamics of historical events."[39]

The Kohutian task is before us. Exactly how to carry it out is a challenge to historians. In Chapter 10 "The Hidden Khomeini," I sought to draw inspiration from the Kohutian spirit (see pp. 139–152). Starting with a description of narcissism from the side of the leader, I analyzed, as the reader may recall, Shiite Islamism and Persian history, remarking on the "age-old feelings of betrayal, injustice, and oppression" embodied in that inheritance and especially on the contrast between feelings of national (really imperial), cultural, and religious grandeur and concurrent feelings of humiliation and injury caused by foreign domination. I then tried to join the two parts—leader and led—concluding that in Khomeini we have a man who alternated between a sense of himself as a grandiose and as a humiliated figure, and whose feelings corresponded with those of a large number of Iranians who were prepared to follow him to the end.

When Kohut writes that "the endopsychic equilibrium of the charismatic leader or of the messiah seems to be of the all-or-nothing type: there are no survival potentialities between the extremes of utter firmness and strength, on the one hand, and utter destruction (psychosis; suicide) on the other," I feel he is talking about Khomeini, in anticipation.[40] The theory of narcissism and the psychology of the self does have the great advantage of speaking about processes potentially shared by leader and led, which may arise out of varied family dynamics, are the same for male and female, and are connected to large-scale historical changes.[41]

In earlier chapters, I asked what "texts" were available, once we had identified the group in which we were interested, that would be the counterpart of the "talk" of an individual patient.[42] In terms of what I am now saying, and in the Kohutian framework, I think the answer is the psychic repository: myths, legends, and ideologies, "talking" not only about Oedipal conflicts but about the most deeply rooted fantasies, fears, and feelings of self, object, and possible self-disintegration.

262

How can we actually *do* the new psychohistory? What kind of empirical work should we be undertaking, and in what way? The answer is, of course, in many ways, with many different materials, and with various theories. Narcissism, for example, is only one, though perhaps the most valuable, theory to be used in our kind of work; but drive theory, with its concern, say, for Oedipal relations, its hysterical and compulsive personalities and populations is not to be simply discarded, but added to (see Chapter 4).

For present purposes, however, I want to return to my idea of the psychic repository. I believe we must establish, so to speak, a "listing" for various groups, of what is in their repository. Let me offer some clumsy examples of what I have in mind. Take the central concept of political science—power. Power is a *human* relationship, defined more in psychological than in material terms. As David Hume tells us, it is public opinion that rules; as the Aztecs in the face of Cortez confirm, psychology counted more than numbers. Power, then, revolves around feelings about domination–subordination, superiority–inferiority, independence–dependence, love–hate, and so on; thus, groups may wish to suppress and exploit others, trounce them, teach them a lesson, and so forth. These feelings, in turn, are expressed in the myths, legends, ideologies, in the symbols, with all of the ambivalences and polarities that comprise the group's repository.

One can express some of these polarized feelings as Erik Erikson does at one point, dealing with the American identity, as external alternatives: "open roads of immigration and jealous islands of tradition; outgoing internationalism and defiant isolationism; boisterous competition and self-effacing cooperation."[43] More broadly, and internally, he later rephrases these polarities as "migratory and sedentary, individualistic and standardized, competitive and cooperative, pious and freethinking, responsible and cynical, etc."[44] In the same article, Erikson talks about attitudes toward nature and the machine, as they relate to feelings of fragmentation, control (as in clockwork regularity of man and machine), and so on.

We see some of the same elements examined by Henry Nash Smith, a cultural historian, as he looks at what I am calling the repository of America in terms of its self-images as a continental nation and a European-oriented member of the Atlantic Community; a populous agricultural society and an empire based on maritime commerce; as inferior to and superior to European nations; and as a garden and a wilderness. Smith also calls attention to the antitheses of nature and civilization, freedom and law, and links them to father–son conflict. He speaks of the myth of the yeoman and of the frontier and of the symbols in which these and other such myths are uttered forth.[45]

We could add others: the American sense of mission, dating back to the

Puritans; the feelings about rebellion and "independence," coming to dramatic expression in 1776 but persisting; the concern with "freedom," especially freedom to "grow," both personally and as a nation; and the wistful sense of abandonment involved in the rebellious acts of asserting independence and freedom. The cowboy as a symbol, for example, is not a mere accident in American history. As the reader will see, I begin to construct "the American Psyche" out of some of these materials in the next chapter.

Here, I want to suggest that, with some such repository, drawn from a careful analysis of the "texts" of myth, legend, and literature, and highly refined so as to align the psychological theory with the "texts," we can then try to activate it, through a study of leader and led. The latter allows us to study actions and interactions, not just the "texts," as expressive of meanings. It reminds us that the repository is being recreated, given new historical form, at a particular moment.

I can now envision two major ways of proceeding from this point. The first is in terms of historical studies, where one can tap into the creative encounter of the leader and led. The second is in terms of present-day "focus groups," where the psychic repository can be explored in an effort to sharpen and focus a possible group psychology.

The first—the historical examples—needs little further explanation. My suggestions as to how to approach the task is implicit in everything that I have been saying up to now. As an illustration, however, let me offer, not such a dramatic instance as Khomeini and the Islamic movement, but the more restrained and limited instance of John Wesley and the Wesleyan Movement.[46] What is the preexisting repository, and how are parts of it activated, and with what polarities involved? How, for example, does Wesley's sense of self, and threatened damnation and disintegration, interact with the psychological state of his followers: narcissistic rage, questioning of authority, need for control, or whatever is involved? How, in the encounter, do Wesley, the leader, and the Wesleyans, the led, come to shape both themselves and their group self?

Other questions will come readily to mind. Let us turn to the second way I envision the field advancing. Like psychoanalysis at its beginning, we need immediate clinical data, live historical "patients," so to speak. With them, we can test out our theories, see what transpires between the repository and its contemporary expression in relation to actual persons and sufferings and present-day historical events. We can seek to elaborate an acceptable group psychology and then apply it to historical examples, such as the Wesleyan case.

What I have in mind is inspired by recent work in what is called attitudinal polling. Most polling, as we know, is fairly mechanized: it asks people how they feel about a variety of matters, and what actions, for example, they might contemplate. The people being queried are individuals, not members of a group responding in a group setting. The result is valuable: wouldn't we like a similar representative sampling of English public opinion at the time of the "Puritan" revolution? But it is limited, in the manner indicated.

We need responses in a group setting. But I have already deprecated the Bion-type small-group approach as a tool for psychohistory. We need a group response that is representative of the larger group, political or religious, and that is historical in nature, responding to large, historical movements. The hint as to how to solve our problem, I would repeat, is available in attitudinal polling.

David Haskell Sawyer, one of the leading practitioners of the art for present-day political leaders (he was hired by Ted Kennedy for the 1980 campaign), explains the method: "This is a technique—borrowed from advertising—where you preselect fifteen or twenty people, on a psycho-demographic basis, and get them all together in a room for a period of time and then ask them to speak their minds on a specific subject." Sawyer's aim is to assist political leaders to lead; he differentiates his work from advertising agencies who attempt to get people to switch brand loyalties. Sawyer continues: "Look, there's a difference between manipulation and emotionality. I think that maybe one could sell a very simple product—say, a kind of soap—by means of packaging and repetition. You know, massive time buys. But I really don't believe that the American voter can be manipulated." And he concludes: "You have to remember that the American voter has become pretty sophisticated in media terms—in being able to evaluate media language. But emotionality is a whole different thing. Emotionality is when you speak directly to people's emotions—to emotions that are already there. That's the key: the emotions are already there."[47]

At first glance, this may seem all very distant from our psychohistorical study of leaders and led. I do not think it is. I believe that we need a number of what Sawyer calls "focus groups," which will be studied and interviewed by a team composed of a psychohistorian and psychoanalyst—perhaps with a Sawyer as a guide—equipped with a provisional psychic repository, a historically live situation, and a potential leader–led relation. We can then empirically explore the "emotions" and the connections we have been talking about in this chapter. We can study the question of what is in the cultural myths and legends and what is in the heads of actual people, in a group, and how a potential leader does or does not tap into a part of that repository.

Once we have struggled through to a better understanding of all this, to a group psychology based on a live leader–led relation, we can turn back to our older history examples, confident in the reality-grounding and validity of our conceptualizations. With these historical cases, and probably only these, we can examine in extended detail and in completed form the ways in which both an individual self and a group self emerge from the creative encounter of a great historical leader and the group that he helps call into being out of the psychic depths. At this point, psychohistory may be able to achieve the true selfhood and identity to which it has been so painfully aspiring.

# CHAPTER SEVENTEEN

# The American
# Psyche

INDIVIDUAL psychology, leader-and-led studies, these carry us just so far; and I have tried in my own work to go with them as far as I could. In the end, however, I have felt the need to push on to what I called in the previous chapter a concern with the psyche, or the psychic repository. It is in terms of such a concept that I believe we best understand the leader–led situation, as well as the nature of, say, a national group psychology itself. As a coda, therefore, I want to begin to test the idea by a brief exemplification.

By psyche, as I suggested in the previous chapter, I mean something special, that is, the existence of a group's "psychic repository," on which it draws unconsciously as well as consciously and which fundamentally shapes its sense of self, its identity, or character. This repository, in turn, can be known through an analysis of myths, legends, creeds, folklore, and literary constructions, as well as rituals, ceremonies, monuments, and so forth. These, of course, embody historical experiences, from which they gain their particular form and content.

A particularly important, I would say crucial, way of looking at these materials is in terms of what I shall call "polarities."[1] These, along with the identification of certain key "themes," are the means I use to organize the diverse materials making up the American Psyche. Polarities are universal in nature and to be found in all societies. Just as all individuals have to wrestle with love and hate, altruism and aggression, and so forth, and yet shape individual identities, so societies have to handle the opposing pulls, for example, of idealism and materialism, of feelings of inferiority and superiority, of definitions of masculinity and femininity, and yet emerge with particular psyches.

Each group, as I have already noted, has its own experiences, its own

267

history, which shapes the particular balance and content of the given polarities. Thus, instead of an individual or modal personality, I shall seek to discern what is in the American psychic repository, for it is this that the newest immigrant, as well as the oldest American, experiences and that makes both of them "American."

Of the materials that enter into the formation of the psychic repository, myths are probably the most fundamental. Much literature has been devoted to the understanding of myth (usually taken, incidentally, to be the antithesis of history).

Myths can be basically divided into two kinds: creation myths and hero myths. The first gives, for example, a poetic explanation for the beginnings of the world—"In the beginning was darkness," or "The great God Ishanami threw a spear from the void into the waters of earth," and so on. The second tells of a culture figure and his or her heroic deeds. The function of the first kind of myth is not to establish "reality" in scientific terms but primarily to give its hearers a sense of order brought out of chaos (although it is true that this can also serve, in a Durkheimian sense, as a model on which society is to be constructed). That of the second is to serve as an inspiration for our own being and behavior.

In dealing with the American Psyche, I am concerned almost solely with the second kind of myth, for at the birth of America science already had prevailed. Indeed, as Alexis de Tocqueville pointed out, America was born not in the mists of ancient times but in the full light of history. Thus, origin myths were present only as religious baggage, so to speak, brought over on the ships from Europe carrying the first white settlers (the Indian origin myths, of course, were not acceptable).

Hero myths present or incorporate polarities and thus choices: between success and failure, heroism and cowardism, etc. They allow us to master psychological problems and thus to "mature"; in other words, to grow up and deal with psychological as well as physical and cultural "reality." In more technical language, one could say they offer us an "ego ideal." In more novelistic terms, we can refer to them as an unconscious group form of *Bildungsroman*.

Bruno Bettelheim emphasizes that "in most cultures, there is no clear line separating myth from folk or fairy tale; all these together form the literature of preliterate societies." Then he goes on to say that "a myth, like a fairy tale, may express an inner conflict in symbolic form and suggest how it may be solved. . . . The myth presents its theme in a majestic way; it carries spiritual force; and the divine is present and is experienced in the form of superhuman heroes who make constant demands on mere mortals." In his view, "Much as we, the mortals, may strive to be like these heroes, we will remain always and obviously inferior to them."[2]

My use of myth can draw inspiration from Bettelheim's definition but also differ from it. America, of course, is not a preliterate society and never has been. Therefore, one might even say that, properly speaking, it cannot have myths. I will settle for looser standards of definition. In speaking, for example, of the "myth" of the frontiersman, or the self-made man, or of Horatio Alger, I mean stories that have taken on group origins, losing their connection to a single creator, if they had one, and that express in symbolic form absolutely fundamental and pressing "inner conflicts" of both the group and the individual. Such myths speak to us mainly in the language of symbols, appealing to our conscious and our unconscious minds.[3] They seem to carry a touch of the "divine"; like rituals, they have about them a kind of "religious" aura, even though they are secular accounts. And finally, they promise that, although we are materialistic mortals, we can achieve heroic stature, and thus a kind of divinity—for idealistic as well as worldly success is the birthright of every American.

If we probe a bit further, however, we discover two troubling aspects to myth. The first is that, although myth allows for and indeed is vital to personal development—a kind of *Bildungsroman*—it also becomes in the process a sort of enthrallment, hiding reality from us, and thus also a form of slavery. From this enthrallment we must break free in order to achieve true independence and adulthood. The second troubling note is that, as a result, myth requires demystifying, a task undertaken professionally by historians. Yet human beings cannot, it appears by the evidence of history itself, live in a completely disenchanted, demystified world. The historians' task thus becomes twofold: they must "reconstruct" in a double sense, first reconstructing the past "as it actually was," which means substituting history for myth; and then they must reconstruct a more realistic world, which realistically allows for myth. It is a Sisyphean task that is imposed upon historians, inherent in the existence of myth, with its superhuman nature, and especially pressing in the construction of a national psyche.

Legends and folklore have less of a "religious," divine quality about them, and literary constructions are obviously human-made and show it. With rituals, which repetitively embody and dramatize a myth or legend through the use of symbols, we again have a strong "religious" overtone, though diminishing as we approach a more formal ceremony, such as a college graduation. Monuments are an obdurate symbolizing of elements of the psychic repository, whereas paintings, currency (think of the symbols on the American dollar bill), and such are significant symbolic representations. All of these materials are what one draws on in trying to understand the American Psyche.

The American Psyche, in my usage, is synonymous with neither the American National Character nor American Identity, though overlaps exist. Let me try to discriminate among them.

National character studies focus on a "modal personality." While attendant to the shaping culture, such studies seek to delineate a "character" manifested by the largest number of individuals. By using projective techniques and clinical interviews, such studies try to supplement, and indeed supplant, subjective impressions, thus claiming a scientific basis of sorts for statements about national character. Practitioners also study, generally through the use of learning and socialization theory, how the modal personality is formed, as well as how changing social institutions affect it. The emphasis tends, however, to be on a static "type," and this runs the danger of becoming a stereotype: the irascible Irish, the phlegmatic German, the inscrutable Oriental.

Identity tends to be a more dynamic concept. It refers to a sustained sense of self held by an individual, and the emphasis is on how that identity is formed through a psychosocial developmental process. It becomes a national identity when held by a sufficient number of individuals. Erik Erikson, for example, handles the subject in highly sophisticated fashion. Stressing the fact that identity is something created, he also recognizes that it is often made up of contradictory elements. Thus, in a typical passage (quoted earlier), Erikson notes that Americans are faced with "alternatives presented by such polarities as: open roads of immigration and jealous islands of tradition; outgoing internationalism and defiant isolationism; boisterous competition and self-effacing co-operation; and many others." While this might seem close to what I am talking about in regard to the American Psyche, it differs greatly in that Erikson's focus is on "an individual ego" and the way in which it "depends on the coincidence of nuclear ego stages with critical changes in the family's geographic and economic vicissitudes."[4]

As I have tried to say forcefully above, my emphases in employing the concept of the American Psyche are different. My approach is actually closer in spirit to that of an intellectual historian, such as Perry Miller, though I have here a more determined psychological intent and method. In summing up the general pattern of development in America, Miller comes close to the sort of thing I have in mind when he states: "Each successive remodeling [of what I myself am calling here the psyche] retains something of the previous form: we echo the covenant not only in the phrase 'God's Country,' but when we pray for the blessing of heaven upon our arms and our industries; we invoke Revolutionary language in our belief that we, of all the world, are preeminently endowed with common sense; we also, by calling ourselves 'nature's noblemen,' imagine ourselves possessed of the pioneer virtues of Natty Bumppo, yet simultaneously suppose ourselves evolving into an industrial paradise, complete with television and the deep freeze. When we try to bundle up these disparate notions into a single definition, we are apt to come up with some such blurb as 'The American Way of Life.'"[5]

What Miller calls the American Way of Life, I refer to as the American Psyche, with the definition and the aim of using it as described above. America, like almost all other nations, claims to be unique. Uniqueness emerges for all from the particular balance of universal polarities and their particular contents. Nevertheless, there may be a relatively special quality in America's claim to be unique. I have already suggested that it is summed up by Tocqueville in his *Democracy in America,* when he declares that "we see a new nation born before our eyes." America's comparative newness—in fact, one of the major themes in the American Psyche is the constant assertion of its being a "Virgin Land"—means that its formation has all been in the light of history; there is no obscure origin, lost in the mists and myths of time.[6] We can see the psychic repository, the very myths and other sources for it, come into existence as a matter of historical record. We can see the formation of what can be regarded as a new civilization.

How might one go about constructing a picture of the American Psyche? I shall deal with some of the polarities present, and occasionally with a theme; each of these elements, of course, is connected to every other, and it is the mosaic, changing over time, that constitutes the particular psyche. What we must always keep an eye on is the way continuity is mixed with metamorphoses or transformations of the content of the persisting polarities.

A few more preliminary observations are necessary. The first concerns two parts of the American "people," whose psyche may not always be represented in the generalizations prevalent in the society: women and blacks.

One of the most important polarities, in fact, is the masculine–feminine, though that is not what I am talking about here. I am referring, rather, to the fact that one half of the population is made up of women, and, for example, when one is speaking of individualism as a dominant trait, one may only be speaking of males.[7] "Minute men" are exactly what they are called, although women also used rifles on the frontier farms. Example after example could be given.

We are, then, faced with a problem. How reliable are the male-oriented polarities we shall be establishing? The answer is that, just as with the North–South problem (discussed below) the dominant view—in this case, the male—has prevailed and shaped the American Psyche (or at least has done so in the past). Nevertheless, it behooves us to be aware of the one-sidedness of our statements about the polarities and themes that emerge out of the materials of myth, legend, and so forth, and play themselves out in the formation of the psychic repository. It also alerts us to the fact that the masculine-feminine polarity itself is one of the critical ones to be considered in a fuller study.

As for blacks, they comprise about 12–13 percent of the American population. Like the American Indians, however, they are one of the most powerful influences on the dominant white-American psyche (as well as having their own intrinsic significance), thus having an importance far beyond their numbers. If the encounter with the Indian is the most formative element, that with the black is the next in importance (and, of course, white on black has its own importance). Again, as with the women's issue, I will not be going into the details of that encounter here. Instead, I want only to flag it and to note that when, for example, Crèvecoeur, the author of *Letters from an American Farmer,* speaks of the American as a "new man" who has shaken off the prejudices of the past and is thereby liberated, he is not speaking of the black man. The black is also made a "new man" in America, also with his past removed from him—but in the process he is left enslaved, not free. Crèvecoeur's *American* farmer is white (as well as male).

One last preliminary problem: change. The earliest experiences are the most important and formative ones. The polarities and themes thereby established persist, no matter how far they may seem to be driven underground. They are the base against which all future melodies are composed. Nevertheless, change can and does take place. It does so in two ways.

The first is in terms of the changed shape, but not content, of the elements in the psychic repository, what a little earlier I referred to as metamorphoses or transformations. For example, the leatherstocking hero may change into the cowboy, and then into the hard-boiled detective, though remaining the same isolated "individual," without women, children, or family of any kind, rootless and "free" from the restraints of civilization.

The second is in terms of major shifts in the weights attached to various of the polarities. For example, that between superiority and inferiority shifts drastically after the Second World War, when America loses almost all conscious recognition of inferiority feelings (though, of course, they persist in the psyche). Even before the Second World War, industrialism and the growth of consumerism portend a major shift in the scale of values and challenge older agrarian and republican commitments. An accommodation becomes, therefore, necessary. So too does the emergence after 1948 and the Truman Doctrine of America as a superpower, possibly hegemonic and definitely military-industrial in its complex.

Once more, without going into details, it must constantly be borne in mind that, just as with women and blacks, the problem of change must, in a fuller account, be given room in our construction of the psychic repository.

The first polarity I want to consider is civilization and wilderness, and possibly the most important thing to be said about America is that it results from an experience with both a real and a psychic wilderness. Like all future Americans, the first colonists were immigrants, and the New World to which they headed symbolized both a possible garden of Eden and a howling desert. In fact, of course, there were two distinct forms of settlement, emanating from one company but two cities: London and Bristol. The first settlement was the Southern, or Virginian, and the second the New England, or Puritan. The extraordinary thing is that one, and not two, nations resulted.

The Southern experience began in 1584-87 with the ill-fated Roanoke colony, and then took root with the Jamestown settlement in 1607. It was of a very different nature from the Puritan, which was to come to America a few years later, for the Virginians had mainly military and trading aims in mind. Both colonizations, however, had to confront the wilderness and its aboriginal inhabitants, the Indians. Both groups of colonists, moreover, came with the same mixed image of the Indian, who was seen as gentle, natural man, on one hand, and as savage cannibal on the other.

Nevertheless, while acknowledging some of the similarities of the two colonizations, there are two reasons we can give a lessened weight here to the Southern experience—though it occurred prior in time and *is of general equal intrinsic importance* with the Puritan—and concentrate on the latter. The first is that the Southerners accidentally discovered the tobacco crop, in 1613, and thus developed as a largely rural, agriculturally exploitive economy, abandoning exhausted land quickly and moving on, with labor being supplied by imported and portable black slaves; thus, in the South, the Indian problem quickly became the Negro slave problem (which, as I suggested earlier, does persist as a major shaping factor in the American Psyche). The second reason is that the plantations developed on the shores of rivers, each removed from the other. For both reasons, there resulted little in the way of cultural centers. In contrast, New England was inhabited by colonists who came as families, developed in terms of villages, towns, and cities, and thus established urban and learned communities—for example, Harvard University was instituted almost immediately—which dominated the intellectual life of early America and established its prevailing myths.

Of the prevailing myths, the first revolves around the leaving of civilization, England, and embarking on what is called an "errand into the wilderness," cast in the form of a "mission." The Puritans, or so declared their spokesmen, came for religious reasons: to establish a community of saints. There is a touch of grandiosity to the claim of John Winthrop, leader of the 1630 Puritan expedition, that they were establishing a "city on a hill," to which all eyes would be directed. In Catholic Europe, men and women might remove themselves from the world by entering into the purity of a monastery; here we have a community establishing itself in full public view, its ascetic practices to be carried out in *this* world (as in Max Weber's famous concept of the Protestant Ethic) and to serve as a model for the rest of the world.

The Old World, seen as a corrupt civilization, was to be rejected. It is a theme that runs through all subsequent American thought, forming a major part of what I am calling the American Psyche. As opposed to the corruption of Europe, a rebirth, a regeneration, of humanity is to take place by a return to nature. Only the Puritan's nature is a "howling wilderness and desert," a biblical landscape as well as an actual America.

In this landscape, the American Indians took on the features of the Christian Devil. Their lives of seeming idleness and sensuality stood as a temptation to the would-be saint. The encounter with the Indian was both real—there were repeated wars and massacres—and symbolic. There was both a need for acculturation—unless the Puritan could adapt to the new land partly by copying the Indian ways, the Puritan would not survive—and for establishing a sense of difference: for to "go" Indian, to abandon civilization entirely, was to yield to Satan's temptation. One way, incidentally, that William Bradford dealt with the problem was to take the Indian's corn, in a feast celebrated then and now as Thanksgiving Day, but to acknowledge no thanks to, no dependence on, the savage: as Bradford declares in his "Of Plymouth Plantation," giving the account, "And here is to be noted a special *providence of God,* and a great mercy to this poor people, that here they got seed to plant them corn the next year, or else they might have starved" (my italics).

Still, relations with the Indians were necessarily a matter of enormous ambivalence, and this ambivalence was made especially manifest in the form of the captivity narrative, which, along with the sermon, was the major genre of early American literature. Between 1677 and 1750, there were more than 750 published accounts of being captured by the Indians (half of those captured were ransomed after periods up to twenty years). These accounts then became the basis of numerous published sermons, for it was very important to interpret correctly these "temptation" experiences, so to speak, to exorcise them. In the narrative, the man or woman is now portrayed as a hero, questing for religious salvation and undergoing a "testing" by the Lord. He or she is regenerated, born again, out of the ordeal.[8]

As for the Indians, they remain as the embodiment of the forces of darkness and must not only be spurned but exterminated. Unexpectedly, the Puritan anticipation of a new life seems to require death, or as Richard Slotkin puts it, a "regeneration through violence." Thus, another theme attaches itself to the civilization–wilderness polarity, the theme of violence that runs henceforth like the proverbial red thread through the American Psyche. We see it surfacing again both in the first American novel, Charles Brockton Brown's *Edgar Huntley,* modeled explicitly after the captivity novel; and, of course, in Fenimore Cooper's Leatherstocking tales, as when Deerslayer must kill his Indian opponent in order to secure his new identity as Hawkeye. It is what D. H. Lawrence has in mind when he calls the American a "killer." If expressed in the form of a polarity, we would probably have to speak in terms of violence and benevolence, for the Puritan–Leatherstocking killer also wishes to convert, that is, to "save," his victim.[9]

The fact is, nevertheless, that in the process of destroying the Indian, the early American did become, to a certain extent, "Indianized," that is, "Americanized." Though with enormous ambivalence, New Englanders grew the Indian's corn and, on the frontier, came to imitate his survival techniques. I have already alluded to the Leatherstocking novels of James Fenimore Cooper, modeled somewhat after the actual figure of Daniel Boone, where this adaptation is given immortal form. What has taken place is a form of cannibalism (the accusation, of course, hurled at the Indians by the whites), of taking in symbolically as well as materially the Indian "spirit." That spirit still haunts us in the names of our rivers and mountains, for example, the Wiscasset River, the Allegheny Mountains, and our states, for example, Massachusetts, Connecticut (not to mention our sports teams). Though incorporated into an emerging American way of life, the Indian and his fate persist as well in the form of guilt, weighing heavily, though largely unconsciously, on the American Psyche.

The American wilderness was, in fact, the wilderness of the soul. For the Puritan, a sense of self had to be achieved, constructed, out of an arduous inner experience. Sacvan Bercovitch writes of this process, and quotes George Goodwin, a seventeenth-century poet, who declares, "I sing my SELF; my *Civil Warrs* within."[10] This constant spiritual warfare, this troubled search for self, is imbedded in the American Psyche; it is one reason why America is so hospitable to psychoanalysis and why, for every American, identity is still to be achieved, not inherited. We speak today of America's narcissism, its constant absorption in self. It is to a large extent merely the modern form of the Puritan's inward turning.

The Puritan freely and publicly confessed to an experience of melancholy, or depression, marked by intense self-loathing to the point of contemplated suicide. It was seen, as I have argued earlier in Chapter 12, "The Iron of Melancholy," not as a psychological breakdown but as a testing by the Lord, to prove oneself worthy of salvation. The powers of darkness wrestled with the powers of light.

It is this inner struggle, intrinsic to the Puritans' faith, brought with them from England, that was then projected onto the American wilderness. Listen to Cotton Mather, in his great *Magnolia Christi Americana* (written circa the 1690s and published 1702), where he speaks of the "church of exiles" driven out of England "into an horrible wilderness." Once entered, however, into these "dark regions of America," these "godly men" will make arise "light in darkness," led as they are by divine providence who "hath irradiated an Indian wilderness." The outer and the inner, the actual wilderness and that of the subjective self, are a battleground for the struggle between God and the Devil, light and dark.

It is a struggle in which many if not most Americans still engage. About 40 million Americans, even in this day of Darwinian evolution and modern science, claim to be born-again Christians, many with a fundamental, or literal, faith in the Bible. As current opinion surveys show, Americans at large are more committed to such religious beliefs as God, an afterlife, Heaven and Hell, and, most significantly, the real presence of the Devil, than any other Western people: whereas about 60–65 percent of Americans attest to such beliefs, only about 30–35 percent of Europeans do.

Looked at historically, we can see that, in the eighteenth and nineteenth centuries, the Puritan sense of self and wilderness took on a particular expression, very much influenced by the emergence of romanticism: the Bible became merged with Nature in the round, not just as an isolated sense of wilderness. Now God's revelation is to be found not only in the Bible, and then applied to the wilds, but in the very landscape itself. Thus, Nature—in fact, the frontier—takes on an independent, Godlike aspect, where God speaks directly to the American, such as Emerson. The projection of the conflict in the self goes on, however, but now in terms of a whole continent and, more recently, even of the whole world. As has often been remarked, the sense of mission in the American Psyche persists. The need to redeem the wilderness from the forces of evil lingers on, as does the thread of violence that runs through the pursuit of regeneration. Language changes; the elements of the psyche remain fixed, only with new layers coming into existence.

All Americans, that is, all non-Indian Americans, have left an old world behind. The theme of separation runs strongly, especially in the early accounts. William Bradford, in "On Plymouth Plantation," speaks eloquently of how "if they looked behind them, there was the mighty ocean which they had passed and was now as a main bar and gulf to separate them from all the civil parts of the world." Implicit in this view is that, having turned their backs on the parent country, Americans must also repudiate its values, must break the affective ties binding them to the old world. Thus, Europe is seen as a continent of corruption, debauchery, and tyranny, from which Americans must stand free.

It is also a source of temptation. If the Indian represents the sensual and the all-too-natural, the European represents the cultured and the civilized. Over a century after Bradford, David Rittenhouse, the Philadelphia scientist, uses a similar image to express his ambivalences. As he says in 1775, "I am ready to wish—vain wish! that nature would raise her everlasting bars between the new and old world; and make a voyage to Europe as impracticable as one to the moon. I confess indeed, that by our connections with

Europe we have made most surprising, I had almost said unnatural, advances toward the meridian of glory; But by those connections too, in all probability, our fall will be premature."[11] Between the Indian and the European poles, the American was, and is, in extreme tension. Toward the former, he feels superior; toward the latter (at least until post Second World War), inferior. Alternately attracted and repulsed, he has been a troubled soul. This theme, of inferiority–superiority, is one to which I shall return.

The tension and torment described above also takes on another dimension, one that can best be described as a polarity between the ideal and the material world. John Winthrop expressed the division well when he spoke of how, if we dissemble with God and "fall to embrace this present world and prosecute our carnal intentions, seeking great things for ourselves and our posterity, the Lord will surely break out in wrath against us." In this view, the Puritan endures the trials of separation, and its attendant anxieties, for religious, or ideal, reasons. Providence, in the form of Nature, in America, sees fit to reward him with its bounty. Suddenly, he is possessed of material wealth; and the lust after worldly goods becomes a threat to his ideals. American historians, such as Perry Miller, speak of a Declension, a fall from the high ideals of the fathers, as occurring within one or two generations of the first settlement. Such a declension leaves a bad conscience.

The cure in part, administered periodically in the course of American history, is the revivalist movement. It preaches the heart over the head, fervor over calculation, God over Mammon—and in the process often advances its adherents' own economic position (one need only think in recent years of the Moral Majority or Jim and Tammy Bakker)! The first such revival occurred in the Great Awakening of the 1740s, when the movement led by Jonathan Edwards swept like a great fire over the Northampton Valley and then out over the country. Since then, some historians have claimed the coming into renewed existence of three or four such revivalist movements. Such movements are awkward compromises of the ideal and the material desires, and it is arguable that America today is in the midst of some such revivalist moment.[12]

Out of this general travail of the American spirit, its need to accommodate ideal and material desires, fought out in a self-war and made manifest in the absorption over self-definition, a general observation emerges. The characteristic form of rebellion in America, aside from 1776, is not revolution, the overthrow and remodeling of political institutions, but revivalism and the conversion experience, reform of the self. We Americans, with our bad conscience, locate the blame (when we are not projecting it on to other "outside" forces, such as communism), sometimes diffuse, sometimes specific, in our own wickedness—a falling away from the covenant with God—and not in either the inequities of our rulers or the failings of our political and social structures.


Surely, one can object, America had a revolution. Indeed, it was founded as a nation as a result of a violent war of independence. The exception, I will argue, proves the rule. To understand this fact, a number of observations are in order here.

First, the evidence is increasing that a strong revivalist element permeated the American Revolution. The prevailing picture has been that the revolution was a consequence of rational, enlightened men asserting their inalienable rights. And so it was, in part. Tom Paine and Thomas Jefferson do not fade from the scene. But we now know that the revolution was also the consequence of religious revivalists, infused with emotion, who turned against the corruption and licentiousness of the parent country and proclaimed the need for American purity, brotherhood, unity, and nationalism. Or, in the words of the evangelicals, a "new birth," requiring a new man, in a new order.[13]

Second, for a long time the colonists saw themselves as "inferior" Englishmen, "children" who needed the protection of the "mother" country. Only gradually, in the 1750–60s, as we noted earlier, did the terms of love and respect turn to terms of hatred and revilement. Once again, the colonists turned to their ideal self, which they opposed to the materialistic, corrupting old country, Great Britain.[14] Both revivalist and rationalist concurred in the picture of "virtuous" Americans rising against an evil, tyrannical despot.

The language is highly familial. It is the "sons of liberty" versus George III, the "father" who has betrayed them, or, alternatively, versus the "mother," Great Britain, who has withdrawn her nurturance—a favorite image is of the colonists as children at their mother's breast. (For a further development of this father–mother theme, see Chapter 14, "Leadership in the American Revolution.") The children must now grow up. They must become free and independent, that is, experience a second birth.[15]

At this point a number of themes converge: the need to return to the ideal and reverse a declension; the need to experience a rebirth; the need for sons to stand free of their parents, especially fathers; and the need to repudiate the traditions and values of the old civilization of Europe. From being an English colonist now emerges an American.

The American Revolution, it must be noted, like almost all such revolutions, was mainly a young man's revolution. Of the Founding Fathers, George Washington was the oldest, forty-four at the outbreak of hostilities. The others were in their thirties, with a handful in their twenties. Experience in a "Continental" army gave them a new, "national," rather than merely "colonial" identity; and it was men such as these who led the fight in the Constitutional Convention for a revision of the Articles of Confederation and the creation of a United States of America.[16]

My last theme here in the effort to sketch even a few of the lineaments of the American Psyche is the theme of inferiority and superiority. I have already touched on it briefly in earlier parts of this analysis; now I want to trace its operations a little further on in the American experience. It is a theme that sounds with especial loudness around the time of the American Revolution and its aftermath, pauses during the Civil War, is renewed in the late nineteenth to early twentieth century, and then fades away after the Second World War and America's emergence as a superpower.

One need only glance at Thomas Jefferson's "Notes on the State of Virginia" (written 1781–82, published 1787) to see his persistent effort to prove that American flora and fauna—its plants and its animals, such as mountain lions—are as big as other versions; that the native Indian is a manly creature; and that the conquerors, the American whites, are also virile, intelligent, and worthy beings. As proof, Jefferson pictures George Washington and Benjamin Franklin as equal to the great men of antiquity. Indeed, America, equal or almost equal to the past, symbolizes for him the greater future. In contrast, and here Jefferson passes to the offense, "The sum of her [England's] glory is fast descending to the horizon . . . and herself seems passing to that awful dissolution, whose issue is not given human foresight to scan." And this on the eve of Great Britain's industrial revolution!

Jefferson's contemporary, Crèvecoeur, also felt compelled, as we saw earlier, to praise America and to do so by disparaging Europe. As we noted, he depicts America's virtues as the obverse of Europe's ancient vices, declaring that "he is an American who, leaving behind him all his ancient prejudices and manners, receives new ones."

Such a new man, the American, wanted a new language. The fear was that accepting English models meant an accompanying influence of corrupt monarchical ideas. Thus, Noah Webster wrote in 1807 that he intended "to detach this country as much as possible from its dependence on the parent country," and to this end he went on to compile Webster's Dictionary, still the basic version of the American language.

Such a new language could become the basis of a new literature. Thus, Fenimore Cooper wrote to an acquaintance in 1831: "You have appreciated my motives, in regard to my own country. . . . Her mental independence is my object." And Henry Wadsworth Longfellow, a few years later, though he himself wished American writing to be part of a world literature, caught the American impulse exactly in the phrases he ascribed to a proponent of American nationalistic literature: "We want a national literature commensurate with our mountains and rivers,—commensurate with Niagara, and the Alleghenies, and the Great Lakes. We want a national epic that shall correspond to the size of the country. . . . In a word, we want a national literature altogether shaggy and unshorn, that shall shake the earth like a herd of buffaloes thundering over the prairies!"[17]

Much of this debate found its quintessential expression in Ralph Waldo Emerson's "The American Scholar" (1837). It was a new declaration of independence, this time spiritual. In Emerson's ringing words, "Perhaps the time is already come . . . when the sluggard intellect of this continent will look from under its iron lids and fill the postponed expectation of the world with something better than the exertions of mechanical skill. Our day of dependence, our long apprenticeship to the learning of other lands, draws to a close."

Emerson's confidence is based on both a sense of America's mission— the "expectation of the world"—and on his view of Nature. America's Nature is representative of God. Emerson stretches this view to a kind of pantheism, when he exclaims that "man is surprised to find that things near are not less beautiful and wondrous than things remote. The near explains the far. The drop is a small ocean."

One need not, therefore, go beyond America to find the exotic and the beautiful. Instead, Emerson glorifies the common, even the vulgar. His is the aesthetic version of Jacksonian democracy, where everyone and everything is equal. One needs only to be self-reliant, to look out at one's own American world, and one will see all that needs to be seen. Shifting the sensory image, Emerson announced that "we have listened too long to the courtly muses of Europe," and then concludes in the next breath that America must prepare itself for "the conversion of the world." His series of claims comes close to making self-reliance a form of parochialism, which transforms a sense of inferiority into a sense of superiority and then into a mission to convert the world to America and Americanism.

Part of this Americanism is a rejection of the past and a constant reach for the novel and the future. It emerges as a side product of the inferiority-superiority polarity, where the past embodied America's inferiority. Jefferson, for example, sounded the new time perspective when he argued that the usufruct of the earth belonged solely to the living and not to the past generations; he even urged a revolution every twenty years or so, to water the tree of liberty, thus acting out anew the shaking off of the old and past.

This argument is taken up again in Hawthorne's novel, *The House of the Seven Gables* (1850–51), when its protagonist, Holgrave, proposes that "if each generation were allowed and expected to build its own houses, that single change, comparatively unimportant in itself, would imply almost every reform which society is now suffering for . . . our public edifices. . . . It were better that they should crumble to ruin once in twenty years, or thereabouts, as a hint to the people to examine into and reform the institutions which they symbolize."

Many more such examples could be given. The point is that America is like the nouveaux riches, who know that if status is judged by past connections and glories, they will always bear the stigma of inferiority. Thus, America, like the new rich, vaunts its present and its future, in which its prowess can assert itself. This trait regarding the young–old polarity, is part of both America's strength and its weakness. One could make a similar comment, as to the presence of both strengths and weaknesses, concerning the other polarities I have briefly treated: wilderness and civilization, benevolence (or religious mission) and violence, ideal and material (which leads to revivalism rather than revolution), God and Devil (reflected in both the inner and outer worlds), and inferiority and superiority, all of which I have only hinted at here, which go to form the American Psyche.

These and other polarities forming the American Psyche are the fundamentals underlying foreign, as well as domestic, policies (and, of course, the two overlap) and to which America's leaders appeal in selected fashion. Such fundamentals lie deep and often seem vague and obscure. They appear, perhaps, as remote from contemporary postures and policies, which seem more the result of long-term national interests, shifting political fortunes, and external events. Without denying the importance of these factors, I would argue for the fundamental shaping force of what I have called the American Psyche.

As a hint to what I have in mind, let me end by alluding to a few episodes in American history where we can see elements of the American Psyche alive and well. Take, for example, the present-day controversy over gun control. Surely, one could argue, Saturday night specials and deadly assault rifles have no place in crowded urban areas and can hardly be said to protect our liberty and lives; rather, the reverse, being used by criminals to destroy us.

Why then do millions of Americans fight against their elimination, as a threat to American freedom? Some of the anti-gun-control fervor comes from the lobbying forces of the makers of guns. Much more, however, comes from the American Psyche. It would be wrong to underestimate the depth and sincerity of feeling involved on the part of average citizens.

In the beginning, the colonists' superiority over the Indian resided in their muskets. Pictures of Thanksgiving all show the men with weapons over their shoulders (note that these are men, not women, though women also seized muskets when needed on the frontier—the gun issue is a *male* issue).

Then there is the American Revolution, when the colonists defended their freedom and became Americans. I have already mentioned "minute men"; there is also the embattled farmer at Lexington, the sharpshooters, and the militiamen. One mark of being a citizen was the right to bear arms, enshrined in the Second Amendment (in fact, this meant the right to form militias, but the legal nicety has been swept aside in the tide of myth). Part of the depreciated European past was its despotism, which could not trust its subjects with arms (which might be turned against the despot); thus, debauched Europe fought with press-gang armies, who melted away after each battle. As citizens, Americans were defending themselves and their freedom. Freedom was equated with the right to bear arms, and the latter with virile "sons of liberty." Anyone who overlooks these resonances of the gun control issue in the American Psyche will have only a superficial understanding of the matter.

Another example, also involving the polarity of freedom versus despotism, is expressed in terms of fear of central government. This feeling, too, has deep roots. It rises from the exaggerated stress on individualism versus society, one of whose forms is to be found in the Leatherstocking myth and its transformations. In recent times, we catch the flavor of this appeal in the demagogic use of the polarity made by James G. Watt, when he was secretary of the interior in the Reagan administration. Speaking to the graduates of the Rev. Jerry Falwell's *Liberty* Baptist Schools (my italics), Watt warned them that they were inheriting a "hurting country" in danger from "the one force that could snuff out spiritual freedom—excessive government." Watt added that antifreedom forces—"you can call them czars, kings, gestapos or dictators"—have been eroding liberty in America. Then he concluded with the observation that "we have seen government used by the enemies of liberty and freedom right here in America—God's chosen place."[18] Placing such rhetoric in the context of the psychic repository illustrates one way in which "leaders" make their appeals.

My last example as to how the elements of the American Psyche persist into the present combines foreign and domestic strands. It relates to the polarity of idealism–materialism and to the theme of America's civilizing mission. I cite first President William McKinley's response to the unexpected taking of the Philippines in 1898. Getting down on his knees, he prayed and, he tells us, realized that "there was nothing left for us to do but take them all, and to educate the Filipinos, and uplift and civilize and Christianize them, and by God's grace do the very best we could by them, as our fellow-men for whom Christ also dies." Even more strikingly, McKinley's sense of mission was echoed—better still, internalized—by the Filipino nationalist leader Pardo de Tavera, who wrote McKinley that "Providence led the United States to these distant islands for the fulfillment of a noble mission, to take charge of the task of teaching us the principles that . . . have made your people the wonder of the world and the pride of humanity."[19]

We see the years change, but not the appeal to the same elements of the psychic repository—trust in Providence, in a new frontier, in America's destiny, and in its missionary nature—in President Reagan's statements of 1984: "America's new strength, confidence, and purpose are carrying hope and opportunity far from our shores. . . . How can we not believe in the goodness and greatness of Americans? How can we not do what is right and needed to preserve this last, best hope of man on earth?"[20]

One could go on and on, reaching back into America's two-hundred-year-old history, and citing, for example, Washington's 1783 circular, asserting America's role as a model, this time not only as a city on a hill but as the "great Experiment" in democracy. As Washington told his fellow citizens, they were "actors on a most conspicuous Theater, which seems to be peculiarly designated by Providence for the display of human greatness and felicity," and then, in language directly reminiscent of Winthrop, concluding, "this is the moment when the eyes of the whole World are turned upon them"; to Lincoln's Gettysburg Address and his appeal to a rededication to the preservation of liberty—"that this nation, under God, shall have a new birth of freedom—and that government of the people . . . shall not perish from the earth"—as an example to others; and to JFK and his New Frontier and willingness to pay any price.[21]

In citing such examples, I am being very American, for it is actually such appeals that emanate from and mirror forth the American Psyche. In a fuller treatment, one would want systematically to explore the entire range of polarities and their historical expression over time and then to indicate how they weave in and out of one another, creating a particular balance, and what that balance is today. Here and now, however, I shall more or less stop, simply making the assertion, which I have tried briefly to illustrate, that, in the realm of the psyche, the past is indeed prologue to the present— and to the future.

One last comment, however. In seeking to understand human history, as it stretches from time past to time present and time future, a viable group psychology that could illuminate the doings of men and women would be of great value. In my view, we do not yet have such a psychology; and Freudian psychoanalysis, as I have remarked in the Introduction, with its gaze largely fixed on the individual, does not offer much hope in this regard, though its insights form an essential starting point. It may be, then, that in practicing psychohistory, the historian is in a better position to construct such a group psychology than are the psychologists themselves. It is this ambitious goal that I also have had in mind as I pursued an understanding of, particularly, the American Psyche, as well as other historical phenomena, an understanding in which the specific and the general must necessarily be united.

# Notes

## Introduction

1. Even in the natural sciences today, we are more aware of the role of the scientist as an influencing factor in his or her observations (see, for example, the work of Heisenberg in physics). Still, the difference I am pointing to should be obvious.
2. For my further discussion of the genetic fallacy problem, see Chapter 6, p. 91; Chapter 7, p. 99; and Chapter 8, p. 121.
3. For why and how a given individual, in this case myself, enters upon such a practice, see the new introduction to the paperback edition of *James and John Stuart Mill: Father and Son in the Nineteenth Century* (Transaction Books: New Brunswick, N.J., 1988; orig. pub., Basic Books: New York, 1975), xvii–xx.
4. Incidentally, I do not think of myself as primarily a psychohistorian but as a historian who uses psychoanalytic psychology in some of my work. Most of my work, in fact, has been in intellectual history, philosophy of history, history of science and technology, and so forth. As I remarked at the very beginning of this Introduction, however, "all history is necessarily psychological." Even when not overtly used, therefore, the psychohistorical perspective should inform the historian's work.
5. See, for example, the literature on Leopold von Ranke, or the Annales School.
6. Two useful volumes are *Psychology and Historical Interpretation*, ed. by William McKinley Runyan (New York, 1988), and *Journal of Personality*, 56 (March 1988): Special Issue, "Psychobiography and Life Narratives," ed. by Dan P. McAdams and Richard L. Ochberg. For the reader interested in some of my own further discussions, see, for example, "Inside the Whales," *Times Literary Supplement*, Special Issue, July 1966: "New Ways in History," 667–669; "Group Psychology and Problems of Contemporary History," *Journal of Contemporary History*, 3 (April 1968), 163–77 (repub. in *Psycho-history: Readings . . .*, ed. Geoffrey Cocks and Travis Crosby (New Haven, CT, 1987); "What Is Psycho-history?," *Transactions of the Royal Historical Society*, 5th series, 21 (1971); "Psychiatry and History," Chapter 48 in *American Handbook of Psychiatry*, ed. Silvano Arieti (2nd ed.), Vol. I (New York, 1974); "Psychoanalytic Theory and History: Groups and Events," in *The Annual of Psychoanalysis*, Vol. VI, 41–57 (International University Series: New York, 1978); and *Psychoanalysis and History* (Englewood Cliffs: NJ, 1963; rev. ed., 1971).
7. Quoted in Peter Gay, *Freud: A Life for Our Time* (New York, 1988), 555.

8. Sigmund Freud and William C. Bullitt, *Thomas Woodrow Wilson* (Cambridge, MA, 1967); Sigmund Freud, "Leonardo Da Vinci and a Memory of His Childhood," in J. Strachey, ed., *The Standard Edition of the Complete Psychological Works of Sigmund Freud* (London, 1964), Vol. XI.

9. Herbert S. Lewis, "Leaders and Followers: Some Anthropological Perspectives," Addison-Wesley Module in Anthropology, No. 50 (1974), 3 and 4.

10. Robert C. Tucker, *Politics As Leadership* (Columbia, MO, 1981), 27. Robert Michels's book is *Political Parties* (New York, 1949). Another excellent and important book is James MacGregor Burns, *Leadership* (New York, 1978).

11. Allan Janik and Stephen Toulmin, *Wittgenstein's Vienna* (New York, 1973), 52.

12. The "his," alas, is deliberate; women seem infrequently to serve as "founding fathers."

13. John Maynard Keynes, *The General Theory of Employment, Interest, and Money* (New York, 1964), 383–84.

14. For my own effort to pursue to the limit Freud's inspiration in this regard, see *The Revolutionary Ascetic* (New York, 1976). The best book on the theoretical problems involved in studying group psychology is Fred Weinstein and Gerald M. Platt, *Psychoanalytic Sociology* (Baltimore, 1973).

## 1. Darwin, the Bedrock of Psychoanalysis

1. Sigmund Freud, "Analysis Terminable and Interminable" (1937), in J. Strachey, ed., *The Standard Edition of the Complete Psychological Works of Sigmund Freud* (London, 1964), Vol. XXIII.

2. Anna Freud, *Difficulties in the Path of Psychoanalysis* (1969), quoted in Lucille B. Ritvo, "The Impact of Darwin on Freud," *Psychoanalytic Quarterly*, 43 (1974), 183.

3. A good starting point in Darwinian studies is *The Darwinian Heritage,* ed. David Kohn (Princeton, NJ, 1985). For Darwin's effect on Freud see, for example, Lucille B. Ritvo, "Impact of Darwin on Freud," and "Darwin as the Source of Freud's Neo-Lamarckianism," *Journal of the American Psychoanalytic Association,* 13 (July 1965); and Frank J. Sulloway, *Freud, Mind of the Biologist* (New York, 1979).

4. Quoted in Stephen Toulmin, *The Return to Cosmology* (Berkeley, CA, 1982), 165.

5. Quoted in Toulmin, *Return to Cosmology,* 146–47.

6. Darwin, in fact, was not at the meeting, pleading ill health as usual for his nonattendance. He was represented, however, by T. H. Huxley; but the taunt, of course, was directed as much at Darwin as at his "bulldog," as Huxley was called.

7. Charles Darwin, *The Descent of Man* (New York, n.d.), 390.

8. Ibid., 471. The quotes that follow are on pp. 473, 476, and 478.

9. Alex Comfort, "Darwin and Freud," in *Darwin and the Naked Lady* (New York, 1962).

10. Charles Darwin, *The Expression of the Emotions in Man and Animals* (Chicago, 1965), 315. The next quotes are from pp. 311 and 339–40.

11. Silvan S. Schweber, "Essay Review: The Correspondence of the Young Darwin," *Journal of the History of Biology* (Fall 1988), and his "John Herschel and Charles Darwin: A Study in Parallel Lives," *Journal of the History of Biology,* 22 (Spring 1989), are excellent contributions to a psychologically informed study of Darwin's life.

12. Starting in 1839, Darwin made notes on his own babies. See *The Correspondence of Charles Darwin: Volume 4* (Cambridge, England, 1988) for their recent publication.

13. Ralph Colp, Jr., *To Be an Invalid* (Chicago, 1977). For further discussion of Darwin's illnesses and especially their possible origins in Chagas' disease, see chapter 2, p. 32, and note 1.

14. Howard E. Gruber, *Darwin on Man: A Psychological Study of Scientific Creativity, Together with Darwin's Early and Unpublished Notebooks,* transcribed and annotated by Paul H. Barrett (New York, 1974), 285. The quotes that follow are from pp. 348, 268, 289, and 281. Cf. Robert Thomas Keegan, *The Development of Charles Darwin's Thinking on Psychology* (University Microfilms International, Ann Arbor, MI, 1988).

15. See, for example, Lucille B. Ritvo, "Carl Claus as Freud's Professor of the New Darwinian Biology," *International Journal of Psycho-Analysis,* 53 (1972).

16. Quoted in Sulloway, *Freud, Mind of the Biologist,* 14.

17. Paul F. Cranefield, "Freud and the School of Helmholtz," *Gesnerus,* 23 (1966) Heft 1/2, 37.

18. Quoted in Paul E. Cranefield, "The Philosophical and Cultural Interests of the Biophysics Movement of 1847," *Journal of the History of Medicine and Allied Science,* 21 (1966), 6.

19. William J. McGrath, *Freud's Discovery of Psychoanalysis: The Politics of Hysteria* (Ithaca, NY, 1986), 115.

20. Darwin, *Origin,* 2.

21. Ibid., 552.

22. Sigmund Freud, "Introductory Lecture on Psycho-Analysis," in J. Strachey, ed., *Standard Edition,* Vol. XV, 51.

23. Lili E. Peller, "Biological Foundations of Psychology: Freud Versus Darwin," *Bulletin of the Philadelphia Association for Psychoanalysis,* 15 (1965), 90.

24. This point needs emphasis. Freud's own narrow interpretation of dreams as invariably wish fulfillments, based on libidinal impulses, etc., is no longer sufficient; nevertheless, what does remain completely valid is his insistence that dreams are not mere somatic events but have *meaning,* a *human* meaning, and can therefore be *interpreted.* Attempts to reduce dreams to mere blips on a

scanning device, or purely physiological "events," correctly point to a necessary physical basis but make the category error of thinking that that is all there is to dreams. For an example of this kind of "mindless" psychiatry, see J. Allan Hobson, *The Dreaming Brain* (New York, 1989), and for a balanced critique of Hobson's work, which does have some good features within its limited perspective, see Brian Farrell's review in *The New York Review of Books,* June 15, 1989, pp. 28–32.

25. *The Republic of Plato,* tr. by Francis Macdonald Cornfield (New York, 1945), 296–97.

26. Wolf Lepenies, "Transformation and Storage of Scientific Traditions in Literature," in *Literature and History,* ed. by Leonard Schulze and Walter Wetzels (Lanham, MD, 1983). The quote that follows is from p. 44.

27. Stephen Jay Gould, *The New York Review of Books,* October 27, 1988, p. 32.

28. Sigmund Freud, "Studies on Hysteria," in J. Strachey, ed., *Standard Edition,* Vol. II, 160–61.

29. I owe the gist of this paragraph to a conversation with my friend Stanley Renshon.

30. *Letters of Sigmund Freud,* ed. by Ernst L. Freud (New York, 1964), 59–60, 65.

31. Carl Schorske, *Fin-de-Siècle Vienna* (New York, 1981), 10–11.

32. George Eliot, *Middlemarch,* quoted in Gillian Beer, *Darwin's Plots* (London, 1983), 165.

33. Mary Midgley, *Beast and Man: The Roots of Human Nature* (Ithaca, NY, 1978), 39.

34. Henry Gleitman, *Psychology,* 2nd ed. (New York, 1986), 410. See too Irenäus Eibl-Eibesfeldt, *Love and Hate,* tr. Geoffrey Strachan (London, 1971), and Melvin Konner, *The Tangled Wing: Biological Constraints on the Human Spirit* (New York, 1982).

35. I am using the term "new science" here in a very different sense from that of my book *A New Science: The Breakdown of Connections and the Birth of Sociology* (New York, 1989). There I make no claim that sociology is a *systematic* body of theory, drawing from observations a number of hypotheses, which are then taken back to the data and evaluated anew in their light, resulting in modified or new hypotheses, if necessary. However, I do call it a "new science," for so it was seen by many of its proponents; and I then try to evaluate it as a particular form of human science, which is much looser, however, than what I am contending is the case with psychoanalysis.

## 2. *Darwin, the Benchuca, and Genius*

1. Recent work has reexamined the case for Chagas' disease. Jared Haft Goldstein argues that Darwin suffered from a minimal form of the disease, which characteristically leaves its victims sensitive to psychological stresses ("Darwin, Chagas, Mind, and Body," *Perspectives in Biology and Medicine,* 32[4], Summer

1989). Dr. Ralph Colp, author of *To Be an Invalid* (Chicago, 1977), informs me that he will be reviewing all of this recent work in a forthcoming article.

## 3. Freud and Nietzsche

1. Copies of *The Interpretation of Dreams,* however, actually appeared in November 1899.
2. Sigmund Freud, *The Interpretation of Dreams,* tr. by James Strachey (London, 1954), 330. The brackets are the translator's.
3. In addition, of course, the phrase "transvaluation of all values" is also used in a number of other places in the proposed book.
4. Ernest Jones, *The Life and Works of Sigmund Freud,* 3 vols. (New York, 1953–1957), I, 356.
5. *The Origins of Psychoanalysis. Letters, Drafts and Notes to Wilhelm Fliess, 1887–1902,* ed. by Marie Bonaparte, Anna Freud, and Ernst Kris (Garden City, NY, 1957), 221.
6. *Standard Edition* (hereafter referred to as *SE*), 24 vols. (London, 1953–74), VI, 26–27.
7. It is amusing to note that, later, after the break with Freud, Adler's followers tried to claim Nietzsche for their own camp. Thus, for example, F. G. Crookshank, in *Individual Psychology and Nietzsche* (London, 1933, p. 9), writes: "In spite of what the Freudians may say—they are notoriously hard to please—Adler is infinitely closer to Nietzsche than is Freud."
8. For the entire discussion, see *Minutes of the Vienna Psychoanalytic Society, Vol. I: 1906–1908,* ed. by Herman Nunberg and Ernst Federn, tr. by M. Nunberg (New York, 1962), 355–361.
9. Ibid., Vol. II: 1908–1910 (New York, 1967), 30–32; Jones, *op. cit.,* II, 344.
10. *SE,* VI, 146–147. Freud had had his attention drawn to this saying of Nietzsche by the "Rat Man," whose case history was published in 1909, just before the addition of the footnote. See *SE,* X, 184.
11. *SE,* XIV, 15–16.
12. Ibid., 333.
13. Even Walter Kaufmann, an admirer and favorable critic of Nietzsche, remarks about the "Pale Criminal," "Too abstract to make sense to Nietzsche's first readers, including even his once close friend Rohde, much of this chapter now seems like reflections on Dostoevski's Raskolnikov." (*The Portable Nietzsche* [New York, 1954], 118). I would emphasize the "now."
14. Sigmund Freud, *New Introductory Lectures on Psychoanalysis,* tr. by W. J. H. Sprott (New York, 1933), 102. The editor of the English translation of *The Ego and the Id,* James Strachey, points out, however, that Groddeck himself seems to have derived "das Es" from an old teacher of his, Ernst Schweninger, a well-known German physician of an earlier generation.

15. Sigmund Freud, *An Autobiographical Study,* tr. by James Strachey (New York, 1963), 114.

16. Jones, *Life,* III, 190 and 460. There is another mention of Nietzsche in a letter to Arnold Zweig of September 30, 1934, but it is not important. See, however, *Letters of Sigmund Freud,* selected and ed. by Ernst L. Freud, tr. by Tania and James Stern (New York, 1960), 421.

17. One attribution that I have not mentioned occurred after Freud's death, when his disciple and biographer, Ernest Jones, compared Freud's conception of the superego to Nietzsche's exposition of the "bad conscience"; see Jones, *Life,* III, 283.

18. Nietzsche's sister, on the other hand, is a different matter. Jones reports how he and Hanns Sachs, during the Weimar Congress of 1911, took the opportunity to call on Frau Elisabeth Förster-Nietzsche. "Sachs told her about the Congress," Jones says, "and commented on the similarity between some of Freud's ideas and her famous brother's" (Jones, *op. cit.,* II, 86). Jones does not tell us about her reaction, but we can imagine the vehemently anti-Semitic Frau Förster-Nietzsche's pleasure at this comparison of her beloved brother to the Viennese Jew, Sigmund Freud.

19. *Gesammelte Werke.* Musarion Ausgabe, 23 vols. (Munich, 1920–1929), XIV, 313.

20. *The Origins of Psychoanalysis,* 213.

21. Letter of July 13, 1917, in *Letters of Sigmund Freud* (New York: Basic Books, 1960), 319, and letter of July 30, 1915, *ibid.,* 310.

22. See Chapter 5, p. 63, for the full text from which this quotation comes. English translations of Nietzsche often mislead the reader into thinking that Nietzsche, too, used energy metaphors. Thus, one translation of #13 of *Beyond Good and Evil* reads: "Above all, a living thing wants to *discharge* its energy: life as such is will to power." (This is the translation by Marianne Cowan [Chicago, 1955]. The translation by Helen Zimmern in the Modern Library volume *The Philosophy of Nietzsche* [New York, n.d.] uses the same word, *discharge.*) But Nietzsche's word is *auslassen,* which has the connotation of "letting off" or "giving vent to," often with anger. It is the word *entladen* that connotes electrical discharge. As for Freud, his use of metaphors is so frequent and obvious as not to need further examples here.

23. *New Introductory Lectures on Psychoanalysis,* 217.

24. For example, Nietzsche had hoped for a pupil in Lou Andreas-Salomé. "I wish to have a pupil in her," Nietzsche declared in 1882, "and, if my life should not last much longer, an heir, and one who will further develop my thought." (From a draft for a letter, Summer 1882, quoted in Erich Podach, *Friedrich Nietzsche und Lou Andreas-Salomé* (Zurich, 1938). Alas, his hopes were doomed to disappointment. Instead, Lou eventually turned to Freud. Introduced to him at the Weimar Congress of the International Psychoanalytic Association in 1911, Lou expressed her intense desire to study psychoanalysis: "I have not been able

to leave psychoanalysis alone, and the deeper I penetrate into it the more it fascinates me." Given permission to attend his Wednesday evening seminars in Vienna, she worked closely with Freud, and also at first with Adler. In time, she herself came to practice psychoanalysis (for details, see further, Jones, *Life,* III, 444). Thus, in many ways, the relationship of Lou Andreas-Salomé to Nietzsche and to Freud can be considered paradigmatic for the subject of this paper.

## 4. The Hysterical Personality and History

1. Alan Krohn, *Hysteria* (New York, 1978). Page numbers noted in text are all from this work.
2. Ilza Veith, *Hysteria: The History of a Disease* (Chicago, 1965).
3. Carroll Smith-Rosenberg, "The Hysterical Woman: Sex Roles and Role Conflict in Nineteenth-Century America," *Social Research,* 39 (1972), 652.
4. For earlier reference to the question of false pregnancies, see pp. 16–17.
5. Wilhelm Reich, *Character-Analysis* (New York, 1963; 3rd ed.).
6. John Demos, "Underlying Themes in the Witchcraft of Seventeenth-Century New England," *The American Historical Review,* 75 (1970), 1311–1326, esp. 1313, 1321, 1322. Since then, Demos has published a full-length book, *Entertaining Satan* (New York, 1982).
7. John Webster, *The Displaying of Supposed Witchcraft* (London, 1677), quoted in Veith, *Hysteria,* 67.
8. See Veith, *Hysteria,* 170, 184.
9. Michel Foucault, *Madness and Civilization: A History of Insanity in the Age of Reason* (trans. Richard Howard) (New York, 1965).
10. Edgar Morin, *Rumour in Orlèans* (trans. Peter Green) (New York, 1971), 42.

## 5. Autobiography and Psychoanalysis

1. John N. Morris, *Versions of the Self* (New York, 1966), 16.
2. Arthur O. Lovejoy, *Essays in the History of Ideas* (Baltimore, 1960), 183, 224.
3. As will the even more recent work of Edith Jacobson and D. W. Winnicott in object relations theory and Heinz Kohut in self-psychology.
4. Freud's seduction theory has occasioned much controversy, especially with Jeffrey M. Masson's *The Assault on Truth: Freud's Suppression of the Seduction Theory* (New York, 1984), an unconvincing book.
5. For other comments on "case history," I refer the reader to Chapter 1.
6. William H. Blanchard, *Rousseau and the Spirit of Revolt* (Ann Arbor, MI, 1967), 247.
7. Erik H. Erikson, "On the Nature of Psycho-Historical Evidence: In Search of Gandhi," in *Psychoanalysis and History,* ed. Bruce Mazlish (New York, 1971) (originally published in *Daedalus,* Summer 1968), 184.

## 6. *The Importance of Being Karl Marx, or Henry Thoreau, or Anybody*

1. Albert Schweitzer, *The Psychiatric Study of Jesus,* trans. Winfred Overholser (Boston, 1948).
2. Richard Lebeaux, *Young Man Thoreau* (Amherst, 1975).
3. A convenient edition is Henry David Thoreau, *Walden; or Life in the Woods* (1854; rpt. New York, 1957). The quotes given are on pp. 3, 4, 29, and 37. The quotes that follow are on pp. 1, 6, 52, and 58.
4. Lebeaux, *Thoreau,* 215.
5. See my earlier comments on Erikson's work, in Chapter 5.
6. Thoreau, *Walden,* 321.
7. Quoted in Lebeaux, *Thoreau,* 245.
8. Thoreau, *Walden,* 321.
9. Quoted in Lebeaux, *Thoreau,* 65.
10. Patrick Hutton, *The Cult of Revolutionary Tradition* (Berkeley, 1981), p. 22.
11. As with Marx, books on Einstein either gloss over or misrepresent his personal relations; great men are not supposed to exhibit less than praiseworthy human qualities. Abraham Pais, in his solid, scientific biography, *Subtle Is the Lord: The Science and the Life of Albert Einstein* (Oxford, 1982), glosses over the matter by saying, "These contacts [with Einstein's children] were not always easy, since Mileva [Einstein's first wife] never reconciled herself to the separation and subsequent divorce" (p. 241). Cf. p. 301.
12. See further on Darwin, of course, Chapter 2.
13. Robert C. Tucker, *The Marx-Engels Reader,* 2nd ed. (New York, 1978), 296.
14. As this is an important point, the interested reader might want to consult, for example, J. H. Hexter, "The Myth of the Middle Class in Tudor England" in *Reappraisals in History* (Evanston, 1961). As another example, I cite the lengthy statement by Elie Kedourie, reviewing a book on modern Iran, by an otherwise excellent scholar, Ervand Abrahamian (*Times Literary Supplement,* December 3, 1982, p. 1327).

> Whether his approach is "neo-Marxist" or plain Marxist, Abrahamian cannot avoid operating with the notion of class. The Marxist notion of class and class-relations, in so far as it is intelligible, is logically tied to that of the ownership (or nonownership) of the means of production. In the Marxist schema a middle class, a bourgeoisie, is the necessary concomitant of capitalism. The middle class is middle because it follows, is indeed conjured up by, the workings of feudalism. As the engine of historical change, it is in turn supplanted by the industrial working class to which "capitalism" willy-nilly gives birth. This account of social and economic change derives its plausibility from its implicit reference to Western European history, where a mercantile and professional bourgeoisie gradually asserted itself and challenged a landed nobility. But how is one to make use of the idea of a middle class in the Middle East, or India, or China—let alone set it up as the motor and mainspring of social and political change?

Consider the difficulties in which Abrahamian gets entangled by his attempt to discern a Persian middle class, and to specify its political role. He first identifies a "traditional middle class": it has ties to the traditional economy and "the traditional Shi'i ideology," and is said to have become aware of itself as a class, conscious of its grievances, when Western economic penetration threatened its commercial interests. But there are two other middle classes. One is a "comprador bourgeoisie" created outside the bazaar by the introduction of European capital and by the capitulations granted to European business men; the other is a "salaried middle class." The latter comprises the intelligentsia and those trained for a profession, who have been affected by Western ideas. They are *munavver alfekr, rushanfekr* (enlightened thinkers), *kravatis* (tie-wearers), *dawlatis* (governmental officials). In the nineteenth century these groups, the author says, formed "a mere stratum"; but during Reza Shah's reign they were transformed into "a social class with similar relationships to the mode of production, the means of administration, and the process of modernization."

Class, as against a mere stratum, is not lightly to be invoked in a Marxist or even a neo-Marxist scheme. A class not only has a relationship to the mode of production, but this relationship determines its political stance, and its position in the class-struggle. Here, however, we have not just one middle class but three. What are the relationships between these three middle classes? Do they struggle against one another, against the class they are supplanting, and against the class which will inevitably supplant them?

Since there is a class waiting to supplant them (as is of course self-evident, according to class-analysis), and since it is (of necessity) the working class, its interests must (precisely because it is a class) find political expression. The Tudeh party is (must be) the voice, the emanation of the working class of Iran. The party was the champion of "workers, peasants, intellectuals, traders, and craftsmen." It is claimed to be the "vanguard of the proletariat and landless peasantry." But if we look more closely at the Party what do we find? We find, as Abrahamian tells us, that "it was the modern middle class that formed the major portion of the party's top, middle, and lower echelons. The modern middle class," he goes on to say, "also made up an important portion of the party's general rank and file and sympathizers." We are also told that—*mirabile dictu*—rapid modernization and industrialization, which drew some 4,000,000 peasants into the cities, tended not to strengthen, but actually to weaken the Tudeh!

If we cling, then, to class-analysis we find ourselves in a topsy-turvy world.

15. Friedrich Nietzsche, *Beyond Good and Evil,* translated by Marianne Cowan (Chicago, 1955), 6.
16. Sigmund Freud, *New Introductory Lectures on Psychoanalysis* (1933 [1932]), Chapter 25, "The Question of a *Weltanschauung,*" in *The Standard Edition of the Complete Psychological Works of Sigmund Freud,* 24 vols., James Strachey (London, 1964), XXII, 178 and 180.
17. *Karl Marx and Friedrich Engels: Collected Works* (New York, 1975–), Vol. I, p. 684. I have used here the translation as given in Marx and Engels's *Collected Works,* which has now become the standard edition in English. The word

translated there as "embitterment" is *Zerrissenheit*. Douglas Scott, who has done an excellent translation of Werner Blumenberg's book on Marx, *Portrait of Marx* (New York, 1972), prefers the English word "confused" rather than "embittered." *Zerrissenheit* means literally "torn condition" and is a Romantic term for "melancholy" or "unhealthy state of mind."

18. Rousseau, Godwin, and others before Marx had made the argument in equally passionate terms. Evil, for example, Rousseau contended, is not in human nature but in society only. We are corrupted by wicked, artificial institutions. It is against this view that Malthus, in turn, wrote his *Population* (Thomas Robert Malthus, *Population: The First Essay* [Ann Arbor, 1959], 62). Malthus's "nature" was not just human nature, though rooted in its propensities to consume and procreate, but certain "givens," mathematical limits to human existence. Marx, as we can see, is resuming the Rousseau–Godwin position and attacking not only Malthus's economics but implicitly his general ideas as well.

19. Tucker, *Reader,* p. 24.

## 7. Jevons's Science and his "Second Nature"

1. Lionel Robbins, "The Place of Jevons in the History of Economic Thought," *The Manchester School,* VII, 1 (1936): 4 and 6.

2. W. S. Jevons, *The Theory of Political Economy* (New York, 1965, 5th ed.) 44. The next quote is on p. 52. See also p. xi.

3. The title of Jevons's seminal work still carries the phrase "Political Economy"; but in the preface to the second edition (1879; the first edition was 1871), he proposes the substitution of the name "Economics" to indicate the movement to a purer "science" (xiv).

4. *The Theory of Political Economy,* 12.

5. Ibid., vii.

6. *Papers and Correspondence of William Stanley Jevons,* ed. by R. D. Collison Black and Rosamond Könekamp, Vol. I, *Biography and Personal Journal* (London, 1972), 98.

7. Jevons had had practical experience with a number of the physical sciences. In fact, his initial studies were in physics and chemistry, at University College, London, and he briefly contemplated a career in these fields. His training in chemistry established his qualifications for his first job, assayer at a new mint to be set up in Australia, where he went at age seventeen, but, once there, he quickly shifted his interest to geology, writing three papers, and to meteorology, making and publishing a number of observations. Hence, the move to economics can be seen, from one perspective, as a continuing progression to the "soft" sciences, but from the other perspective, of classics, history, and poetry, as a firming up of a commitment to "true" science.

8. *The Theory of Political Economy,* 3.

9. Ibid., 23.

10. *Papers and Correspondence of William Stanley Jevons,* ed. by R. D. Collison Black, Vol. II, *Correspondence 1850–1862* (London, 1973), 321.
11. *The Theory of Political Economy,* 23.
12. *The Theory of Political Economy,* 38.
13. Ibid., 18.
14. Ibid., xvii–xviii.
15. *Papers and Correspondence of William Stanley Jevons,* II, 291.
16. Ibid., 316. For a similar impact of Buckle on James Clerk Maxwell and his work, see Theodore M. Porter, "A Statistical Survey of Gases: Maxwell's Social Physics," *HSPS,* 12:1 (1981): 85–87.
17. *The Theory of Political Economy,* 20.
18. *Papers and Correspondence of William Stanley Jevons,* II, 306.
19. Ibid., 359–360.
20. Ibid., 23.
21. Ibid., 39.
22. Ibid., 348.
23. *Papers and Correspondence of William Stanley Jevons,* I, 1.
24. Ibid., 53.
25. Ibid., 38.
26. Ibid., 100.
27. Ibid., 112.
28. Ibid., 133.
29. Ibid., 66.
30. *Papers and Correspondence of William Stanley Jevons,* II, 233.
31. *Papers and Correspondence of William Stanley Jevons,* I, 66.
32. Ibid., 130–131.
33. *Papers and Correspondence of William Stanley Jevons,* II, 307.
34. *Papers and Correspondence of William Stanley Jevons,* I, 131.
35. Ibid., 203.
36. Ibid., 28.
37. Quoted in T. W. Hutchinson, *A Review of Economic Doctrines. 1870–1929* (Oxford, 1953), 33.
38. *Papers and Correspondence of William Stanley Jevons,* I, 183.
39. Ibid., 27.
40. *Papers and Correspondence of William Stanley Jevons,* II, 180.
41. Ibid., 238.
42. *Papers and Correspondence of William Stanley Jevons,* I, 200.
43. *Papers and Correspondence of William Stanley Jevons,* II, 276–277.
44. Ibid., 180.
45. Ibid., 222.
46. *Papers and Correspondence of William Stanley Jevons,* I, 155.
47. *Papers and Correspondence of William Stanley Jevons,* II, 288.
48. Ibid., 312.

## 8. The Iron Cage of Max Weber

1. Arthur Mitzman, *The Iron Cage: An Historical Interpretation of Max Weber* (New York, 1969). Page numbers noted in text are all from this work.
2. *Daedalus* (Summer 1968).
3. Mitzman continued to try to make his case in *Sociology and Estrangement: Three Sociologists of Imperial Germany* (New York, 1973).
4. Fred Weinstein and Gerald Platt, *The Wish to Be Free* (Berkeley, CA, 1969).
5. For my own more extended views on Weber, see *A New Science: The Break-down of Connections and the Birth of Sociology* (New York, 1989).
6. Cf. Erik H. Erikson, "The Legend of Hitler's Childhood," *Childhood and Society* (New York, 1963).
7. Quoted in *From Max Weber,* trans. and ed. by H. H. Gerth and C. Wright Mills (New York, 1952), 71.
8. Friedrich Nietzsche, *Beyond Good and Evil,* trans. by Marianne Cowan (Chicago, 1955), 3.
9. Reinhard Bendix, *Max Weber: An Intellectual Portrait* (Garden City, N.Y., 1962), 47–48.
10. H. H. Gerth and C. Wright Mills, *From Max Weber* (New York, 1952), 7.
11. See Chapter 12, pp. 171–172, for some further reference to Weber's trip to America and its importance.
12. *American Historical Review* 66 (1961), 4.
13. Hugh Stretton, *The Political Sciences* (New York, 1970).
14. Gerth and Mills, *From Max Weber,* 8–9.
15. Ibid., 143.
16. *Max Weber: The Theory of Social and Economic Organization,* trans. by A. M. Henderson and Talcott Parsons (New York, 1966), 89–90.
17. *The Protestant Ethic and the Spirit of Capitalism,* trans. by Talcott Parsons (New York, 1958), 29, 90.
18. Gerth and Mills, *From Max Weber,* 149.
19. Ibid., 151.

## 9. Prolegomena to Psychohistory

1. E. Victor Wolfenstein, *The Revolutionary Personality: Lenin, Trotsky, Gandhi* (Princeton, 1967).
2. Peter Loewenberg, *Decoding the Past* (New York, 1983), has some interesting things to say about "The Education of a Psychohistorian."
3. The role of judgment in history is perhaps best handled in Louis Mink, "The Autonomy of Historical Understanding," *History and Theory,* 5(1) 1966.
4. For one of the best discussions of Freud's application of psychoanalysis to political and historical subjects, see the relevant chapters in Philip Rieff, *Freud:*

*The Mind of the Moralist* (1960). A recent book of interest on this subject is Paul Roazen, *Freud: Political and Social Thought* (1968).

5. See, for example, the collection of articles on the *Authoritarian Personality,* edited by Christie and Jahoda (1954).

6. One of the best efforts to view the "authoritarian personality" in terms of concrete political conditions, with the result being varied political behavior, is Seymour Martin Lipset, *Political Man* (1960).

7. Chalmers Johnson, *Revolution and the Social System* (Hoover Institute Studies, 3 [1964], 22–26). Harry Eckstein, "On the Etiology of Internal War," *History and Theory,* 4(2), 1965, is another important work on the typology of revolutions.

8. In my own effort at a typology of a revolutionary personality—which I called *The Revolutionary Ascetic* (New York, 1976)—I did try to situate it in the context of different types of revolution, but may also have short-changed the account of the social systems, an inherent tendency of all typologies.

9. Back in October 1967, a Conference on Leadership, under the direction of Professor Dankwart Rustow (Columbia University), was held, with a special emphasis on the psychological dimension of the leader-led relation. The papers were published in the Summer 1968 issue of *Daedalus*. My own effort to deal with a facet of this problem, "James Mill and the Utilitarians," is included in this collection.

10. James David Barber, *The Presidential Character* (Englewood Cliffs, N.J., 1972).

11. There is a difference between Freud's construction of "oral," "anal," and "genital" character types, based on his clinical work, and the construction of political types, based on extrapolation of private motives to public agencies. That difference is exactly what is involved in the Lasswellian dilemma.

12. For the psychoanalyst's problem of outside verification, see Samuel Novey's "The Significance of the Actual Historical Event in Psychiatry and Psycho-analysis," *British Journal of Medical Psychology,* 37(4), 1964.

13. Cf. my "Group Psychology and Problems of Contemporary History," *Journal of Contemporary History,* April 1968.

## 11. Orwell inside the Whale

1. *The Collected Essays, Journalism and Letters of George Orwell,* edited by Sonia Orwell and Ian Angus (New York, 1968) Four volumes. IV (1945–1950), 460.

2. *Collected Essays,* IV, 502.

3. *Collected Essays,* IV, 475.

4. *Collected Essays,* IV, 217.

5. Alexis de Tocqueville, *Democracy in America,* ed. J. P. Mayer, translated by George Lawrence (Garden City, 1969), 691–92.

6. Eugene Zamiatin, *We,* translated by Gregory Zilboorg (New York, 1924), 3.

7. *Collected Essays,* IV, 213.

8. *Collected Essays,* I (1920–1940), 532.
9. *Collected Essays,* I, 532.
10. *Collected Essays,* I, 530, 531.
11. *Collected Essays,* IV, 466.
12. George Orwell, *1984* (New York: New American Library), 216. Page numbers noted in the text are all from this work.
13. *Collected Essays,* I, 376.
14. Jeremy Bentham, *Works,* ed. John Bowring (London, 1843), IV, 40.
15. Quoted in Michael Ignatieff, *A Just Measure of Pain* (New York, 1978), 197–98.
16. *Collected Essays,* I, 380–81.
17. *Collected Essays,* I, 4.
18. *Collected Essays,* I, 448.
19. *Collected Essays,* I, 5.
20. *Collected Essays,* I, 521.
21. Murray Sperber, "Gazing into the Glass Paperweight: The Structure and Psychology of Orwell's *1984,*" *Modern Fiction Studies,* 26 (Summer 1980), 214.
22. *Collected Essays,* IV, 334, 351.
23. *Collected Essays,* IV, 359.
24. *Collected Essays,* IV, 337.
25. Sperber, 214.
26. *Collected Essays,* I, 533.
27. *Collected Essays,* I, 526.
28. *Collected Essays,* I, 524.
29. *Collected Essays,* I, 534.

## 12. *The Iron of Melancholy*

1. Alexis de Tocqueville, *Democracy in America,* trans. Henry Reeve (New York, 1900), II, 142, 147.
2. John Owen King III, *The Iron of Melancholy: Structures of Spiritual Conversion in America from the Puritan Conscience to Victorian Neurosis* (Middletown, Conn., 1983), 457. Page numbers noted in text are all from this work.
3. See Perry Miller, "The Shaping of the American Character," in *Nature's Nation* (Cambridge, Mass., 1967); Edmund S. Morgan, *Visible Saints: The History of a Puritan Idea* (New York, 1963); Sacvan Bercovitch, *The Puritan Origins of the American Self* (New Haven, 1975); and Philip Greven, *The Protestant Temperament* (New York, 1977).
4. Quoted in Steven Marcus, *Freud and the Culture of Psychoanalysis* (Boston, 1984), 84.
5. All quotes from Cotton Mather are from his *Memorable Providences, Relating to Witchcrafts and Possessions* (Boston, 1689) in *Narratives of the Witchcraft Cases (1648–1706),* ed. George Lincoln Burr (New York, 1914), 98–99, 104, 107.

6. Quoted in Ilza Veith, *Hysteria* (Chicago, 1970), 67.
7. Mather, 109–110.
8. Cf. my Chapter 4, "The Hysterical Personality and History."
9. For details of the Thomas Putnam family and their role in the Salem witchcraft episode, see Paul Boyer and Stephen Nissenbaum, *Salem Possessed: The Social Origins of Witchcraft* (Cambridge, MA, 1974).
10. John Bunyan, *The Pilgrim's Progress* (Harmondsworth, Eng., 1982), 65–66.

## 13. *Crèvecoeur's New World*

1. See my comment on the neglect of women in Chapter 17, "The American Psyche."
2. See Leo Marx, *The Machine and the Garden* (New York, 1964) for a classic treatment of the pastoral image.

## 14. *Leadership in the American Revolution*

1. Dankwart A. Rustow, "The Study of Elites. Who's Who, When and How," *World Politics,* 18 (1966), 690–717. Cf. Harold D. Lasswell, *Psychopathology and Politics* (New York, 1960) and Daniel Lerner, with the collaboration of Ithiel de Sola Pool and George K. Schueller, *The Nazi Elite,* Hoover Institute Studies, series B: Elite Studies, no. 3 (Stanford, 1951).
2. The best attempt to provide overall objective data on American Revolutionary leadership is James Kirby Martin's *Men in Rebellion: Higher Governmental Leaders and the Coming of the American Revolution* (New Brunswick, N.J., 1973).
3. Charles S. Sydnor, *American Revolutionaries in the Making* (New York, 1965), 98. Originally published as *Gentlemen Freeholders.*
4. Stanley Elkins and Eric McKitrick, "The Founding Fathers: Young Men of the Revolution," in *The Reinterpretation of the American Revolution,* ed. Jack A. Greene (New York, 1968) emphasizes the "Continental" experience as a shaping force.
5. A special group treated in an interesting manner is in Pauline Maier, *The Old Revolutionaries* (New York, 1980).
6. Seymour Martin Lipset, *The First New Nation* (Garden City, N.Y., 1967), 21.
7. Henry T. Tuckerman, *Essays, Biographical and Critical* (Boston, 1857), quoted in Marcus Cunliffe, *George Washington, Man and Monument* (Boston, 1958), 223.
8. E. J. Hobsbawm, in *New Society* (May 22, 1969).
9. Sigmund Freud, *Group Psychology and the Analysis of the Ego,* in *The Standard Edition of the Complete Psychological Works,* trans. and ed. James Strachey, vol. 18 (London, 1955), 123–24.

10. Louis Hartz, *The Liberal Tradition in America* (New York, 1955); Wesley Frank Craven, *The Legend of the Founding Fathers* (New York, 1956).
11. Edmund S. Morgan, "The Puritan Ethic and the Coming of the American Revolution," in Jack P. Greene, ed., *The Reinterpretation of the American Revolution, 1763–1769* (New York, 1968), 241.
12. Richard Bushman, "Corruption and Power in Provincial America," in Library of Congress Symposia on the American Revolution, 1st, 1972, *The Development of a Revolutionary Mentality* (Washington: Library of Congress, 1972), 72.
13. Edwin G. Burrows and Michael Wallace, "The American Revolution: The Ideology and Psychology of National Liberation," *Perspectives in American History* 6 (1972):167–306; Bernard Bailyn, "Boyd's Jefferson: Notes for a Sketch," *New England Quarterly* 33 (1960):380–400, and "Butterfield's Adams: Notes for a Sketch," *William and Mary Quarterly,* 3d ser. 19 (1962):238–56; Cf. Bailyn's comments in "Common Sense," in Library of Congress Symposia on the American Revolution, 2d, 1973, *Fundamental Testaments of the American Revolution* (Washington: Library of Congress, 1973), p. 17. Further on Jefferson, of course, there is also Fawn M. Brodie, *Thomas Jefferson: An Intimate History* (New York, 1974).
14. Gordon Wood, "Rhetoric and Reality in the American Revolution," *William and Mary Quarterly,* 3d ser. 23 (1966):3–32; reprinted in *Revolution: A Comparative Study,* ed. Lawrence Kaplan (New York, 1973), 128–29.
15. Burrows and Wallace, "American Revolution," 209, 304.
16. Bernard Bailyn, quoted in Greene, ed., *Reinterpretation of the American Revolution,* 55.
17. Alexis de Tocqueville, *Democracy in America,* 2 vols. (New York, 1900), 2:202.
18. Burrows and Wallace, "American Revolution," 203.
19. See Herbert Moller, "Youth as a Force in the Modern World," *Comparative Studies in Society and History* 10(1968):237–60.
20. Quoted in Burrows and Wallace, "American Revolution," 194, 292.
21. Quoted in Merrill Jensen, *The Founding of a Nation* (New York, 1968), 199.
22. Burrows and Wallace, "American Revolution," 202, 213.
23. Quoted in Jensen, *Founding of a Nation,* 12.
24. James Thomas Flexner, *George Washington: The Forge of Experience (1732–1775)* (Boston, 1965), 7.
25. Erik H. Erikson, "Reflections on the American Identity," in *Childhood and Society,* 2d ed. (New York, 1963), 296.
26. Quoted in Burrows and Wallace, "American Revolution," 290.
27. *Journal of Interdisciplinary History* (Winter 1971).
28. Ibid., 213.
29. Cunliffe, *George Washington,* 185.
30. Ibid., 210.
31. Douglas Southall Freeman, *George Washington, a Biography,* 7 vols. (New York, 1948–57), 1:71–72.

32. Cunliffe, *George Washington,* 189.

## 15. A Psychohistorical Inquiry

1. The Wicker comment is in the *New York Times Magazine,* January 19, 1969, 21; Rovere's also in the *New York Times Magazine,* July 20, 1969, 4.
2. There is a growing literature in this field, most of it stemming from the pioneering work by Erik H. Erikson, *Childhood and Society* (New York, 1950). My own position is further put forth in the introduction to Bruce Mazlish (ed.), *Psychoanalysis and History* (Englewood Cliffs, 1963), and in Chapter 9, "Prolegomena to Psychohistory." Compare Cushing Strout, "Ego Psychology and the Historian," *History and Theory,* 7 (1968), 281–297.
3. Sigmund Freud and William Bullitt, *Thomas Woodrow Wilson: A Psychological Study* (Boston, 1967).
4. View expressed by Tovah Silver Marion in a letter to *The Boston Globe,* November 26, 1968. The "psychotherapist" in question is Dr. Arnold A. Hutschnecker. His article, "The Mental Health of Our Leaders," *Look,* 33 (July 15, 1969), 51–54, is more revealing of Dr. Hutschnecker, as a sort of Pavlovian and Freudian synthesizer, than of President Nixon. He was very discreet about his "treatment" of Nixon, and no clear picture of the relationship emerges. Although he had published a book on psychosomatic medicine in 1951, Dr. Hutschnecker describes himself as still engaged in internal medicine when consulted by Nixon. The doctor's casual reference to a "discussion" in 1955 seems to set at least that date as part of the consultations, but one cannot even be sure of that. In any case, he states that "during the entire period that I treated Mr. Nixon, I detected no sign of mental illness in him," a comforting if innocuous statement. On my reading, Dr. Hutschnecker was obviously a man of high moral standards, who reassured Nixon as to his strength and his goals and tried to encourage that side of him that tended toward peace. As Dr. Hutschnecker writes, "I now believe that if he chooses to resist the military-industrial complex, as Eisenhower did, he could become the man to put together, finally, Wendell Willkie's 'one world.'" To sum up, though, the article tells us little about Nixon's psychology.

   There is another problem connected with Nixon's relation to Dr. Hutschnecker. In Joe McGinniss, *The Selling of the President, 1968* (New York, 1969), we are told about Nixon's horror of psychiatrists. In seeking to "sell the President," panel television shows were worked out for Nixon. Inadvertently, on one occasion a psychiatrist was added. McGinniss treats us to the following reaction of Nixon's aides: "'Jesus Christ,' he [Roger Ailes] said, 'you're not going to believe this but Nixon hates psychiatrists.' 'What?' 'Nixon hates psychiatrists. He's got this thing apparently. They make him very nervous. You should have heard Len [Garment] on the phone when I told him I had one on the panel. Did you hear him? If I ever heard a guy's voice turn white, that was it.' 'Why?' 'He said he didn't want to go into it. But apparently Nixon wouldn't even let one in the same room. Jesus Christ, could you picture him on a live TV show finding out he's being questioned by a shrink?'" (I used the version in *Harper's,* 239 [August, 1969], 54.)

5. Incidentally, a news release informed us that "the U.S. Information Agency has been circulating abroad a film of President-elect Richard Milhous Nixon which pictures him as an 'intellectual introvert not unlike' President Woodrow Wilson. The 24-minute film carried the endorsement of Nixon headquarters." For a good analysis of the Georges' work and of the problems surrounding all such work, as perceived from the point of view of political science, see Fred I. Greenstein, *Personality and Politics* (Chicago, 1969), esp. Chapter 3.

6. Erik H. Erikson, *Young Man Luther* (New York, 1962); *Gandhi's Truth: On the Origins of Militant Nonviolence* (New York, 1969).

7. For a comparison of the original book by Earl Mazo and the rewritten version by Earl Mazo and Stephen Hess, see the somewhat partisan and antagonistic review by Marvin Kitman in the *New York Times Book Review,* January 19, 1969. In *Six Crises* (New York, 1962), Nixon was helped in the writing by Alvin Moscow. According to the account by Mark Harris, *Mark the Glove Boy* (New York, 1964), Nixon wrote only one of the six chapters entirely by himself, and in the others relied on Moscow to convert his outline into an original draft (see 34–35). This fact, of course, colors any interpretation of *Six Crises,* but I am proceeding on the assumption that it was at the time the most personal of Nixon's revelations. Seemingly, the earliest book on Nixon is Philip Andrews, *This Man Nixon* (Philadelphia, 1952), a 63-page affair, with some interesting photographs. Then there were James Keogh, *This Is Nixon* (New York, 1956), also with photographs; Ralph de Toledano, *Nixon* (New York, 1956), highly admiring of its subject; William A. Reuben, *The Honorable Mr. Nixon* (New York, 1958), which is a hostile account of Nixon's role in the Hiss case; Bela Kornitzer, *The Real Nixon: An Intimate Biography* (New York, 1960), claimed to be based on a number of taped interviews and was about the only book on Nixon that openly stated as its major interest Nixon's personality and family background, though it had some strange omissions; William Costello, *The Facts about Nixon: An Unauthorized Biography* (New York, 1960), which, while openly critical of Nixon was a fairly substantial work; Steward Alsop, *Nixon and Rockefeller: A Double Portrait* (Garden City, 1960), which emphasized Nixon as politician; and George Johnson, *Richard Nixon* (Derby, 1961). What was striking about *all* of these books was their repetition, with variations that made one wonder who was being accurate, of exactly the same stories about Nixon, with no attribution of source that measured up to the standard with which a historian would feel comfortable. The only serious psychological study of Nixon was James David Barber's paper delivered at the 65th Annual Meeting of the American Political Science Association in September 1969, and first published in a partial version as "Analyzing Presidents: From Passive-Positive Taft to Active-Negative Nixon," *Washington Monthly,* 1 (October, 1969), 33–54.

In addition to these works directly on Nixon, one could consult such accounts of campaigns in which he was involved as Theodore White, *The Making of a President, 1960* (New York, 1961), and *The Making of a President, 1968* (New York, 1969); David English and the staff of the London *Daily Express, Divided They Stand* (New York, 1969); McGinniss, *The Selling of the President;* and so forth.

8. Earl Mazo and Stephen Hess, *Nixon: A Political Portrait* (New York, 1968), 32. Further references to this work will be indicated by M-H, followed by page number(s).

9. Stephen E. Ambrose, *Nixon: The Education of a Politician* (New York, 1987), 101–104, adds to our knowledge of this episode.

10. For a magisterial treatment of this problem, see Erik H. Erikson, "On the Nature of Psycho-Historical Evidence: In Search of Gandhi," *Daedalus,* 97 (1968), 695–730.

11. Nixon spent one summer—Mazo and Hess give his age as fourteen (M-H, 12)—during the two years with his mother and brother in Prescott, Arizona, putting his nascent oratorical skills to work as a barker at a concession in the Slippery Gulch Rodeo (see Costello, *The Facts about Nixon,* 23). I do not believe, however, that this would much affect the feeling that I postulated for Nixon of perceiving, on the unconscious level, his mother as "deserting" him. (Incidentally, existing published sources did not allow me to establish with certainty the precise dates involved. Keogh, *This Is Nixon,* 25, for example, claims Harold got tuberculosis at age eighteen and died five years later. On the face of it, Mazo and Hess's dates are more acceptable.)

12. The use here of these "musts," and others that follow, runs all the risks that I cautioned against in Chapter 9, but which cannot be avoided, given the nature of the materials. The "must" draws its probability from general clinical evidence and the theories derived from them. Proof that it actually applies to Nixon would require specific data that we do not have (although some of it may be forthcoming in the future). In lieu of such specific data, our confidence in the "must" resides in effects evinced later in Nixon's life that correspond with our hypothesized cause and with its fit with other elements in the jigsaw puzzle, so to speak, that we put together to picture his personality. It is noteworthy that the analysis of Nixon presented in this way seems to have been more prescient in its results than other kinds of analysis. Still, caution is obviously advised.

13. See, for example, Robert Lifton, "On Death and Death Symbolism" and "The Hiroshima Bomb," reprinted in *History and Human Survival* (New York, 1970), and *Death in Life: Survivors of Hiroshima* (New York, 1967). For Nixon's own account of his feelings about his brother Arthur, see the composition that, at age seventeen, he wrote about his sibling; it is reproduced in Kornitzer, *The Real Nixon,* 61–66.

14. Richard M. Nixon, *Six Crises* (New York, 1968), 317. Further references to this work will be indicated by N, followed by page number(s).

15. Compare Edward Fiske's article in the *New York Times,* January 26, 1969, p. 54.
16. *New York Times Magazine,* June 8, 1969, p. 108.
17. Ambrose, *Nixon,* 58, gives further information about the loss of importance of religion for Nixon.
18. *New York Times Magazine,* June 8, 1969, 111.
19. "Billy Graham's Own Story: 'God Is My Witness,' Part One," *McCall's,* (April, 1964), 124. Cf. John Pollock, *Billy Graham: The Authorized Biography* (London, 1966), 18.
20. Kornitzer, *The Real Nixon,* 78–79.
21. On a less psychological level, Nixon's Quaker background must be viewed in connection with his entrance to Whittier College, a small Quaker institution that played a strong role in his development, and with such figures in his later political life as Herbert Hoover, a fellow Californian and Quaker, who from early on seems to have taken a special interest in Nixon.
22. See Mazo and Hess, *Nixon,* 258, for a beginning analysis.
23. Marie Smith, "Nixon's California Home," *Boston Sunday Globe,* July 6, 1969.
24. See, for example, Harold D. Lasswell, *Psychopathology and Politics* (Chicago, 1930).
25. It is interesting, in this connection, to compare Martin Luther King's litany, "I have a dream." Surely, one task for future psychohistorians might be to analyze the various versions of the "American Dream."
26. Lawrence F. Schiff, "Dynamic Young Fogies—Rebels on the Right," *Trans-Action,* 4 (November 1966), 32.
27. Ibid., 32–33.
28. Although the police chief's daughter, Old Florence Welch, never wrote her memoirs, she did, subsequent to my article, reminisce and give interviews, some of which material I incorporated into my full-length book *In Search of Nixon* (New York, 1972), see also Brodie, *Richard Nixon;* Ambrose, *Nixon.*
29. In another account Dr. Upton reportedly added, "But it was a sincere performance, and there is nothing perfidious or immoral about being a good actor" (Kornitzer, *The Real Nixon,* 107); however, this addition does not undercut the point I am making.
30. It is interesting to note that Nixon's foreign policy adviser, Henry A. Kissinger, in his psychological study of Bismarck, points out that "the apostle of the claims of power was subject to fits of weeping in a crisis." ("The White Revolutionary: Reflections on Bismarck," *Daedalus,* 97 [1968], 890.) A reading of this article opens up fascinating speculations as to the comparisons and "transferences" Kissinger may be making between Bismarck and Nixon; for example, compare also the observation that "it was not that Bismarck lied—this is much too self-conscious an act—but that he was finely attuned to the subtlest currents of any environment and produced measures precisely adjusted to the need to prevail. The key to Bismarck's success was that he was always sincere" (898). (In all

fairness, I ought to indicate that some of my "transferences," though in a different context, may be spotted in my own article, "James Mill and the Utilitarians," ibid., 1036–1061.) Aside from "transferences," a close reading of Kissinger's article sheds light on some of his, and therefore perhaps President Nixon's, fundamental foreign policy attitudes. See further my book, *Kissinger, The European Mind in American Policy* (New York, 1976), for the Nixon-Kissinger relation, especially pp. 211–218.

31. See T. Adorno, et al., *The Authoritarian Personality* (New York, 1950), and, on Hitler, for example, Robert G. L. Waite, "Adolf Hitler's Anti-Semitism: A Study in History and Psychoanalysis," in Benjamin B. Wolman (ed.), *Psychoanalytic Interpretation of History* (New York, 1971) and "Adolf Hitler's Guilt Feelings: A Problem in History and Psychology," in *The Journal of Interdisciplinary History,* 1(2), Winter 1971.

32. A further comparison to Khomeini's fears of infection leaps to mind; see Chapter 10. However, if the psychology involved is similar, the political setting is different.

33. Clearly, much of Nixon's behavior, even in the area of "smearing" and feeling "smeared," is typical behavior of *all* politicians (which poses some interesting questions as to the nature of politics). The problem is in deciding whether the degree of feeling raises it to another level, and justifies the term "projection."

34. For my views on the nature of autobiography and its relation to psychohistory, see "Autobiography and Psycho-analysis," Chapter 5. By 1978, Nixon did reach the point of publishing his *Memoirs* (New York, 1978).

35. A well-known analysis of the Soviet Politburo in the terms that I have been using is, of course, Nathan Leites, *A Study of Bolshevism* (Glencoe, 1953).

36. Quite a while after writing this paragraph, I came across some confirmation of my guess as to the actual phrase used by Nixon. Alsop, *Nixon and Rockefeller,* 63, claims "three people who should know" have Nixon saying "pee or get off the pot." My own hunch is still that the language was even stronger than this. After all, one of Nixon's triumphs in college was bringing in a "four holer" to his fraternity.

37. The entire discussion of the last few pages raises again the issue of what is characteristic of all politicians and what is particularly personal to Nixon, a sticky issue for all psychohistorical work. The need to believe well of oneself, to think of oneself as principled and fair, and to avoid self-examination seems to be a characteristic necessity of politicians as a group; a minimum requirement of their egos to sustain them, as the journalist David Broder suggested to me, against "the terrific competitive pressures of their profession." So too, simple political necessity forces them often to take public positions during a campaign diametrically opposed to what they know to be right and truthful. Once again, then, the question of "degree" arises. More than this, however, the question of "fit" also arises: the way in which an individual's personality allows him to be a "typical" politician (Adlai Stevenson obviously had difficulties in this respect),

and the ways in which the behavior of politicians "fits" the expectations of their constituents.

## 16. *Leader and Led, Individual and Group*

1. John Maynard Keynes, *The Economic Consequences of the Peace* (New York, 1971; originally published in 1920); Alexander L. and Julliette L. George, *Woodrow Wilson and Colonel House: A Personality Study* (New York, 1956); Edmund Wilson, *Patriotic Gore* (New York, 1962).
2. See Chapters 1 and 3 for a further discussion of this particular point.
3. Inspired by Lasswell, the Georges did their famous study of Woodrow Wilson and Colonel House and James David Barber his *The Lawmakers* (New Haven, Conn., 1965), a study of Connecticut legislators, and *The Presidential Character* (Englewood Cliffs, N.J., 1972), which attempted to set up a typology of American leaders, based on a Passive/Active, Positive/Negative matrix.
4. In all fairness, it must be added that the Lasswellian characteristics given above were tendencies, not total commitments. Thus, in practice, the Georges explicitly wished to view Wilson in light of the political situation at the time, which favored "political reforms and strong leadership" (318), and they claimed to refine Lasswell's hypothesis by identifying the special conditions under which Wilson's power-need operated. The problem still remains, however, that, in their otherwise exemplary study, they viewed the political situation in purely rational, nonpsychological terms, without analyzing the desire for "reform" and "strong leadership" in psychohistorical terms. In short, psychohistory is applied only to the leader and not to the led; and, naturally in these circumstances, not to the interaction between them.
5. Robert C. Tucker, "The Georges' Wilson Reexamined: An Essay on Psychobiography," *American Political Science Review,* 71 (June 1977).
6. Erik H. Erikson, *Young Man Luther* (New York: W. W. Norton, 1958); *Gandhi's Truth* (New York, 1969).
7. In back of the psychohistorical inquiry must stand a classification into different types of leaders—political, religious, intellectual, artistic, etc.—as well as a sociological analysis, such as offered by Max Weber, who identifies charismatic, rational-bureaucratic, and traditional types of leadership. I shall not enter further into this matter here, but simply post the alert that the psychohistorian, in practice, must make clear what kind of leader he is studying. For present purposes, I am generalizing primarily about political or religious leaders, at the head of relatively large-scale historical groups.
8. *Early Writings of Walter Lippmann,* with introduction by Arthur Schlesinger, Jr. (New York, 1970), 179 and 185.
9. Henry Fairlie, *The Kennedy Promise* (Garden City, N.Y., 1973), 65.
10. Ibid., 78.
11. Heinz Kohut, "Creativeness, Charisma, Group Psychology: Reflections on the

Self-analysis of Freud" in *Freud: The Fusion of Science and Humanism,* eds. John E. Gedo and George H. Pollock (*Psychological Issues,* Monograph 34/35) (New York, 1976). The quotation that follows is on p. 404.

12. Cf. Henry Nash Smith, *Virgin Land* (Cambridge, Mass., 1976), viii. My effort to "sort those out" in a preliminary way, and, in general, to develop the concept of the psychic repository is to be found in the next chapter.

13. Erik H. Erikson, "Reflections on the American Identity," in *Childhood and Society,* 2nd ed. (New York, 1963), especially pp. 285 ff.

14. Smith, *Virgin Land,* xi.

15. Cleanth Brooks, R. G. B. Lewis, Robert Penn Warren, *American Literature* (New York: St. Martin's Press, 1973), 670.

16. *The New York Times,* 21 December 1979.

17. In other cases leaders will seek to define themselves as "successors" to a great predecessor, as Stalin did for a while with Lenin. Great imitative successors to great leaders are rare, I believe, for reasons adumbrated in such a work as Robert Jay Lifton, *Revolutionary Immortality: Mao Tse-tung and the Chinese Cultural Revolution* (New York, 1968); but the problem requires separate treatment from what I am according it here.

18. Bruce Mazlish, *The Revolutionary Ascetic* (New York, 1976).

19. D. A. Hamer, "Gladstone: The Making of a Political Myth," *Victorian Studies,* 22 (Autumn 1978), 29.

20. Ibid., 30.

21. I have quoted from the original manuscript; the quotations that follow are on pp. 3, 17, 29 and 17. The article was published in *New Directions in Psychohistory,* ed. Mel Albin (Lexington, Mass., 1980).

22. Cf. for a similar argument the paper by Fred Weinstein, "The Sociological Implications of Charismatic Leadership," delivered June 7, 1980, at the Conference on Psychohistorical Meanings of Leadership, Michael Reese Hospital, Chicago.

23. *The New York Times,* 15 March 1980.

24. *The New York Times Book Review,* 4 November 1979, p. 22.

25. *The Psychohistory Review,* 8 (Winter 1979), 16–26.

26. Robert L. Moore, *John Wesley and Authority: A Psychological Perspective* (Missoula, Mont., 1979), 190.

27. Ibid.

28. For example, Robert Southey, the poet laureate, as Geoffrey Carnall puts it, viewed Methodism as preaching "a means by which the lowest sort of tradesmen—bakers, barbers, tailors, even servants and labourers—are promoted to social eminence. These people find themselves in positions of influence for which by 'birth, education, knowledge, and intellect' they are quite unfit" (Geoffrey Carnall, *Robert Southey and His Age* [Oxford, 1960], 70–71). Southey went on to compare the Methodist societies to the radical Corresponding Societies at the time of the French Revolution because of a supposedly similar democratic character.

29. The North Koreans, for example, understood this matter well and acted in a reverse manner toward their American prisoners of war: they deliberately removed the American leaders from any influence, thereby destroying the authority structure and the command organization, and thus the roles that gave a sense of meaning and identity to the ordinary soldier. Such individuals were then presumed ready for "brainwashing," i.e., the creation of a new set of values and a new identity.

30. William Langer, "The Next Assignment," *The American Historical Review,* 63 (January 1958).

31. *Group for the Use of Psychology in History Newsletter,* 3 (March 1975), 4.

32. Heinz Kohut, *The Analysis of the Self* (New York, 1971).

33. *The Psychoanalytic Study of the Child,* Vol. 27 (New York, 1972).

34. Heinz Kohut, *The Restoration of the Self* (New York, 1977), 129. For Kohut's writings especially on history, see his *Self-Psychology and the Humanities,* ed. Charles B. Strozier (New York, 1985), and the review of this book by Lewis D. Wurgaft in *History and Theory,* 26 (1987).

35. Ibid., 269.

36. Ibid., 103.

37. Kohut, "Creativeness," 408.

38. Ibid., 415.

39. Ibid., 419.

40. Kohut, "Creativeness," 410.

41. One problem for such theory, however, and for object relations as well, is that it is pre-Oedipal, in the sense of finding the etiology of what it studies in the first year or so of life. Such early experience is almost never recoverable to us in a direct way, as is, for example, the Oedipal experience. Adult recollections can reverberate to the Oedipal conflict, can "recapture" that experience, so to speak, in a way not possible for the pre-Oedipally rooted feelings of separation, abandonment, merger, and so forth. The latter are recoverable, but in terms of generalized situations, which we "remember" in a nonpersonal way as a kind of "threshold" feeling. Such matters are at a less immediate and formulatable level than the materials of drive theory. They are less the stuff of which great dramas are made. At best, they speak of a diffuse feeling or mood, not a conflict. Their "hero" is not the child or adolescent fighting the father, or struggling through the identity crisis, but the person of late middle age, whose self is threatened with disintegration and whose salvation lies in renewable grandiosity or idealization. So for the individual, it is also so for the group or groups to which he or she belongs. It is of this stuff that great history is made.

42. See the Introduction, p. 4, and Chapter 9, pp. 137–138. Cf. Bruce Mazlish, "Psychoanalytic Theory and History: Groups and Events," in *The Annual of Psychoanalysis* (New York, 1978), 41–57.

43. Erikson, *Childhood and Society,* 285.

44. Ibid., 286.

45. Smith, *Virgin Land,* passim.
46. On Wesley, I have already mentioned Robert L. Moore's book, and commented on the importance of organization for the personal development of followers.
47. *The New Yorker,* February 18, 1980, pp. 112, 114.

## 17. The American Psyche

1. Michael Kammen, in *People of Paradox,* (New York, 1980), also uses the term "polarities," along with "antinomies," "dualisms," and "biformities," to express some of what I have in mind. But his intentions are not first and foremost psychological, or at least not systematically so. Erik Erikson, of course, is systematically psychological and does use the term "polarities" in this context. While I have drawn inspiration from his usage, I am trying to go beyond it, drawing less on individual psychology than on an attempt to construct a different, non-Freudian (though still informed by Freudian ideas) group psychology.
2. Bruno Bettelheim, *The Enchantment of Fairy Tales* (New York, 1976), 25–26.
3. Richard Slotkin, in *Regeneration through Violence* (Middletown, CT, 1973), defines them as "stories drawn from history, that have acquired through usage over many generations a symbolizing function that is central to the cultural functioning of the society that produces them" (p. 16).
4. Erik Erikson, *Childhood and Society* (New York, 1963), 286. It is worth noting that Erikson's life-cycle theory, with its eight stages marked by such descriptions as basic truth versus distrust, intimacy versus isolation, etc., is based on incipient polarities that apply to the group as well as to the individual.
5. Perry Miller, *Nature's Nation* (Cambridge, MA, 1967), 12.
6. In fact, of course, America is not totally unique in this regard, as a moment's thought about the other Americas—South and North, i.e., Canadian—will remind us. They too were born, so to speak, in historic time. What is unique, however, is that the United States boasts so fiercely and frequently of its uniqueness.
7. See David Potter, "American Women and American Character," in *History and American Society,* ed. Don E. Fehrenbacher (New York, 1973).
8. Richard Slotkin, *Regeneration through Violence,* is *the* book on this subject, and much of my inspiration is derived from it. The captivity narrative-sermon as a form of "testing" echoes the general concern with Puritan salvation as a temptation ordeal and testing; see Chapter 12, "The Iron of Melancholy."
9. It is also worthy of note that both Brown and Cooper, as well as the Leatherstocking real-life prototype, Daniel Boone, were Quakers—with their dedication to peace. Talk about ambivalence!
10. Sacvan Bercovitch, *The Puritan Origins of the American Self* (New Haven, CT, 1975), 19. Goodwin's poetry finds its echo in Whitman's famous "I sing myself," though transposed into a very different key. Puritans, of course, remained in England as well as coming to the United States, and engaged there in an actual external "civil war." The American Puritan's differences from his English

counterpart were (1) emigration meant a special form of uprooting; (2) the Indian encounter, as suggested, was unique; (3) in New England, the Puritan was in a majority position; and (4) gradually his religion became a form of ethnicity, i.e., WASPism, or Brahminism.

11. Quoted in Kammen, *People of Paradox,* 211.
12. See William McLaughlin, "Pietism and the American Character," *American Quarterly,* 17(2), Pt. 1 (Summer 1965), and his review-essay, "The American Revolution as a Religious Revival: 'The Millennium in One Country,'" *The New England Quarterly,* 40(1) (March 1967).
13. See Rhys Isaac, "Preachers and Patriots: Popular Culture and the Revolution in Virginia," in *The American Revolution,* ed. Alfred F. Young (DeKalb, IL, 1976).
14. See T. H. Breen, "'Baubles of Britain': The American and Consumer Revolutions of the Eighteenth Century," *Past and Present,* No. 119 (May 1988).
15. For the familial imagery involved in the period, see Edwin G. Burrows and Michael Wallace, *The American Revolution: The Ideology and Psychology of National Liberation,* Vol. 6 (Perspectives in American History) (Cambridge, MA, 1972).
16. For the generational conflict between Federalists and anti-Federalists, see Stanley Elkins and Eric McKittrick, "The Founding Fathers: Young Men of the Revolution," in *The Reinterpretation of the American Revolution 1763–1789,* ed. Jack P. Greene (New York, 1968). On colonial and revolutionary military matters, see, for example, Daniel J. Boorstin, *The Americans: The Colonial Experience* (New York, 1958); John Shy, "The American Military Experience: History and Learning," *The Journal of Interdisciplinary History,* 1(2) (Winter 1971); E. Wayne Carp, *To Starve the Army at Pleasure* (Chapel Hill, NC, 1984).
17. The Cooper quotation is from Stephen Railton, *Fenimore Cooper* (Princeton, NJ, 1987), 13; and the Longfellow from *Kavanagh,* quoted in Howard Mumford Jones, *O Strange New World* (New York, 1967), 347. In the arts, the Hudson River School of painting took on the task as well, painting the Niagaras and mountains called for in the new nationalism. (See, for example, *American Paradise* [New York: The Metropolitan Museum of Art, 1987].) It should be noticed, of course, that this appeal also forms part of the discovery of God in Nature, which leads Perry Miller to call America "Nature's Nation."
18. Quoted in the *Boston Globe,* May 10, 1983.
19. Quoted in Ian Buruma, "The Bartered Bride," *The New York Review of Books,* June 1, 1989, p. 8. The whole of this article should be read.
20. Ronald Reagan, 1984 State of the Union speech.
21. The quotations from Washington and Lincoln can be found in Richard N. Current, "Lincoln, the Civil War, and the American Mission," in *The Public and the Private Lincoln,* ed. by Cullom Davis et al. (Carbondale, IL, 1979), 141, 145.

# Name Index

Adams, John, 190
Adler, Alfred, 49, 250, 251
Agnew, Spiro, 241
Andreas-Salomé, Lou, 41, 49

Bailyn, Bernard, 187, 188
Barber, James David, 136
Baumgarten, Eduard, 108
Bazargan, Mehdi, 148, 149
Bentham, Jeremy, 158
Bettelheim, Bruno, 268, 269
Bradford, William, 275, 277
Brentano, Franz, 21
Breuer, Joseph, 52, 70
Brücke, Ernst, 20
Buckle, Henry Thomas, 21, 98
Bullitt, William, 4, 199
Burnham, James, 155
Burns, James MacGregor, 149
Burrows, Edwin G., 187, 188, 189

Chambers, Whittaker, 212, 222, 227, 228, 246
Channing, William Ellery, 121
Charcot, Jean Martin, 29
Claus, Carl, 19
Colp, Ralph, Jr., 18
Comfort, Alex, 15
Cooper, James Fenimore, 175, 275, 281
Cranefield, Paul, 20
Crèvecoeur, Michel Guillaume St. Jean de, 7, 173ff., 191, 272, 280
Cunliffe, Marcus, 194, 195

Darwin, Charles, 13ff., 31ff., 67, 88, 90, 115
Darwin, Francis, 19, 32
Darwin, Robert, 32, 34, 36
Demos, John, 54
Dickens, Charles, 156
Dostoevsky, Feodor, 157
Douglas, Helen Gahagan, 226
du Bois-Reymond, Emil, 20

Einstein, Albert, 7, 87, 88, 90
Eisenhower, Dwight David, 233, 235, 236ff., 255
Eliot, George, 28
Emerson, Ralph Waldo, 85, 281
Engels, Friedrich, 79
Erikson, Eric H., 8, 25, 66, 75, 107, 119, 128, 141, 166, 169, 191, 192, 200, 251, 254, 263, 270

Fliess, Wilhelm, 39
Foucault, Michel, 56, 166, 168
Freud, Anna, 13, 65, 66
Freud, Martha (Bernays), 28, 69
Freud, Sigmund, 4, 7, 38ff., 51, 63, 67, 68ff., 112, 114, 124, 134, 144, 166, 171, 185, 199, 220, 249
Fromm, Eric, 155, 159

Gandhi, Mohandas Karamchand Mohatma, 130ff.
George, Alexander, 137, 200, 249
George, Juliette, 200, 249
George, Stefan, 111
Goethe, Johann Wolfgang von, 60, 61
Goldwater, Barry, 199
Gould, Stephen Jay, 25
Graham, Billy, 207, 208
Greven, Philip, 166
Groddeck, George, 44

Ha'iri, Mehdi, 143, 144
Ha'iri, Yazid, 143
Hartmann, Heinz, 65, 66
Helmholtz, Hermann, 20
Hiss, Alger, 212, 222, 227
Hitler, Adolf, 141, 149, 227, 261
Hobsbawm, Eric, 184, 186
Horney, Karen, 251
Hutton, Patrick, 87
Huxley, Aldous, 154, 155

James, William, 62, 165, 168, 172
Jefferson, Thomas, 178, 187, 254, 280, 282
Jesus Christ, 80, 86, 88
Jevons, William Stanley, 95ff.
Johnson, Chalmers, 135
Jones, Ernest, 69, 71ff.
Jones, Jim, 6, 80
Jung, Carl, 49

Kennedy, John F., 224, 230, 244, 245, 255, 284
Keynes, John Maynard, 6, 7, 249
Khomeini, Ayatollah Rohollah, 139ff.
Khrushchev, Sergevich, 222, 228, 235
King, John Owen, 165ff.
Kohut, Heinz, 253, 260ff.
Krohn, Alan, 51ff.

Lacan, Jacques, 23
Langer, William, 260
Lasswell, Harold, 127, 134, 250
Lebeaux, Richard, 81, 83
Lenin (Vladimir Ilich Ulyanov), 130ff., 185
Lincoln, Abraham, 242, 284
Lytton, Edward Bulwer-Lytton, 102, 103

McGrath, William J., 21
McKinley, William, 284
Marx, Karl, 79ff.
Mather, Cotton, 169, 170, 186, 276
Miller, Henry, 160, 161
Miller, Perry, 270, 271, 278
Mitzman, Arthur, 107ff., 172
Morris, John N., 60, 62

Namier, Lewis, 133
Nietzsche, Friedrich, 17, 38ff.
Nixon, Frank, 205, 207ff.
Nixon, Hannah (Milhous), 203, 205, 207ff.
Nixon, Patricia (Ryan), 213, 219ff.
Nixon, Richard, 198ff.

Orwell, George, 153ff.

Pascal, Roy, 66, 74
Pavlov, Ivan, 25, 159
Pinel, Philippe, 55, 56

Reich, Wilhelm, 52
Rousseau, Jean-Jacques, 65, 176
Rushdie, Salman, 151

Sawyer, David Haskell, 265
Schiff, Lawrence F., 217, 218
Schnitzler, Arthur, 28, 120
Schopenhauer, Arthur, 44
Schorske, Carl, 28, 120
Schweitzer, Albert, 81
Sedgwick, Adam, 14
Shy, John, 192, 193
Smith, Adam, 95, 96, 97
Smith, Henry Nash, 254, 263
Smith-Rosenberg, Carol, 52
Southey, Robert, 59
Stevenson, Adlai, 232, 233
Swift, Jonathan, 155, 161

Thoreau, Henry David, 81ff.
Tocqueville, Alexis de, 154, 165, 173, 189, 268, 271
Tolstoy, Count Lev Nikolaevich, 115, 122
Trotsky, Leon, 129ff.
Tucker, Robert C., 5, 6, 251, 255

Voorhis, Jerry, 225, 242

Wallace, Alfred Russel, 88
Wallace, Michael, 187, 188, 189
Washington, George, 194ff., 280, 284
Weber, Alfred, 118
Weber, Helene (Fallenstein), 112, 113, 114
Weber, Marianne, 108, 114
Weber, Max, 107ff., 165, 168, 171, 183, 185
Weber, Max, Sr., 111, 112, 113, 114
Webster, Noah, 280
Wesley, John, 258, 259, 264
Whewell, William, 26
Wilberforce, Bishop Samuel, 14
Wilson, Edmund, 249
Wilson, (Thomas) Woodrow, 4, 127
Winthrop, John, 167, 186, 278
Wolfenstein, Victor, 127ff.
Wordsworth, William, 60
Wundt, Wilhelm, 24

Zamiatin, Eugene, 154, 155
Zweig, Arnold, 45

# Subject Index

Acting: and political leaders, 221, 222; and roles, 223
"Actual reality," 67
Adolescence, 61, 62, 217
Aggressive impulses: in Nixon, 214, 235; in witchcraft, 54
Ambivalence: toward the American Indian, 275; in Crèvecoeur, 175; in Nixon, 211, 213, 233, 236
America: its mission, 274, 281; and inferiority-superiority polarity, 281; and Nature, 277; and New England, 274; and revivalist movements, 278; and Southern experience, 273; as "Virgin Land," 271; and wilderness, 276; women and blacks in, 271, 272
American Dream, the, and Nixon, 216, 229, 246
American Psyche, 8, 175, 245, 264, 267ff.; and myths, 254; origins of, 177; and polarities, 263, 267ff.
American Revolution, 278, 279, 280; leadership in, 181ff.; and Nixon, 216; psychological dimensions, 181ff.; and revivalist movement, 279
"American Revolution: The Ideology and Psychology of National Liberation, The," 187
Asceticism: worldly, 172. *See also* Revolutionary ascetic
*Authoritarian Personality, The,* 134
Authoritarianism: and "authoritarian personality," 227; and Billy Graham, 208; and German fathers, 113; and Nixon, 208; patriarchal, 188
*Autobiographical Study, An,* 68
Autobiography, 54, 59ff.; Darwin's, 33; definition of, 62; Freud's, 44; as literature, 74; and Orwell, 160, 161; and romanticism, 59

*Beagle,* 31, 32, 35
Behavioral modification, 158–159

Benchuca, 31, 32, 37
Benthamism, 97, 157
*Bildungsroman,* 268, 269; and Goethe, 61
*Brave New World,* 154

*Capital,* 90
Captivity narrative, 275
Case history, 26, 27, 28, 67
Causality, 25; and corresponding processes, 25
Certainty, 22
Charisma, 183; and Kohut, 261; and Weber, 115, 118
Childhood, 61
Class struggle, 91
Collecting, and Darwin, 35
Communism, and Nixon, 225ff.
Comparative revolution, 135, 182; Iranian, 139, 140. *See also* Revolutionary personality
Consilience, 26
Conversion symptoms, 52, 53, 56, 58
Corresponding processes, 25, 120; and Erikson, 128. *See also* Causality
Countertransference, 52, 75, 202
Creativity, 34, 87
Crisis, and Nixon, 231, 232

Darwinian evolution, 13, 14; and Jevons, 101; and Lord Kelvin, 22; and morality, 15; and race, 14; and sexual selection, 29. *See also* Psychoanalysis
Daydreams, and Nixon, 214–215
Death: fears in Darwin, 33, 34, 37; fears in Nixon, 204; and regeneration through violence, 275; and "survivor guilt," 204; and George Washington, 195; and wishes, 237
*Democracy in America,* 154, 165, 173
Demographic revolution, 190
Depth psychology, 66
*Descent of Man, The,* 14

Desertion, effect of on Nixon, 204
Determinism, 25; and memory, 65
"Displaced libido," 145; and Khomeini, 146
Dreams, 64
Dystopias, 154, 155

Economics: and history, 97, 98; as a moral science, 96; and rationalism; 117; as a science, 95ff.
Ego, 44, 66
Ego and the Id, The, 52
Ego ideals, 259
Ego psychology, 53, 58; effect on history, 181
Elite studies, 181, 182
Enlightenment, 176; and witchcraft, 55
Etiological fallacy, 91, 99, 121. See also Genetic fallacy
Expression of the Emotions in Man and Animals, The, 15, 19, 28

False pregnancy, 17, 52
"Family romance," 140; in Khomeini, 150
Father figure: and American Revolution, 189ff.; and Nixon, 236
Focus group, 264; and attitudinal polling, 265
Founding fathers, 189
Free association, 23, 64, 138; in Ernest Jones, 72
Free Associations, 71ff.
Freedom-Happiness argument, 155; and Utilitarian pleasure-pain, 157

Genetic fallacy, 3. See also Etiological fallacy
Grandiosity, in Khomeini, 140
Group psychology, 8, 253, 264, 266
Group Psychology and the Analysis of the Ego, 134, 185

Hermeneutics, 13, 25, 27
Historicism, 123
History: and evidence, 133; intellectual, 110; and Jevons, 97; problems of, 137; and psychoanalysis, 55; and psychology, 51
History of the Psycho-Analytic Movement, 42, 68
Human nature, in Marx, 93, 94

Human sciences. See Science, social
Hypnosis, 16; Darwin and, 18, 31
Hysteria, 29, 51ff., 171; and "conversion symptoms," 52; and history, 51, 58; and hysterical personality, 52, 57; and mass hysteria, 57; and passivity, 53; and shamanism, 55; and Victorian society, 52, 56; and witchcraft, 54

Id, 44; and ego and superego, 66
Ideal type, 124
Identification, 87, 113; in Darwin, 35; by Khomeini, 142; with father by Nixon, 205, 207, 228, 235
Identity, 141; American, 270; and Crève-coeur, 173ff.; and crisis, in Nixon, 229, 241; and Khomeini, 140; of political leaders, 252, 253, 255
Ideology, and leaders, 257, 258
Indians (American), 272, 274; and Crève-coeur, 176; projection on to, 193
Individualism, and women in America, 272
Infantile sexuality, 65
Inferiority: and American Revolution, 279, 280; compensation for, 213; and low self-esteem, 251; and superiority, 273, 278, 281, 282
Intellectuals, as leaders, 6, 7
Interpretation, 132
Interpretation of Dreams, The, 23, 39, 70, 114
Iranian Revolution, 149, 150, 151
Iron cage, in Max Weber, 124, 172
Iron of Melancholy, The, 165ff.
Islamic Government, 145, 146, 149
Islamic revolution, 149, 150, 151

"Just So" stories. See Psychoanalysis, as a short story

Labor theory of value, 95
Leaders, 198; in American Revolution, 193; charismatic, 183, 184; and crisis, 232; and ego ideals, 259; and groups, 252; and identification, 87; and ideology, 257; and imitation of their lives, 86; intellectuals as, 6, 7; and led, 136, 249ff.; nature of, 144–145; and organization, 258; and political identity, 252; and psychic repository, 284; as revolutionary ascetics,

185; and roles, 223; as symbol, 144, 256. *See also* Psychic repository

Leadership, 9; and acting ability, 221; in American Revolution, 181ff.; and James MacGregor Burns, 149; and "fit," 136; moral, 149; nature of, 5, 136; and psychoanalysis, 6; and psychohistory, 249ff. *See also* Intellectuals

Leatherstocking, 175, 275, 283

*Letters from an American Farmer,* 173ff., 272

Libidinal impulses, 111; few, 144; in witchcraft, 54

Life cycle, 66

Life history, 32; of George Washington, 197

*Madness and Civilization,* 168

Marginal utility; theory of, 95

Meaning, 23

Melancholy, 62; in America, 165ff., 276; and capitalism, 172; and death fears, 195; as form of discourse, 166

Memory, 63; and autobiography, 60; and dreams, 64; in Orwell, 159; and George Washington, 195

Mesmerism. *See* Hypnosis

Modernity, and Max Weber, 111

Modernization, and revolution, 186

"Mourning and Melancholia," 115

Myth: American, 173; and American Psyche, 254, 267; and Crèvecoeur, 180; of the Indians, 176; and Khomeini, 139–140, 148, 151; kinds of, 268, 274

Narcissism, 52, 58, 260ff.; and America, 276; and grandiose and idealizing tendencies, 150; and Khomeini, 140, 150; and witches, 56

"Narcissistic rage," 146

Narrative, 27, 69

National character, 166; American, 270

Natural science. *See* Science, natural

Nature: in America, 277; Emerson's view of, 281

Neurosis, 169; introduction of the term, 55; Victorian, 165ff.

"New man," 173, 177, 191; in American Revolution, 279; and new language, 280

Object relations theory, 58

Oedipal conflict, 27, 53, 54, 188, 191; in

America, 189; and demographic change, 190; and drive theory, 263; in Freud, 71; and infantile sexuality, 65; and Kohut, 261; and Nixon, 205, 207; and Sophocles' *Oedipus Rex,* 24; and George Washington, 195–196; and Max Weber, 109, 115

"On the Nature of Psycho-Historical Evidence: In Search of Gandhi," 75

Organization: and leaders, 258; and personal development, 258

*Origin of Species, The,* 14, 33, 37

Overdetermination, 26, 113, 138; and psychoanalysis, 137

Overwork, and Max Weber, 114

Paranoid suspicions: in Khomeini, 147; in Nixon, 204, 227; in George Washington, 197. *See also* Poisoning

Passivity: myth of in hysteria, 53, 54, 56, 57; and Orwell, 160, 161, 162

Personality: and knowledge, 107; revolutionary, 107; and science, 7; and scientific theories, 87

Personality and politics, 5, 199, 250

Philosophy, as confession of philosopher, 92

Philosophy of science, 88. *See also* Science

Poisoning: fear of, 147, 192. *See also* Paranoid suspicions

Polarities, 311nn. 1 and 4; and American Psyche, 267ff.; civilization and wilderness, 273; and Erikson, 263; freedom and despotism, 283; God and Devil, 282; idealism and materialism, 278, 284; individualism and society, 283; inferiority and superiority, 278, 280, 282; violence and benevolence, 275; young and old, 282

Power, concept in political science, 263

Progress, and Jevons, 104

"Project for a Scientific Psychology," 20

Projection: and Indians (American), 193; and Nixon, 227

*Protestant Ethic and the Spirit of Capitalism, The,* 110, 118, 165

*Psychiatric Study of Jesus, The,* 81

"Psychic reality," 67, 137

Psychic repository, 8, 263, 267ff.; and leaders, 8; and polarities, 263; transformations in, 272

Psychoanalysis, 199; Adlerian, 6, 213; and autobiography, 59ff.; critics of, 3, 4, 52;

and Darwin, 13; Darwinian basis of, 2ff., 9, 13ff., 22; as "experiment," 27; historian's need for training in, 133; and historical evidence, 55; and intellectual history, 110; mechanistic model of, 21; and melancholia, 171; nature of, 1ff.; and normal and abnormal, 30; and nineteenth-century physics, 50; and physical-chemical forces, 20; and Plato's *Republic*, 23; questions concerning, 4, 199; as a science, 2ff., 50, 52; and self, 63; as a short story, 4, 26, 27, 28, 29, 43, 68; and "talk," 49; and "texts," 4, 8; and the unconscious, 24. *See also* Darwinian evolution; Hermeneutics; Melancholy; and Reductionism

Psychobiography, 203

Psychohistory, 1ff., 199ff.; criticisms of, 130, 131, 256; and Darwin, 32; and evidence, 133; nature of, 181, 249; possibility of, 137, 201, 263; and prediction, 136; problems of, 136–137; and reductionism, 137; and the revolutionary personality, 127ff.; and "texts," 262, 264; and therapy, 137; validity of, 137

Psychology: associational, 60; Darwin's, 18; Freudian, 8; group, 8; and history, 51; individual, 8; and Marx, 93

"Psychology of knowledge," 107, 108, 124

*Psychopathology and Politics,* 127, 250

Puritans: and ethos, 187, 274; and Indians (American), 274

Quakerism, and Nixon, 209, 210, 231

Race, 14

Rationality, and Max Weber, 111, 117, 123–124

*Recollections of the Development of my Mind and Character,* 33

Reductionism, 14, 25, 120, 124; and psychohistory, 137, 256

Religion: and Khomeini, 142ff.; and Nixon, 208

Repression, 63

Resistance, 63

Revivalist movement: in America, 278; in American Revolution, 279

Revolutionary ascetic, 184-185, 191; in American Revolution, 186, 188; Khomeini as, 145

Revolutionary personality, 127ff.

*Revolutionary Personality, The,* 127ff.

Romanticism: in America, 277; and autobiography, 59; and romantic empiricism, 59

*Satanic Verses, The,* 151

Science: difference from philosophy, 47; of economics, 95ff.; and Jevons, 103, 105; moral, 157; and narrative, 27; and a "new science," 290 fn.; and poetic vision, 36; and systems, 47. *See also* Science, natural; Science, social; Scientific method; and Scientific revolution

Science, natural: and causality, 25; and Marx, 91; and personality, 7, 88, 287ff.; research papers in, 26; and validity of a theory, 87

Science, social, 8–9; and Vicomte de Bonald, 158; as confession of social scientist, 92; and Marx, 84, 86, 89, 91, 94; and personality, 7; and *Realpolitik,* 122; and theory of class struggle, 91; and Thoreau, 84; and values, 122; and Max Weber, 121

Scientific method, 30; and Darwin, 36; and observation, 36

Scientific revolution, psychoanalysis as, 30, 47

Self, 74; and autobiography, 60, 76; divided, 62, 63; grandiose, 260; injury to, 146; and Marx, 94; and Nixon, 229; and personal development, 259; and psychoanalysis, 63; psychology of, 260 (*see also* Narcissism); Puritan, 166ff.; and wilderness of, 276, 277

Self-fulfilling prophecy, 91

Self-interest, in Jevons, 101, 102

Separation, theme of in America, 277

Sexual selection, 14, 29

Sexuality, 55, 120; in Islamic culture, 145; and Helene Weber, 112

Shamanism, and hysteria, 55

Shiite Muslims, 142, 148, 262

*Six Crises,* 202ff.

Sociobiology, 29

Sociology of knowledge, 107, 124

Stages of development, 61, 65; and infantile sexuality, 65

Structuralism, 168, 171, 172; and Foucault, 168; in John Owen King's work, 166, 168

*Studies on Hysteria,* 17, 26, 28, 52

*Sturm und Drang,* 61, 62

Sublimation, 110

Sufi mysticism, 144; and Khomeini, 151
Superego, 119; and Erikson, 66
Superman, 48
"Survivor guilt," 204

*Thomas Woodrow Wilson,* 200
Thought experiments, 80
*Totem and Taboo,* 43, 134
Transference, 52, 75, 119, 202
"Transvaluation of all Values," 39
"Tutelary State," in Tocqueville, 154

Unconscious, 63
Unintended consequences, 123

Utopias, 154

Value-free inquiry, 120, 123; and Max
    Weber, 121
Values, and social science, 122
*Varieties of Religious Experience, The,* 165,
    172
Violence, regeneration through, 275

*Walden,* 81
*We,* 154; reviewed by Orwell, 155
*Will to Power, The,* 39
Witchcraft, 55, 169–170; and hysteria, 54;
    and Cotton Mather, 169
*Woodrow Wilson and Colonel House,* 200,
    249

# Bibliographical Note

THE following chapters originally appeared in somewhat different form in these publications:

Chapter 2, "Darwin, the Benchuca, and Genius," in *Horizon* (Summer 1975);

Chapter 3, "Freud and Nietzsche," in *The Psychoanalytic Review* 55, no. 3 (1968), copyright © 1968 by the National Psychological Association for Psychoanalysis, Inc., permission to reprint granted by The Guilford Press;

Chapter 4, "The Hysterical Personality and History," in *The Journal of Interdisciplinary History* XI (Summer 1980), used with the permission of the editors of *The Journal of Interdisciplinary History* and The MIT Press, Cambridge, Massachusetts, copyright © 1980 by The Massachusetts Institute of Technology and the editors of *The Journal of Interdisciplinary History*;

Chapter 5, "Autobiography and Psychoanalysis," in *Encounter* (October 1970);

Chapter 6, "The Importance of Being Karl Marx, or Henry Thoreau, or Anybody," in *The Meaning of Karl Marx* (New York: Oxford University Press, 1984), copyright © 1984 by Bruce Mazlish, used by permission of Oxford University Press;

Chapter 7, "Jevons's Science and His 'Second Nature,'" in *Journal of the History of the Behavioral Sciences* 22, no. 2 (April 1986), used with permission of CPPC, 4 Conant Square, Brandon VT 05733;

Chapter 8, "The Iron Cage of Max Weber," in *History and Theory* X, no. 1 (1971);

Chapter 9, "Prolegomena to Psychohistory," in *Encounter* (September 1968);

Chapter 10, "The Hidden Khomeini," in *New York Magazine* (December 24, 1979);

Chapter 11, "Orwell Inside the Whale," in *North Dakota Quarterly* (Spring 1987);

Chapter 12, "The Iron of Melancholy," in *History and Theory* XXIV, no. 2 (1985);

Chapter 13, "Crèvecoeur's New World," in *The Wilson Quarterly* (Autumn 1982);

Chapter 14, "Leadership in the American Revolution," in *Leadership in the American Revolution* (Washington, D.C.: Library of Congress, 1974);

Chapter 15, "A Psychohistorical Inquiry: The 'Real' Richard Nixon," in *The Journal of Interdisciplinary History* I (Autumn 1970);

Chapter 16, "Leader and Led, Individual and Group," in *The Psychohistory Review* 9, no. 3 (Spring 1981).

# About the Author

$B$RUCE Mazlish became a psychohistorian in response to William Langer's presidential address to the American Historical Association—if he were young, Langer said, he would explore the frontiers of the psychology of history. Mazlish accepted the challenge and the result was his *Psychoanalysis and History,* published in 1963.

Mazlish holds the Thomas Meloy Chair in Rhetoric and is Professor of History at the Massachusetts Institute of Technology. In 1987 he received the Toynbee Prize for distinction in contributions to the social sciences. He is the author of, among other books, *The Western Intellectual Tradition* (with Jacob Bronowski); *In Search of Nixon: A Psychohistorical Study; James and John Stuart Mill: Father and Son in the Nineteenth Century;* and, most recently, *A New Science: The Breakdown of Connections and the Birth of Sociology.*

He was graduated from Columbia University (B.A. 1944, M.A. 1947), tried out for the Washington Senators, covered sports for the *Washington Daily News,* taught secondary school, and returned to Columbia, receiving his Ph.D. in history in 1955. He has taught at MIT from 1950, with two years (1953–55) as Director of the American School in Madrid. He lives in Cambridge, Massachusetts.